D1308879

THREE TOPICS IN THE THEORY OF INTERNATIONAL TRADE

Distribution, Welfare and Uncertainty

STUDIES IN
INTERNATIONAL ECONOMICS

Editors

JAGDISH N. BHAGWATI
JOHN S. CHIPMAN

Advisory Board

WILLIAM H. BRANSON   PETER B. KENEN
RICHARD COOPER   TAKASHI NEGISHI
MURRAY C. KEMP   YASUO UEKAWA

Volume 2

NORTH-HOLLAND PUBLISHING COMPANY – AMSTERDAM · OXFORD
AMERICAN ELSEVIER PUBLISHING COMPANY, INC. – NEW YORK

THREE TOPICS IN THE THEORY OF INTERNATIONAL TRADE

Distribution, Welfare and Uncertainty

MURRAY C. KEMP

1976

NORTH-HOLLAND PUBLISHING COMPANY – AMSTERDAM · OXFORD
AMERICAN ELSEVIER PUBLISHING COMPANY, INC. – NEW YORK

© NORTH-HOLLAND PUBLISHING COMPANY – 1976

Library of Congress Catalog Card Number 75–23116
ISBN North-Holland for this series 0 7204 8500 2
ISBN North-Holland for this volume 0 7204 0502 9
ISBN American Elsevier for this volume 0 444 10967 6

Publishers

NORTH-HOLLAND PUBLISHING COMPANY – AMSTERDAM
NORTH-HOLLAND PUBLISHING COMPANY, LTD. – OXFORD

Sole distributors for the U.S.A. and Canada

AMERICAN ELSEVIER PUBLISHING COMPANY, INC.
52 VANDERBILT AVENUE
NEW YORK, N.Y. 10017

Library of Congress Cataloging in Publication Data

Kemp, Murray C
   Three topics in the theory of international trade--
distribution, welfare, and uncertainty.

   (Studies in international economics)
   1. Commerce--Addresses, essays, lectures. 2. International economic relations--Addresses, essays, lectures.
3. Investments--Addresses, essays, lectures. I. Title.
HF1007.K43 1976   382.1   75-23116
ISBN 0-444-10967-6

PRINTED IN THE NETHERLANDS

INTRODUCTION TO THE SERIES

This series is intended to embrace all aspects of international economic analysis: theoretical, empirical and econometric. It will equally encompass contributions to pure and monetary theory.

The series will include the publication of collected essays, conference proceedings of exceptional professional quality and interest, and edited volumes addressed to specific phenomena of importance in the analysis of international economics. It will particularly encourage, however, the publication of hitherto unpublished studies which represent fresh and valuable contributions to the analysis of international economic problems.

The *Journal of International Economics* now provides an excellent outlet for original scientific work in international economics in article length form. For pamphlet length contributions, the different series published by the *International Finance Section* at Princeton have long been of exceptional value, even though they have not generally extended beyond international monetary issues. It is the hope of the editors that the launching of this series, *Studies in International Economics*, will now fill the lacuna in the systematic publication of monograph and volume length research output of international economists, and succeed in doing so consistently with the high quality that the promotion of scientific study of international economic issues requires.

THE EDITORS

For Thérèse

PREFACE

Most of the papers collected here have been written during the past ten years. Some have been published before. Each is concerned directly or indirectly with some aspect of the theory of international trade and investment. More specifically, the papers report on several attempts to relax the strict terms of the textbook-codified version of what is usually called the Heckscher–Ohlin approach to international trade.

The papers are arranged in three parts covering, respectively, the implications of trade for the distribution of income among factors, the gains from trade and investment, and the interactions of trade and uncertainty. Each part contains an introduction. I have tried to keep the introductions short by confining myself to sketches of the background to some papers and to brief guides to work which, in my view, has substantially advanced our understanding of the topics I have treated.

In the case of papers published for the second time, known obscurities, errors and misprints have been removed. Otherwise, the papers are republished in their original form, without any attempt to update or upgrade them. For this reason, it has seemed appropriate to retain as chapter headings the titles of the original papers.

Several of the papers are joint products, monuments to friendships made in many places. Where a paper has been written jointly that fact is recorded in the first footnote. To Jagdish Bhagwati, Wilfred Ethier, Ken-ichi Inada, Chulsoon Khang, Nissan Liviatan, Takashi Negishi, Hideo Suzuki, Yasuo Uekawa, Henry Wan and Leon Wegge go my thanks for their agreement to the present publication or republication of their work. Yasuo Uekawa has read all papers published here for the first time and has made many valuable suggestions for their improvement.

Finally, it is a pleasure to record my thanks to the several organizations which have given me permission to reprint articles first published in journals or books under their copyright. Where a chapter contains material not published for the first time, the place of original publication is stated in the first footnote of that chapter.

CONTENTS

PART I

INTERNATIONAL TRADE
AND THE DISTRIBUTION OF INCOME

Introduction to Part I

The relationship between commodity prices and the distribution of income between factors of production has interested economists at least since the post-Napoleonic debate over the English corn laws. To the formal analysis of the relationship important contributions were made by Cairnes, Bastable, Taussig, Heckscher, Ohlin and Haberler. In a sense, their work culminated in 1941 in the well-known proposition of Stolper and Samuelson. That proposition has been the point of departure for nearly all further analysis.

Stolper and Samuelson worked with a model of markets and production which is now thoroughly familiar to all trade theorists. Let us recall the salient features of the model:

(i) Just two primary factors and two products are recognized; there are no produced inputs.

(ii) Production has no time structure.

(iii) Joint products are ruled out, as are factors specific to a particular industry[1].

(iv) Both prices and production relationships are assumed to be non-random.

(v) Both factor markets are cleared.

Since these features of the model are of dubious realism, one is led to ask whether they can be modified without destroying the precision and sweep of the theorem. The essays of this part were written with this question in mind[2].

Related investigations have been carried out by Chipman, Ethier, Kemp and Wegge, Kuhn, Inada and Uekawa. References may be found at the end of chs. 3 and 4.

---

[1] In the latter respect, Stolper and Samuelson are much less ambitious than older writers like Bastable and Haberler.

[2] None of the essays comes to grips with the problem of unemployment (see (v) above). An early paper of the author's (Tariffs, income and distribution, *Quarterly Journal of Economics*, 70 (1), (Feb. 1956), 139–155) seems to be the only attempt in this direction, but is inadequate in its omission of money and in its reliance on equilibrium analysis.

Chapter 1

ON THE RELATION BETWEEN COMMODITY PRICES AND FACTOR REWARDS*

1. Introduction

Consider a competitive economy with two commodities produced in positive amounts, two non-produced factors of production, and production functions concave and homogeneous of degree one. According to the Stolper–Samuelson theorem (Stolper et al., 1941), an autonomous increase in the price of one product gives rise to an increase in the real reward of one factor and to a decline in the real reward of the other. Specifically, an increase in the price of the ith product results in an increase in the real reward of whichever factor is used with greater relative intensity in the ith industry; and since one is free to number factors in any order, it is possible to associate the ith factor with the ith product (at least in a sufficiently small neighbourhood of an initial equilibrium).

This is an exceedingly useful theorem. In a two-by-two model one finds oneself appealing to it in just about every exercise involving the distribution of income. The original article by Stolper and Samuelson was devoted to a single application of the theorem, the relation between tariff protection and real

* *International Economic Review*, 10 (Oct. 1969), 407–413, with L. L. Wegge. We are greatly indebted to Professor and Mrs. George Szekeres for mathematical assistance, and to Michio Morishima for suggesting a proof of theorem 3 much shorter than the one we had constructed. We should like to acknowledge also numerous helpful conversations with Ken-ichi Inada. Finally, we wish to acknowledge the general stimulation of Paul Samuelson's fundamental papers on trade theory and on the principle of Le Châtelier (see especially Samuelson, 1953, 1960).

We have enjoyed privileged access to unpublished papers by Chipman (1969) and Uekawa (1971). The present paper is a revised version of part of an earlier paper of the same title referred to by Uekawa. It differs from its predecessor in omitting a section dealing with a general sufficient condition for the Stolper–Samuelson conclusions (a condition which has been weakened by Uekawa) and two sections dealing with cases in which products and factors are unequal in number.

Finally, we should like to acknowledge that Kuhn (1968) has independently stated condition (7) and theorem 2 of the present paper. Kuhn's paper became known to us only after our own work had been completed.

wages[1]. But the theorem plays an equally important role in determining the incidence of a sales tax in a closed economy (Benham, 1935; Johnson, 1956; Kemp, 1964), and in making clear the distributional implications of capital accumulation (Solow, 1961).

The theorem would be even more useful if it could be extended to the case of n products and n factors. Can we in that more general case claim that an increase in the price of the ith good results in an unambiguous increase in the real reward of that factor (the ith) which is used relatively intensively in the ith industry, and in an unambiguous decline in the real rewards of all other factors?

The answer to this question depends on the way in which one generalizes the concept of relative factor intensity and on the related restriction on the matrix of input–output coefficients. If one adopts what seems to us to be the most natural generalization, the Stolper–Samuelson conclusions carry over in full strength if $n = 3$ and in weakened form if $n = 4$. For $n > 1$, moreover, the proposed restriction is implied by the Stolper–Samuelson conclusions.

The bulk of the paper is devoted to a justification of these assertions.

2. The model

In this section we set out the assumptions, notation and basic relationships to be used throughout the paper[2]. y_i is the amount of commodity i produced, a_{ij} is the amount of factor j used in the production of one unit of product i, w_j is the money reward (rental) of the jth factor, p_i is the money price of the ith product. It will be assumed that all of these quantities are positive.

Given $w = (w_1, w_2, \ldots, w_n)$, producers select those a_{ij}'s which minimize the unit cost c_i of product i. Thus $a_{ij} = a_{ij}(w)$, where $a_{ij}(w)$ is homogeneous of degree zero; and $c_i = \Sigma_j w_j a_{ij}(w) = g_i(w)$, say, where g_i is homogeneous of degree one and concave. Moreover, $\partial g_i / \partial w_j = a_{ij}$ (Samuelson, 1953, p. 15). Under competition, with all goods produced, therefore,

$$c_i = \sum_{j=1}^{n} w_j a_{ij}(w) = g_i(w) = p_i \tag{1}$$

or, in vector notation,

$$p = g(w) \tag{2}$$

---

[1] Hence their classification of factors into 'scarce' and 'abundant'. From our more general point of view the scarcity or abundance of a factor is irrelevant.

[2] This section follows Chipman (1969) closely.

with the Jacobian

$$\partial g / \partial w = [a_{ij}] \equiv A. \tag{3}$$

It will, however, be more convenient to work with the logarithms of prices. Introducing the notation $\pi = \ln p$ and $\omega = \ln w$, we may rewrite (2) and (3) as

$$\pi = \ln g(e^{\omega}) = \phi(\omega) \tag{2'}$$

and

$$\partial \phi / \partial \omega = \phi'(\omega) = \hat{p}^{-1} A \hat{w}, \tag{3'}$$

where $\hat{p}$ and $\hat{w}$ are diagonal matrices, so that the ijth element of ϕ' is

$$\alpha_{ij} = w_j a_{ij} / p_i. \tag{4}$$

Let $[\alpha_{ij}]$, the matrix of distributive shares, be denoted by S. It is obvious that the row sums of S are one; that is, S is a stochastic matrix. It follows that the inverse S^{-1} also has unit row sums[3].

In terms of this notation one can say that an increase in the price of the ith product gives rise to an unambiguous increase in the real reward of the ith factor and to an unambiguous decline in the real reward of the jth factor ($j \neq i$) if and only if the inverse matrix S^{-1} possesses negative off-diagonal elements and diagonal elements in excess of unity.

3. Extensions of the Stolper–Samuelson theorem

Stolper and Samuelson, in their consideration of the two-by-two case, assumed that

$$a_{11}/a_{12} > a_{21}/a_{22} \quad \text{and} \quad \alpha_{11}/\alpha_{12} > \alpha_{21}/\alpha_{22}. \tag{5}$$

In words, the first factor is used relatively intensively in the first industry, and the second factor is used relatively intensively in the second. Moreover, it follows from a remark in section 1 that it is always possible to number the factors in such a way that the inequality has the sense of (5), so that it is not necessary to consider the possibility that the first factor is used relatively intensively in the second industry, etc.

From (5) it follows that A^{-1} and S^{-1} possess negative off-diagonal elements and positive diagonal elements. And since the row sums of S^{-1} are equal to one,

---

[3] Let 1 be the column vector consisting of n ones. Then if the $n \times n$ matrix S has row sums equal to unity, $S1 = 1$, whence $S^{-1}1 = S^{-1}(S1) = (S^{-1}S)1 = 1$. The proof is Chipman's (1969).

the diagonal elements must be greater than one. In fact, (5) is necessary as well as sufficient for the Stolper–Samuelson result.

Our first problem is to generalize the concept of relative factor intensity: that is, we need to generalize (5) so that it may be interpreted as requiring that the *i*th factor is used relatively intensively in the *i*th industry. Evidently non-singularity of the matrix S is not enough; further restrictions are necessary. There are several ways in which the concept might be generalized[4]; however, it seems most natural to say that factor i is used relatively intensively in the *i*th industry, and is associated with that industry, if and only if

$$\max\,(\alpha_{si}/\alpha_{sj}) = \alpha_{ii}/\alpha_{ij}, \qquad j = 1, .\,. , n. \tag{6}$$

If (6) holds for all i, so that[5]

$$\alpha_{ii}/\alpha_{ij} > \alpha_{si}/\alpha_{sj}, \qquad j \neq i, \qquad s \neq i; \qquad i = 1, \ldots, n, \tag{7}$$

we have the required generalization. In the special two-by-two case (7) reduces to (5).

A necessary and sufficient condition for the Stolper–Samuelson conclusions is that S^{-1} be a strong irreducible Minkowski matrix. Hence all *necessary* conditions for the Stolper–Samuelson conclusions are properties of such matrices. Among these properties the following are of special interest: (i) S is a P matrix, (ii) the inequalities (7) are satisfied, (iii) $\alpha_{ii} > \alpha_{ji}, j \neq i$. Property (i) has been established by Chipman (1969)[6]. It remains to establish (ii) and (iii).

Theorem 1. If S^{-1} has positive diagonal elements and negative off-diagonal elements, condition (7) is satisfied.

Proof. Suppose that S^{-1} has the required sign pattern and is therefore a strong irreducible Minkowski matrix. Then every principal submatrix of S^{-1} is a strong irreducible Minkowski matrix. Hence S, and the inverse of every

---

[4] Cf. Chipman, (1969) and Uekawa (1971). Johnson (1969) seems to deny the possibility of generalization.

[5] For $n > 2$ condition (7) may be written more compactly as

$$\alpha_{ii}/\alpha_{ij} > \alpha_{si}/\alpha_{sj}, \qquad i \neq j \neq s; \qquad i = 1, \ldots, n.$$

The 'missing' relation, with $s = j$, follows from $\alpha_{ii}/\alpha_{ij} > \alpha_{si}/\alpha_{sj}$ and $\alpha_{jj}/\alpha_{ji} > \alpha_{sj}/\alpha_{si}$. Thus (7) contains just $n(n-1)(n-2)$ independent relations.

It is worth noting also that (7) holds if and only if

$$\alpha_{ii}/\alpha_{ji} > \alpha_{is}/\alpha_{js}, \qquad j \neq i, \qquad s \neq i; \qquad i = 1, \ldots, n.$$

[6] An alternative proof could make use of the known relationship between the minors of a non-singular matrix and the complementary cofactors of the inverse.

principal submatrix of S^{-1}, is positive. From Jacobi's theorem, for any determinant Δ and its minors

$$\Delta_{11}\Delta_{js} - \Delta_{1s}\Delta_{j1} = \Delta_{11,js}\Delta.$$

Hence

$$\frac{\Delta_{11}}{\Delta}\frac{(-1)^{j+s}\Delta_{js}}{\Delta} - \frac{(-1)^{1+s}\Delta_{1s}}{\Delta}\frac{(-1)^{1+j}\Delta_{j1}}{\Delta} = \frac{(-1)^{j+s}\Delta_{11,js}}{\Delta_{11}}\frac{\Delta_{11}}{\Delta}. \tag{8}$$

Applying (8) to S^{-1}, and noting that $(-1)^{j+s}\Delta_{11,js}/\Delta_{11}$ is an element of the inverse of an $(n-1)$-dimensional principal submatrix of S^{-1} and therefore positive, we conclude that $\alpha_{11}\alpha_{sj} - \alpha_{s1}\alpha_{1j} > 0$. The same argument may be applied to each principal submatrix of S^{-1}. QED

Theorem 2. If S^{-1} has positive diagonal elements and negative off-diagonal elements, $\alpha_{ii} > \alpha_{ji}$ $(j \neq i)$.

Proof. From theorem 1, (7) is satisfied. Hence

$$\alpha_{ii}\alpha_{js} = \alpha_{is}\alpha_{ji} > 0, \qquad s \neq i, \qquad j \neq i.$$

Summing over $s \neq i$,

$$\alpha_{ii} \sum_{\substack{s=1 \\ s \neq i}}^{n} \alpha_{js} - \alpha_{ji} \sum_{\substack{s=1 \\ s \neq i}}^{n} \alpha_{is} > 0.$$

That is, $\alpha_{ii}(1 - \alpha_{ji}) - \alpha_{ji}(1 - \alpha_{ii}) > 0$. Hence $\alpha_{ii} > \alpha_{ji}$. QED

We now prove two *sufficiency* theorems, one for the case $n = 3$, the other for the case $n = 4$.

Theorem 3. For $n = 3$, (7) implies that S^{-1} has negative off-diagonal elements and diagonal elements greater than one.

Proof. From (7), the cofactors of the diagonal elements of S are positive and the cofactors of the off-diagonal elements are negative. It therefore suffices to show that S has a positive determinant. Now

$$|S| = \begin{vmatrix} \alpha_{11} & \alpha_{12} & \alpha_{13} \\ \alpha_{21} & \alpha_{22} & \alpha_{23} \\ \alpha_{31} & \alpha_{32} & \alpha_{33} \end{vmatrix} = \frac{1}{\alpha_{23}} \begin{vmatrix} \alpha_{11}\alpha_{23} - \alpha_{21}\alpha_{13} & \alpha_{12}\alpha_{23} - \alpha_{13}\alpha_{22} & 0 \\ \alpha_{21} & \alpha_{22} & \alpha_{23} \\ \alpha_{31} & \alpha_{32} & \alpha_{33} \end{vmatrix}$$

From (7), however, $\alpha_{11}\alpha_{23} - \alpha_{21}\alpha_{13} > 0$ and $\alpha_{12}\alpha_{23} - \alpha_{13}\alpha_{22} < 0$; moreover, the cofactors associated with these two elements are positive and negative respectively. Hence $|S| > 0$.
                                                                                QED

From theorems 1 and 3 we infer that for $n = 3$ condition (7) is both necessary and sufficient for the Stolper–Samuelson conclusions.

At the outset of our investigations we had hoped that, for $n \geq 4$ also, (7) would yield the Stolper–Samuelson conclusions. Our hopes were, however, soon frustrated. When $n = 4$, (7) no longer ensures that the off-diagonal elements of S^{-1} are negative. Consider the counter example

$$S = \frac{1}{22} \begin{bmatrix} 8 & 1 & 6.5 & 6.5 \\ 6.2 & 1.8 & 7 & 7 \\ 7 & 1 & 8 & 6 \\ 7 & 1.05 & 6 & 7.95 \end{bmatrix}.$$

The matrix satisfies (7) and has unit row sums; but the first column of S^{-1} is $(22/32.78) \times (21.33, 22.43, -11.89, -12.77)$, whence the $(2, 1)$th element of S^{-1} is positive and larger than the $(1, 1)$th element.

There is no way to negate a counter example. However, we were reluctant to concede that nothing at all can be said about the case $n = 4$. In the above example, and in all others we have constructed, not only are the diagonal elements of the inverse greater than one, but at least two off-diagonals are negative in each column and the diagonal element is larger in absolute value than the negative elements in the same column. We can prove that this is always so for four-by-four matrices satisfying (7). The economic sense of this is as follows: given the factor intensity condition (7), an increase in the price of the ith product results in an unambiguous increase in the real reward of the associated factor (the ith); the real reward of at least two other factors must decline, but at a rate which is less than the rate of increase in the reward of the ith factor.

More formally, we have been able to prove

Theorem 4. For $n = 4$, (7) implies (a) that the determinant and therefore all principal minors of S are positive (so that S is a P-matrix and factor–price equalization is assured), (b) that the diagonal elements of S^{-1} are greater than one, (c) that in each column of S^{-1} at least two elements are negative, (d) that in each column of S^{-1} the diagonal element is larger in absolute value than the negative elements, but may be smaller than the other positive element, if there is one.

Here we prove (b) only. Proofs of (a), (c) and (d) are provided in Kemp (1964).

Proof of theorem 4(b). It suffices to show that the first diagonal element of S^{-1} is greater than one. Let the ijth cofactor of S be represented by S_{ij}. Then

$$|S| = \begin{vmatrix} 1 & \alpha_{12} & \alpha_{13} & \alpha_{14} \\ 1 & \alpha_{22} & \alpha_{23} & \alpha_{24} \\ 1 & \alpha_{32} & \alpha_{33} & \alpha_{34} \\ 1 & \alpha_{42} & \alpha_{43} & \alpha_{44} \end{vmatrix} \quad \text{(add all other columns to the first and recall that } S \text{ is a stochastic matrix)}$$

$$= \begin{vmatrix} 1 & \alpha_{12} & \alpha_{13} & \alpha_{14} \\ 0 & \alpha_{22}-\alpha_{12} & \alpha_{23}-\alpha_{13} & \alpha_{24}-\alpha_{14} \\ 0 & \alpha_{32}-\alpha_{12} & \alpha_{33}-\alpha_{13} & \alpha_{34}-\alpha_{14} \\ 0 & \alpha_{42}-\alpha_{12} & \alpha_{43}-\alpha_{13} & \alpha_{44}-\alpha_{14} \end{vmatrix} \quad \text{(subtract the first row from each of the remaining rows)}$$

$$= \begin{vmatrix} \alpha_{22} & \alpha_{23} & \alpha_{24} \\ \alpha_{32} & \alpha_{33} & \alpha_{34} \\ \alpha_{42} & \alpha_{43} & \alpha_{44} \end{vmatrix} - \alpha_{12} \begin{vmatrix} 1 & \alpha_{23} & \alpha_{24} \\ 1 & \alpha_{33} & \alpha_{34} \\ 1 & \alpha_{43} & \alpha_{44} \end{vmatrix} - \alpha_{13} \begin{vmatrix} \alpha_{22} & 1 & \alpha_{24} \\ \alpha_{32} & 1 & \alpha_{34} \\ \alpha_{42} & 1 & \alpha_{44} \end{vmatrix} - \alpha_{14} \begin{vmatrix} \alpha_{22} & \alpha_{23} & 1 \\ \alpha_{32} & \alpha_{33} & 1 \\ \alpha_{42} & \alpha_{43} & 1 \end{vmatrix}$$

$$= S_{11} - \alpha_{12}B_{12} - \alpha_{13}B_{13} - \alpha_{14}B_{14},$$

say. Now the first diagonal element of S^{-1} is $S_{11}/|S|$. Evidently this element is greater than one if and only if $(\alpha_{12}B_{12} + \alpha_{13}B_{13} + \alpha_{14}B_{14})$ is positive. Adding the first two terms, we obtain

$$\alpha_{12}B_{12} + \alpha_{13}B_{13} = (\alpha_{13}\alpha_{22} - \alpha_{12}\alpha_{23} + \alpha_{12}\alpha_{43} - \alpha_{13}\alpha_{42})(\alpha_{44} - \alpha_{34})$$
$$+ (\alpha_{12}\alpha_{33} - \alpha_{13}\alpha_{32} - \alpha_{12}\alpha_{43} + \alpha_{13}\alpha_{42})(\alpha_{44} - \alpha_{24}). \tag{9}$$

The first of the four bracketed expressions may be written

$$\xi \equiv \alpha_{13}\alpha_{22}(1 - \mu_2) - \alpha_{12}\alpha_{23}(1 - \mu_3),$$

where $\mu_2 \equiv \alpha_{42}/\alpha_{22}$ and $\mu_3 \equiv \alpha_{43}/\alpha_{23}$. Now (7) implies that the diagonal element is the largest in each column (see the proof of theorem 2); hence $\mu_2 < 1$. Moreover, it follows from (7) that $\mu_2 < \mu_3$. Evidently ξ is positive if $\mu_3 \geq 1$; but, from (7) and the fact that $(1 - \mu_3) < (1 - \mu_2)$, it is positive also if $\mu_3 < 1$. The third bracketed component of (9) has a structure similar to that of the first; hence it, too, is positive. The second and fourth bracketed expressions are already known to be positive. Hence $(\alpha_{12}B_{12} + \alpha_{13}B_{13})$ is positive. By similar reasoning, $(\alpha_{13}B_{13} + \alpha_{14}B_{14})$ and $(\alpha_{12}B_{12} + \alpha_{14}B_{14})$ are positive. It follows by addition that $(\alpha_{12}B_{12} + \alpha_{13}B_{13} + \alpha_{14}B_{14})$ is positive. QED

4. Concluding remark

It is well known that in the two-by-two case an increase in a country's endowment of the ith factor, commodity prices held constant, will give rise to an increase in the output of that industry (the ith) in which the ith factor is used relatively intensively, and to a decline in the output of the other industry (Rybcznski, 1955). This result is dual to the Stolper–Samuelson relationship between commodity prices and factor rewards described in section 3. In fact

$$\partial y_i / \partial V_j = \partial w_j / \partial p_i, \qquad i, j = 1, 2, \tag{10}$$

where V_j is the country's endowment of the jth factor. We now know (Samuelson, 1953, p. 10) that (10) holds for any i and j ($i, j = 1, \ldots, n$). It follows that any conclusions we have established concerning the sign of the price relationship $\partial w_j / \partial p_i$ apply equally to the quantity relationship $\partial y_i / \partial V_j$.

References

Benham, F. (1935), Taxation and the relative shares of factors of production, *Economica*, new series, II, May, 198–203.

Chipman, J. S. (1969), Factor price equalization and the Stolper–Samuelson theorem, *International Economic Review*, 10, Oct., 399–406.

Johnson, H. G. (1958), *International Trade and Economic Grwoth*, Allen and Urwin, London.

Johnson, H. G. (1956), The general equilibrium analysis of sales taxes: a comment, *American Economic Review*, 46, March, 151–156.

Kemp, M. C. (1964), *The Pure Theory of International Trade*, Prentice-Hall, Englewood Cliffs.

Kemp, M. C. (1969), *The Pure Theory of International Trade and Investment*, Prentice-Hall, Englewood Cliffs.

Kuhn, H. W. (1968), Lectures on mathematical economics, in: Dantzig, G. B. and A. F. Veinott, Jr. (Eds.), *Mathematics of the Decision Sciences*, Part 2, American Mathematical Society, Providence, R. I., 49–84.

Rybczynski, T. N. (1955), Factor endowments and relative factor prices, *Economica*, new series, 22, Nov., 336–341.

Samuelson, P. A. (1953), Prices of factors and goods in general equilibrium, *Review of Economic Studies*, 21, Oct., 1–20.

Samuelson, P. A. (1960), An extension of the Le Chatelier principle, *Econometrica*, 39, April, 368–379.

Solow, R. M. (1961), Note on Uzawa's two-sector model of economic growth, *Review of Economic Studies*, 24, Oct., 48–50.

Stolper, W. F. and P. A. Samuelson, (1941), Protection and real wages, *Review of Economic Studies*, 9, Nov., 58–73. Reprinted in Ellis, H. S. and L. A. Metzler (Eds.), *Readings in the Theory of International Trade*, The Blakiston Co., Philadelphia, 333–357.

Uekawa, Y. (1971), On the generalization of the Stolper–Samuelson theorem, *Econometrica*, 39, March, 197–218.

Chapter 2

GENERALIZATIONS OF THE STOLPER–SAMUELSON AND SAMUELSON–RYBCZYNSKI THEOREMS IN TERMS OF CONDITIONAL INPUT–OUTPUT COEFFICIENTS*

1. Introduction

Consider a competitive economy with two commodities produced in positive amounts, two non-produced factors of production, and production functions concave and homogeneous of degree one. Corresponding to each vector of factor rewards $W = (w_1, w_2)$ there is an input–output matrix

$$A(W) = \begin{bmatrix} a_{11} & a_{12} \\ a_{21} & a_{22} \end{bmatrix} > 0,$$

where $a_{ij}(W)$ is the cost-minimizing input of the ith factor per unit of the jth output. Under our assumptions,

$$P = WA, \tag{1a}$$

where $P = (p_1, p_2) > 0$ is the vector of commodity prices. Moreover, with full employment of both factors of production

$$V = AY, \tag{1b}$$

where $Y = (y_1, y_2)' > 0$ is the vector of outputs and $V = (v_1, v_2)' > 0$ is the vector of factor endowments.

According to the Stolper–Samuelson theorem (Stolper and Samuelson, 1941; Samuelson, 1953), a small increase in the price of the ith product, with all other product prices frozen, is associated with an increase in the real reward of whichever factor is used relatively intensively in the ith industry and with a

* *International Economic Review*, 10 (Oct. 1969), 414–425, with L. L. Wegge.

decline in the real reward of the factor used relatively unintensively in the ith industry. The Samuelson–Rybczynski theorem (Rybczynski, 1955; Samuelson, 1953), on the other hand, states that a small increase in the community's endowment of the ith factor of production, all product prices and all other factor endowments frozen, is associated with an increase in the output of whichever industry is relatively intensive in its use of the ith factor and with a decline in the output of the industry relatively unintensive in its use of the ith factor. In terms of our notation, the sign pattern of A^{-1} is

$$\begin{bmatrix} + & - \\ - & + \end{bmatrix} \quad \text{if and only if } a_{11}/a_{21} > a_{12}/a_{22}, \tag{2a}$$

$$\begin{bmatrix} - & + \\ + & - \end{bmatrix} \quad \text{if and only if } a_{11}/a_{21} < a_{12}/a_{22}. \tag{2b}$$

In the simple two-by-two case (2a) and (2b) are equivalent statements: one can be derived from the other simply by renumbering factors or products. When we seek to generalize, however, it is important that the distinction be maintained. Thus we have shown (Kemp and Wegge, 1969) for the three-by-three case that the sign pattern is

$$\begin{bmatrix} + & - & - \\ - & + & - \\ - & - & + \end{bmatrix} \quad \text{if and only if } a_{ss}/a_{is} > a_{sj}/a_{ij}, \qquad i, j \neq s, \tag{3a}$$

and Inada (1971) has shown that it is

$$\begin{bmatrix} - & + & + \\ + & - & + \\ + & + & - \end{bmatrix} \quad \text{if and only if } a_{ss}/a_{is} < a_{sj}/a_{ij}, \qquad i, j \neq s, \tag{3b}$$

but it is impossible to reduce one sign pattern to the other (and one system of inequalities to the other) simply by renumbering factors or products.

In this note we derive two alternative necessary and sufficient conditions, one for A^{-1} to have the (Minkowski) sign pattern

$$\begin{bmatrix} + & - & \cdots & - \\ - & + & \cdots & - \\ \cdots & \cdots & \cdots & \cdots \\ - & - & \cdots & + \end{bmatrix}, \tag{4a}$$

and one for A^{-1} to have the (Metzler) sign pattern

$$\begin{bmatrix} - & + & \cdots & + \\ + & - & \cdots & + \\ + & + & \cdots & - \end{bmatrix},$$ (4b)

where n, the number of products and primary factors of production, is arbitrary.

If and only if the first condition is satisfied, it is possible to order products and factors so that: (a) a small increase in the ith product price, with all other product prices frozen, is associated with an increase in the real reward of the ith factor of production and with a decrease in the real reward of every other factor; and (b) a small increase in the endowment of the ith factor, all product prices and all other factor endowments frozen, is associated with an increase in the output of the ith commodity and with a decline in every other output. The condition is simply that all conditional input–output coefficients, appropriately defined, be positive.

If and only if the second condition is satisfied, it is possible to order products and factors so that: (a') a small increase in the ith product price, with all other product prices frozen, is associated with a decline in the real reward of the ith factor of production and with an increase in the real reward of every other factor; and (b') a small increase in the endowment of the ith factor, all product prices and all other factor endowments frozen, is associated with a decline in the output of the ith commodity and with an increase in every other output. The condition is simply that all conditional input–output coefficients be negative.

It is shown also that the original ($n = 2$) versions of the Stolper–Samuelson and Samuelson–Rybcynski theorems are valid for arbitrary n if, in the pairwise comparison of factor intensities, the input–output coefficients are of the conditional variety. Finally, it is shown that the condition derived in our earlier work (Kemp and Wegge, 1969) (and expressed by the inequalities in (3a)), applied to all three-by-three arrays of conditional input–output coefficients of order $n - 3$, is both necessary and sufficient for the (Minkowski) sign pattern (4a) if $n \geqq 3$; and that the same condition, applied to the same arrays, is both necessary and sufficient for the (Metzler) sign pattern (4b), if $n \geqq 4$, it being understood that in this case the arrays are negative.

2. Conditional input–output coefficients

2.1. Conditional input–output coefficients of the first order

The familiar input–output coefficient a_{ij} measures the change in the demand for the ith factor of production per unit increase in the jth output, with all other outputs frozen. It also measures the change in the jth product price per unit increase in the ith factor reward, with all other factor rewards frozen.

We now denote by $a_{(ij)(s)}$ the change in the demand for the ith factor of production per unit increase in the jth output when the sth output is adjusted to keep constant the total demand for the sth factor ($s \neq i$, $s \neq j$). It is not difficult to see that

$$a_{(ij)(s)} = a_{ij} - a_{is} a_{ss}^{-1} a_{sj}. \tag{5}$$

Thus a unit increase in the jth output requires a_{sj} units of the sth factor; this amount will be forthcoming if the sth output is curtailed by $a_{ss}^{-1} a_{sj}$; the contraction of the sth industry in turn releases $a_{is} a_{ss}^{-1} a_{sj}$ units of the ith factor; the *net* increase in the demand for the ith factor is therefore $a_{ij} - a_{is} a_{ss}^{-1} a_{sj}$.

We have defined $a_{(ij)(s)}$ in terms of quantity variations. But an alternative definition in terms of dual price variations is also available. Thus we could have defined $a_{(ij)(s)}$ as the change in the jth product price per unit change in the ith factor reward when the sth factor reward is adjusted to keep constant the price of the sth product ($s \neq i$, $s \neq j$), and we could have shown that $a_{(ij)(s)}$ defined in this way also is equal to $a_{ij} - a_{is} a_{ss}^{-1} a_{sj}$.

Suppose now that the inequalities of (3a) are satisfied. Then $a_{is} a_{ss}^{-1} a_{sj}$, the amount of the ith factor released by the sth industry, is smaller than $a_{ir} a_{sr}^{-1} a_{sj}$, the amount that any other industry r would release if charged with the provision of the required amount of the sth factor. In this case, therefore, $a_{(ij)(s)}$ measures the largest possible change in the demand for the ith factor per unit change in the jth output, and is optimal in that sense. Suppose, alternatively, that the inequalities of (3b) are satisfied. Then $a_{is} a_{ss}^{-1} a_{sj}$, which is now interpreted as the reduction in the jth unit cost as the result of the reduction in the sth factor reward, is larger than $a_{ir} a_{sr}^{-1} a_{sj}$, the reduction in the jth unit costs as the result of the reduction in any other factor reward (the rth) designed to stabilize the sth product price. In this second case, therefore, $a_{(ij)(s)}$ measures the smallest possible change in the jth product price per unit change in the ith factor reward, and is optimal in *that* sense.

$a_{(ij)(s)}$ will be referred to as a first-order conditional input–output coefficient – first-order, because the total demand for just one factor (the sth) is frozen. Consistently with the terminology, we may think of a_{ij} as a zero-order coefficient.

2.2. *Conditional input–output coefficients of arbitrary order*

Extending the above definition, we define $a_{(ij)(s_1 \ldots s_k)}$ as the change in the demand for the ith factor of production per unit increase in the jth output when

k other outputs (the $(s_1, \ldots, s_k)$th) are adjusted to keep constant the total demand for the $(s_1, \ldots, s_k)$th factors $(s_r \neq i, s_r \neq j)$. The kth order conditional input–output coefficient defined in this way is given by[1]

$$
a_{(ij)(s_1 \ldots s_k)} = a_{ij} - (a_{is_1}, \ldots, a_{is_k})
\begin{bmatrix}
a_{s_1s_1} & \cdots & a_{s_1s_k} \\
\vdots & & \vdots \\
a_{s_ks_1} & \cdots & a_{s_ks_k}
\end{bmatrix}^{-1}
\begin{bmatrix}
a_{s_1j} \\
\vdots \\
a_{s_kj}
\end{bmatrix},
\qquad s_r \neq i; \quad s_r \neq j.
$$

$$(6)$$

Moreover, the higher-order conditional input–output coefficients can be obtained from the lower-order coefficients recursively, just as the first-order coefficients were obtained from the zero-order coefficients

$$
a_{(ij)(s_1 \ldots s_{k+1})} = a_{(ij)(s_1 \ldots s_k)} - a_{(is_{k+1})(s_1 \ldots s_k)} a_{(s_{k+1}s_{k+1})(s_1 \ldots s_k)}^{-1} a_{(s_{k+1}j)(s_1 \ldots s_k)}. \tag{7}
$$

The proof is found in appendix 1.

Alternatively, we might have defined $a_{(ij)(s_1 \ldots s_k)}$ as the change in the jth product price per unit change in the ith factor reward when the $(s_1, \ldots, s_k)$th factor rewards are adjusted to keep constant the prices of the $(s_1, \ldots, s_k)$th products $(s_r \neq i, s_r \neq j)$. We could have shown that $a_{(ij)(s_1 \ldots s_k)}$ defined in this way also may be calculated from formula (6), thus arriving at a generalization of the last of Samuelson's reciprocity relations (Samuelson, 1953, p. 10).

When the inequalities (3a) or (3b) are satisfied, the kth-order conditional input–output coefficients bear the expected optimality interpretations.

2.3. Reformulation of the Stolper–Samuelson and Samuelson–Rybczynski theorems in terms of conditional input–output coefficients

Before proceeding to our principal theorems we note that

$$
a_{(ii)(s_1 \ldots s_{n-1})}^{-1} = b_{ii},
$$

and

$$
\begin{bmatrix}
a_{(ii)(s_1 \ldots s_{n-2})} & a_{(ij)(s_1 \ldots s_{n-2})} \\
a_{(ji)(s_1 \ldots s_{n-2})} & a_{(jj)(s_1 \ldots s_{n-2})}
\end{bmatrix}^{-1}
=
\begin{bmatrix}
b_{ii} & b_{ij} \\
b_{ji} & b_{jj}
\end{bmatrix},
\qquad i, j = 1, \ldots, n; \qquad i \neq j. \tag{8}
$$

---

[1] A unit increase in the jth output requires amounts $(a_{s_1j}, \ldots, a_{s_kj})$ of the factors of production $(s_1, \ldots, s_k)$. These amounts are made available by adjustments to outputs $(s_1, \ldots, s_k)$. The required adjustments emerge as the solution to

$$
\begin{bmatrix}
a_{s_1s_1} & \cdots & a_{s_1s_k} \\
\vdots & & \vdots \\
a_{s_ks_1} & \cdots & a_{s_ks_k}
\end{bmatrix}
\begin{bmatrix}
x_{s_1} \\
\vdots \\
x_{s_k}
\end{bmatrix}
=
\begin{bmatrix}
a_{s_1j} \\
\vdots \\
a_{s_kj}
\end{bmatrix}.
$$

The amount of the ith factor released by industries $(s_1, \ldots, s_k)$ is then $(a_{is_1}x_{s_1} + \cdots + a_{is_k}x_{s_k})$ and the net increase in demand for the ith factor is $a_{ij} - (a_{is_1}x_{s_1} + \cdots + a_{is_k}x_{s_k})$, that is, expression (6).

where

$$\begin{bmatrix} b_{11} & \cdots & b_{1n} \\ \vdots & & \vdots \\ b_{n1} & \cdots & b_{nn} \end{bmatrix} \equiv B \equiv A^{-1}.$$

Thus the Stolper–Samuelson and Samuelson–Rybczynski theorems, originally formulated for $n = 2$, are valid for arbitrary n if in the pairwise comparison of factor intensities *conditional* input–output coefficients of order $(n - 2)$ are employed. Specifically: (a) a small increase in the ith product price, with all other product prices frozen, is associated with an increase in the real reward of the ith factor of production and with a decline in all other factor rewards; and (b) an increase in the endowment of the ith factor, all product prices and all other factor endowments frozen, is associated with an increase in the ith output and with a decline in all other outputs, if all conditional input–output coefficients in (8) are positive and if

$$a_{(ii)(s_1 \ldots s_{n-2})} a_{(jj)(s_1 \ldots s_{n-2})} > a_{(ij)(s_1 \ldots s_{n-2})} a_{(ji)(s_1 \ldots s_{n-2})}, \tag{9a}$$

that is, if

$$a_{(ii)(s_1 \ldots s_{n-2j})} > 0. \tag{9b}$$

Similarly: (a′) a small increase in the ith product price, with all other product prices frozen, is associated with a decline in the real reward of the ith factor of production and with an increase in all other factor rewards; and (b′) an increase in the endowment of the ith factor, all product prices and all other factor endowments frozen, is associated with a decline in the ith output and with an increase in all other outputs if all conditional input–output coefficients in (8) are negative and if (9a) is satisfied, i.e. if $a_{(ii)(s_1 \ldots s_{n-2j})} < 0$. Finally, we may write

$$\begin{bmatrix} a_{(hh)(s_1 \ldots s_{n-3})} & a_{(hi)(s_1 \ldots s_{n-3})} & a_{(hj)(s_1 \ldots s_{n-3})} \\ a_{(ih)(s_1 \ldots s_{n-3})} & a_{(ii)(s_1 \ldots s_{n-3})} & a_{(ij)(s_1 \ldots s_{n-3})} \\ a_{(jh)(s_1 \ldots s_{n-3})} & a_{(ji)(s_1 \ldots s_{n-3})} & a_{(jj)(s_1 \ldots s_{n-3})} \end{bmatrix}^{-1} = \begin{bmatrix} b_{hh} & b_{hi} & b_{hj} \\ b_{ih} & b_{ii} & b_{ij} \\ b_{jh} & b_{ji} & b_{jj} \end{bmatrix}, \tag{10}$$

and, drawing on Inada (1971) and Kemp and Wegge (1969), conclude: that A^{-1} has the (Minkowski) sign pattern (3a) if the $(n - 3)$-order conditional input–output coefficients of (10) are positive, $n \geq 3$, and if the inequalities of (3a), with $(n - 3)$-order conditional input–output coefficients substituted, are satisfied; and that A^{-1} has the (Metzler) sign pattern (3b) if the $(n - 3)$-order conditional input–output coefficients of (10) are negative, $n \geq 4$, and if the inequalities of (3a), with $(n - 3)$-order conditional input–output coefficients substituted, are satisfied.

The common sense of (8) and (10) may be found by noting that a_{ij} and b_{ij} are defined in different environments, one being precisely the opposite of the other. In defining a_{ij} we keep fixed all output levels except the jth, leaving factor demands variable; in defining b_{ij}, on the other hand, we hold constant all resource endowments except the jth, leaving outputs variable. Thus, when we analyse the conditions under which the Stolper–Samuelson conclusions hold, we must recalculate the input–output coefficients, replacing the fixity of output levels with the fixity of input demands. This is accomplished by the construction of conditional input–output coefficients.

Notice that in this subsection we have stated sufficient conditions only. It will be shown in section 3, however, that for the (Minkowski) sign pattern (4a) it is necessary that all conditional input–output coefficients be positive, and that for the (Metzler) sign pattern (4b) it is necessary that all conditional input–output coefficients be negative. Thus the conditions stated here will be shown to be both necessary and sufficient for the generalized Stolper–Samuelson and Samuelson–Rybczynski conclusions.

3. The generalized Stolper-Samuelson and Samuelson-Rybczynski theorems

It is now possible to state and prove our principal results. We begin with two theorems which relate to the *weak* Minkowski sign pattern ($b_{ii} \geq 0$, $b_{ij} \leq 0$ for $i \neq j$) and which, therefore, generalize versions of the Stolper–Samuelson and Samuelson–Rybczynski theorems slightly weaker than those discussed in sections 1 and 2.

We have listed in appendix 2 definitions of Minkowski and related matrices, as well as those of their properties relied on in the present section.

Theorem 1. The inverse matrix $B \equiv [b_{ij}]$ of a matrix $A \equiv [a_{ij}]$, where $AY = V$ for some $Y > 0$, $V > 0$, has the weak Minkowski sign pattern $b_{ii} \geq 0$, $b_{ij} \leq 0$, $i \neq j$, if and only if

$$a_{(ij)(s_1 \ldots s_{n-2})} \geq 0, \quad i, j = 1, \ldots, n; \quad i \neq j; \quad s_r \neq i, j. \tag{11a}$$

and

$$a_{(ii)(s_1 \ldots s_{n-2})} > 0 \quad and \quad a_{(ii)(s_1 \ldots s_{n-1})} > 0, \quad i = 1, \ldots, n; \quad s_r \neq i. \tag{11b}$$

Proof. Let $T \equiv \hat{V}^{-1} A \hat{Y}$, where $\hat{V}$ and $\hat{Y}$ are diagonal matrices such that the (i, j)th element of T is $t_{ij} = a_{ij} y_i / v_i$. Then the row sums of $T^{-1} = \hat{Y}^{-1} B \hat{V}$ are all equal to one and T^{-1} has the same sign pattern as B. Hence B has the required weak Minkowski sign pattern if and only if T^{-1} is a proper Minkowski matrix, i.e. a matrix with non-negative diagonal elements, non-positive off-diagonal elements and positive row sums. From Minkowski's theorem (see appendix 2), the determinant of a proper Minkowski matrix is positive; hence T^{-1} has a positive determinant and positive principal minors. It follows that the principal minors of B, and therefore of A also, are positive. From appendix 1, however, all conditional input–output coefficients in (11b) are ratios of principal minors of A. Thus (11b) is necessary.

Equation (1b) may be expressed in partitioned form as

$$\begin{bmatrix} V_1 \\ V_2 \end{bmatrix} = \begin{bmatrix} A_{11} & A_{12} \\ A_{21} & A_{22} \end{bmatrix} \begin{bmatrix} Y_1 \\ Y_2 \end{bmatrix},$$

where A_{11} is a $k \times k$ principal submatrix of A. Solving for Y_1, the system may be written equivalently as

$$\begin{bmatrix} Y_1 \\ V_2 \end{bmatrix} = \begin{bmatrix} A_{11}^{-1} & -A_{11}^{-1}A_{12} \\ A_{21}A_{11}^{-1} & A_{22} - A_{21}A_{11}^{-1}A_{12} \end{bmatrix} \begin{bmatrix} V_1 \\ Y_2 \end{bmatrix}$$

$$= \begin{bmatrix} B_{11} - B_{12}B_{22}^{-1}B_{21} & B_{12}B_{22}^{-1} \\ -B_{22}^{-1}B_{21} & B_{22}^{-1} \end{bmatrix} \begin{bmatrix} V_1 \\ Y_2 \end{bmatrix}, \tag{12}$$

where the second equality follows from the standard relations between a partitioned matrix with non-vanishing principal minors and its inverse. The necessity of (11a) and the sufficiency of (11) may now be established by choosing a partition with $k = n - 2$ and noticing that the elements of $A_{22} - A_{21}A_{11}^{-1}A_{12}$ are the conditional input–output coefficients of order k.   QED

We now state a corollary which depends on the special properties of proper Minkowski matrices and proper M matrices.

Corollary 1. The inverse matrix $B \equiv [b_{ij}]$ of a matrix $A \equiv [a_{ij}]$, where $AY = V$ for some $Y > 0$, $V > 0$, has the weak Minkowski sign pattern $b_{ii} \geq 0$, $b_{ij} \leq 0$, $i \neq j$, if and only if

$$a_{ij} \geq a_{(ij)(s_1)} \geq a_{(ij)(s_1 s_2)} \geq \cdots \geq a_{(ij)(s_1 \ldots s_{n-2})} \geq 0, \qquad i, j = 1, \ldots, n;$$
$$i \neq j; \qquad s_r \neq i, j \tag{13a}$$

and

$$a_{ii} \geq a_{(ii)(s_1)} \geq a_{(ii)(s_1 s_2)} \geq \cdots \geq a_{(ii)(s_1 \ldots s_{n-1})} > 0, \qquad i = 1, \ldots, n; \qquad s_r \neq i. \tag{13b}$$

Proof. If B is a proper M matrix, so is any principal submatrix of B, say B_{22}. Moreover, the inverse of a proper M matrix is non-negative and has positive diagonal elements. In particular, $B_{22}^{-1} = A_{22} - A_{21}A_{11}^{-1}A_{12}$ is non-negative and has positive diagonal elements. The Le Châtelier–Samuelson (1960) orderings (13a) and (13b) then follow from the recursive relations (7). In particular, (13b) is the condition that A be a P matrix.   QED

Theorem 2. If the inverse matrix $B \equiv [b_{ij}]$ of a matrix $A \equiv [a_{ij}]$, where $AY = V$ for some $Y > 0$, $V > 0$, has the weak Minkowski sign pattern $b_{ii} \geq 0$, $b_{ij} \leq 0$, $i \neq j$, then $a_{ij} = 0$ implies that A is reducible.

Proof. Consider a partition of A with $k = 1$ and the rows and columns in natural order. Then, from (12),

$$(1/a_{11})(a_{12}, a_{13}, \ldots, a_{1n})B_{22} = -(b_{12}, b_{13}, \ldots, b_{1n}), \tag{14}$$

where B_{22} is a proper M matrix. (14) may be viewed as a system of $(n - 1)$ equations in the unknowns $a_{1j}, j = 2, \ldots, n$. From appendix 2, if $b_{1j}, j = 2, \ldots, n$, is non-negative, so is $a_{1j}, j = 2, \ldots, n$. Further, if $a_{1j} = 0$ then $b_{1j} = 0$, for any j. If L is the index set of all vanishing a_{1j} and K is the index set of all non-vanishing (i.e. positive) a_{1j}, then the matrix $b_{kl}, k \in K, l \in L$, is a null matrix. Together with $b_{1l} = 0, l \in L$, this implies that B, and therefore A, is reducible. If $b_{1j} = 0$ for all j, B and A are trivially reducible.   QED

Thus if to the weak Minkowski sign pattern we add the further requirement that B be irreducible, then A must be strictly positive; moreover, at least one of the weak inequalities in (13a) must be replaced by a strict inequality, although $a_{(ij)(s_1 \ldots s_{n-2})}$ could still be zero.

We now revert to the strong Minkowski sign pattern of sections 1 and 2, with $b_{ii} > 0$, $b_{ij} < 0(i \neq j)$ and, therefore, every principal submatrix of B irreducible. Then for any partition of A, the elements $A_{22} - A_{21}A_{11}^{-1}A_{12}$ of (12) are strictly positive and, from the recursive relations (7), both (13a) and (13b) must hold with strict inequalities. In fact, conditions (13a) and (13b) are no longer independent. More precisely, we have

Theorem 3. For $n \geq 3$, the inverse matrix $B \equiv [b_{ij}]$ of a matrix $A \equiv [a_{ij}]$, where $AY = V$ for some $Y > 0$, $V > 0$, has the strong Minkowski sign pattern $b_{ii} > 0$, $b_{ij} < 0$, $i \neq j$, if and only if

$$a_{ij} > a_{(ij)(s_1)} > a_{(ij)(s_1 s_2)} > \cdots > a_{(ij)(s_1 \ldots s_{n-2})} > 0, \qquad i, j = 1, \ldots, n;$$
$$i \neq j; \qquad s_r \neq i, j. \tag{15a}$$

and

$$a_{ii} > 0, \qquad i = 1, \ldots, n. \tag{15b}$$

Proof. The inverse of a proper irreducible M matrix is positive. B_{22} is such a matrix. Hence, from (12), for all k the elements of $A_{22} - A_{21}A_{11}^{-1}A_{12}$ are strictly positive. Thus B has the strong Minkowski sign pattern if and only if

$$a_{(ij)(s_1 \ldots s_k)} > 0, \qquad i \neq j; \qquad s_r \neq i, j; \qquad k = 0, 1, \ldots, n-2, \tag{16a}$$

and

$$a_{(ii)(s_1 \ldots s_k)} > 0, \qquad s_r \neq i; \qquad k = 0, 1, \ldots, n-1. \tag{16b}$$

The conditions (16a) and (16b) are valid for all n; in particular, (16b) is the requirement that A be a P matrix. However, if $n \geq 3$ conditions (16b) follow from (16a). To see this, let

$$C_k = \begin{bmatrix} a_{(hh)(s_1 \ldots s_k)} & a_{(hi)(s_1 \ldots s_k)} & a_{(hj)(s_1 \ldots s_k)} \\ a_{(ih)(s_1 \ldots s_k)} & a_{(ii)(s_1 \ldots s_k)} & a_{(ij)(s_1 \ldots s_k)} \\ a_{(jh)(s_1 \ldots s_k)} & a_{(ji)(s_1 \ldots s_k)} & a_{(jj)(s_1 \ldots s_k)} \end{bmatrix}, \qquad s_r \neq i, j, h,$$

be a positive array of kth-order input–output coefficients. Then relations (16a),

$$a_{(ij)(s_1 \ldots s_k h)} \equiv a_{(ij)(s_1 \ldots s_k)} - a_{(ih)(s_1 \ldots s_k)}a_{(hh)(s_1 \ldots s_k)}^{-1}a_{(hj)(s_1 \ldots s_k)} > 0,$$

$$a_{(ih)(s_1 \ldots s_k j)} \equiv a_{(ih)(s_1 \ldots s_k)} - a_{(ij)(s_1 \ldots s_k)}a_{(jj)(s_1 \ldots s_k)}^{-1}a_{(jh)(s_1 \ldots s_k)} > 0,$$

imply

$$a_{(jj)(s_1 \ldots s_k h)} \equiv a_{(jj)(s_1 \ldots s_k)} - a_{(jh)(s_1 \ldots s_k)}a_{(hh)(s_1 \ldots s_k)}^{-1}a_{(hj)(s_1 \ldots s_k)} > 0,$$

so that the positivity of the off-diagonal $(k+1)$th-order conditional input–output coefficients implies the positivity of the diagonal $(k+1)$th-order coefficients. It follows that C_k satisfies the conditions expressed by (3a) and, therefore, has a positive determinant. This in turn implies the positivity of the diagonal conditional input–output coefficients of order $(k+2)$. Thus

$$\det C_k = a_{(hh)(s_1 \ldots s_k)}a_{(ii)(s_1 \ldots s_k h)}a_{(jj)(s_1 \ldots s_k hi)},$$

and the assertion is proved by rotating subscripts and letting k assume the values $0, 1, \ldots, n-3$.

The Le Châtelier–Samuelson (1960) ordering (15a) then follows from the recursive relations (7). QED

That completes our discussion of the Minkowski case. It should be noted that, in each of theorems 1–3, the full-employment relations $AY = V$, $Y > 0$, $V > 0$ can be replaced by the dual price relations $P = WA$, $P > 0$, $W > 0$, which correspond more closely to the terms of the original Stolper–Samuelson theorem.

It should be noted also that Uekawa (1971) has derived a necessary and sufficient condition for a version of the Minkowski sign pattern intermediate to what we have referred to as the weak and strong versions. Specifically, Uekawa considers the pattern $b_{ij} \leq 0$ $(i \neq j)$, with $b_{ij} < 0$ for at least one i for each j, thus ruling out the case in which B is diagonal. In terms of our notation, his condition is that the row vector $-B_{12}B_{22}^{-1} = A_{11}^{-1}A_{12}$ should be non-negative and B_{22} positive, where A_{11} is of order $(n-1)$. With B_{22} a scalar, Uekawa's condition follows immediately from (12). However, while we have relied on the properties of Minkowski matrices, Uekawa's paper is substantially self-contained.

Our final theorem concerns the Metzler sign pattern. We confine ourselves to the strong version of the Metzler sign pattern, with A strictly positive, since it is for such matrices that Inada (1971) has proved global univalence.

Theorem 4. For $n \geq 4$, the inverse matrix $B \equiv [b_{ij}]$ of a positive matrix $A = [a_{ij}]$ has the strong Metzler sign pattern $b_{ii} < 0$, $b_{ij} > 0$, $i \neq j$, if and only if

$$0 > a_{(ij)(s_1 \ldots s_{n-2})} > \cdots > a_{(ij)(s_1 s_2)} > a_{(ij)(s_1)} \qquad i, j = 1, \ldots, n;$$
$$i \neq j; \qquad s_r \neq i, j, \tag{17a}$$

and

$$0 > a_{(ii)(s_1)} \qquad i = 1, \ldots, n; \qquad s_1 \neq i. \tag{17b}$$

Proof. Suppose B has the strong Metzler sign pattern. Then, from Inada (1971), every principal submatrix B_{22}, except B itself, has a negative inverse; that is, $-B_{22}$ is an irreducible proper M matrix. It is necessary therefore that all conditional input–output coefficients of order greater than zero be negative.

From the negativity of all conditional input–output coefficients of orders $(n-1)$ and $(n-2)$ it follows that (9a) is satisfied and, therefore, that B has the strong Metzler sign pattern. Thus the negativity of all conditional input–output coefficients of order greater than zero is also sufficient for the Metzler sign pattern.

Thus A^{-1} has the strong Metzler sign pattern if and only if

$$a_{(ij)(s_1 \ldots s_k)} < 0, \qquad i \neq j; \qquad s_r \neq i, j; \qquad k = 1, \ldots, n-2, \tag{18a}$$

and

$$a_{(ii)(s_1 \ldots s_k)} < 0, \qquad s_r \neq i; \qquad k = 1, \ldots, n-1. \tag{18b}$$

But (18b) follows from (18a) and (17b), as may be checked by replacing C_k by $-C_k$, $k = 1, \ldots, n - 3$, in theorem 3. Thus B has the Metzler sign pattern if and only if (18a) and (17b) are satisfied. The ordering (17a) then follows from (7).

QED

In the Metzler case there remain unsolved problems which cannot be handled by the methods which succeeded in the Minkowski case. In particular, the Metzler sign pattern is quite consistent with zeros on the main diagonal of A. In such a case conditional input–output coefficients are undefined and we are without a univalence theorem.

Appendix 1

Any conditional input–output coefficient may be expressed as a ratio of determinants,

$$a_{(ij)(s_1 \ldots s_k)} = \left. \begin{vmatrix} a_{s_1 s_1} & \cdots & a_{s_1 s_k} & a_{s_1 j} \\ \vdots & & \vdots & \vdots \\ a_{s_k s_1} & \cdots & a_{s_k s_k} & a_{s_k j} \\ a_{i s_1} & \cdots & a_{i s_k} & a_{ij} \end{vmatrix} \middle/ \begin{vmatrix} a_{s_1 s_1} & \cdots & a_{s_1 s_k} \\ \vdots & & \vdots \\ a_{s_k s_1} & \cdots & a_{s_k s_k} \end{vmatrix} \right.$$

as may be verified by taking the Cauchy expansion of the numerator, in terms of the elements of the last row and last column, and comparing with (6). In particular, diagonal conditional input–output coefficients are ratios of principal minors.

Denote by $|A|$ and by $N_{(ij)(s_1 \ldots s_{k+1})}$ the numerator of $a_{(ij)(s_1 \ldots s_{k+1})}$ as defined above, and partition A so that A_{11} is $k \times k$. A_{11} is non-singular; hence

$$N_{(ij)(s_1 \ldots s_{k+1})} = |A_{11}| \cdot |A_{22} - A_{21} A_{11}^{-1} A_{12}|$$

or

$$a_{(ij)(s_1 \ldots s_{k+1})} = \left. \begin{vmatrix} a_{(s_{k+1} s_{k+1})(s_1 \ldots s_k)} & a_{(s_{k+1} j)(s_1 \ldots s_k)} \\ a_{(i s_{k+1})(s_1 \ldots s_k)} & a_{(ij)(s_1 \ldots s_k)} \end{vmatrix} \middle/ a_{(s_{k+1} s_{k+1})(s_1 \ldots s_k)} \right.,$$

which is (7).

Appendix 2

The following definitions and theorems have been used in the text. For details of proofs and for further references, especially to the earlier work of Levy, Minkowski, Markov and Besikovitch, see Ostrowski (1937–1938).

1. A matrix M^* is a Minkowski matrix if its diagonal elements are non-negative and its off-diagonal elements non-positive, and if all of its row sums are non-negative. If all row sums are strictly positive, M^* is called a proper Minkowski matrix; in all other cases it is said to be improper.

Levy (1899) and Minkowski (1900) showed that the determinant of a proper Minkowski matrix is positive. On the other hand, Markov (1908) proved that the determinant of an irreducible Minkowski matrix vanishes if and only if all its row sums are equal to zero. This is the point at which Solow's well-known paper (Solow, 1952) fits in.

2. A matrix $M \equiv [m_{ij}]$ with non-negative diagonal elements and non-positive off-diagonal elements is an M-matrix if all of its principal minors are non-negative. If its determinant is positive the matrix is called a proper M-matrix; otherwise, it is said to be improper.

The $(n-1)$th-order cofactors of an M matrix are non-negative. If M is a proper M matrix then all of its principal minors are positive and the system of equations

$$Mx = a, \qquad a \geqq 0,$$

has a non-negative solution. If a is semi-positive then $x_k = 0$ implies $a_k = 0$. If L is the index set for all vanishing x_k and K the index set for all non-vanishing (i.e. positive) x_k then the elements m_{ij}, $i \in L$, $j \in K$, are all equal to zero, which means that M is reducible. In particular, all $(n-1)$th-order cofactors of an irreducible proper M matrix are positive.

A proper Minkowski matrix is also a proper M matrix. Moreover, a proper M matrix M can be obtained from a proper Minkowski matrix M^* by multiplying the columns of M^* by appropriately chosen positive numbers. This construction underlies McKenzie's definition (McKenzie, 1960) of a diagonally dominant matrix; it is a special case of a transformation, used in Chipman (1969) and in this paper, which multiplies both rows and columns.

3. Hawkins and Simon (1949) showed that the system of equations,

$$Ax = y, \qquad a_{ii} > 0, \qquad a_{ij} < 0, \qquad y_i > 0,$$

has a solution $x_i > 0$, all i, if and only if all principal minors of A are positive. Necessity follows from the fact that $A^* \equiv [a_{ij}x_j/y_i]$ is a proper Minkowski matrix and A therefore a proper M matrix. Sufficiency follows from the positivity of the cofactors of A, as noted under paragraph 2 above. The same theorem holds if A is irreducible with non-negative diagonal elements and non-positive off-diagonal elements, and is proved in the same way.

References

Chipman, J. S. (1969), Factor price equalization and the Stolper–Samuelson theorem, *International Economic Review*, 10, Oct. 399–406.

Hawkins, D. and H. A. Simon, (1949), Note: some conditions of macroeconomic stability, *Econometrica*, 17, July–Oct., 245–248.

Inada, K. (1971), The production coefficient matrix and the Stolper–Samuelson condition, *Econometrica*, 39, March, 219–240.

Kemp, M. C. and L. L. Wegge (1969), On the relation between commodity prices and factor rewards, *International Economic Review*, 10, Oct., 407–413.

McKenzie, L. W. (1960), Matrices with dominant diagonals and economic theory, in K. J. Arrow, et al., (Eds.), (1960), *Mathematical methods in the Social Sciences, 1959*. Stanford University Press, Stanford, 47–62.

Ostrowski, A. (1937–1938), Über die Determinanten mit überwiegender Hauptdiagonale, *Commentarii Mathematici Helvetici*, 10, 69–96.

Rybczynski, T. N., (1955), Factor endowments and relative factor prices, *Economica*, new series, 22, Nov., 336–341.

Samuelson, P. A. (1953), Prices of factors and goods in general equilibrium, *Review of Economic Studies*, 21, Oct., 1–20.

Samuelson, P. A. (1960), An extension of the Le Chatelier principle, *Econometrica*, 28, April, 368–379.

Solow, R. M. (1952), On the structure of linear models, *Econometrica*, 20, Jan., 29–46.

Stolper, W. F. and Samuelson, P. A. (1941), Protection and real wages, *Review of Economic Studies*, 9, Nov., 58–73.

Uekawa, Y. (1971), Generalization of the Stolper–Samuelson theorem, *Econometrica*, 39, March, 127–218.

Chapter 3

P AND PN MATRICES, MINKOWSKI AND METZLER MATRICES, AND GENERALIZATIONS OF THE STOLPER–SAMUELSON AND SAMUELSON–RYBCZYNSKI THEOREMS*

1. Introduction

The title of our paper is long enough to serve as its introduction. We need add only that the paper is concerned with problems similar to those recently examined by Chipman (1969), Kemp and Wegge (1969), Kemp (1969, appendix to ch. 1), Wegge and Kemp (1969), Kuhn (1968), Uekawa (1971) and Inada (1971). Concentrating on matrices which are non-negative, we establish a parallel between those which are also P matrices and those which are also PN matrices, and a further parallel between matrices which have the Minkowski property of possessing inverses with non-negative diagonal elements and non-positive off-diagonal elements and those which have the Metzler property of possessing inverses with non-positive diagonal elements and non-negative off-diagonal elements. We then establish several generalizations of the Stolper–Samuelson and Samuelson–Rybczynski theorems. Some of these generalizations involve the recognition of produced inputs (intermediate goods); all of them are in terms of products and primary factors which are arbitrary (but equal) in number.

The purely mathematical derivations are collected in section 2. The economics is left to section 3.

2. Mathematics

Throughout this section we are concerned with a square matrix A of order n. If it exists, the inverse is denoted by $A^{-1} \equiv (a^{ij})$. The following additional

  * *Journal of International Economics*, 3 (Feb. 1973), 53–76, with Y. Uekawa and L. L. Wegge. We are grateful to Professor Yoshio Kimura and to an unknown referee for useful comments.

notation is needed:

a^i = ith row vector of a matrix A;

a_j = jth column vector of a matrix A;

$v(i)$ = vector obtained from a vector v by deleting the ith component;

$A(^i_j)$ = matrix obtained from a matrix A by deleting the ith row and the jth column;

$A(i;v)$ = matrix obtained from A by replacing the ith column vector with the vector v;

N = set $\{1, 2, \ldots, n\}$;

$N(i)$ = subset of N obtained by deleting the element i;

J = subset of N;

$J(i)$ = subset of N which does not contain the element i;

$\bar{J}$ = complement of J relative to N;

$\bar{J}(i)$ = complement of $J(i)$ relative to $N(i)$;

I_J = diagonal matrix obtained from the identity matrix by replacing each jth row e^j by $-e^j$, $j \in J$;

A_J = submatrix of the matrix A which includes the jth column vector of A, $j \in J$;

x_J = a subvector of the vector x which consists of the jth component of x, $j \in J$;

e = sum vector $[1, 1, \ldots, 1]$;

$\emptyset$ = null set;

$\subset$ = proper inclusion.

By $x > 0$ we mean $x_i > 0$ for all i. By $x \geq 0$ we mean: $x_i \geq 0$ for all i and $x_i > 0$ for at least one i. By $x \geqq 0$ we mean $x_i \geqq 0$ for all i. By $A \geqq 0$ we mean: $a_{ij} \geqq 0$ for all i and all j.

Definition 1. The square matrix A is said to be a P matrix if all of its principal minors are positive.

Definition 2. The square matrix A of order $n(\geqq 2)$ is said to be a PN matrix if every principal minor of order k, $2 \leqq k \leqq n$, is not zero and has the sign of $(-1)^{k-1}$.

Remark. If the non-negative matrix A is a PN matrix then A has positive off-diagonal elements. For example, suppose that $a_{ij} = 0$ for some i and some j, $i \neq j$. Then the second-order principal minor $\begin{vmatrix} a_{ii} & 0 \\ a_{ji} & a_{jj} \end{vmatrix}$ is non-negative, a contradiction.

Definition 3. The square matrix A is said to have the Minkowski property if it possesses an inverse with $a^{ii} \geqq 0$ and $a^{ij} \leqq 0$, $i \neq j$.

Definition 4. The square matrix A is said to have the Metzler property if it possesses an inverse with $a^{ii} \leq 0$ and $a^{ij} \geq 0$, $i \neq j$.

Henceforth, A will be assumed to be non-negative. In addition, several alternative conditions will be imposed on A. Economic interpretations of some of these conditions will be provided in section 3.

Condition 1. For any non-empty proper subset J of N, there exist $x_j > 0$, $j = 1, 2, \ldots, n$, depending on J, such that

$$\sum_{i \in J} a_{ij} x_i > \sum_{i \in \bar{J}} a_{ij} x_i \quad \text{for any } j \in J, \tag{1a}$$

$$\sum_{i \in \bar{J}} a_{ij} x_i > \sum_{i \in J} a_{ij} x_i \quad \text{for any } j \in \bar{J}. \tag{1b}$$

That is, for any J, $\emptyset \subset J \subset N$, the inequality

$$x[I_J A I_J] > 0 \tag{2}$$

has a positive solution.

Condition 2. For any non-empty proper subset J of N, there exist $x_j > 0$, $j = 1, 2, \ldots, n$, depending on J, such that

$$\sum_{j \in J} a_{ij} x_j < \sum_{j \in \bar{J}} a_{ij} x_j \quad \text{for any } i \in J, \tag{3a}$$

$$\sum_{j \in \bar{J}} a_{ij} x_j < \sum_{j \in J} a_{ij} x_j \quad \text{for any } i \in \bar{J}. \tag{3b}$$

That is, for any J, $\emptyset \subset J \subset N$, the inequality

$$[I_J A I_J] x < 0 \tag{4}$$

has a positive solution.

Condition 2 is dual to condition 1.

Condition 3. For any non-empty proper subset J of N and any given positive $\bar{x}_{\bar{J}} > 0$, the inequality

$$[x_J \bar{x}_{\bar{J}}][I_J A I_J] > 0 \tag{5}$$

has a solution $x_J > 0$.

Condition 4. For any non-empty proper subset J of N and any given positive $\bar{x}_{\bar{J}} > 0$, the inequality

$$[I_J A I_J] \begin{bmatrix} x_J \\ \bar{x}_{\bar{J}} \end{bmatrix} < 0 \tag{6}$$

has a solution $x_J > 0$.

Further conditions will be considered below.

Theorem 1. The non-negative square matrix A is a P matrix if and only if A satisfies condition 1.

Proof. See Uekawa (1971, theorem 1).

Lemma 1. If a non-negative square matrix A satisfies condition 2 then any principal submatrix of A satisfies condition 2.

Proof. It suffices to show that, for any i, $A\binom{i}{i}$ satisfies condition 2. Suppose that, for some $J(i)$, $A\binom{i}{i}$ does not satisfy condition 2. Then the inequality

$$[I_{J(i)}A\binom{i}{i}I_{J(i)}]x(i)<0 \tag{7}$$

cannot possess a non-negative solution. For if the inequality has a non-negative solution then it has a positive solution. From duality (Gale, 1960, theorem 2.10), then, the inequality

$$y(i)[I_{J(i)}A\binom{i}{i}I_{J(i)}]\geqq 0 \tag{8}$$

has a semi-positive solution $y(i)\geqq 0$. Now either $y(i)I_{J(i)}a_i(i)\geqq 0$ or $y(i)I_{J(i)}a_i(i)<0$. Let $J=J(i)$ if $y(i)I_{J(i)}a_i(i)\geqq 0$ and let $J\equiv J(i)\cup\{i\}$ if $y(i)I_{J(i)}a_i(i)<0$. Then the inequality

$$y[I_J A I_J]\geqq 0 \tag{9}$$

has a semi-positive solution $y\geqq 0$, with $y_i=0$. This implies that inequality (4) does not have a positive solution, a contradiction. QED.

Lemma 2. If a non-negative square matrix A satisfies condition 2 then A is non-singular.

Proof. Suppose that A is singular. Then there exists a vector $y\neq 0$ such that

$$yA=0. \tag{10}$$

Let $J=\{j:y_j\geqq 0\}$, so that $\bar{J}=\{j:y_j<0\}$. By assumption, A is non-negative and satisfies condition 2; hence its off-diagonal elements are positive, so that

$$J\neq\emptyset \quad\text{and}\quad \bar{J}\neq\emptyset. \tag{11}$$

From (11), inequality (9) is satisfied as an equality. Thus, from duality (Gale,

1960, theorem 2.10), inequality (4) does not have a positive solution, a contradiction.

QED

Theorem 2. A non-negative square matrix A is a PN matrix if and only if A satisfies condition 2.

Proof. Sufficiency. For $n = 2$ the proof is immediate. Suppose that $n > 3$. From lemmas 1 and 2, $A\binom{i}{i}$ is non-singular. Hence the equation

$$a^i(i) = y(i)A\binom{i}{i} \tag{12}$$

has a solution $y(i)$. Let $J(i) = \{j : y_j > 0,\ i \neq j\}$, so that $\bar{J}(i) = \{j : y_j \leq 0,\ i \neq j\}$. Since $A\binom{i}{i}$ is a non-negative matrix with positive off-diagonal elements,

$$J(i) \neq \emptyset. \tag{13}$$

From lemma 2, A is non-singular; hence either $a_{ii} > y(i)a_i(i)$ or $a_{ii} < y(i)a_i(i)$. Suppose that $a_{ii} > y(i)a_i(i)$. Then

$$a_{ii} + \sum_{k \in \bar{J}(i)} (-y_k)a_{ki} - \sum_{k \in J(i)} y_k a_{ki} > 0,$$

$$a_{ij} + \sum_{k \in \bar{J}(i)} (-y_k)a_{kj} - \sum_{k \in J(i)} y_k a_{kj} = 0 \quad \text{for } j \in \bar{J}(i), \tag{14}$$

$$-a_{ij} - \sum_{k \in \bar{J}(i)} (-y_k)a_{kj} + \sum_{k \in J(i)} y_k a_{kj} = 0 \quad \text{for } j \in J(i).$$

From (14), with $\bar{J} = \bar{J}(i) \cup \{i\}$, inequality (9) has a semi-positive solution; this is so whether $\bar{J}(i) \neq \emptyset$ or $\bar{J}(i) = \emptyset$. Hence A does not satisfy condition 2, a contradiction. Thus

$$a_{ii} < y(i)a_i(i). \tag{15}$$

Eqs. (12) and (15) imply that

$$\text{sign det } A = -\text{sign det } A\binom{i}{i} \quad \text{for any } i. \tag{16}$$

Any principal submatrix of A also satisfies (16). This, together with lemma 1 and the fact that the principal minors of order 2 are negative, implies that A is a PN matrix.

Necessity. We proceed by induction. It is clear that condition 2 is satisfied if $n = 2$. Consider then a particular value of n greater than 2, and suppose that for a value of n one less, condition 2 is satisfied, but that this is not true for this particular value of n. Then, from duality (Gale, 1960, theorem 2.10), for some J,

$0 \subset J \subset N$, the inequality

$$y[I_J A I_J] \geqq 0 \tag{17}$$

has a solution $y \geq 0$. In fact y must be positive, as we proceed to show. Let $M = \{j : y_j > 0\}$, $M \neq \emptyset$, and $\bar{M} = \{j : y_j = 0\}$. Further, let $\hat{J} = M \cap J$ and $\hat{\bar{J}} = M \cap \bar{J}$. Then $\hat{J} \neq \emptyset$ and $\hat{\bar{J}} \neq \emptyset$ since A is a PN matrix and therefore has positive off-diagonal elements. Let $\hat{A}$ be a principal submatrix of A with indices in $\hat{J} \cup \hat{\bar{J}}$. Then, from (17), the inequality

$$\hat{y}[I_J \hat{A} I_J] \geqq 0 \tag{18}$$

has a positive solution. From duality, $\hat{A}$ does not satisfy condition 2. If $\bar{M} \neq \emptyset$, the order of $\hat{A}$ is less than n, a contradiction. Thus $\bar{M} \neq \emptyset$, that is, $\hat{A} = A$. Hence any solution of (17) must be positive.

Let $B \equiv [I_J A I_J]^{-1}$. Since $I_J A I_J$ is a PN matrix, any row of B, say the first row b^1, must contain some negative elements. Let t be the minimum of $(-y_i/b_{1i})$ over all negative components of b^1, and suppose that this minimum is attained for $i = k$. Then $t > 0$, $z \equiv y + tb^1 \geqq 0$ and $z_k = 0$. Notice that $z[I_J A I_J] = y[I_J A I_J] + t(\delta_{1i}) \geqq 0$, where the δ_{ij} are the Kronecker deltas. Thus $z \geq 0$, $z_k = 0$, is a solution of inequality (17), a contradiction. Hence condition 2 must be satisfied.

QED

Theorems 1 and 2 establish a parallel between P and PN matrices.

Lemma 3. If a non-negative square matrix A has the Minkowski property then (a) A is a P matrix and (b) any kth-order principal submatrix of A, $k \geq 2$, has the Minkowski property.

Proof. (a) See Uekawa (1971, the last part of lemma 4). For the special case in which A is assumed to have the strong Minkowski property ($a^{ii} > 0$ and $a^{ij} < 0$, $i \neq j$), so that A is necessarily positive, see Chipman (1969, p. 405), Kemp (1969, theorem 1A.1), and Inada (1971, corollary 2).

(b) See Uekawa (1971, lemma 6) and part (a) of this lemma. For the special case in which A is assumed to have the strong Minkowski property, see Inada (1971, theorem 1).

Lemma 4. A non-negative square matrix A has the Minkowski property if and only if, for any given k and J, $k \notin J$, $\emptyset \subset J \subset N$, there exist $x_i^{(k)} \geqq 0$, $i \in J$, *depending on k and J, such that*

$$\sum_{i \in J} a_{ij} x_i^{(k)} \geqq a_{kj} \quad \text{for any } j \in J, \tag{19a}$$

$$\sum_{i \in J} a_{ij} x_i^{(k)} \leqq a_{kj} \quad \text{for any } j \in \bar{J}, \tag{19b}$$

with a strict inequality for j = k.

Proof. See Uekawa (1971, theorem 5).

Theorem 3. The non-negative square matrix A has the Minkowski property if and only if A satisfies condition 3.

Proof. Necessity. Suppose that A has the Minkowski property. Then, from lemma 4, for any k and J, $k \notin J$, and for any given $\bar{x}_k > 0$, there exist $x_i^{(k)} \geqq 0$, $i \in J$, depending on k and J, such that

$$\sum_{i \in J} a_{ij} x_i^{(k)} \geq a_{kj} \bar{x}_k \quad \text{for any } j \in J, \tag{20}$$

$$\sum_{i \in J} a_{ij} x_i^{(k)} \leqq a_{kj} \bar{x}_k \quad \text{for any } j \in \bar{J},$$

with a strict inequality for $j = k$. Summing the inequalities (20) over $k \notin J$, we obtain, respectively,

$$\sum_{i \in J} a_{ij} x_i \geqq \sum_{k \notin J} a_{kj} \bar{x}_k \quad \text{for all } j \in J, \tag{21a}$$

$$\sum_{i \in J} a_{ij} x_i < \sum_{k \notin J} a_{kj} \bar{x}_k \quad \text{for all } j \in \bar{J}, \tag{21b}$$

where $x_i = \Sigma_{k \notin J} x_i^{(k)} \geqq 0$ for $i \in J$. From lemma 3(a), A is a P matrix and, in particular, has positive diagonal elements. In (21a), therefore, it is possible to replace $x_i \geqq 0$, $i \in J$, with $x_i + \epsilon$, ϵ positive but sufficiently small, and thus ensure that the inequalities (21) are strict. Then (21a) and (21b) imply that A satisfies condition 3.

Sufficiency. Suppose that A satisfies condition 3. Then A satisfies condition 1; from theorem 1, therefore, A is a P matrix. Let A_{ij} be the cofactor of a_{ij}. It suffices to show that, for any i and j, $i \neq j$, $A_{ij} \leqq 0$. Suppose without loss of generality that $i = 1$ and $j = 2$, and consider the matrix

$$B(t) \equiv \begin{bmatrix} a_{21} + t a_{11} & a_{23} + t a_{13} & \dots & a_{2n} + t a_{1n} \\ a_{31} & a_{33} & \dots & a_{3n} \\ \vdots & \vdots & & \vdots \\ a_{n1} & a_{n3} & \dots & a_{nn} \end{bmatrix}, \tag{22}$$

where $t > 0$. A satisfies condition 3; hence $B(t)$ satisfies condition 1, so that $B(t)$ is a P matrix. In particular, $\det B(t) > 0$ for $t > 0$. Hence

$$A_{12} = -\lim_{t \to 0} \det B(t) \leq 0. \tag{23}$$

QED

Lemma 5. If the non-negative square matrix A with positive off-diagonal elements has the Metzler property then:
  (a) $a^{ii} \leq 0$ and $a^{ij} > 0$, $i \neq j$, for $n = 2$,
      $a^{ii} < 0$ and $a^{ij} \geq 0$, $i \neq j$, for $n \geq 3$;
  (b) any kth order principal submatrix of A, $k \geq 2$, has the Metzler property;
  (c) A is a PN matrix.

Proof. (a) For $n = 2$ the proposition is immediate. Suppose that $n \geq 3$ and that, for some i, $a^{ii} = 0$. Let $J(i) = \{j : a^{ij} > 0, j \neq i\}$. Since A is non-singular, $J(i) \neq \emptyset$. Consider the (i, k)th component of $A^{-1}A = I$, with $i \neq k$. We have

$$\sum_{j \in J(i)} a^{ij} a_{jk} = 0, \qquad k \neq i. \tag{24}$$

Now $a^{ij} > 0$, $j \in J(i)$; hence $a_{jk} = 0$ for $j \in J(i)$ and $k \neq i$. Thus for $n \geq 3$ there exists k such that $a_{jk} = 0$, $k \neq j$ and $j \in J(i)$, a contradiction.

  (b) For $n = 2$ the proposition is immediate. Consider then a particular value of n greater than 2. It suffices to prove that, for any i, $A\binom{i}{i}$ has the Metzler property. Without loss of generality, let $i = 1$. We have $n \geq 3$; hence, from lemma 5(a), $a^{ii} < 0$ for any i. Following Inada (1971, theorem 1), consider the matrix

$$M = \begin{bmatrix} 1 & 0 & \dots & 0 \\ \dfrac{-a^{21}}{a^{11}} & 1 & \dots & 0 \\ \dfrac{-a^{n1}}{a^{11}} & 0 & \dots & 1 \end{bmatrix}. \tag{25}$$

Now $MA^{-1}A = M$, that is,

$$
\begin{bmatrix} a^{11} & a^{12} & \ldots & a^{1n} \\ 0 & b^{22} & \ldots & b^{2n} \\ \vdots & \vdots & & \vdots \\ 0 & b^{n2} & \ldots & b^{nn} \end{bmatrix}
\begin{bmatrix} a_{11} & a_{12} & \ldots & a_{1n} \\ a_{21} & a_{22} & \ldots & a_{2n} \\ \vdots & \vdots & & \vdots \\ a_{n1} & a_{n2} & \ldots & a_{nn} \end{bmatrix}
=
\begin{bmatrix} 1 & 0 & \ldots & 0 \\ \dfrac{-a^{21}}{a^{11}} & 1 & \ldots & 0 \\ \vdots & \vdots & & \vdots \\ \dfrac{-a^{n1}}{a^{11}} & 0 & \ldots & 1 \end{bmatrix},
$$

$$(26)$$

where $b^{ij} \equiv a^{ij} - a^{i1}a^{1j}/a^{11}$, $i, j = 2, \ldots, n$. From (26),

$$
\begin{bmatrix} b^{22} & \ldots & b^{2n} \\ \vdots & & \vdots \\ b^{n2} & \ldots & b^{nn} \end{bmatrix}
\begin{bmatrix} a_{22} & \ldots & a_{2n} \\ \vdots & & \vdots \\ a_{n2} & \ldots & a_{nn} \end{bmatrix}
\equiv I.
\tag{27}
$$

Now A has positive off-diagonal elements, and it is clear that $b^{ij} \geq 0$, $i \neq j$; hence, from (27), $b^{ii} \leq 0$. Thus $A(^1_1)$ has the Metzler property.

(c) From (26) and (27), the principal minors of A are not zero and alternate in sign, beginning with a minus sign for $k = 2$. QED

Theorem 4. Consider the non-negative square matrix A with positive off-diagonal elements. The following three statements are equivalent:

(i) A has the Metzler property.

(ii) For any given k and J, $k \notin J$, $\emptyset \subset J \subset N$, there exist $x_j^{(k)} \geq 0$, $j \in J$, depending on k and J, such that

$$\sum_{j \in J} a_{ij} x_j^{(k)} \leq a_{ik} \quad \text{for any } i \in J, \tag{28a}$$

$$\sum_{j \in J} a_{ij} x_j^{(k)} \geq a_{ik} \quad \text{for any } i \in \bar{J}, \tag{28b}$$

with a strict inequality for $i = k$.

(iii) A satisfies condition 4.

Proof. The implication (i) $\Rightarrow$ (ii). For $n = 2$ the implication is immediate. Suppose that $n \geq 3$. Consider the principal submatrix of A

$$
\hat{A} = \begin{bmatrix} a_{ii} & a_{ik} & a_{ij_1} & \ldots & a_{ij_r} \\ a_{ki} & a_{kk} & a_{kj_1} & \ldots & a_{kj_r} \\ a_{j_1 i} & a_{j_1 k} & & & \\ \vdots & \vdots & & A_{JJ} & \\ a_{j_r i} & a_{j_r l} & & & \end{bmatrix},
\tag{29}
$$

where $J = \{j_1 \ldots j_r\}$ is any given non-empty proper subset of $N(i)$ and A_{JJ} is a principal submatrix of A with indices in J. From lemma 5(b) and 5(c), both $\hat{A}$ and $\hat{A}\binom{i}{i}$ have the Metzler property and are PN matrices. From lemma 5(a) and (29),

$$\hat{a}^{\,ik} = \frac{-1}{\det \hat{A}} \begin{vmatrix} a_{ik} & a_{ij_1} & \ldots & a_{ij_r} \\ a_{j_1 k} & & & \\ \vdots & & A_{JJ} & \\ a_{j_r k} & & & \end{vmatrix} \geq 0,$$

$$\hat{a}^{\,ii} = \frac{1}{\det \hat{A}} \begin{vmatrix} a_{kk} & a_{kj_1} & \ldots & a_{kj_r} \\ a_{j_1 k} & & & \\ \vdots & & A_{JJ} & \\ a_{j_r k} & & & \end{vmatrix} < 0. \tag{30}$$

Suppose that J has only one component. $\hat{A}$ is a PN matrix, so that sign $\det \hat{A} = (-1)^{3-1} > 0$; hence, from (30), the implication holds. Suppose that J has more than one component. From lemma 5(b), $\hat{A}\binom{i}{i}$ has the Metzler property. From lemma 5(a), therefore, the system

$$a_{kk} < \sum_{j \in J} a_{ij} x_j^{(k)},$$

$$a_{ik} = \sum_{j \in J} a_{ij} x_j^{(k)} \quad \text{for any } i \in J \tag{31}$$

has a non-negative solution[1]. The implication follows from (30) and (31) and the fact that sign $\det \hat{A} = $ sign $\det A_{JJ}$.

The implication (ii) $\Rightarrow$ (iii). From statement (ii), for any k and J, $k \not\in J$, and any given $\bar{x}_k > 0$, there exist $x_j^{(k)} \geq 0$, $j \in J$, depending on k and J, such that

$$\sum_{j \in J} a_{ij} x_j^{(k)} \leq a_{ik} \bar{x}_k \quad \text{for any } i \in J,$$

$$\sum_{j \in J} a_{ij} x_j^{(k)} \geq a_{ik} \bar{x}_k \quad \text{for any } i \in \bar{J}, \tag{32}$$

with a strict inequality for $i = k$. Summing the inequalities (32) over $k \not\in J$, we

---

[1] If $A \geq 0$ has the Metzler property, the system $a_{ii} < a^i(i)x(i)$, $a_i(i) = A\binom{i}{i}x(i)$ has a non-negative solution when $n \geq 3$. For let $x_j = -a^{ij}/a^{ii}$, $j \neq i$. Then the above inequality can be seen to hold, for $a^{ii} < 0$ and $a^{ij} \geq 0$, $i \neq j$.

obtain, respectively,

$$\sum_{j \in J} a_{ij} x_j \leqq \sum_{k \in J} a_{ik} \bar{x}_k \quad \text{for any } i \in J, \tag{33a}$$

$$\sum_{j \in J} a_{ij} x_j > \sum_{k \in J} a_{ik} \bar{x}_k \quad \text{for any } i \in \bar{J}, \tag{33b}$$

where $x_j = \sum_{k \in J} x_j^{(k)} \geqq 0$ for $j \in J$. Statement (ii) implies that A has positive off-diagonal elements. In (33a), therefore, it is possible to replace $x_j \geqq 0$, $j \in J$, with $(1-t)x_j + \epsilon$, t and ϵ positive but sufficiently small, and thus ensure that the inequalities (33) are strict, for the right-hand side of (33a) is positive. Thus (33a) and (33b) imply that A satisfies condition 4.

The implication (iii) $\Rightarrow$ (i). Since A satisfies condition 2, A is a PN matrix, from theorem 2. Let A_{ij} be the cofactor of a_{ij}. Then, $A_{ii}/\det A \leqq 0$ with a strict inequality for $n \geqq 3$. It therefore suffices to show that, for any i and j, $i \neq j$, $A_{ij}/\det A \geqq 0$. Suppose without loss of generality that $i = 1$ and $j = 2$, and consider the matrix

$$B(t) \equiv \begin{bmatrix} a_{21} + ta_{22} & a_{23} & \cdots & a_{2n} \\ a_{31} + ta_{32} & a_{33} & \cdots & a_{3n} \\ \vdots & \vdots & & \vdots \\ a_{n1} + ta_{n2} & a_{n3} & \cdots & a_{nn} \end{bmatrix}, \tag{34}$$

where $t > 0$. Since A satisfies condition 4, $B(t)$ satisfies condition 2, so that $B(t)$ is a PN matrix. In particular, sign $\det B(t) = (-1)^{n-2}$ for $t > 0$. Since sign $\det A = (-1)^{n-1}$,

$$a^{21} = A_{12}/\det A = -[\lim_{t \to 0} \det B(t)]/\det A \geqq 0. \qquad \text{QED}$$

Theorems 3 and 4 establish a parallel between non-negative matrices with the Minkowski property and non-negative matrices with the Metzler property.

In the remainder of this section, we consider simultaneously two square matrices A and C, each of order n. We continue to assume that A is non-negative; C, on the other hand, is assumed to be a Leontief matrix, in the sense of

Definition 5. The square matrix $C = (c_{ij})$ is said to be a Leontief matrix if $c_{ij} \leqq 0$, $i \neq j$, and if $Cu > 0$ for some $u > 0$.

In addition, several alternative conditions will be imposed on A and C jointly. Economic interpretations of some of these conditions will be provided in section 3. We shall establish a parallel between matrices $C^{-1}A$ which are P matrices and those which are PN matrices, and a further parallel between matrices $C^{-1}A$ which have the Minkowski property and those which have the Metzler property[2].

Condition 5. For any non-empty proper subset J of N, the equation

$$A_J x_J - A_{\bar{J}} x_{\bar{J}} = C_J y_J - C_{\bar{J}} y_{\bar{J}} \tag{35}$$

has a positive solution $x > 0$, $y > 0$.

Condition 6. For any non-empty proper subset J of N, the equation

$$A_J x_J - A_{\bar{J}} x_{\bar{J}} = C_{\bar{J}} y_{\bar{J}} - C_J y_J \tag{36}$$

has a positive solution $x > 0$, $y > 0$.

Condition 7. For any non-empty proper subset J of N and any given positive $\bar{x}_J$, the equation

$$A_J x_J - A_{\bar{J}} \bar{x}_{\bar{J}} = C_J x_J - C_{\bar{J}} y_{\bar{J}} \tag{37}$$

has a positive solution $x_J > 0$, $y > 0$.

Condition 8. For any non-empty proper subset J of N and any given positive $\bar{x}_{\bar{J}} > 0$, the equation

$$A_J x_J - A_{\bar{J}} \bar{x}_{\bar{J}} = C_{\bar{J}} y_{\bar{J}} - C_J y_J \tag{38}$$

has a positive solution $x_J > 0$, $y > 0$.

Theorem 5. *Let A be a non-negative square matrix and C a Leontief matrix, each of order n. Then the matrix $D \equiv C^{-1}A$ is a P matrix if and only if A and C satisfy condition 5.*

Proof. C has a dominant diagonal; hence C^{-1} is non-negative; hence D is non-negative. From theorem 1, then, D is a P matrix if and only if, for any non-empty proper subset $\bar{J}$ of N, the equation

$$[I_J C^{-1} A I_{\bar{J}}] x = y \tag{39}$$

has a solution $x > 0$ and $y > 0$. But (39) can be written as

$$A[I_{\bar{J}} x] = C[I_J y], \tag{40}$$

and therefore as

$$A_J x_J - A_{\bar{J}} x_{\bar{J}} = C_J y_J - C_{\bar{J}} y_{\bar{J}}. \tag{41}$$

QED

---

[2] It is shown in the appendix that for $C^{-1}A$ to be a P matrix (PN matrix) it is neither necessary nor sufficient that A be a P matrix (PN matrix).

Theorem 6. Let A be a non-negative square matrix and C a Leontief matrix, each of order n. Then the matrix $D \equiv C^{-1}A$ is a PN matrix if and only if A and C satisfy condition 6.

Theorem 7. Let A be a non-negative square matrix and C a Leontief matrix, each of order n. Then the matrix $D \equiv C^{-1}A$ has the Minkowski property if and only if A and C satisfy condition 7.

Theorem 8. Let A be a non-negative square matrix and C an indecomposable Leontief matrix, each of order n. Then the matrix $D \equiv C^{-1}A$ has the Metzler property if and only if A and C satisfy condition 8.

Theorems 6–8 can be proved in a straightforward way, along the lines of the proof provided for theorem 5.

3. Economics

The original statements of the dual Stolper–Samuelson and Samuelson–Rybczynski theorems are in terms of a simple two-by-two neoclassical technology. In particular, joint production is ruled out and produced inputs (intermediate goods) are suppressed (or submerged in the primary input–final output coefficients). Recently the theorems have been generalized by the admission of more than two primary factors of production and more than two final products, with factors and products equal in number. (See Kuhn, 1968; Chipman, 1969; Kemp and Wegge, 1969; Wegge and Kemp, 1969; Kemp, 1969; Uekawa, 1971; and Inada, 1971.) Under these conditions the Stolper–Samuelson problem (in a weak version) is to find technological restrictions which imply the existence of a numbering of factors or products such that an increase in the price of the ith product results in an unambiguous increase (or no change) in the real reward of the ith factor and an unambiguous decline (or no change) in the real rewards of all other factors *or*, alternatively, in an unambiguous decrease (or no change) in the real reward of the ith factor and an unambiguous increase (or no change) in the real rewards of all other factors.

In this section our mathematical results are shown to yield further generalizations of the two theorems. We consider an economy in which each of n commodities is produced with the aid of n primary factors of production and of n produced inputs and in which all coefficients of production are allowed to depend on factor rewards and commodity prices. It is assumed that returns to scale are constant and returns to proportions diminishing.

The following notation is needed almost immediately.

v_{ij} = amount of the jth primary factor used in the least-cost production of a unit of the ith commodity;

x_{ij} = amount of the jth (produced) commodity used in the least-cost production of a unit of the ith commodity;

p_i = money price of the ith (produced) commodity;

w_j = money reward (rental) of the ith primary factor.

A circumflex indicates relative changes; thus $\hat{x} \equiv dx/x$, etc.

Given $w \equiv (w_1, w_2, \ldots, w_n)$ and $p \equiv (p_1, p_2, \ldots, p_n)$, producers select those v_{ij}'s and x_{ij}'s which minimize the unit cost of producing the ith commodity. Thus $v_{ij} = v_{ij}(w, p)$ and $x_{ij} = x_{ij}(w, p)$, where $v_{ij}(\ )$ and $x_{ij}(\ )$ are homogeneous of degree zero; and the minimum unit cost of producing the ith commodity is $\Sigma_j w_j v_{ij}(w, p) + \Sigma_j p_j x_{ij}(w, p) = h_i(w, p)$, say, where $h_i(w, p)$ is homogeneous of degree one and concave. Moreover,

$$\partial h_i / \partial w_j = v_{ij}, \qquad \partial h_i / \partial p_j = x_{ij}. \tag{42}$$

Under competition, with all goods produced,

$$p_i = \sum_j w_j v_{ij}(w, p) + \sum_j p_i x_{ij}(w, p), \tag{43}$$

or, in matrix notation,

$$p = Vw + Xp, \tag{44}$$

where $V \equiv (v_{ij})$ and $X \equiv (x_{ij})$. From (42) and (43),

$$dp_i = \sum_j v_{ij}\, dw_j + \sum_j x_{ij}\, dp_i, \tag{45}$$

whence

$$\hat{p}_i = \sum_j \left(\frac{w_j v_{ij}}{p_i} \right) \hat{w}_j + \sum_j \left(\frac{p_j x_{ij}}{p_i} \right) \hat{p}_j \tag{46}$$

or, in matrix notation,

$$(I - B)\hat{p} = A\hat{w}, \tag{47}$$

where $A = (a_{ij}) \equiv (w_j v_{ij}/p_i)$ and $B = (b_{ij}) \equiv (p_i x_{ij}/p_i)$. In the absence of intermediate goods, $B = 0$ and (47) reduces to

$$\hat{p} = A\hat{w}. \tag{47'}$$

We can now apply our earlier mathematical results. For the time being, we ignore produced inputs and focus on eq. (47'). By definition, a_{ij} is the share of the jth primary factor in the cost of producing the ith commodity. Evidently A is non-negative; it is, in fact, a stochastic matrix. Let us now turn back to theorems 3 and 4 of section 2. There we find ready-made generalizations of our weak version of the Stolper–Samuelson theorem[3]. It remains only to provide economic interpretations of conditions 3 and 4. Consider condition 3[4]. We note first that the share matrix A has the Minkowski (Metzler) property if and only if the input–output matrix V has it. Hence we may just as well consider the interpretation of condition 3 as applied to V. Suppose that we group the n commodities into two composite goods J and $\bar{J}$, the grouping being done in any way whatever; and let us interpret x_i as the output of the ith commodity, so that $v_{ij}x_i$ is the amount of the jth factor hired by the ith industry. Then condition 3 states that, for any non-trivial J and any set of positive outputs $\bar{x}_i$, $i \in \bar{J}$, there exists a set of positive outputs x_i, $i \in J$, such that more of the jth factor, $j \in J$, and less of the jth factor, $j \in \bar{J}$, is used in producing the composite good J than in producing the composite good $\bar{J}$. An alternative interpretation is obtained by noting that V has the Minkowski (Metzler) property if and only if $V' = (v_{ij})$, the transpose of V, has it, so that we may just as well consider the interpretation of condition 3 as applied to V'. Let us now group the n primary factors of production into two composite factors J and $\bar{J}$, the grouping being done in any way whatever, and interpret x_i as the rental of the ith factor, so that $v_{ij}x_i = v_i x_i$ is the cost of the ith factor to the jth industry, per unit of output. Then condition 3, applied to V', states that, for any non-trivial J and any set of positive factor rentals $\bar{x}_i$, $i \in \bar{J}$, there exists a set of positive factor rentals x_i, $i \in J$, such that the composite factor J contributes more to the cost of the ith commodity, $i \in J$, and less to the cost of the ith commodity, $i \in \bar{J}$, than does the composite factor $\bar{J}$. Condition 4 lends itself to analogous interpretations.

Let us now re-admit produced inputs and return to eq. (47). We shall assume that each industry uses at least one primary factor (so that, for each i, there exists at least one j such that $a_{ij} > 0$). Evidently, $I - B$ is a Leontief matrix. It therefore possesses an inverse, so that we may write

$$\hat{p} = [I - B]^{-1}A\hat{w} = C^{-1}A\hat{w} = D\hat{w}, \tag{48}$$

where $C \equiv I - B$ and $D \equiv C^{-1}A$. We have observed already that D is non-negative; it is, in fact, a stochastic matrix[5]. In this more general case, therefore,

---

[3] Recall, however, that if A has the Minkowski (Metzler) property and if $n > 2$ then A^{-1} has strictly positive (negative) diagonal elements. See lemmas 3 and 5.

[4] The interpretations here sketched are based on Uekawa's interpretations of his condition 1. See Uekawa (1971, p. 204).

[5] Let $[p]$ be the diagonal matrix with p_i in the ith diagonal position, and let $[w]$ be the diagonal matrix with w_j in the jth diagonal position. We have

$$(I - B)^{-1}Ae = (I - B)^{-1}[p]^{-1}V[w]e = (I - B)^{-1}[p]^{-1}(I - X)[p]e = Ie = e,$$

since

$$(I - B)^{-1} = (I - [p]^{-1}X[p])^{-1} = [p]^{-1}(I - X)^{-1}[p].$$

the weak Stolper–Samuelson conclusions are obtained if and only if D has the Minkowski or Metzler property. Now the matrix D has a clear economic interpretation. The (ij)th element of D describes the total (primary plus secondary) relative effect on the ith commodity price of a change in the jth factor reward; it is therefore the share of the jth primary factor in the cost of producing the ith commodity when the cost of each produced input is properly allocated to the primary factors which, directly or indirectly, produced it. One therefore might sensibly apply all existing theorems directly to the matrix D.

In spite of these comforting observations, one may be interested in conditions on the matrices A and B (rather than on D itself) which imply that D has the Minkowski (Metzler) property. We begin by observing that, in the special case $n = 2$, D has the Minkowski (Metzler) property if and only if A has that property. (This may be confirmed by direct calculation or by noting that, for any primary factor, the true or net factor intensity of one commodity, allowing for the factor intensity of the produced input, is a positively weighted average of its apparent or gross factor intensity and of the net factor intensity of the other commodity. See Kemp (1969, ch. 7). Moreover, as is well known, A has the Minkowski (Metzler) property if and only if the first commodity is relatively intensive in its use of the first (second) primary factor, that is, if and only if v_{11}/v_{12} is greater than (less than) v_{21}/v_{22}. Thus D has the Minkowski (Metzler) property if and only if the first commodity is relatively intensive in its use of the first (second) primary factor. The existence of produced inputs makes no difference to the statement of the Stolper–Samuelson theorem. When $n \geq 3$, on the other hand, for D to have the Minkowski (Metzler) property it is neither necessary nor sufficient that A have that property[6]. Then theorems 7 and 8 provide us with the required generalizations of the Stolper–Samuelson theorem. It remains only to provide economic interpretations of conditions 7 and 8. Consider condition 7. Suppose without loss of generality that the numbering of primary factors is given. Then for every non-trivial partitioning of N into J and $\bar{J}$ and every pattern of decreases in the rentals of factors j, $j \in J$, there exists a numbering of products such that one can find a pattern of increases in the rentals of primary factors j, $j \in J$, consistent with increases in the prices of commodities i, $i \in J$, and decreases in the prices of commodities i, $i \in \bar{J}$. Thus theorem 7 tells us that if we systematically reduce the $n \times n$ case to the 2×2 by considering all possible blocks or consolidations of products and primary factors, and if we impose (the Minkowski version of) the Stolper–Samuelson conclusions on the blocks then (the Minkowski version of) the

[6] See examples 1 and 2 of the appendix.

Stolper–Samuelson conclusions applies to the individual, unconsolidated products and factors. Similarly for condition 8 and the Metzler version of the generalized Stolper–Samuelson theorem implicit in theorem 8.

So far we have concentrated on generalizations of the Stolper–Samuelson theorem. However, the dual price–rental and endowment–output relationships enable us to generalize the Samuelson–Rybczynski theorem in precisely the same way. Let $v = (v_i)$ be the vector of aggregate factor endowments, $x = (x_i)$ the vector of gross outputs, x^0 the vector of net outputs, and x^{00} the vector of real values added. Then

$$xV = v. \tag{49}$$

Also,

$$x^0 = x(I - X) \tag{50}$$

so that

$$x^0 V^0 = v. \tag{51}$$

where

$$V^0 \equiv (I - X)^{-1} V. \tag{52}$$

Finally, if physical units are chosen so that prices and rentals are unity and if $[Xe]$ is the diagonal matrix with $\Sigma_j x_{ij}$ in the ith diagonal place,

$$x^{00} = x(I - [Xe]) \tag{53}$$

so that

$$x^{00} V^{00} = v, \tag{54}$$

where

$$V^{00} \equiv (I - [Xe])^{-1} V. \tag{55}$$

Eqs. (49), (51) and (54) point the way to three alternative generalizations of the Samuelson–Rybczynski theorem. Differentiating (49), (51) and (54) logarithmically, we obtain, respectively,

$$\hat{x}\Lambda = \hat{v}, \tag{56}$$

$$\hat{x}^0 \Lambda^0 = \hat{v} \tag{57}$$

and

$$\hat{x}^{00} \Lambda^{00} = \hat{v}, \tag{58}$$

where

$$\Lambda = [x]V[v]^{-1}, \tag{59}$$

$$\Lambda^0 = [x^0]V^0[v]^{-1}, \tag{60}$$

$$\Lambda^{00} = [x^{00}]V^{00}[v]^{-1} \tag{61}$$

and $[x]$ is the diagonal matrix with x_i in the ith diagonal place, etc. It is easy to show that Λ, Λ^0, Λ^{00} are non-negative matrices with column sums equal to one. If, then, output is defined in gross terms, theorems 3 and 4 provide suitable generalizations of the Samuelson–Rybczynski theorem. If output is defined in net terms, theorems 7 and 8 provide suitable generalizations. And if output is defined as real value added, theorems 3 and 4 again provide suitable generalizations. All told, we have distinguished six alternative generalizations of the Samuelson–Rybczynski theorem – for each of three concepts of output one has a choice of Minkowski and Metzler approaches. Almost needless to say, input–output matrices which on one definition and approach yield the desired sign pattern in the inverse may not do so on an alternative definition and approach, at least when $n > 2$.[7]

Appendix

In this appendix we show by example that, when $n \geq 3$, for D to have the Minkowski (Metzler) property it is neither necessary nor sufficient that A have that property, and that, when $n \geq 3$, for D to be a P matrix (PN matrix) it is neither necessary nor sufficient for A to be a P matrix (PN matrix).

   Example 1 (Minowski property).

$$\text{(a)} \quad A = \begin{bmatrix} 0.2 & 0.1 & 0.1 \\ 0.1 & 0.2 & 0.1 \\ 0.1 & 0.1 & 0.2 \end{bmatrix}, \quad B = \begin{bmatrix} 0 & 0 & 0.6 \\ 0.4 & 0.2 & 0 \\ 0 & 0.1 & 0.5 \end{bmatrix},$$

---

[7] See examples 1 and 2 of the appendix. Chang and Mayer have shown that, when $n = 2$, net and gross outputs necessarily change in the same direction. When $n = 2$, real value added also moves in the same direction as net output. (This may be inferred from (49) and (54), bearing in mind that pre-multiplication of V by a diagonal matrix with positive diagonal elements does not change the Minkowski–Metzler properties of V.) We have shown, in effect, that these propositions do not generalize.

$$A^{-1} = \begin{bmatrix} 15/2 & -5/2 & -5/2 \\ -5/2 & 15/2 & -5/2 \\ -5/2 & -5/2 & 15/2 \end{bmatrix}, \qquad A^{-1}(I-B) \equiv D^{-1}$$

$$\equiv \begin{bmatrix} 17/2 & -7/4 & -23/4 \\ -11/2 & 25/4 & 1/4 \\ -3/2 & -11/4 & 21/4 \end{bmatrix}.$$

A has the Minkowski property, *D* has not.

(b) $A = \begin{bmatrix} 0.2 & 0.1 & 0.1 \\ 0.1 & 0.1 & 0.1 \\ 0 & 0.1 & 0.2 \end{bmatrix}, \qquad B = \begin{bmatrix} 0.5 & 0 & 0.1 \\ 0 & 0.6 & 0.1 \\ 0.6 & 0.1 & 0 \end{bmatrix},$

$$A^{-1} = \begin{bmatrix} 10 & -10 & 0 \\ -20 & 40 & -10 \\ 10 & -20 & 10 \end{bmatrix}, \qquad A^{-1}(I-B) \equiv D^{-1} = \begin{bmatrix} 5 & -4 & 0 \\ -4 & 17 & -12 \\ -1 & -9 & 11 \end{bmatrix}.$$

D has the Minkowski property, *A* has not.

Example 2 (Metzler property).

(a) $A = \begin{bmatrix} 0 & 0.2 & 0.1 \\ 0.2 & 0.1 & 0.2 \\ 0.1 & 0.2 & 0.1 \end{bmatrix}, \qquad B = \begin{bmatrix} 0.2 & 0.2 & 0.3 \\ 0.2 & 0.1 & 0.2 \\ 0 & 0.4 & 0.2 \end{bmatrix},$

$$A^{-1} = \begin{bmatrix} -10 & 0 & 10 \\ 0 & -10/3 & 20/3 \\ 10 & 20/3 & -40/3 \end{bmatrix}, \qquad A^{-1}(I-B) \equiv D^{-1}$$

$$= \begin{bmatrix} -8 & -2 & 11 \\ 2/3 & -17/3 & 18/3 \\ 20/3 & 28/3 & -45/3 \end{bmatrix}.$$

A has the Metzler property, *D* has not.

(b) $A = \begin{bmatrix} 0.1 & 0.1 & 0.2 \\ 0.1 & 0 & 0.2 \\ 0.1 & 0.2 & 0 \end{bmatrix}, \qquad B = \begin{bmatrix} 0.5 & 0 & 0.1 \\ 0 & 0.6 & 0.1 \\ 0.1 & 0.5 & 0.1 \end{bmatrix},$

$$A^{-1} = \begin{bmatrix} -20 & 20 & 10 \\ 10 & -10 & 0 \\ 10 & -5 & -5 \end{bmatrix}, \qquad A^{-1}(I-B) \equiv D^{-1}$$

$$= \begin{bmatrix} -11 & 3 & 9 \\ 5 & -4 & 0 \\ 5.5 & 0.5 & -5 \end{bmatrix}.$$

D has the Metzler property, A has not.

Example 3 (P matrices).

(a) $A = \begin{bmatrix} 0.2 & 0.1 & 0 \\ 0.1 & 0.1 & 0.1 \\ 0.2 & 0 & 0.1 \end{bmatrix}$, $\quad B = \begin{bmatrix} 0.3 & 0.4 & 0 \\ 0.1 & 0.2 & 0.4 \\ 0.1 & 0.2 & 0.4 \end{bmatrix}$,

$\det A = 0.003$.

$$A^{-1} = \begin{bmatrix} 10/3 & -10/3 & 10/3 \\ 10/3 & 20/3 & -20/3 \\ -20/3 & 20/3 & 10/3 \end{bmatrix}, \quad D^{-1} = \begin{bmatrix} 7/3 & -14/3 & 10/3 \\ 7/3 & 16/3 & -20/3 \\ -17/3 & 22/3 & -2/3 \end{bmatrix}.$$

A is a P matrix, D is not.

(b) $A = \begin{bmatrix} 0.1 & 0.2 & 0.1 \\ 0 & 0.1 & 0.2 \\ 0.2 & 0.2 & 0.3 \end{bmatrix}$, $\quad B = \begin{bmatrix} 0.3 & 0.3 & 0 \\ 0.4 & 0.1 & 0.2 \\ 0.1 & 0.2 & 0 \end{bmatrix}$,

$\det A = 0.005$.

$$A^{-1} = \begin{bmatrix} -2 & -8 & 6 \\ 8 & 2 & -4 \\ -4 & 4 & 2 \end{bmatrix}, \quad D^{-1} = \begin{bmatrix} 1.2 & -7.8 & 7.6 \\ 5.2 & 0.2 & -4.4 \\ -4.6 & 4.4 & 1.2 \end{bmatrix}.$$

D is a P matrix, A is not.

Example 4 (PN matrices).

(a) $A = \begin{bmatrix} 0.1 & 0.2 & 0.1 \\ 0.1 & 0 & 0.2 \\ 0.1 & 0.3 & 0 \end{bmatrix}$, $\quad B = \begin{bmatrix} 0.2 & 0 & 0.4 \\ 0 & 0.6 & 0.1 \\ 0.1 & 0.5 & 0 \end{bmatrix}$,

$\det A = 0.001$.

$$A^{-1} = \begin{bmatrix} -60 & 30 & 40 \\ 20 & -10 & -10 \\ 30 & -10 & -20 \end{bmatrix}, \quad D^{-1} = \begin{bmatrix} -152 & -8 & 61 \\ 17 & 1 & -17 \\ 26 & 6 & -31 \end{bmatrix}.$$

A is a PN matrix, D is not.

(b) $A = \begin{bmatrix} 0.1 & 0.1 & 0.2 \\ 0.1 & 0.1 & 0.1 \\ 0 & 0.2 & 0.1 \end{bmatrix}$, $\quad B = \begin{bmatrix} 0.4 & 0 & 0.2 \\ 0 & 0.6 & 0.1 \\ 0.1 & 0.5 & 0.1 \end{bmatrix}$, det $A = 0.002$.

$$A^{-1} = \begin{bmatrix} -5 & 15 & -5 \\ -5 & 5 & 5 \\ 10 & -10 & 0 \end{bmatrix}, \qquad D^{-1} = \begin{bmatrix} -2.5 & 8.5 & -5 \\ -3.5 & -0.5 & 5 \\ 6 & -4 & -1 \end{bmatrix}.$$

D is a PN matrix, A is not.

Addendum: Extensions of the Heckscher–Ohlin theorem

In section 3 of the text it has been shown that it is possible to extend to $n \times n$ economies two of the best-known propositions of static descriptive trade theory. Concerning a third pillar of orthodoxy, nothing was ventured. Is it possible to generate an $n \times n$ version of the Heckscher–Ohlin theorem? To this question I here offer a very timid affirmative[8].

Even in a $2 \times 2 \times 2$ context there are two versions of the Heckscher–Ohlin theorem – one based on a comparison of factor endowment ratios, the other on a comparison of autarkic factor rental ratios. It is known that neither version is valid without special restrictions on technology and preferences. (See Jones, 1956; Inada, 1967; and Kemp 1969, ch. 3.) Consider the version based on a comparison of endowment ratios. For the validity of this version it more than suffices that preferences be homothetic and the same in both countries and that the two countries share a common technology.

Let us now suppose that l countries share a common technology and common homothetic preferences and that each country produces and trades freely in each of n commodities. Endowment vectors may differ from country to country, and not just in scale. For the time being, intermediate goods are

---

[8] The Heckscher–Ohlin theorem relates international flows of *commodities* to relative *factor scarcities*. In the present note an attempt is made to establish such a relationship in an $n \times n$ world. However, this is not the only way in which one might proceed. Thus, building on earlier work of Travis, Melvin, Vanek and Baldwin, Horiba (1974) has formulated a Heckscher–Ohlin-like proposition which relates international flows of *factor content* to relative *factor scarcities* and has extended the proposition to accommodate n factors and m commodities ($m \geqq n$).

Our analysis has been partially anticipated by McKenzie (1966, pp. 100–101). However, McKenzie argues that if trading countries share a common technology and preferences then '[the] directions of trade . . . are complementary to the directions of specialization in production'. The conclusion follows from the premises only if they are strengthened by additional restrictions on international disparities in factor endowments or on the common preferences. In the present note, for example, preferences are supposed to be homothetic.

ignored. In world equilibrium

$$x^j V = v^j, \qquad j = 1, \ldots, l, \tag{A1}$$

where x^j is the vector of net outputs of the jth country and v^j is the endowment vector of that country. Summing over countries,

$$x V = v, \tag{A2}$$

where $x \equiv \Sigma \, x^j$ is the vector of world outputs (equals world consumption) and $v \equiv \Sigma \, v^j$ is the vector of world factor endowments. Since the trading countries share common homothetic preferences, any particular country, say the jth, must consume the same proportion, say π^j, of each commodity, so that the consumption vector of the jth country is $\pi^j x$. From (A1) and (A2),

$$(x^j - \pi^j x) V = v^j - \pi^j v, \tag{A3}$$

where $x^j - \pi^j x$ is the export vector of the jth country and $v^j - \pi^j v$ is the difference between the actual endowment of the jth country and what it would have been if all endowments had been positive multiples one of the other, that is, if each primary factor had been shared in the same manner. Evidently $v^j - \pi^j v$ must contain positive entries if it contains negative entries, and vice versa. Indeed if w is the common equilibrium vector of factor rentals then

$$(v^j - \pi^j v) w = 0. \tag{A4}$$

Let us write (A3) more compactly as

$$\Delta x^j V = \Delta v^j \tag{A3$'$}$$

and define the sets

$$J^j = \{i : \Delta v_i^j > 0\} \tag{A4a}$$

and

$$\bar{J}^j = \{i : \Delta v_i^j < 0\}. \tag{A4b}$$

From (A3$'$), if V is of full rank,

$$\Delta x^j = \Delta v^j V^{-1}, \tag{A5a}$$

whence, dropping the superscript j and defining $(v^{ki}) = V^{-1}$,

$$\sum_{i \in J^j} \Delta x_i = \sum_{k \in J^j} \left(\sum_{i \in J^j} v^{ki} \right) \Delta v_k + \sum_{k \in \bar{J}^j} \left(\sum_{i \in J^j} v^{ki} \right) \Delta v_k. \tag{A5b}$$

If now condition 3 is satisfied we may infer from theorem 3 that

$$\sum_{i \in J^j} v^{ki} \begin{cases} \geq 1 & \text{if } k \in J^j, \\ \leq 0 & \text{if } k \in \bar{J}^j \end{cases} \tag{A6}$$

and, therefore, that

$$\sum_{i \in J^j} \Delta x_i > 0 \quad \text{if } J^j \text{ is not empty.} \tag{A7a}$$

Under the same condition,

$$\sum_{j \in \bar{J}^j} \Delta x_i < 0 \quad \text{if } J^j \text{ is not empty.} \tag{A7b}$$

Thus *if condition 3 is satisfied and if trading countries have the same technology and the same homothetic preferences and if each country produces and trades freely in all commodities then, for any particular country j, those commodities each of which is associated with a factor with which the country is relatively well (respectively, poorly) endowed* (that is, those commodities i, $i \in J^j$ (respectively, $i \in \bar{J}^j$)) *on balance must be exported (respectively, imported).* The qualifier 'on balance' is essential: it does not follow from the listed assumptions that *each* commodity i, $i \in J^j$ (respectively, $i \in \bar{J}^j$), must be exported by country j.

If intermediate goods are admitted, one may turn to condition 7 and theorem 7 to obtain a similar extension of the Heckscher–Ohlin theorem.

References

Chang, W. W. and W. Mayer (1973), Intermediate goods in a general equilibrium trade model, *International Economic Review*, 14(2), June, 447–459.

Chipman, J. S. (1969), Factor price equalization and the Stolper–Samuelson theorem, *International Economic Review*, 10(3), Oct., 399–406.

Gale, David (1960), *The Theory of Linear Economic Models*, McGraw-Hill, New York.

Horiba, Y. (1974), General equilibrium and the Heckscher–Ohlin theory of trade: the multi-country case, *International Economic Review*, 15(2), June, 440–449.

Inada, K. (1971), The production coefficient matrix and the Stolper–Samuelson condition, *Econometrica* 39(2), March, 219–240.

Inada, K. (1967), A note on the Heckscher–Ohlin theorem, *Economic Record*, 43(101), March, 88–96.

Jones, R. W. (1956), Factor proportions and the Heckscher–Ohlin theorem, *Review of Economic Studies*, 24(1), Oct., 1–10.

Kemp, M. C. and L. L. F. Wegge (1969), On the relation between commodity prices and factor rewards, *International Economic Review*, 10(3), Oct., 407–413.

Kemp, M. C. (1969), *The Pure Theory of International Trade and Investment*, Prentice-Hall, Englewood Cliffs.

Kuhn, H. W. (1968), Lectures on mathematical economics, in: Dantzig, G. B. and A. F. Veinott (eds.), *Mathematics of the Decision Sciences*, Part 2, (Providence, R. I.: American Mathematical Society) 49–84.

McKenzie, L. W. (1966), International trade: mathematical theory, in: *Encyclopaedia of the Social Sciences*, University of Chicago Press, Chicago, 96–104.

Uekawa, Yasuo, (1971), Generalization of the Stolper–Samuelson theorem, *Econometrica*, 39(2) March, 197–218.

Wegge, L. L. F. and M. C. Kemp (1969), Generalizations of the Stolper–Samuelson and Samuelson–Rybczynski theorems in terms of conditional input–output coefficients, *International Economic Review*, 10(3), Oct., 414–425.

Chapter 4

RELATIVELY SIMPLE GENERALIZATIONS OF THE STOLPER–SAMUELSON AND SAMUELSON–RYBCZYNSKI THEOREMS*

1. Introduction

The Stolper–Samuelson theorem has been much generalized[1]. Almost without exception, however, the generalizations are to economies with primary factors equal in number to final products and with non-singular and otherwise severely restricted input–output matrices.

The generalizations established below are relatively free of these disabilities. Commodities and factors can be found in any numbers, equal or unequal; the rank of the input–output matrix is required merely to be greater than one, meaning that in equilibrium not all industries share a common technical process or activity. Under this rank condition and further weak restrictions on the input–output matrix it is shown that a small autonomous increase in any commodity price, with factor endowments and other commodity prices held constant, gives rise to an unambiguous improvement in the real reward of at least one factor and to an unambiguous deterioration of the real reward of at least one factor. In effect, the proposition sets forth weak sufficient conditions for *conflict* between income categories when a commodity price increases[2].

* With Henry Y. Wan, Jr.
[1] See, for example, the references collected at the end of this note.
[2] The present note is related to work carried out jointly by Kemp with Leon Wegge (Kemp, 1969), appendix to ch. 2). A more immediate stimulus has been provided by a recent paper by Ethier (1974) in which the proposition established in section 1 was proved for non-singular input–output matrices. Ethier's result had been stated and proved by James Meade in a brief unpublished memorandum of early 1968. With Professor Meade's permission the memorandum is printed as an appendix to this paper.
    Our method of proof owes much to Meade's memorandum and to the advice of Chulsoon Khang. The comments of Wilfred Ethier, Yasuo Uekawa and Yew-Kwang Ng helped us eliminate some of the errors and obscurities which abounded in earlier drafts.

2. The simplest case

Consider an open economy in full-employment, competitive equilibrium and producing (actually or incipiently) the full range of n commodities with the aid of m primary or unproduced factors of production, where $m \geqq n$ and $m, n > 1$. The vector of equilibrium commodity prices is denoted by p and is normalized on the n-dimensional natural simplex ($\Sigma\, p_i = 1$), so that any non-trivial change in prices must involve some increases and some decreases. If the vector of equilibrium factor rentals is denoted by w, and if a_{ij} denotes the equilibrium amount of the ith factor used in the production of one unit of the jth commodity, we have

$$p = wa. \tag{1}$$

Here $a = (a_{ij})$ is the $m \times n$ technology matrix; it depends on w and is assumed to be positive and of rank $r > 1$. It is assumed that the vector of factor endowments cannot be written as a positive linear combination of less than s, $1 < s \leqq r$, columns of a.

The initial equilibrium is disturbed by a small autonomous increase in the price of some commodity, say the first. (This is equivalent, of course, to a small decrease, in uniform proportion, in all other commodity prices.) The economy settles into a new equilibrium with a different set of factor rentals. It is possible that, in the new equilibrium, the production of some commodities is unprofitable. We may be sure, however, that at least $s > 1$ commodities are produced (actually or incipiently), including the first commodity, and that suffices for our conclusion that at least one factor benefits from the disturbance and at least one suffers. The demonstration is easy.

Without loss we may suppose that the first q commodities are produced in the new equilibrium ($q \geqq s > 1$). To maintain the competitive equality of price and average cost in the first industry it is necessary that

$$dw_j / w_j \geqq dp_1 / p_1 > 0 \quad \text{for some } j. \tag{2}$$

To maintain the equality of price and average cost in the second industry it is therefore necessary that

$$dw_k / w_k < dp_2 / p_2 < 0 \quad \text{for some } k. \tag{3}$$

Hence at least one factor suffers. Finally, we may infer from (3) that, to maintain the equality of price and average cost in the first industry, it is necessary that the weak inequality in (2) hold as a strong inequality. Hence at least one factor must benefit.

The assumption that a is positive is unnecessarily strong. Any pattern of zeros consistent with the rank and other restrictions on a can be tolerated. In particular, factors specific to an industry (or, more generally, groups of factors specific to a group of industries) are allowed. Thus this section formalizes and extends the older analysis of, for example, Bastable and Haberler.

3. The proposition extended to capitalistic economies

The proposition carries over undiluted to open economies with any kind of capital structure, that is, with produced inputs of any durability and time- or use-pattern of depreciation, provided that attention is restricted to the comparison of alternative steady states. Perhaps it will suffice to sketch the proof for the simplest circulating-capital case. Then, instead of (1), we have

$$p = wa + \rho p b, \tag{4}$$

where ρ is one plus the (constant) rate of interest, b is the $n \times n$ matrix of produced-input–output coefficients. Provisionally, the matrix a is taken to be positive and of rank $r > 1$, and it is assumed that the endowment vector cannot be expressed as a positive linear combination of less than s, $1 < s \le r$, columns of $a(I - b)^{-1}$. (From the Hawkins–Simon conditions, $(I - b)$ is non-singular; hence the rank of $a(I - B)^{-1}$ is r, the rank of a.) Suppose again that p_1 increases slightly and that a new equilibrium establishes itself. In the new equilibrium at least s industries are active; suppose that the first q industries are active. From (4) and the fact that $dp_i < 0$ for $i = 2, \ldots, n$,

$$0 < \frac{dp_1}{p_1} = \sum \alpha_{i1} \frac{dw_i}{w_i} + \sum \beta_{i1} \frac{dp_i}{p_i} \le \sum \alpha_{i1} \frac{dw_i}{w_i} + \beta_{11} \frac{dp_1}{p_1} \tag{5a}$$

and

$$0 > \frac{dp_2}{p_2} = \sum \alpha_{i2} \frac{dw_i}{w_i} + \sum \beta_{i2} \frac{dp_i}{p_i} \ge \sum \alpha_{i2} \frac{dw_i}{w_i} + \sum \beta_{i2} \frac{dp_2}{p_2}, \tag{5b}$$

where α_{ij} is the share of the ith primary factor in the cost of producing the jth product and β_{ij} is the share of the ith produced input in the cost of the jth product. (For example, $\beta_{ij} = \rho b_{ij} p_i / p_j$). From (5a),

$$0 < dp_1/p_1 \le \sum \alpha_{i1}^*(dw_i/w_i), \tag{6}$$

where $\alpha_{i1}^* \equiv \alpha_{i1}/(1 - \beta_{11}) > 0$. It is easy to check that

$$\sum \alpha_{i1}^* = \left(1 - \sum \beta_{i1}\right) \Big/ (1 - \beta_{11}) \le 1. \tag{7}$$

From (5b), on the other hand,

$$0 > \frac{dp_2}{p_2} \geqq \sum \alpha_{i2}^* \frac{dw_i}{w_i} \tag{8}$$

where $\alpha_{i2}^* \equiv \alpha_{i2}/(1 - \sum \beta_{i2}) > 0$ and it is easy to check that

$$\sum \alpha_{i2}^* = \left(1 - \sum_{i=1}^{n} \beta_{i2}\right) \Big/ \left(1 - \sum_{i=2}^{n} \beta_{i2}\right) \leqq 1. \tag{9}$$

From (6) and (7),

$$dw_j/w_j \geqq dp_1/p_1 > 0 \quad \text{for some } j. \tag{10}$$

From (8)–(10),

$$dw_k/w_k < dp_2/p_2 < 0 \quad \text{for some } k. \tag{11}$$

Hence at least one factor suffers. Finally, we may infer from (6), (7) and (11) that (10) must hold as a strict inequality. Hence at least one factor must benefit.

It should be noted again that the assumption that a is positive is unnecessarily strong. It much more than suffices that $a(I - b)^{-1}$, the $m \times n$ matrix of total (direct plus indirect) primary factor requirements, be positive.

4. Further extensions

The analysis has run in terms of an autonomous increase in a single commodity price. However, the proposition is valid for simultaneous increases, in uniform proportion, in several prices, provided that the number of prices which increase be less than s (that is, provided that the number of prices which decrease be greater than $n - s$) and provided that the disturbance is small. If these conditions are met, some commodities with reduced prices will be produced in the new equilibrium and the proofs of sections 1 and 2 apply without modification.

We can now state our

Generalized Stolper–Samuelson theorem. Confining ourselves to alternative steady states, suppose that n commodities are produced (actually or incipiently) with the aid of m primary factors (m, n $\geq$ 2; m $\gtreqless$ n) and of produced inputs of arbitrary time- and use-durability. Suppose further that in an initial equilibrium the vector of primary factor endowments can be expressed as a positive linear combination of not less than s (s > 1) columns of a(I − b)$^{-1}$, the positive m × n matrix of total (direct plus indirect) primary factor requirements. Then a small *increase, in uniform proportion, of k commodity prices (that is, a small decrease, in uniform proportion, of n − k commodity prices), s > k, with the rate of interest constant, gives rise to an unambiguous increase in the real reward of at least one factor and to an unambiguous decline in the real reward of at least one factor.*

Since only price changes in uniform proportion are admitted, it might be objected that we are still effectively in a world of just two commodities and that therefore the proposed generalization is bogus. Note, however, that the partitioning of the set of n commodities into subsets of k and $n − k$ commodities can be achieved in many different ways (to be precise, in $\frac{1}{2}\Sigma_{k=1}^{s}\{n!/[(n − k)!k!]\}$ different ways) and that the theorem covers each and every partition. Moreover, as may be easily checked, the conclusion of the theorem holds even if $k(k < s)$ commodities increase in price in terms of the remaining $n − k$ commodities (the relative prices of which are constant), with the increases in *non*-uniform proportion[3]. As a corollary, if $m = n = s$ then any non-trivial change in the price vector leaves at least one factor worse off and at least one factor better off.

We have not yet been prepared to say that the real reward of a factor increases or decreases unless it increases or decreases in terms of each and every commodity. Let us now weaken the criterion slightly and admit that the real reward of a factor increases if it increases in terms of some commodity and decreases in terms of no commodity; similarly for decreases in real rewards. Then, the conclusion of the above theorem follows from very weak assumptions indeed. In particular we need impose on technology only the trivial restrictions that the matrix $a(I − b)^{-1}$ contain at least one positive element in each column (so that, directly or indirectly, each industry makes use of at least one primary factor) and that $s > 1$; a and even $a(I − b)^{-1}$ may be quite riddled with zeros. The proof is easy, and is withheld.

We now state our

Generalized Stolper–Samuelson theorem (weak version). Confining ourselves to alternative steady states, suppose that n commodities are produced (actually or incipiently) with the aid of m primary factors (m, n ≧ 2; m ≷ n)

---

[3] If $n − k(s > k)$ commodities decrease in price in terms of the remaining k commodities (the relative prices of which are constant), with the decreases in non-uniform proportion, it can be shown that at least one factor is better off after the change. However, without stronger assumptions, it cannot be shown that at least one factor is worse off. Here, then, our conditions are not sufficient to establish a conflict of interest between income classes. The explanation may be found in the possibility that the commodity which has suffered the greatest relative price cut is not produced in the new equilibrium.

and of produced inputs of arbitrary time- and use-durability. Suppose further that in an initial equilibrium the vector of primary factor endowments can be expressed as a positive linear combination of not less than $s(s > 1)$ columns of $a(I - b)^{-1}$, the non-negative $m \times n$ matrix of total (direct plus indirect) primary factor requirements. Suppose finally that, directly or indirectly, each industry makes use of at least one primary factor. Then a small increase, in uniform proportion, of k commodity prices (that is, a small decrease, in uniform proportion, of $n - k$ commodity prices), $s > k$, with the rate of interest constant, gives rise to an increase in the real reward of at least one factor and to a decline in the real reward of at least one factor, where the increase and decrease are understood to satisfy the weaker revised criterion.

The conclusion of this theorem also holds if the k relative price increases are in non-uniform proportion. As a corollary, if $m = n = s$ then any non-trivial change in the price vector leaves at least one factor worse off and at least one factor better off in the weaker sense.

The two theorems can be extended without difficulty to cover any number of non-traded goods. Generally, this would require the introduction of final demand for the non-traded goods and would take us beyond the supply considerations which have occupied us so far. Let us therefore confine our attention to non-traded pure intermediate goods. Suppose that there are n traded final goods, q non-traded intermediate goods and m primary factors. Let a_1 be the $m \times n$ matrix of primary input–final output coefficients, a_2 the $q \times n$ matrix of produced input–final output coefficients, c the $m \times q$ matrix of primary input–intermediate output coefficients, p the n-dimensional vector of prices of final products, π the q-dimensional vector of prices of intermediate goods, and w the m-dimensional vector of rentals of primary factors. In an initial equilibrium, with all goods produced (actually or incipiently),

$$p = wa_1 + \pi a_2, \tag{12}$$

$$\pi = wc, \tag{13}$$

whence

$$p = w(a_1 + ca_2) = wd, \tag{14}$$

where $d \equiv a_1 + ca_2$ is a $m \times n$ matrix of total (direct plus indirect) primary factor-final output coefficients. Clearly d plays the same role here as has a hitherto.

We note also that the two theorems carry over without change to an economy encumbered with any mixture of excise, sales and trade taxes and subsidies, provided only that the rates of tax and subsidy are constant, independent of the price changes, and that factor rewards are taken gross, before the distribution of (positive or negative) tax proceeds. The demonstration offers no novelties[4].

Finally, the two theorems remain valid even if the rewards received by each factor differ from industry to industry, provided only that the several rewards of a factor bear relationships of proportionality to each other which are constant, independent of changes in commodity prices. Then, at least one factor is better off after the change in prices, in the sense that its real reward *in whatever industry* is higher; and at least one factor is worse off after the change in prices, in the sense that its real reward *in whatever industry* is lower[5].

[4] It is possible to prove theorems analogous to those already established but describing the effects of excise taxes and subsidies or of trade taxes and subsidies in a small open economy. In the interests of brevity, let us return to the assumptions of section 1. Let p_i now stand for the producers' price of the ith commodity, p_i' for the consumers' price and p_i'' for the constant world price; and let t_i stand for the *ad valorem* rate of excise tax on the ith commodity and τ_i for the rate of duty on imports of the ith commodity. (If the ith commodity is exported, the rate of export duty, expressed on the internal price as base, is $-\tau_i/(1+\tau_i)$.) Then

$$p_i(1+t_i) = p_i' = p_i''(1+\tau_i) \tag{i}$$

so that, if the excise tax on the first commodity is lowered,

$$dp_1/p_1 = -dt_1/(1+t_1) > 0 = dp_i'/p_i' \qquad i = 1, \ldots, n. \tag{ii}$$

Under the assumptions of section 1 it then follows that

$$dw_j/w_j \geqq dp_1/p_1 > 0 \quad \text{for some } j \tag{iii}$$

and

$$dw_k/w_k < 0 \quad \text{for some } k. \tag{iv}$$

From (ii)–(iv) we may infer that at least one factor is left unambiguously better off and one unambiguously worse off. Similarly, if the rate of duty levied on imports of the first commodity is raised,

$$dp_1/p_1 = dp_1'/p_1' = d\tau_1/(1+\tau_1) > 0 \tag{v}$$

and we obtain (iii) and (iv) again. From (iv), the weak inequality in (iii) must be strict. Hence one factor is made better off, one worse.

[5] It is possible to establish propositions analogous to those of the text but describing the effects of changes in relative interindustrial differences in factor rewards. As in footnote 4, and for the same reasons, we return to the assumptions of section 1; but let us suppose that the first factor receives a reward in the jth industry equal to $\lambda_j w_1 (\lambda_j > 0)$. Now imagine that λ_j decreases slightly, with commodity prices held constant. In the new equilibrium, at least $s(s > 1)$ commodities are produced, including the first and, let us say, the second. Hence

$$0 < -\theta_{11}\hat{\lambda}_1 = \theta_{11}\hat{w}_1 + \theta_{21}\hat{w}_2 + \cdots + \theta_{m1}\hat{w}_m, \tag{vi}$$

$$0 = \theta_{12}\hat{w}_1 + \theta_{22}\hat{w}_2 + \cdots + \theta_{m2}\hat{w}_m. \tag{vii}$$

5. Generalized Samuelson–Rybczynski theorems

Having arrived at satisfying generalizations of the Stolper–Samuelson theorem we are conditioned to expect that 'corresponding' or 'dual' extensions of this theorem will not be hard to find. Relatively simple generalizations of the Samuelson–Rybczynski theorem can indeed be produced. However, the strict duality of the Stolper–Samuelson and Samuelson–Rybczynski theorems does not survive generalization. The generalized theorems are dual only in a very attenuated sense, even (as Ethier (1974) has noted) when $m = n$ (provided that $m > 2$).

In seeking to extend the Samuelson–Rybczynski theorem to an $m \times n$ world we may follow either of two paths. On one approach we study the implications for commodity outputs of small variations in the endowment vector with both commodity prices and factor rentals held constant. This approach has the virtue of following Samuelson–Rybczynski in holding factor rentals constant, but departs from the two-by-two tradition in not necessarily maintaining the full employment of each factor. On the alternative approach, factor rewards are allowed to adjust to endowment changes so that full employment is maintained. Each approach is faithful to the two-by-two tradition in one respect but not in the other. When $m \neq n$ it is impossible to capture both features of the original problem. In this section only the first of the paths is explored.

We take as given a vector of n commodity prices, a vector of m primary factor rentals and a vector v of m factor endowments. The prices and rentals determine the positive matrix a of primary factor–output coefficients. Choosing factor units so that all equilibrium marginal rates of substitution are one, we normalize the endowment vector on the n-dimensional natural simplex ($\Sigma \, v_i = 1$). Again it is supposed that v cannot be expressed as a positive linear

---

From (vi) and (viii),

$\hat{w}_k > 0$ for some k,

$\hat{w}_l < 0$ for some l.

Moreover, if $k = 1$ and w_1 is the only rental to increase then

$\hat{w}_1 > -\hat{\lambda}_1$.

Thus at least one factor is made better off, at least one worse off, by the change in λ_1.

The proposition can be extended to accommodate cuts in $k (k < s)$ of the λ_i's, the cuts not necessarily in uniform proportion, to allow for produced inputs, and to accommodate zeros in the input–output matrices.

combination of less than s, $1 < s \leqq r$, columns of a. In an initial equilibrium, with each factor fully employed, we have

$$ax = v,\tag{15}$$

where x is a (not necessarily unique) vector of m equilibrium gross outputs. The initial equilibrium is disturbed by a small *decrease* in the endowment of one primary factor, say the first (and, therefore, by a small uniform increase in all other endowments). In the new equilibrium some factors may be less than fully employed. The number of such factors is, in general, indeterminate since the new equilibrium need not be unique. However, there always exist equilibria in which exactly s factors are fully employed and $m - s$ under-employed, and we confine our attention to such equilibria. In particular, we may be sure that the first factor is fully employed. To maintain balance between the availability and requirements of the first factor it is necessary that

$$\mathrm{d}x_j/x_j \leqq \mathrm{d}v_1/v_1 < 0 \quad \text{for some } j.\tag{16}$$

Consider now another of the s factors which are fully employed in the new equilibrium, say the second factor. To maintain balance between the availability and requirements of the second factor it is necessary, in view of (16), that

$$\mathrm{d}x_k/x_k > \mathrm{d}v_2/v_2 > 0 \quad \text{for some } k.\tag{17}$$

That is, at least one industry expands. Finally, we may infer from (17) that, to maintain balance between availability and requirements of the first factor, it is necessary that the weak inequality in (16) hold as a strong inequality. That is, at least one industry contracts in greater proportion than the endowment of the first factor.

The extension of the proposition to a uniform proportionate contraction in the endowments of several primary factors, less than s in number, and to steady states with any capital structure presents no novelties. Thus we can state our

Generalized Samuelson–Rybczynski theorem. Confining ourselves to alternative steady states, suppose that n commodities are produced (actually or incipiently) with the aid of m primary factors ($m, n \geqq 2$; $m \gtreqless n$) and of produced inputs of arbitrary time- and use-durability. Suppose further that in an initial equilibrium the vector of primary factor endowments can be expressed as a positive linear combination of not less than $s(s > 1)$ columns of a, the positive $m \times n$ matrix of direct primary factor requirements. Then a slight depletion, in uniform proportion, of k factor endowments (that is, an increase, in uniform *proportion, of m − k factor endowments), s > k, with all factor rentals and the rate of interest constant, gives rise to a decrease in the output of at least one industry, the decrease in output being relatively greater than the decrease in some endowments and to a more than proportionate increase in the output of at least one industry, the increase in output being relatively greater than the increase in some endowments.*

Again a weaker version of the theorem is available, again the depletion of endowments need not be in uniform proportion, and again non-traded goods can be accommodated.

Addendum: Memorandum by J. E. Meade (1968)

Accept Kemp's assumptions (and in particular the assumption that each factor is needed in some quantity to produce each product). Start in equilibrium with money product prices p_x, p_y, $p_z \ldots$ and money factor prices w_k, w_l, $w_m \ldots$. Let p_x rise by dp_x; p_y, p_z, etc. stay constant. *Assume production functions such that something of each product is produced both before and after the change in p_x.* (This rules out, for example, the possibility that X and Y are both produced with the same factor proportions.) Then it is easy to show that at least one factor price must go down absolutely, and that at least one factor price must go up in a proportion greater than dp_x/p_x.

   Proof. Since p_x goes up, the cost of p_x must go up. Therefore at least one factor price must go up. Suppose w_k goes up. Since k is needed to produce Y, Z, etc. and since the costs of Y, Z, etc. are unchanged, the price of some factor must go down. Suppose w_l goes down. Since L enters into the cost of X and since the total cost of X rises in the proportion dp_x/p_x, the price of some factor must rise by more than dp_x/p_x. Suppose w_m goes up by more than dp_x/p_x. Then M gains in terms of all products and L loses in terms of all products.

   The relevant condition on the production side is that underlined above. The condition is sufficient. Is it necessary[6]?

References

Chipman, J. S. (1969), Factor price equalization and the Stolper–Samuelson theorem, *International Economic Review*, 10 (3), Oct., 399–406.

[6] To Professor Meade's question this paper offers a negative answer (M.C.K. and H.Y.W.).

Ethier, W. (1974), Some of the theorems of international trade with many goods and factors, *Journal of International Economics*, 4 (2), May, 199–206.

Inada, K. (1971), The production coefficient matrix and the Stolper–Samuelson condition, *Econometrica* 39 (2), March, 219–240.

Kemp, M. C. (1969), *The Pure Theory of International Trade and Investment*, Prentice-Hall, Englewood Cliffs.

Kemp, M. C. and L. L. F. Wegge (1969), On the relation between commodity prices and factor rewards, *International Economic Review*, 10 (3), Oct., 407–413.

Kemp, M. C. (1973), Heterogeneous capital goods and long-run Stolper–Samuelson theorems, *Australian Economic Papers*, 12, Dec., 253–260.

Kuhn, H. W. (1968), Lectures on mathematical economics, in: Dantzig, G. B. and A. V. Vienott, Jr. (eds), *Mathematics of the Decision Sciences*, Part 2, American Mathematical Society, Providence, R. I., 49–84.

Uekawa, Y., M. C. Kemp, and L. L. Wegge (1973), P- and PN-matrices, Minkowski- and Metzler-matrices, and generalizations of the Stolper–Samuelson and Samuelson–Rybczynski theorems, *Journal of International Economics* 3 (1), Feb., 53–76.

Wegge, L. L. F. and M. C. Kemp (1969), Generalizations of the Stolper–Samuelson and Samuelson–Rybczynski theorems in terms of conditional input–output coefficients, *International Economic Review* 10 (3), Oct., 414–425.

Chapter 5

HETEROGENEOUS CAPITAL GOODS AND LONG-RUN STOLPER–SAMUELSON THEOREMS*

1. Introduction

Many propositions of trade theory have been derived from a simple model of production which accommodates two 'final' products and two primary (non-produced) factors of production (labour and land, say) but in which produced means of production have no place. This is true in particular of the Stolper–Samuelson theorem.

Here an attempt is made to extend the traditional model by introducing produced means of production while remaining within an essentially two-by-two framework. The task can be approached in at least two ways. One may retain both primary factors, hold the rate of interest constant, then examine the implications for the rentals of the primary factors of autonomous changes in commodity prices. Or one may drop one primary factor (land, say) in favour of 'capital', then examine the implications for the wage rate *and the rate of interest* of changes in commodity prices.

Here both approaches will be explored and it will be shown that conclusions of the Stolper–Samuelson type can be obtained from models which accommodate produced inputs of any finite durability and any time pattern of productivity. The price of this extra generality may appear to be a severe one – our conclusions relate only to comparisons of alternative steady states. However, it might well be argued that conclusions based on the original Heckscher–Ohlin model are also of this kind.

* *Australian Economic Papers*, 12 (Dec. 1973), 253–260. I wish to acknowledge an enjoyable and, for me, highly profitable correspondence with K. Acheson, W. Ethier, R. Manning, J. S. Metcalfe, I. Steedman and Y. Uekawa.

2. Two primary factors

It seems most natural to retain the traditional assumption of two primary
factors. Thus we suppose that each of two industries produces a single
commodity with the aid of two indispensable primary factors and, moreover,
that each commodity serves as an essential and more or less durable input in
each industry. Once it is allocated to a particular industry, a batch of produced
inputs is completely immobile between industries. The two primary factors, on
the other hand, are taken to be completely mobile between industries. No
special assumptions are made about the relationship between the productivity
of a machine and the length of time it has been in use (we can even admit the
possibility that, for a time, productivity increases); nor do we rule out the
possibility of trade-offs between the economic lifetime of a machine and the
intensity with which it is used. In particular we do not suppose that there exists
a formula, independent of prices, for summing or aggregating produced inputs,
of the same type but different vintages or work histories, employed by a
particular industry. It is assumed only that each produced input has a maximum
economic life span; either equipment eventually disintegrates or, more generally, given the state of technology there exists for each type of equipment
assigned to any particular industry a working age beyond which it ceases to be
profitable whatever the pattern of market prices and however tenderly it has
been nursed. Both the maximum economic life span of a particular type of
equipment and the time pattern of its productivity may depend on the industry
to which it is allocated. Each primary factor is supposed to be immortal or
of constant productivity through time. Time is divided into periods of equal
duration. It is supposed that the rentals of primary factors are paid at the end of
each period and that produced means of production are bought by the industry
using them and paid for on delivery. However, only the detail of the argument
would change if instead it were supposed that primary factor rentals are paid at
the beginning of each period or that produced means of production are rented
on long-term contract, either from producers or from specialist suppliers[1].
    The following notation will be used:

p_j = price of the *j*th product ($j = 1, 2$);
w_i = rental of one unit of *i*th primary factor of production for one period ($i = 1$,
    2);
r = rate of interest for one period ($r > 0$);

---

[1] For a detailed justification of the second claim, see footnote 2.

a_{ij} = amount of the *i*th primary factor used in producing one unit of the *j*th commodity (*i*, *j* = 1, 2);

b_{ij} = amount of the *i*th commodity, in new condition, used in producing one unit of the *j*th commodity (*i*, *j* = 1, 2);

θ_{ij} = relative share of the *i*th primary factor in the cost of producing the *j*th commodity (*i*, *j* = 1, 2);

ψ_{ij} = relative share of the *i*th commodity in the cost of producing the *j*th commodity (*i*, *j* = 1, 2).

Relative changes are indicated by a circumflex. For example, $\hat{x} \equiv dx/x$.

It is assumed that, in long-run competitive equilibrium, price is equal to the average cost of the two primary factors plus the average cost of new produced means of production, i.e.[2]

$$p_j = \sum_{i=1}^{2} a_{ij} w_i + r \sum_{i=1}^{2} b_{ij} p_i, \qquad j = 1, 2, \tag{1}$$

where the a_{ij} and b_{ij} depend on the w_i and p_i and on r.

---

[2] The appropriate equilibrium condition for long-run or steady-state analysis is not obvious. If time has a beginning, if entry is free and if in the beginning all producers are endowed with a balanced assemblage of machines of different types and vintages, then (1) is a condition of competitive equilibrium. The beginning of time need not be interpreted quite literally but might be equated to the date of conquest or any other exogenous event with the implication that debts are written off.

It has been assumed that produced inputs are purchased outright. The assumption is not restrictive. As we have noted in the text, it might have been assumed, alternatively, that such inputs are rented on long-term contract. Let us choose units so that to one unit of new equipment of type *i* assigned to industry *j* there is associated exactly one unit of equipment of type *i* and period of use *t* assigned to industry *j*, where *t* is any integer between 1 and, say, $T_{ij} + 1$, the maximum economic life of equipment of type *i* in industry *j*. And let $w_{ijt}(\tau)$ be the rental paid at the beginning of period τ for equipment of type *i* and period of use *t* in industry *j*. Then, in place of (1) we have

$$p_j(\tau) = \sum_{i=1}^{2} a_{ij} w + r \sum_{i=1}^{2} b_{ij} \sum_{t=0}^{T_{ij}} w_{ijt}(\tau). \tag{i}$$

However, in investment equilibrium,

$$p_j(\tau) = \sum_{t=0}^{T_{ij}} (1+r)^{-t} w_{ijt}(\tau + t), \tag{ii}$$

that is, the cost of a piece of equipment must equal the present value of its (perfectly foreseen) earnings. Moreover arbitrageurs will maintain the following relationship between the rentals of equipment of the same type, location and period in use:

$$w_{ijt}(\tau) = (1+r)^{-k} w_{ijt}(\tau + k). \tag{iii}$$

Substituting from (iii) into (ii) and thence into (i), we arrive back at (1) of the text.

Differentiating (1), holding r constant,

$$dp_j = \sum a_{ij}\, dw_i + r \sum b_{ij}\, dp_i + \sum (da_{ij})w_i + r \sum (db_{ij})p_i, \qquad j = 1, 2, \qquad (2)$$

where the da_{ij} and db_{ij} are constrained by the production function of the jth industry. From the first-order conditions of cost minimization, however, the last two terms on the right of (2) sum to zero so that, converting to relative changes,

$$\hat{p}_j = \sum \theta_{ij}\hat{w}_i + \sum \psi_{ij}\hat{p}_i, \qquad j = 1, 2 \qquad (3)$$

or, in matrix notation,

$$\hat{p}(I - \psi) = \hat{w}\theta, \qquad (4)$$

where

$$\theta \equiv \begin{pmatrix} \theta_{11} & \theta_{12} \\ \theta_{21} & \theta_{22} \end{pmatrix}, \qquad \psi \equiv \begin{pmatrix} \psi_{11} & \psi_{12} \\ \psi_{21} & \psi_{22} \end{pmatrix}, \qquad \hat{p} \equiv (\hat{p}_1, \hat{p}_2),$$

$$\hat{w} \equiv (\hat{w}_1, \hat{w}_2). \qquad (5)$$

For the viability of the system it is necessary that $\det(I - \psi)$ be positive. Hence $(I - \psi)^{-1}$, and therefore $\theta(I - \psi)^{-1}$, is a positive matrix. In fact $\theta(I - \psi)^{-1}$ is a stochastic matrix; for, letting $e \equiv (1, 1)$, we have $e(I - \psi) = e\theta$, whence $e\theta(I - \psi)^{-1} = e$. Moreover, the sign of $\det \theta(I - \psi)^{-1}$ is the sign of $\det \theta$. It is well known that the sign of $\det \theta$ depends on the relative intensities with which the primary factors are employed in the two industries. Specifically, $\det \theta$ is positive or negative as the first industry is relatively intensive in its use of the first or second primary factor of production respectively. Putting these facts together, we arrive at conclusions of the Stolper–Samuelson type: An increase in the relative price of the jth commodity gives rise to an increase (decrease) in the real reward of whichever primary factor is employed relatively intensively in the jth industry.

While θ is the matrix of *direct* primary factor shares, $\theta(I - \psi)^{-1}$ can be interpreted as the matrix of true (direct plus indirect) shares. Thus we have proved that, whether one calculates on the basis of direct or true (total) primary factor inputs, the relative factor intensities of the two industries are the same. This generalizes a well-known proposition relating to simple intermediate-goods models (Kemp, 1969, p. 152).

3. A single primary factor

Let us now drop one of the two primary factors. If a_j is the amount of the primary factor needed to produce one unit of the jth commodity and if w is the rental of that factor, we have, instead of (1),

$$p_j = a_j w + r \sum_{i=1}^{2} b_{ij} p_i, \qquad j = 1, 2. \tag{6}$$

If now we treat r as a variable, we obtain, in place of (3),

$$\hat{p}_j = \theta_j \hat{w} + \psi_j \hat{r} + \sum \psi_{ij} \hat{p}_i \tag{7}$$

where θ_j is the share of the primary factor in the cost of producing the jth commodity, $\psi_j \equiv \Sigma \psi_{ij}$ is the share of capital in the cost of producing the jth commodity, and $\hat{r} \equiv dr/r$. Switching to matrix notation,

$$\hat{p}(I - \psi) = (\hat{w} \quad \hat{r})\rho, \tag{8}$$

where

$$\rho \equiv \begin{pmatrix} \theta_1 & \theta_2 \\ \psi_1 & \psi_2 \end{pmatrix}. \tag{9}$$

Evidently the matrix ρ plays here a role similar to that of θ in the preceding section. By familiar reasoning, if det ρ is positive (the first industry is relatively intensive in its use of the primary factor of production) then $(I - \psi)\rho^{-1}$ has positive diagonal and negative off-diagonal elements; and if det ρ is negative (the first industry is relatively intensive in its use of capital) then $(I - \psi)\rho^{-1}$ has negative diagonal and positive off-diagonal elements. Moreover, the first column of $(I - \psi)\rho^{-1}$ adds to one and the second column to zero. We may conclude, therefore, that an increase in the jth commodity price gives rise to an increase (decrease) in the real rental of the primary factor of production and to a decrease (increase) in the rate of interest if the jth industry is relatively intensive in its use of the primary factor (capital).

4. Disconnected remarks concerning the above propositions

We have been comparing steady states. The theorems proved are local in scope and valid whatever the growth rate of the economy. However, the age distribution of equipment depends on the growth rate. Therefore, if the growth rate changes, so may equilibrium factor rentals and, in the second case studied, the rate of interest. It then follows that the relative primary factor intensities of the two industries may depend on the growth rate. The theorems are valid for all growth rates, but the data to be fed into the theorems may depend on the rate of growth assumed.

Similarly, the proposition established in section 2 is valid for all rates of interest. However, the relative primary factor intensities of the two industries may depend on the particular value assigned to the rate of interest. An increase or decrease in the rate of interest, with both commodity prices constant, changes the relative cost of the composite capital good and brings about accommodating changes in the equilibrium rentals of the primary factors. It is quite possible for the initial and new factor rewards to be associated with quite different relative primary factor intensities of the two industries.

It has been assumed that equipment is immobile between industries. The assumption seems reasonable, at least in relation to the alternative polar assumption of complete mobility. However, the assumption is not essential. The conclusions of sections 2 and 3 are valid even if mobility is perfect. However, a formal proof of this fact is lengthy, for the notation must allow for the possibility that a piece of equipment repeatedly switches industries and earns a rental which depends on its entire working history.

It has been shown in effect that the Stolper–Samuelson theorem can be reinterpreted to apply to an economy with a much richer productive structure than that of the standard two-by-two Heckscher–Ohlin model. From this it does *not* follow that all $n \times n$ generalizations of that theorem may be similarly reinterpreted. However, it *is* true that all $n \times n$ generalizations of the theorem *with intermediate goods of the simple Leontief type admitted* may be reinterpreted in this way. For references to such generalizations, see Uekawa et al. (1973).

5. Bibliographical notes

Important earlier investigations have been carried out by Acheson (1970) and by Metcalfe and Steedman (1972a, 1972b). Metcalfe and Steedman (1972b) show that conclusions of the Stolper–Samuelson kind hold for a model incorporating circulating capital as well as two primary factors of production. Acheson (1970) shows that conclusions of the Stolper–Samuelson kind hold for a model incorporating perfectly durable instruments and one primary factor of production; specifically, each industry employs the primary factor and the durable commodity produced by the other industry, but does not employ its own durable product. That is, Metcalfe and Steedman (1972b) and Acheson (1970) give proofs of special cases of the theorems proved in sections 2 and 3, respectively[3]. On the other hand, Metcalfe and Steedman (1972a) consider a model involving circulating capital and a single primary factor of production and show by example that in general conclusions of the Stolper–Samuelson kind cannot be expected to hold. The apparent contradiction between this result and that of section 3 may be resolved by noting that in the Metcalfe–Steedman example there are more than two products (two consumption goods

[3] We are here interested chiefly in those sections of Acheson's paper which are devoted to the Stolper–Samuelson and Samuelson–Rybczynski theorems. We therefore offer only footnote comment on the final section of the paper, which is concerned with the possibility of factor price equalization in his model. Acheson shows that, if capital is measured in terms of one of the products, the capital–labour ratio in the industry producing the *numéraire* may be a non-monotonic function of the wage–interest ratio. He correctly infers that it is possible for an incompletely specialized economy with a given aggregate capital–labour ratio to be in equilibrium at more than one wage–interest ratio and to display factor intensity reversals. These possibilities are, of course, quite surprising for anyone brought up on the standard Heckscher–Ohlin-Samuelson model or, indeed, on the model of section 2 above. However, factor intensity reversals of the type unearthed by Acheson can be ruled out if one is prepared to impose a certain factor intensity condition on the physical input–output coefficients. Now under the conditions of section 3 it seems natural to say that the first industry is relatively labour-intensive if and only if for each produced input the ratio of labour to produced input is higher in the first industry than in the second industry, that is, if and only if

$$a_1/b_{11} > a_2/b_{12} \quad \text{and} \quad a_1/b_{21} > a_2/b_{22}. \tag{10}$$

Similarly, one would wish to say that the second industry is relatively labour-intensive if and only if the inequalities of (10) are reversed:

$$a_1/b_{11} < a_2/b_{12} \quad \text{and} \quad a_1/b_{21} < a_2/b_{22}. \tag{11}$$

But if (10) is satisfied for all compatible commodity prices, wage rates and rates of interest then

$$wa_1/\sum p_i b_{i1} > wa_2/\sum p_i b_{i2} \tag{12}$$

always, that is, factor intensity reversals of the Acheson type are impossible. Similarly, if (11) is satisfied for all compatible commodity prices, wage rates of interest,

$$wa_1 \bigg/ \sum p_i b_{i1} < wa_2 \bigg/ \sum p_i b_{i2} \tag{13}$$

always, and factor intensity reversals of the Acheson type are again ruled out. Thus if one is prepared to assume that in the sense of (10) or (11) one industry is uniformly more intensive in its use of labour than the other industry then one need not worry about factor intensity reversals of the Acheson type. In assuming that $b_{ii} \equiv 0$, $i = 1, 2$, Acheson denied both (10) and (11).

On the other hand, the condition that (10) or (11) be satisfied is merely sufficient, not necessary, to rule out factor intensity reversals of the Acheson type. For example, (12) may be satisfied for all wage–interest ratios even though the two inequalities of (10) never point in the same direction (of course, it is necessary that, at each wage–interest ratio, at least one inequality points to the right).

plus produced means of production). The Metcalfe–Steedman result flows not from the heterogeneity of capital or from the existence of a positive rate of interest but from the abandonment of the two-by-two world of Stolper and Samuelson.

6. Further thoughts

An obvious question remains for consideration. It has been shown that one important proposition derived from the standard two-by-two model of production carries over to a fully structured capitalistic extension of that model. Are other familiar propositions derivable from that model similarly robust? It will now be shown that all comparative statical propositions concerning prices which may be derived from the standard model share the robustness of the Stolper–Samuelson theorem.

We begin by introducing a parameter α which is equal to one initially and increases in which indicate technical improvements. Then (1) may be rewritten in extended form as

$$p_j = \sum_{i=1}^{2} a_{ij}(w_1, w_2; p_1, p_2; r; \alpha)w_i + r\sum_{i=1}^{2} b_{ij}(w_1, w_2; p_1, p_2; r)p_i, \qquad j = 1, 2.$$

$$(14)$$

Two cases must be distinguished according as commodity prices or factor rentals are treated as variables.

Suppose that factor rentals are treated as variables. We wish to calculate the effect on those variables of changes in the parameters of the system, namely the two commodity prices and α. Differentiating (14) totally with respect to α, we obtain, after manipulations familiar from section 2,

$$\hat{w} = -e(\partial\theta/\partial\alpha)\theta^{-1}\hat{\alpha}, \tag{15}$$

where

$$\frac{\partial\theta}{\partial\alpha} \equiv \begin{pmatrix} \dfrac{\partial\theta_{11}}{\partial\alpha} & \dfrac{\partial\theta_{12}}{\partial\alpha} \\ \dfrac{\partial\theta_{21}}{\partial\alpha} & \dfrac{\partial\theta_{22}}{\partial\alpha} \end{pmatrix} = \begin{pmatrix} \theta_{11}\tilde{a}_{11} & \theta_{12}\tilde{a}_{12} \\ \theta_{21}\tilde{a}_{21} & \theta_{22}\tilde{a}_{22} \end{pmatrix} \tag{16}$$

and

$$\tilde{a}_{ij} \equiv (1/a_{ij})/(\partial a_{ij}/\partial\alpha). \tag{17}$$

Evidently (15) has the same form whether or not there are produced means of production. Any proposition concerning the distributional implications of technical improvements, derived from the standard two-by-two model, carries over to any capitalistic generalization of that model. This conclusion generalizes parts of propositions 2 and 3 of Kemp and Uekawa (1972). Differentiating (14) next with respect to p_1 and p_2, we obtain

$$\hat{w} = \hat{p}(I - \psi)\theta^{-1} \tag{18}$$

which we know to yield conclusions of the Stolper–Samuelson type whether or not produced means of production are present.

Suppose alternatively that commodity prices are treated as variables, so that our task is to calculate the effects on those prices of parametric changes in factor rentals and α. Differentiating (14) with respect to w_1 and w_2 we obtain, as expected,

$$\hat{p} = \hat{w}\theta(I - \psi)^{-1} \tag{19}$$

which is a simple transformation of (18). Differentiating (14) with respect to α, we obtain

$$\hat{p} = e(\partial\theta/\partial\alpha)(I - \psi)^{-1}\hat{\alpha}. \tag{20}$$

Since $(I - \psi)^{-1}$ is a positive matrix and since $\partial\theta/\partial\alpha$ is semi-negative, the direction of change of prices is the same whether or not there are produced means of production. Moreover, substituting for $\partial\theta/\partial\alpha$ from (16) and spelling out $(I - \psi)^{-1}$, we obtain

$$\hat{p}_1 - \hat{p}_2 = \frac{(\theta_{11} + \theta_{21})(\theta_{12} + \theta_{22})}{\det (I - \psi)} \left(\frac{\theta_{11}\tilde{a}_{11} + \theta_{21}\tilde{a}_{21}}{\theta_{11} + \theta_{21}} - \frac{\theta_{12}\tilde{a}_{12} + \theta_{22}\tilde{a}_{22}}{\theta_{12} + \theta_{22}} \right) \hat{\alpha} \tag{21}$$

which has the same form whether or not $b = 0$.

What has been shown to be true of propositions involving prices only is also true of propositions concerning inputs and outputs (the Samuelson–Rybczynski theorem is an example). However, it is not true of propositions involving both prices and inputs or outputs. A proposition of this kind, valid for the standard two-by-two model, may be invalid for a more general capitalistic model. For example, it is *not* true, even for a model incorporating intermediate goods of the simple Leontief type, that an increase in the jth commodity price gives rise to an increase in the gross output of the jth industry (see Chang and Meyer, 1973). Moreover, when we consider $n \times n$ models even propositions concerning prices only, valid for models without produced means of production, are not necessarily valid for more general models. (For examples, see

Uekawa, et al.) It is true, however, that all comparative statical propositions which are valid for $n \times n$ models with intermediate goods of the simple Leontief type are also valid for more general capitalistic $n \times n$ economies; and this is so whether the propositions are restricted to prices or not.

Addendum: The relationship between the rate of interest and the rentals of primary factors of production

Consider a competitive constant-returns economy which produces two commodities non-jointly with the aid of two primary factors of production and of circulating capital. Suppose that commodity prices are given (by world markets or by analyst's fiat). Suppose further that the economy is in an initial stationary state with rate of interest r_0 and that with each rate of interest in a sufficiently small neighbourhood or r_0 there is associated an alternative stationary state. Associated with each such rate of interest there are equilibrium stationary-state rentals of the two primary factors. How do these rentals respond to a small increase in the rate of interest? Must both rentals decline or may one increase? What determines the direction of change of *relative* primary factor rentals?

In considering these questions, we take a step beyond the analysis of the so-called factor–price frontier, which is defined for a single primary factor[4].

Differentiating (1) with $p_j (j = 1, 2)$ constant, we obtain, after some manipulation,

$$\hat{w}\theta + \hat{r}(\psi_1 \quad \psi_2) = 0 \tag{22}$$

whence

$$\hat{w}_1 = -\frac{\psi_2 \theta_{22}}{|\theta|}\left(\frac{\psi_1}{\psi_2} - \frac{\theta_{21}}{\theta_{22}}\right)\hat{r},$$

$$\hat{w}_2 = \frac{\psi_2 \theta_{12}}{|\theta|}\left(\frac{\psi_1}{\psi_2} - \frac{\theta_{11}}{\theta_{22}}\right)\hat{r} \tag{23}$$

From (23) and the fact that $\theta_{1i} + \theta_{2i} + \psi_i = 1$,

$$\hat{w}_1 - \hat{w}_2 = [(\psi_2 - \psi_1)/|\theta|]\hat{r}. \tag{24}$$

Let us say that the first (second) industry is relatively intensive in its use of the first primary factor in relation to the second primary factor if $|\theta|$ is positive

---

[4] Burmeister (1974) has introduced the notion of a 'factor price frontier *surface*' and has noted that if the rental of one primary factor is held constant then any change in the rate of interest must cause the rental of the remaining primary factor to move in the opposite direction.

(negative), and let us say that the first (second) industry is relatively intensive in its use of the ith primary factor in relation to capital if $\theta_{i1}/\theta_{i2} - \psi_1/\psi_2$ is positive (negative). Then from (23) and (24) we have

Proposition 1. (a) An increase in the rate of interest gives rise to opposite changes in the rentals of the two primary factors of production if and only if one industry employs both primary factors relatively intensively in relation to capital, and it depresses both factor rentals if each industry employs one primary factor relatively intensively in relation to capital and the other primary factor relatively unintensively in relation to capital. An increase in the rate of interest cannot raise both factor rentals.

(b) An increase in the rate of interest gives rise to an increase in the relative rental of the ith primary factor if and only if the ith primary factor is employed relatively intensively (in relation to the other primary factor) in the industry which employs capital relatively sparingly.

The second part of the proposition is illustrated by fig. 1.

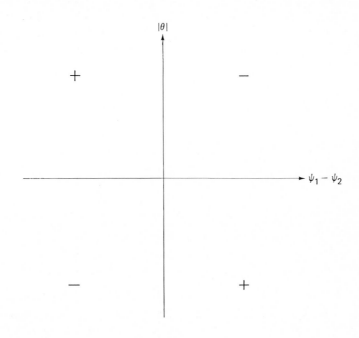

Fig. 1. Sign of $w_1 - w_2$.

References

Acheson, K. (1970), The aggregation of heterogeneous capital goods and various trade theorems, *Journal of Political Economy*, 78(2), March/April, 565–571.

Burmeister, E. (1974), Synthesizing the neo-Austrian and alternative approaches to capital theory: a survey, *Journal of Economic Literature*, 12(2), June, 413–456.

Chang, W. W. and W. Meyer (1973), Intermediate goods in a general equilibrium trade model, *International Economic Review*, 14(2), June, 447–459.

Kemp, M. C. (1969), *The Pure Theory of International Trade and Investment*, Prentice-Hall, Englewood Cliffs.

Kemp, M. C. and Y. Uekawa (1972), Produced inputs and their implications for trade theory, *Economic Record*, 48(4), Dec., 561–569.

Metcalfe, J. S. and I. Steedman (1972a), Heterogeneous capital and the Heckscher–Ohlin–Samuelson theory of trade, in: Parkin, J. M. and A. R. Nobay (eds.), *Essays in Modern Economics, Proceedings of the AUTE Conference, Aberystwyth.*

Metcalfe, J. S. and I. Steedman (1972b), Reswitching and primary input use, *Economic Journal*, 82(1), March, 140–157.

Uekawa, Y., M. C. Kemp and L. L. Wegge (1973), P- and PN-matrices, Minkowski- and Metzler-matrices and generalizations of the Stolper–Samuelson and Samuelson–Rybczynski theorems, *Journal of International Economics*, 3(1), Feb., 53–76.

Chapter 6

A CONVEXITY PROPERTY OF THE TWO-BY-TWO MODEL OF PRODUCTION*

1. Introduction

The best-known properties of the relationships which prevail between primary factor rentals and commodity prices in a two-by-two neo-classical model of production are summarized in the Stolper–Samuelson theorem. In particular, it is known that if factor intensities differ between industries the general-equilibrium *mutatis mutandis* elasticity of any factor rental with respect to any commodity price is either negative or greater than one. In the present note we explore the convexity–concavity properties of those relationships and, specifically, provide a sufficient condition for the rental of the ith factor ($i = 1, 2$) to be a convex function of the commodity price, both rentals and the commodity price being expressed in terms of a common *but arbitrary numéraire*. We then apply our findings to establish some connections between price variability and the distribution of income between factors. Specifically, we derive sufficient conditions for the average rental of the ith factor, in terms of whatever (composite or non-composite) *numéraire*, to be greater with variable prices than with constant prices. Finally, we extend the Stolper–Samuelson and Samuelson–Rybczynski theorems to accommodate commodity-price and factor-endowment variability, respectively.

2. Convexity of the price–rental relationships

Consider a country which produces two commodities under constant returns with the aid of two indispensable primary factors of production. In competitive

* *Journal of International Economics*, 5(3) (Aug. 1975), 255–261, in shortened form. With Chulsoon Khang.

equilibrium with both goods produced, the average cost of production must equal price in each sector. Choosing the first commodity as *numéraire*, we have

$$a_{11}w_{11} + a_{21}w_{21} = 1, \qquad a_{12}w_{11} + a_{22}w_{21} = p, \tag{1}$$

where a_{ij} is the cost-minimizing amount of the ith factor employed in the production of a unit of the jth commodity ($i, j = 1, 2$), w_{ij} is the rental of the ith factor in terms of the jth commodity, and p is the relative price of the second commodity. Evidently a_{ij} is a function homogeneous of degree zero in w_{11} and w_{21} (and in w_{12} and w_{22}). For future reference we define the ratio of factor rentals $\omega \equiv w_{1j}/w_{2j}\,(j = 1, 2)$.

Let us now vary p parametrically and observe the responses of w_{11} and w_{21}. Differentiating (1) totally, and noting the cost-minimizing conditions

$$w_{11}\,\mathrm{d}a_{11} + w_{21}\,\mathrm{d}a_{21} = 0, \qquad w_{11}\,\mathrm{d}a_{12} + w_{21}\,\mathrm{d}a_{22} = 0, \tag{2}$$

we find that

$$a_{11}\,\mathrm{d}w_{11} + a_{21}\,\mathrm{d}w_{21} = 0, \qquad a_{12}\,\mathrm{d}w_{11} + a_{22}\,\mathrm{d}w_{21} = \mathrm{d}p. \tag{3}$$

Again differentiating totally, we obtain

$$\begin{aligned}
\mathrm{d}a_{11}\,\mathrm{d}w_{11} + \mathrm{d}a_{21}\,\mathrm{d}w_{21} + a_{11}\,\mathrm{d}^2w_{11} + a_{21}\,\mathrm{d}^2w_{21} = 0, \\
\mathrm{d}a_{12}\,\mathrm{d}w_{11} + \mathrm{d}a_{22}\,\mathrm{d}w_{21} + a_{12}\,\mathrm{d}^2w_{11} + a_{22}\,\mathrm{d}^2w_{21} = 0,
\end{aligned} \tag{4}$$

where, of course, $\mathrm{d}^2p = 0$.

Denoting by θ_{ij} the relative share of the ith factor in the cost of producing the jth commodity ($i, j = 1, 2$), and indicating relative changes by a circumflex, we may write (2) and (4) as

$$\theta_{11}\hat{a}_{11} + \theta_{21}\hat{a}_{21} = 0, \qquad \theta_{12}\hat{a}_{12} + \theta_{22}\hat{a}_{22} = 0 \tag{2'}$$

and

$$\begin{aligned}
-(\theta_{11}\hat{a}_{11}\hat{w}_{11} + \theta_{21}\hat{a}_{21}\hat{w}_{21}) = a_{11}\,\mathrm{d}^2w_{11} + a_{21}\,\mathrm{d}^2w_{21}, \\
-(\theta_{12}\hat{a}_{12}\hat{w}_{11} + \theta_{22}\hat{a}_{22}\hat{w}_{21}) = (a_{12}/p)\,\mathrm{d}^2w_{11} + (a_{22}/p)\,\mathrm{d}^2w_{21},
\end{aligned} \tag{4'}$$

respectively. Moreover, under competitive conditions,

$$\hat{a}_{11} - \hat{a}_{21} = \sigma_1(\hat{w}_{21} - \hat{w}_{11}), \qquad \hat{a}_{12} - \hat{a}_{22} = \sigma_2(\hat{w}_{21} - \hat{w}_{11}), \tag{5}$$

where σ_i is the elasticity of factor substitution in the ith industry ($i = 1, 2$). Solving the first equations of (2') and (5) for $\hat{a}_{11}$ and $\hat{a}_{21}$, and the second equations for $\hat{a}_{12}$ and $\hat{a}_{22}$, we obtain

$$\hat{a}_{11} = \theta_{21}\sigma_1(\hat{w}_{21} - \hat{w}_{11}), \qquad \hat{a}_{21} = -\theta_{11}\sigma_1(\hat{w}_{21} - \hat{w}_{11}),$$
$$\hat{a}_{12} = \theta_{22}\sigma_2(\hat{w}_{21} - \hat{w}_{11}), \qquad \hat{a}_{22} = -\theta_{12}\sigma_2(\hat{w}_{21} - \hat{w}_{11}). \tag{6}$$

Substituting from (6) into (4'), and simplifying,

$$a_{11} d^2w_{11} + a_{21} d^2w_{21} = \theta_{11}\theta_{21}\sigma_1(\hat{w}_{21} - \hat{w}_{11})^2,$$
$$(a_{12}/p) d^2w_{11} + (a_{22}/p) d^2w_{21} = \theta_{12}\theta_{22}\sigma_2(\hat{w}_{21} - \hat{w}_{11})^2, \tag{7}$$

whence, solving for d^2w_{11} and d^2w_{21},

$$d^2w_{11} = \frac{w_{21}(\hat{w}_{21} - \hat{w}_{11})^2}{[(a_{11}/a_{21}) - (a_{12}/a_{22})]} (\theta_{11}\sigma_1 - \theta_{12}\sigma_2),$$

$$d^2w_{21} = -\frac{w_{21}\theta_{11}\theta_{12}(\hat{w}_{21} - \hat{w}_{11})^2}{\theta_{21}\theta_{22}[(a_{11}/a_{21}) - (a_{12}/a_{22})]} (\theta_{21}\sigma_1 - \theta_{22}\sigma_2). \tag{8}$$

Finally, we note that

$$\theta_{11} \gtreqless \theta_{12} \quad \text{as} \quad (a_{11}/a_{21}) \gtreqless (a_{12}/a_{22}). \tag{9}$$

Applying this result to (8), we may conclude that the function $w_{i1}(p)$ is convex if and only if the weighted elasticity of factor substitution is greater in whichever industry employs the ith factor relatively intensively, the weights being the shares in total costs of the ith factor. The proposition does not depend on the choice of *numéraire*; that is, under exactly the same condition $w_{i2}(1/p)$ is a convex function of $1/p$. Thus, defining π_i as the price of the jth commodity in terms of the other, we have

Proposition 1. The function $w_{ij}(\pi_j)$ is convex if and only if the weighted elasticity of factor substitution is greater in whichever industry employs the ith factor relatively intensively, the weights being the shares of the ith factor in the total costs of the two industries.

3. Price variability and the distribution of income

In addition to proposition 1 we shall need in this section the well-known

Jensen's inequality. Let y be a real-valued stochastic variable with expected value $\bar{y}$, and let g be a real-valued strictly convex (concave) function of y. Then the expected value of g(y) is greater (less) than $g(\bar{y})$.

Moreover, throughout this section nominal commodity prices p_1 and p_2 are constrained to lie on the natural simplex

$$p_1 + p_2 = 1. \tag{10}$$

This normalization implies a composite *numéraire* consisting of one unit of each commodity. By appropriately varying units of measurement, it is possible to change in any desired way the relative weights assigned to the two commodities in the *numéraire* basket.

Suppose now that the commodity prices facing producers are random variables with known distributions. (One may imagine that the country is a small one, facing unstable world prices; but that situation is not the only one to which our analysis applies.) Suppose further, that producers react immediately and costlessly to changes in factor rentals and commodity prices, and that factor rentals adjust without delay to maintain market clearance. The assumption is, of course, absurdly unrealistic, but it does enable us to separate and highlight some of the irreducible effects of variability, with all the complications of *uncertainty* skimmed off[1].

We begin by showing that expected national income, in terms of whatever *numéraire*, is not less with variable prices than with constant prices. From this we may infer that the expected reward of at least one factor is not less with variable prices. In view of Jensen's inequality and of the normalization (10), it suffices to show that national income is a convex function of p_1. Let p_{sup} and p_{inf} be, respectively, the supremum and infimum of the set of prices consistent with the incomplete specialization of production. National income is $Y = p_1 X_1 + (1 - p_1) X_2$, where X_i is the output of the ith commodity $(i = 1, 2)$. If $(1 - p_1)/p_1 = p \geqq p_{\text{sup}}$, that is, if $p_1 \leqq (1 + p_{\text{sup}})^{-1}$, then only the second commodity is produced and national income reduces to $(1 - p_1)X_2$, a linear function of p_1. If, at the other extreme, $(1 - p_1)/p_1 = p \leqq p_{\text{inf}}$, that is, if $p_1 \geqq (1 + p_{\text{inf}})^{-1}$, then only the first commodity is produced and national income reduces to $p_1 X_1$, also a linear function of p_1. For values of p_1 consistent with the incomplete specialization of production, that is, for $(1 + p_{\text{inf}})^{-1} < p_1 < (1 + p_{\text{sup}})^{-1}$, it may be verified that[2] $dY/dp_1 = X_1 - X_2$ and that $d^2Y/dp_1^2 = (dX_1/dp_1 - dX_2/dp_1)$ which, of course, is positive. The relationship between Y and p_1 is illustrated in fig. 1. Clearly the function $Y(p_1)$ is convex and, for $(1 + p_{\text{inf}})^{-1} > p_1 >$

---

[1] In an important recent paper Rothenberg and Smith (1971) assumed that one factor responds without delay, while the other is totally unresponsive, to short-run fluctuations in real rewards.

[2] Use is made of the well-known fact that $(d/dp)(X_1 + pX_2) = X_2$.

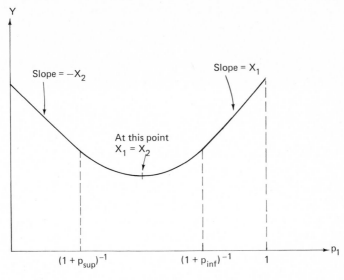

Fig. 1.

$(1 + p_{\text{sup}})^{-1}$, strictly convex. Let us now contrast a variable-price situation with one in which p_1 is constant at its expected value $\bar{p}_1$. Applying Jensen's inequality to the facts summarized in fig. 1, we arrive at

Proposition 2. Expected national income, however measured, is not less with variable prices; moreover, if the probability of $(1 + p_{\text{inf}})^{-1} > p > (1 + p_{\text{sup}})^{-1}$ is positive or if the probabilities of $p_1 \geqq (1 + p_{\text{inf}})^{-1}$ and $p_2 \leqq (1 + p_{\text{sup}})^{-1}$ are (both) positive then expected national income, however measured, is greater with variable prices.

Everywhere in this proposition, 'national income' can be replaced by 'income of at least one factor'.

We turn now to the effects of price variability on the expected rentals of particular factors. The rental of the ith factor, in terms of the composite *numéraire*, is, let us say, $w_i^* = p_1 w_{i1}$. It follows that

$$dw_i^*/dp_1 = w_{i1} + p_1(dw_{i1}/dp)\, dp/dp_1$$

and, since $dp/dp_1 = -1/p_1^2$ and $d^2p/dp_1^2 = 2/p_1^3$,

$$d^2 w_i^*/dp_1^2 = p_1(d^2 w_{i1}/dp^2)(dp/dp_1)^2. \tag{11}$$

That is, w_i^* is a convex function of p_1 if and only if w_{i1} is a convex function of p. Applying Jensen's inequality to proposition 1 and eq. (11) we obtain

Proposition 3. If the weighted elasticity of factor substitution is greater in whichever industry employs the ith factor relatively intensively, the weights being the shares in total costs of the ith factor, then the expected rental of the ith factor, in terms of whatever (pure or composite) numéraire, is not less with variable prices than with constant; moreover, if the probability of $(1 + p_{inf})^{-1} > p_1 > (1 + p_{sup})^{-1}$ is positive or if the probabilities of $p_1 \geq (1 + p_{inf})^{-1}$ and $p_1 \leq (1 + p_{sup})^{-1}$ are (both) positive then the expected rental of the ith factor, however the rental is measured, is greater with variable prices.

Recalling that $\theta_{1j} + \theta_{2j} = 1$, we obtain the following

Corollary. If $(\theta_{11}/\theta_{12}) \geq (\sigma_2/\sigma_1) \geq 1$, with at least one strong inequality, or if $1 \geq (\sigma_2/\sigma_1) \geq (\theta_{11}/\theta_{12})$, with at least one strong inequality, then the expected rental of each factor, however the rental is measured, is not less with variable prices than with constant. If, in addition, the probability of $(1 + p_{inf})^{-1} > p_1 > (1 + p_{sup})^{-1}$ is positive or the probabilities of $p_1 \geq (1 + p_{inf})^{-1}$ and $p_1 \leq (1 + p_{sup})^{-1}$ are (both) positive then the expected rental of at least one factor, however the rental is measured, is greater with variable prices; under the further restriction that $\sigma_1 = \sigma_2$, the expected rental of each factor, however the rental is measured, is greater with variable prices.

The corollary is illustrated in fig. 2. Roughly, the more alike are the two elasticities of factor substitution and the more disparate are the factor ratios of the two industries, the more likely it is that neither expected rental will decline with price variability.

In proposition 3 a comparison is made between a situation of complete price constancy and one displaying a measure of variability. It is possible to state a more general proposition in which the comparison is between more and less variability, with more variability defined in terms of a 'mean-preserving spread' in the probability distribution of p_1. Moreover, it is worth noting that proposition 3 contains merely sufficient conditions. For the conclusions there set out it is not necessary that the functions $w_{ij}(\pi_j)$ and $w_i^*(p_1)$ be convex.

We have derived conditions under which price variability gives rise to a higher expected income for a particular factor of production. It perhaps bears saying that a higher expected income does not by itself imply a higher level of wellbeing.

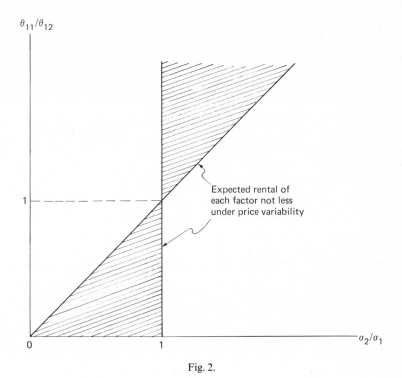

Fig. 2.

4. A stochastic Stolper–Samuelson theorem

We have examined the distributive implications of a change in price variability. Holding the mean of p_j constant, we allowed the spread of prices to change and then calculated the effects of the change on expected real factor rentals. We now turn the question about and ask what will be the distributive effects of a change in expected p_j, with the price spread held constant.

Suppose that the mean of p_1 changes from $\bar{p}_1$ to $\bar{p}_1 + \delta$, with $\delta > 0$; and that, before and after the change, all values of p_1 with positive probability density are consistent with the incomplete specialization of production. The density associated with any particular value of p_1, say p^*_1, before the disturbance is the same as that associated with $p^*_1 + \delta$ after the disturbance. Hence the density associated with $p^*_1 w_{i1}(p^*_1)$ before the disturbance is the same as that associated with $(p^*_1 + \delta)w_{i1}(p^*_1 + \delta)$ after the disturbance. Moreover, $p^*_1 w_{i1}(p^*_1) \lessgtr (p^*_1 + \delta)w_{i1}(p^*_1 + \delta)$ according as the first industry is or is not relatively intensive in its use of the ith factor of production. We now have

Proposition 4. Suppose that all prices with positive probability density are compatible with the incomplete specialization of production and that there occurs a spread-preserving increase in the mean of p_j. Then the expected real rental of the ith factor, in terms of whatever numéraire, will increase or decrease according as that factor is used relatively intensively or unintensively in the jth industry.

The familiar Stolper–Samuelson theorem emerges as a special case as the price spread goes to zero.

A comparable generalization of the dual Samuelson–Rybczynski theorem is available. This time we hold commodity prices constant and examine the implications of changes in the means of random factor endowments V_i, $i = 1, 2$. Let us assume that $\omega(p_1) \cdot V_1 + V_2$ or, after suitable choice of units, $V_1 + V_2$, is constant. Suppose now that the mean of V_1 changes from $\bar{V}_1$ to $\bar{V}_1 + \epsilon$, with $\epsilon > 0$; and that, before and after the change, all values of V_1 with positive probability densities are consistent with the incomplete specialization of production. Then, by reasoning parallel to that of the preceding paragraph, we may verify

Proposition 5. Suppose that all factor endowments with positive probability densities are compatible with the incomplete specialization of production and that there occurs a spread-preserving increase in the mean of V_i. Then the expected output of the jth industry will increase or decrease according as that industry is or is not relatively intensive in its use of the ith factor.

Reference

Rothenberg, T. J. and K. R. Smith, (1971), The effect of uncertainty on resource allocation, *Quarterly Journal of Economics*, 85 (3), Aug., 440–459.

Chapter 7

A NOTE ON JOINT PRODUCTION AND THE THEORY OF INTERNATIONAL TRADE*

1. Introduction

Many of the propositions which comprise the pure theory of international trade collapse in the face of joint production. In particular, this is true of those elegant display pieces the dual Stolper–Samuelson and Samuelson–Rybczynski theorems. Indeed, the usual statements of those propositions make no sense in a context of joint production, for there the key notion of the relative factor intensity of an industry is not defined. Since jointness is almost certainly a fact of life, one can only be pessimistic about the relevance of some highly esteemed parts of trade theory.

Likewise the fate of these two propositions in the face of arbitrary numbers of factors and commodities is of interest. Recent work (Ethier, 1974 and Kemp and Wan, 1975) has established unambiguous comparative statics results of the Stolper–Samuelson and Samuelson–Rybczynski type in a multifactor, multisectoral framework, but little has been deduced about the dual nature of these two propositions.

In this note we investigate the problem of duality in a multi-commodity, multi-factor context and develop three propositions, mouse-like in their proportions, but at least guaranteed to stand up to jointness[1]. Roughly speaking, if one simply assumes (one-half of) the conclusions of the Stolper–Samuelson theorem then one can deduce (one-half of) the conclusions of the

*With Wilfred Ethier. We are grateful to Yasuo Uekawa for helpful comments on an earlier draft.

[1]The propositions are stated and proved for timeless economies with completely degenerate capital structures. However the propositions carry over to comparisons of alternative steady-growth paths in economies with technologies of the general Malinvaud (1953) type, provided only that the rate of interest is held constant throughout.

Samuelson–Rybczynski theorem, and conversely. The propositions are shown to be valid for any number of primary factors and any number of products[2].

The following notation will be used:

x_i = net output of the ith commodity ($i = 1, \ldots, n$):

v_j = total endowment of the jth primary factor of production ($j = 1, \ldots, m$);

p_i = price of the ith commodity, in terms of an arbitrary unit of account ($i = 1, \ldots, n$);

w_j = reward of the jth primary factor, in terms of the same unit of account ($j = 1, \ldots, m$).

The boundary of the set of production possibilities is defined by

$$\psi(x_1, \ldots, x_n; v_1, \ldots, v_m) = 0. \tag{1}$$

It is assumed that, for any given endowment ($v_1, \ldots, v_m$) > 0, (1) defines a locus which is strictly concave to the origin. Then outputs are uniquely determined by commodity prices and the factor endowment. Moreover, since real factor rewards are equal to marginal products ($w_j/p_i = -\partial\psi/\partial v_j / \partial\psi/\partial x_i$), they, too, are uniquely determined by prices and the endowment. Finally, we are able to write down the basic reciprocity relations[3]

$$\partial w_j/\partial p_i = \partial x_i/\partial v_j, \qquad i = 1, \ldots, n; \qquad j = 1, \ldots, m. \tag{2}$$

From (2) we easily obtain

$$\frac{p_i}{w_j} \frac{\partial w_j}{\partial p_i} - 1 = \frac{p_i}{w_j} \left(\frac{\partial x_i}{\partial v_j} - \frac{w_j}{p_i} \right) \tag{3}$$

which, in view of the marginal productivity interpretation of w_j/p_i, yields

Proposition 1. An increase in the price of the ith commodity unambiguously raises the real reward of the jth factor if and only if an increase in the endowment of that factor raises the output of the ith commodity by so much that the aggregate value of the output of all other commodities falls.

(The output of particular commodities other than the ith may rise.)

---

[2] Kuga (1972) has examined the robustness of another standard proposition of trade theory, the factor–price equalization theorem. Also relevant to the present discussion are Samuelson (1966), Hirota and Kuga (1971), Burmeister and Turnovsky (1971) and Kuga (1973). For careful definitions of jointness, see especially Hirota and Kuga (1971).

[3] See Samuelson (1953–1954, p. 10). Since for the most part Samuelson rules out joint products it is important to note that his demonstration of the reciprocity relations is quite general. However the assumption of strict concavity does seem to be essential to the demonstration.

Note that, even with the assumption of strict concavity, it is not possible to show that a price change which works to the advantage (disadvantage) of one factor necessarily works to the disadvantage (advantage) of some other factor. Against the welter of possibilities, all we can be sure of is that a price change cannot leave all factors better off or all factors worse off[4].

From (2) we also obtain

$$\frac{v_j}{x_i}\frac{\partial x_i}{\partial v_j} - 1 = \frac{v_j}{x_i}\left(\frac{\partial w_j}{\partial p_i} - \frac{x_i}{v_j}\right) \tag{4}$$

which yields

Proposition 2. An increase in the endowment of the jth factor raises the output of the ith commodity in greater proportion if and only if an increase in the price of the ith commodity raises the reward of the jth factor by so much that the aggregate payment to all other factors falls.

(The reward of particular factors other than the *j*th may rise.)

Note that it is not possible to show that an increase in the endowment of the *j*th factor which gives rise to a more than proportionate increase in the output of the *i*th commodity necessarily gives rise to a contraction in the output of some other commodity. All we can be sure of is that not all outputs increase in greater proportion than the factor and not all outputs decrease[5].

We note for completeness that the reciprocity relations (2) themselves at once yield

Proposition 3. An increase in the price of the ith commodity unambiguously reduces the real reward of the jth factor if and only if an increase in the endowment of that factor reduces the output of the ith commodity.

In conclusion we remind the reader that the assumption of strict concavity is not trivial. It is known that if production is non-joint and if $m < n$ then the locus of production possibilities is not strictly concave (see Samuelson, 1953–1954). Hence the above propositions do not apply to the non-joint case unless factors are at least as numerous as products. But if this is so then we also

---

[4] Strictly, a price change cannot leave one or more factors unambiguously better (worse) off and all others at least as well (badly) off in terms of each commodity.

[5] Strictly, an increase in v_j cannot result in a more than proportionate increase in the output of one or more commodities and an equi-proportionate increase in all other outputs, nor can it give rise to a decline in one or more outputs without an increase in one or more outputs.

know (Ethier, 1972; Kemp and Wan, 1975) that unambiguous relationships to which the propositions can be applied do indeed exist.

References

Burmeister, E. and S. J. Turnovsky (1971), The degree of joint production, *International Economic Review*, 12, 99–105.
Ethier, W. (1974), Some of the theorems of international trade with many goods and factors, *Journal of International Economics* 4, 199–206.
Hirota, M. and K. Kuga (1971), On an intrinsic joint production, *International Economic Review*, 12, 87–98.
Kemp, M. C. and H. Y. Wan, Jr. (1975), Relatively simple generalizations of the Stolper–Samuelson and Samuelson–Rybczynski theorems, ch. 4 above.
Kuga, K. (1972), The factor–price equalization theorem, *Econometrica*, 40, 723–736.
Kuga, K. (1973), More about joint production, *International Economic Review*, 14, 196–210.
Malinvaud, E. (1953), Capital accumulation and efficient allocation of resources, *Econometrica*, 21, 233–268.
Samuelson, P. A. (1966), The fundamental signularity theorem of non-joint production, *International Economic Review*, 7, 34–41.
Samuelson, P. A. (1953–1954), Prices of factors and goods in general equilibrium, *Review of Economic Studies*, 21, 1–20.

PART II

THE GAINS FROM
INTERNATIONAL TRADE AND INVESTMENT

Introduction to Part II

Careful and general statements, and complete demonstrations, of propositions relating to the gains from trade are of very recent origin. Until Samuelson's (1939) paper, the literature consisted of minor variations on the classical Torrens–Ricardo theme and of the Torrens–Mill–Sidgwick–Edgeworth–Bickerdike analysis of optimal tariffs. Samuelson's paper contains a proof of the potential gainfulness of free trade for a small country and has been a principal inspiration of later work in the field.

Samuelson confined himself to small countries without taxes, externalities or other distortions, without transport costs and with constant returns to scale, Moreover, he confined himself almost exclusively to the comparison of autarkic and free-trade equilibria. Finally, his analysis was timeless; therefore he could not consider the implications for trade gains of phenomena which can reveal themselves only in time – investment and population growth, the wasting and replenishment of natural resources, human learning, the coexistence of different generations each with a finite life expectancy.

In the papers collected in part II, I report on several attempts to weaken Samuelson's assumptions and to answer a wider range of questions. All but the last three papers deal with questions of trading gain in a static, essentially timeless context. In chs. 17–19, however, I indicate several directions in which one might go in seeking to escape from that framework. Also relevant are chs. 23 and 24, in which questions of trading gain under uncertainty are considered.

With two important exceptions, the essays in Part II are reprinted with only typographical errors corrected. The first exception is section 4 of ch. 8 from which an error, first noted by Krueger and Sonnenschein (1967), has been removed. The revised version of that section generalizes the relevant proposition of Krueger and Sonnenschein by allowing for variable supplies of primary factors. That the Krueger–Sonnenschein proposition could be generalized in this way was noted in an unpublished manuscript by Suzumura (1969). The second exception is section 3 of ch. 16, which has been modified in the light of comments by Jones (1967) and Rakowski (1970). And the third exception is section 2 of ch. 15 from which an error, noted by Michihiro Ohyama, has been removed.

A warning is in order. Some of the proofs in chs. 8–10 are incomplete in that it is simply assumed (not demonstrated, as an implication of other assumptions) that to each possible competitive equilibrium under one set of conditions there corresponds a Pareto-comparable competitive equilibrium under an alternative set of conditions. That the gap can be filled is shown in ch. 11.

Chapter 11 contains a list of most of the important post-1939 contributions to the essentially timeless aspects of the subject. However, to that list must be added Grandmont et al. (1972), Negishi (1972), Ohyama (1972) and Fishburn (1973). Going beyond statics, it may be noted first that there is a rapidly growing literature in which it is sought to treat the problem of ch. 16 in a growth setting, that is, to determine the optimal time paths of tariffs and of taxes on foreign investment earnings. However, this extended problem has been resolved only in quite special cases. In particular, it has been customary to neglect the interaction through time of mutually trading and investing countries. See, for example, the essays of Bade (1972, 1973), Bardhan (1967), Hamada (1966, 1969), Osana (1972) and Pitchford (1970). Only Manning (1972) has broken with this restrictive assumption: however, he was driven by the complexity of the problem to adopt equally restrictive assumptions concerning the saving behaviour of the policy-making country. It may be noted also that Gale (1971, 1974) has examined some of the implications for trade gains of overlapping generations and that Negishi (1972, ch. 6), Long (1975), and Clemhout and Wan (1970) and Bardhan (1971) have examined, in an 'infant industry' context, the implications of human learning.

What remains to be done? One can date commodities and thus effortlessly extend all existing theorems to a world with any finite number of time periods and with perfect foresight. And by introducing contingency markets of the Arrow–Debreu type one can even accommodate uncertainty. There remains, however, the task of reformulating and answering questions concerning trade gains in a context of infinite time. Since individuals have finite lifetimes, we are led to consider economies which possess general Malinvaud technologies and an infinite sequence of Samuelsonian overlapping generations. Evidently one cannot now appeal to Debreu's ch. 5. However, there are available appropriate extensions of the Arrow–Debreu theorems: see for example, the first three theorems of Stigum (1973). On the basis of these recent developments it seems that it will be possible to provide generalizations of most theorems concerning the gains from trade. For example, I conjecture that, for economies of the type described, fully anticipated free trade is potentially superior to no trade. To be sure, we already have several demonstrations that the steady state of free trade may be inferior to the steady state of autarky. But such propositions pay no attention to the transition from one steady state to the other, and transitions may never end. We also have demonstrations that unexpected free trade or free trade with arbitrarily imposed saving patterns or rates of interest may be inferior to autarky. Evidently none of these propositions prejudices the above conjecture.

References

Bade, R. (1972), Optimal growth and foreign borrowing with restricted mobility of foreign capital, *International Economic Review*, 13, Oct., 544–552.

Bade, R. (1973), Optimal foreign investment and international trade, *Economic Record*, 49, March, 62–75.

Bardhan, P. (1967), Optimal foreign borrowing, in: K. Shell (ed.), *Essays on the Theory of Optimal Economic Growth*, MIT Press, Cambridge, Mass., 117–128.

Bardhan, P. (1971), On optimum subsidy to a learning industry: an aspect of the theory of infant-industry protection, *International Economic Review*, 12, Feb., 54–70.

Clemhout, S. and H. Y. Wan, Jr. (1970), Learning-by-doing and infant industry protection, *Review of Economic Studies*, 37, Jan., 33–56.

Fishburn, G. (1973), The gains from trade for a small country under conditions of price distortion and externalities, University of New South Wales.

Gale, D. (1971), General equilibrium with imbalance of trade, *Journal of International Economics*, 1, May, 141–158.

Gale, D. (1974), The trade imbalance story, *Journal of International Economics*, 4, May, 119–137.

Grandmont, J. M., et al. (1972), Symposium on the gains from trade, *Journal of International Economics*, 2, May, 109–180.

Hamada, K. (1966), Economic growth and long-term international capital movements," *Yale Economic Essays*, 6, Spring, 49–96.

Hamada, K. (1969), Optimal capital accumulation by an economy facing an international capital market, *Journal of Political Economy*, 77, July/Aug., 684–697.

Jones, R. W. (1967), International capital movements and the theory of tariffs and trade, *Quarterly Journal of Economics*, 81, Feb., 1–38.

Krueger, A. and H. Sonnenschein (1967), The terms of trade, the gains from trade and price divergence, *International Economic Review*, 8, Feb., 121–127.

Long, N. V. (1975), Infant industry protection, dynamic internal economies, and the non-appropriability of consumers' and producers' surpluses, *Economic Record*, 51, June, 256–262.

Manning, R. (1972), Optimal taxation when borrowing alters the foreign supply curve for capital, *Economic Record*, 48, Sept., 400–410.

Negishi, T. (1972), *General Equilibrium Theory and International Trade*, North-Holland, Amsterdam.

Ohyama, M. (1972), Trade and welfare in general equilibrium, *Keio Economic Studies*, 9, 37–73.

Osana, H. (1972), Optimal capital accumulation in an open economy, *Keio Economic Studies*, 9, 15–42.

Pitchford, J. D. (1970), Foreign investment and the national advantage in a dynamic context, in: MacDougall I. A. and R. H. Snape (eds.), *Studies in International Economics*, North-Holland, Amsterdam, 193–206.

Rakowski, J. J. (1970), Capital movements in a tariff-ridden international economy, *American Economic Review*, 60, Sept., 753–760.

Samuelson, P. A. (1939), The gains from international trade, *Canadian Journal of Economics and Political Science*, 5, May, 195–205.

Stigum, B. P. (1973), Competitive equilibria with infinitely many commodities, *Journal of Economic Theory*, 6, Oct., 415–445.

Suzumura, K. (1969), The price divergence and gains from trade under collective rationality, Hitotsubashi University.

Chapter 8

THE GAIN FROM INTERNATIONAL TRADE*

1. Introduction

In a brilliant paper of 1939 Paul Samuelson proved, under certain assumptions concerning technology, that for a small country unable to influence world prices, free trade is, in a clearly defined sense, better than no trade.

In this note I shall offer a generalization of Samuelson's theorem. In particular, it will be shown that free trade *or trade distorted by (non-negative) import or export duties or quantitative import or export restrictions* is, in Samuelson's sense, better than no trade, *regardless of the size of the trading country*. The theorem will be shown to be valid whether or not the country imports raw materials, or is a net lender or borrower – possibilities from which Samuelson abstracted in his initial exposition.

For the most part my method of proof parallels that introduced by Samuelson. My indebtedness to his 1939 paper will, I hope, be abundantly clear.

2. Samuelson's 1939 theorem

It will be convenient to begin with a bare statement of Samuelson's theorem.

We shall consider a single economy consisting of one or more individuals enjoying a certain unchanging amount of technological knowledge, so that we may take as data the production functions relating the output of each commodity to the amounts of inputs devoted to its production. Any number of commodities is assumed; there may also be any number of inputs or productive services. These are not necessarily fixed in amount, but may have supply functions in terms of various economic prices. Moreover, for our purposes the differentiation of the factors of production can proceed to any degree; thus, labour services of the same man in different

* *Economic Journal*, 82 (Dec. 1962), 803–819. I have greatly profited from several conversations with Paul Samuelson. I have also had privileged access to the article of Professor Samuelson's published in this issue of the *Economic Journal*.

occupations are not regarded as the same factor of production unless the provider of these services is indifferent as between these two uses. [As a limiting case, factors may be occupationally completely immobile.] Similarly, in order that the productive services rendered by different individuals may be considered the same service, it is necessary that in every use they be infinitely substitutable.

In order to ensure that perfect competition is possible, we rule out increasing returns, and assume that all production functions show constant returns with respect to proportional changes of *all* factors. Each individual acts as if he were a small part of the markets which he faces and takes prices as given parameters which he cannot influence by changes in his own supplies or demands. It is assumed that for each individual there exists an *ordinal* preference scale in which enter all commodities and productive services, and that subject to the restraints of fixed prices he always selects optimal amounts of each and every commodity and every productive service (some zero in amount). Each individual is better off if he receives more of every commodity while rendering less of every productive service. No attempt is made to render the 'utilities' and 'disutilities' of different persons comparable[1].

It is assumed, in addition, (Samuelson, 1939, pp. 198 and 199) that

. . . there exists an outside market in which there prevail certain arbitrarily established (relative) prices at which this country can buy or sell various commodities in unlimited amounts without changing those quoted prices.

The theorem follows:

Although it cannot be shown that every individual *is* made better off by the introduction of trade, it can be shown that through trade every individual *could* [by resort to lump-sum taxes and subsidies] be made better off (or in the limiting case, no worse off). In other words, if a unanimous decision were required in order for trade to be permitted, it would always be possible for those who desired trade to buy off those opposed to trade, with the result that all could be made better off[2].

3. Extension of the theorem to variable terms of trade

I shall demonstrate in this section that Samuelson's theorem can be proved for countries of any size whatever. All other assumptions of section 2 are retained.

The following notation will be useful[3]. The amount consumed of the ith commodity is denoted by z_i, the amount produced by $\bar{z}_i$. The consumption vector is then

$$z = (z_1, z_2, \ldots, z_n)$$

and the production vector is

$$\bar{z} = (\bar{z}_1, \bar{z}_2, \ldots, \bar{z}_n).$$

---

[1] Samuelson (1939, pp. 195–196). The sentence in square brackets is inserted.
[2] Samuelson (1939, pp. 198–199). The phrase in square brackets is inserted.
[3] The notation of the present paper conforms as closely as is practicable to that of Samuelson (1939). There are, however, some discrepancies. In particular, my z corresponds to his x.

The vector of domestic commodity prices is

$$p = (p_1, p_2, \ldots, p_n).$$

The vector of factor inputs is

$$a = (a_1, a_2, \ldots, a_s)$$

and the vector of factor prices is

$$w = (w_1, w_2, \ldots, w_s).$$

Values of the variables under autarky are indicated by the superscript 0, free trade values by primes.

In the absence of trade

$$\bar{z}^0 - z^0 = 0. \tag{1}$$

But under balanced free trade the amount consumed of any particular commodity need not equal the amount produced. It is necessary only that the value of imports be equal to the value of exports or, what is the same thing, that the value of consumption be equal to the value of production[4].

$$p'(\bar{z}' - z') = 0. \tag{2}$$

Turning to the keystone of the proof, we observe that, given constant returns to scale and the possibility of independently carrying on production in separate processes, the set S production possibilities is convex (Samuelson, 1953). Under perfect competition and free trade, S will be supported by the price plane

$$p'(\bar{z} - \bar{z}') - w'(a - a') = 0 \tag{3}$$

at the free trade production point $(\bar{z}'; a')$. It follows that $p'\bar{z} - w'a$, considered as a linear function defined on S, reaches a maximum at $(\bar{z}'; a')$. This means that at the free trade prices the competitive quantities of commodities and factor services maximize for the economy as a whole the algebraic difference between the total value of output and total factor cost, as compared to any other commodity and factor combinations in S, in particular the autarkic combination (Samuelson, 1939, p. 197). This result may be written

$$0 = p'\bar{z}' - w'a' \geq p'\bar{z}^0 - w'a^0 \tag{4}$$

and is illustrated, for the special two-commodities, fixed-factors case, by fig. 1.

---

[4] $p'\bar{z}'$ is to be understood as the inner product $\Sigma_{i=1}^{n} p_i'\bar{z}_i'$, $p'z'$ as $\Sigma_{i=1}^{n} p_i'z_i'$.

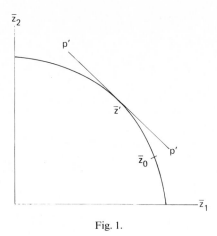

Fig. 1.

Substituting from (1) and (2) in (4), we obtain the basic equation

$$p'z' - w'a' \geq p'z^0 - w'a^0: \tag{5}$$

at free trade prices, the community's autarkic consumption pattern would have cost not more than the actual free trade consumption pattern.

What can be inferred from (5)? Not very much, but enough for our purposes: that it is impossible, by simply redistributing the collection of goods actually chosen under autarky, to make everyone better off than in the chosen free trade position[5]. This is readily illustrated, for the two-persons case, by means of Samuelson's utility possibility curves. In fig. 2 the point u^0 indicates the distribution of utilities which actually emerges under autarky and the dotted curve g^0g^0 is the utility possibility curve corresponding to the collection of goods actually chosen under autarky. g^0g^0 passes south-west of u', the utility mixture of free trade.

Imagine that under autarky some other distribution of income had prevailed. Corresponding to it would be a new set of demands, a new production mixture and hence a new utility possibility curve, say h^0h^0 in fig. 2. If trade is opened up and if, simultaneously, appropriate lump sum taxes and subsidies are introduced, z' will reappear and, with it, u'. Evidently h^0h^0, like g^0g^0, passes south-west of u'.

Consider now the envelope pp of all *point* utility possibility curves like g^0g^0 and h^0h^0. This envelope is the utility possibility curve of the autarkic *situation*

[5] Samuelson (1950, especially pp. 1–9). Note that it *cannot* be inferred from eq. (5) that it is possible, by simply redistributing the collection of goods actually chosen under free trade, to make everyone better off than in the chosen autarkic position.

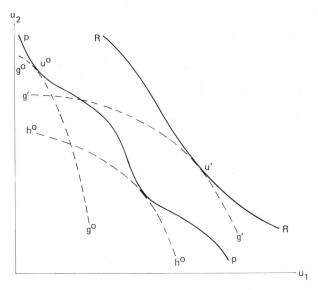

Fig. 2.

(Samuelson, 1950, pp. 12ff). It, too, must pass south-west of u'. Thus it is impossible under autarky to make everyone better off than at the particular free trade point z' (or u'). Put otherwise, it would not be advantageous (it might be impossible) for those who expect to be hurt by the introduction of trade to bribe the rest of the community into foregoing the free trade point z' (or u').

But evidently a similar statement can be made with respect to *any* free trade point attainable by means of appropriate lump sum taxes and transfers. In other words, the utility possibility locus of the free trade *situation*, say RR, cannot lie inside pp, the utility possibility locus of the autarkic situation[6].

---

[6] RR and pp may possibly touch at one or more points. Note that $g'g'$, the *point* utility possibility curve corresponding to the collection of goods actually chosen under free trade, may not only cut pp but may pass south-west of u^0. (Cf. footnote 5 on p. 94.) This point has been emphasized by Olsen (1958); Olsen went astray, however, in arguing that it is inconsistent with Samuelson's 1939 results. Mr. Olsen has indicated in correspondence that he now accepts the analysis of the present paper.

That RR cannot lie inside pp is denied by Enke (1961) who holds that, given individual indifference curves of 'extreme curvature', 'a change to *free* trade from no trade will...lessen welfare for all after compensation'. Mr. Enke's mistake is in supposing that the compensated and uncompensated free trade consumption mixtures (represented by Z' in his fig. 1) are identical and, by implication, denying the necessity of the compensated mixture lying 'above' the autarkic community indifference curve.

Thus we have proved that, for some systems of taxes and subsidies, (5) would hold for every individual. (z^0, z', a^0 and a' must now be interpreted as vectors of quantities of commodities bought and supplied by individuals.) Every individual would be revealed as better off or (in the limiting case in which $z' = z^0$ and $a' = a^0$) no worse off under compensated free trade than under autarky.

Note that nowhere in the above proof was it assumed that the trading country has no influence on world prices; at no point was it necessary to assume that trade can in fact take place along the $p'p'$ curve of fig. 1. Note also that while inputs and outputs are permitted to vary in response to changes in world prices, the proof does not *require* that such adjustment takes place. Specifically, the theorem holds even for fixed, totally unresponsive inputs and outputs.

4. A footnote to sections 2 and 3

It has been stated in section 2 (and proved in section 3) that exposure to world prices which differ from those which happened to prevail under autarky carries with it a clearly defined benefit. Suppose that it is beyond the power of the individual country to influence world prices. Then the following interesting questions arise: (i) Is it possible to show that the benefit increases with an improvement of the terms of trade? (ii) Is it possible to show that the benefit is greater the more prices 'deviate' from those of the autarkic state[7]?

(i) Evidently a prerequisite of any analysis of the first question is agreement on the sense in which in a world of many commodities the terms of trade can be said to improve or deteriorate. Let p' and p'' be two vectors of world commodity prices, w' and w'' the corresponding vectors of domestic factor rewards. Then we shall say that a change from p' to p'' involves an improvement in the terms of trade if and only if

$$p''(\bar{z}' - z') > 0. \tag{6}$$

Now it is clearly impossible to show that everyone is necessarily better off at a chosen consumption point z'' than at any chosen point z'. The analysis of section 2 suggests, however, that the utility possibility locus of the p'' situation might be shown to lie 'outside' that of the p' situation. This is indeed the case.

---

[7] Samuelson (1939, p. 203) has stated that this is so for the very special case in which individuals are alike with respect to tastes, abilities and ownership of the factors of production.

We wish to show that, if p' consumption is restricted so that inequality (6) is satisfied, then

$$p''z'' - w''a'' \geq p''z' - w''a'. \tag{7}$$

From the discussion of section 2,

$$p''\bar{z}'' - w''a'' \geq p''\bar{z}' - w''a' \tag{8}$$

and

$$p''(z'' - \bar{z}'') = 0. \tag{9}$$

From these materials the proof may be pieced together:

$$p''z'' - w''a'' = p''\bar{z}'' - w''a'' \quad \text{(from (9))}$$
$$\geq p''\bar{z}' - w''a' \quad \text{(from (8))},$$
$$= p''z' + p''(\bar{z}' - z') - w''a'' \geq p''z' - w''a' \quad \text{(from (6))}.$$

Hence eq. (7).

Figure 3 illustrates the theorem for the simple two-commodities, fixed-factors case. Assumption (6) means that the chosen point z' cannot lie on the heavy part of the p' line of fig. 3(a). Restricted in this way, the utility possibility

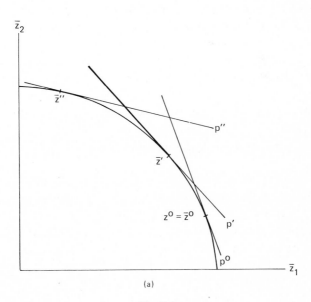

(a)

Fig. 3(a).

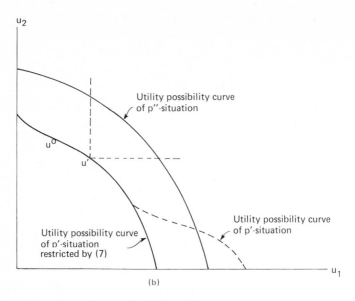

Fig. 3(b).

curve of the p' situation must lie inside the utility possibility curve of the p'' situation, as in fig. 3(b).

Note that nowhere in the above proof was it assumed that each commodity is either imported or exported: purely domestic goods, for which $z_i = \bar{z}_i$, are admitted.

(ii) If exposure to prices which differ from those which would have prevailed under autarky is beneficial, one might have supposed that the benefit is greater the more prices deviate from those of the autarkic state. Unfortunately, this attractive speculation is false unless heavily qualified.

Evidently a prerequisite of any analysis of the question is agreement on the sense in which one set of prices can be said to diverge more than another from the autarkic set. Of several conventions which suggest themselves, the following is both plausible and analytically convenient[8]. Again let p' and p'' be two vectors of world prices, w' and w'' the corresponding vectors of domestic

[8] It should suffice to dispel the doubts expressed by Caves (1960, p. 266): 'The danger of circularity in reasoning becomes great, unless some way of expressing "greater deviation of world from autarkic prices" can be found which does not *define* an increase in welfare.' Note that preliminary normalisation of the price vector is unnecessary. The only weakness of the definition that I can detect is its failure to rank all p' and p''; for some p' and p'' it may not be possible to say that p' deviates from p^0 by more than does p'', or that p'' deviates by more than p', or that p' and p'' deviate equally.

factor prices. p'' will be said to deviate from p^0, the autarkic set, by more than does p' if p' can be expressed as a positive linear combination of p^0 and p'':

$$p' = \mu^0 p^0 + \mu'' p'', \qquad \mu^0, \mu'' > 0. \tag{10}$$

Given this definition, it can be shown that, provided autarkic and p' consumption points are constrained to satisfy the weak axiom of revealed preference, so that

$$p^0 z^0 - w^0 a^0 < p^0 z' - w^0 a', \tag{11}$$

no possible utility point of the p' situation can lie north-east of a possible utility point of the p'' situation. From the convexity of S we obtain further inequalities analogous to (4):

$$p^0 \bar{z}' - w^0 a' \leq 0 \tag{12a}$$

and

$$p'' \bar{z}' - w'' a' \leq 0. \tag{12b}$$

From (11) and (12a), and the fact that $p^0 z^0 - w^0 a^0 = 0$,

$$p^0 (\bar{z}' - z') < 0. \tag{13}$$

Multiplying (12b) by $\mu > 0$ and (10) by $\mu'' > 0$, and adding, then applying (10) and (2), we obtain

$$p'' z' - w'' a' < 0 \tag{14}$$

whence

$$0 = p'' z'' - w'' a'' > p'' z' - w'' a', \tag{15}$$

as required.

5. Restricted trade is superior to no trade

So far it has been proved only that for any country compensated free trade is better than no trade. In this section I shall argue the more general proposition that compensated free trade or compensated restricted trade is better than no trade. (It is understood, of course, that the restrictions are not prohibitive.) The manner in which trade is restricted is unimportant; the same conclusions hold for (non-negative) tariffs, quantitative commodity controls or exchange restrictions. The assumption of perfect competition is retained.

If imports are restricted it is necessary to distinguish the domestic and world prices of imports. Imagine that, for any assigned set of trade restrictions and for any assigned system of lump sum taxes and subsidies, the first m commodities,

$$x = (z_1, z_2, \ldots, z_m)$$

are exported, and that the remainder

$$y = (z_{m+1}, z_{m+2}, \ldots, z_n)$$

are imported[9]. Then

$$z = (x; y).$$

If, as before, p denotes the vector of *domestic* prices, we may write

$$p = (p_1, p_2, \ldots, p_m; p_{m+1}, p_{m+2}, \ldots, p_n) = (p_x; p_y).$$

The vector of world prices is then

$$q = (q_1, q_2, \ldots, q_m; q_{m+1}, q_{m+2}, \ldots, q_n) = (q_x; q_y) = (p_x; q_y),$$

where

$$q_y \leq p_y. \tag{16}$$

Primes now indicate the magnitudes of the restricted trade situation. With the aid of this extended notation, (1) may be expanded as

$$\bar{x}^0 - x^0 = 0, \qquad \bar{y}^0 - y^0 = 0 \tag{1a}$$

and (2) may be expanded as

$$p_x'(\bar{x}' - x') + q_y'(\bar{y}' - y') = 0 \quad \text{or} \quad p_x'x' + q_y'y' = p_x'\bar{x}' + q_y'\bar{y}'. \tag{2a}$$

Finally, (4) becomes

$$p_x'\bar{x}' + p_y'\bar{y}' - w'a' \geq p_x'\bar{x}^0 + p_y'\bar{y}^0 - w'a^0. \tag{4a}$$

Now it follows from (2a), (11) and the fact that $y' \geq \bar{y}'$ that

$$p_x'x' + p_y'y' \geq p_x'\bar{x}' + p_y'\bar{y}'. \tag{2b}$$

Substituting from (1a) and (2b) in (4a),

$$p_x'x' + p_y'y' - w'a' \geq p_x'x^0 + p_y'y^0 - w'a^0$$

[9] The proof could be modified to accommodate non-traded goods.

that is,

$$p'z' - w'a' \geq p'z^0 - w'a^0. \tag{5}$$

From this point the proof progresses along familiar lines.

If exports rather than imports are restricted, the proof must be modified, but follows essentially the same lines. The vector of world prices is now

$$q = (q_1, q_2, \ldots, q_m; q_{m+1}, q_{m+2}, \ldots, q_n) = (q_x; q_y) = (q_x; p_y),$$

where

$$q_x \geq p_x. \tag{16a}$$

Eq. (2) may be expanded as

$$q'_x(\bar{x}' - x') + p'_y(\bar{y}' - y') = 0 \quad \text{or} \quad q'_x x' + p'_y y' = q'_x \bar{x}' + p'_y \bar{y}'. \tag{2c}$$

From (2c), (16a) and the fact that $\bar{x}' \geq x'$ we may infer (2b) again. From this point the proof proceeds as for the case of restricted imports.

Note that in constructing the above proofs it has not been found necessary to refer to the tariff proceeds (if any), the profits derived from the sale of import or export licences (if any) or the profits derived from exchange dealings (if any).

6. Extension of the proof to cover imported raw materials

In the proofs of sections 3 and 5 it has been assumed implicitly that the trading country makes no use of imported raw materials. This is, of course, a blatantly unrealistic assumption. Fortunately, as must be intuitively obvious, the proofs can easily be modified to accommodate the possibility of imported materials. It will suffice to prove the proposition that compensated free trade is superior to no trade. The extension to the case of restricted trade is straightforward.

Let $\hat{a} = (\hat{a}_1, \hat{a}_2, \ldots, \hat{a}_t)$ represent the vector of imported raw materials, and $\hat{w} = (\hat{w}_1, \hat{w}_2, \ldots, \hat{w}_t)$ the corresponding vector of raw material prices. Then (2) must be rewritten as

$$p'(\bar{z}' - z') - \hat{w}'\hat{a}' = 0 \tag{2d}$$

and (4) as

$$p'\bar{z}' - w'a' - \hat{w}'\hat{a}' \geq p'\bar{z}^0 - w'a^0. \tag{4d}$$

Substituting in (4d) from (1) and (2d), we obtain

$$p'z' - w'a' \geq p'z^0 - x'a^0$$

and the proof proceeds as in section 3.

7. The accommodation of capital movements

In all proofs furnished so far, balanced trade has been assumed. In this section the implications of capital movements are considered. Attention is confined to the case of free trade and capital *imports*. Extension of the proofs to cover restricted trade and capital exports is straightforward.

In the special and very simple case in which the 'capital' to be moved can be thought of as a constant vector of commodities[10], $K = (K_1, K_2, \ldots, K_n) \geq 0$, eqs. (1) and (2) become, respectively,

$$\bar{z}^0 - z^0 + K = 0 \tag{1e}$$

and

$$p'(\bar{z}' - z' + K) = 0. \tag{2e}$$

Substitution into (4) from (1e) and (2e) yields (5), as before.

When the object to be transferred is a sum of money, however, the proof becomes slightly more complicated. 'Autarky' must be redefined to permit imports equal in value to the sum to be transferred, say T. Imagine that, under autarky thus defined, the last $(n - m)$ commodities are imported. Exports are, of course, prohibited, so that imports $y^0 - \bar{y}^0$ are limited in value to T:

$$py^0 - (y^0 - \bar{y}^0) = T. \tag{1f}$$

As before,

$$\bar{x}^0 - x^0 = 0. \tag{1g}$$

Eq. (2) takes the revised form[11]

$$p'_x x' + p'_y y' = p'_x \bar{x}' + p'_y \bar{y}' + T. \tag{2e}$$

With the introduction of free trade import prices will rise; that is, $p'_y > p^0_y$. Hence, from (1f),

$$p'_y(y^0 - \bar{y}^0) > T. \tag{1h}$$

[10] As it can, for example, when reparations are assessed and paid in kind.
[11] That when free trade is introduced the list of imports will expand is of no importance here.

Substituting in (4a) for $\bar{x}^0$ from (1g), for $p'_y\bar{y}^0$ from (1h), and for $(p'_x\bar{x}' + p'_y\bar{y}')$ from (2e), we obtain

$$p'z' - w'a' \geq p'z^0 - w'a^0 \tag{5}$$

as before.

8. The gain from restricting trade

It has been shown that situations of free or restricted trade are superior to the autarkic situation. This leaves open the question whether the various trading situations can be ranked. What can be said of the relative desirabilities of the free-trading situation, the trading situation characterized by a uniform 5% import duty, and that characterized by a 10% duty, etc.?

In the special case in which a country's terms of trade are independent of that country's offer, a particularly simple answer can be given: the free trade situation is superior to the 5% situation, which in turn is superior to the 10% situation, and so on. The reason is very simple: under free trade all the necessary marginal conditions of a Paretian national optimum are satisfied. In particular, the marginal rate of transformation between commodities in production is equal to the marginal rate of transformation between commodities in international trade (the marginal terms of trade) and to their marginal rate of substitution in consumption. A tariff destroys the equality between the marginal terms of trade and the other two marginal rates of transformation. And the greater the rate of duty, the greater the resulting inequality. This is illustrated, for the special two-commodities, fixed-factors case, by fig. 4(a), and for the two-persons case by fig. 4(b). Note that fig. 4(b) allows for the possibility that there exist one or more distributions of income under which no trade takes place. Clearly, if such a distribution exists any tariff will be a dead letter and the utility possibility curves must all touch at one or more points. (In terms of fig. 4(a), W must be recognized as an isolated, tariff-ridden consumption possibility.) Of course, such a distribution need not exist *for the particular terms of trade considered*, in which case the utility possibility curves must lie uniformly one outside the other.

When, however, world prices depend upon the amounts offered and demanded by the tariff-imposing country, complications appear. For in this case the average and marginal rates of transformation through trade diverge; and it is to the average rates that under free trade the marginal rates of substitution and transformation through domestic production are equated. Hence a single-

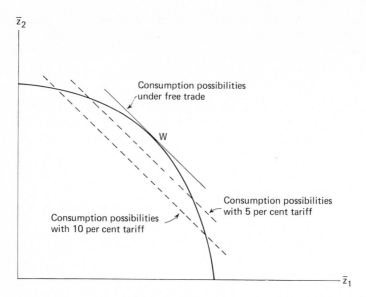

Fig. 4(a).

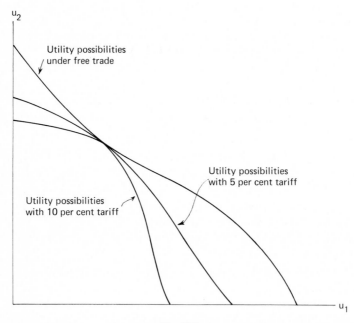

Fig. 4(b).

country Paretian optimum is not necessarily reached under free trade. The possibility emerges that an appropriate system of taxes and subsidies on imports and exports, combined with lump sum redistributive transfers between individuals, would leave everyone in the tariff-ridden country better off than in a particular free trade situation.

Suppose[12], then, that world prices in terms of some *numéraire*, which we assume to be the first commodity, are functions of the quantities imported and exported by a particular country,

$$q_i^1 = q_i^1(E_1, E_2, \ldots, E_n), \qquad i = 2, 3, \ldots, n$$

(E_i is positive if the country is a net importer of the ith commodity, negative if the country is a net exporter). The necessity of international payments equilibrium is expressed by

$$E_1 + \sum_{i=2}^{n} E_i q_i^1(E_1, E_2, \ldots, E_n) = 0.$$

It follows that the marginal rates of commodity transformation through trade are

$$-\frac{\mathrm{d}E_i}{\mathrm{d}E_j} = \left(q_j^1 + \sum_{s=2}^{n} E_s \frac{\partial q_s^1}{\partial E_j}\right) \Big/ \left(q_i^1 + \sum_{s=2}^{n} E_s \frac{\partial q_s^1}{\partial E_i}\right)$$

$$= \frac{q_j^1}{q_i^1} \left[\frac{1 + \sum_s \dfrac{\alpha_s}{\alpha_j} \cdot \dfrac{1}{\xi_{js}}}{1 + \sum_s \dfrac{\alpha_s}{\alpha_i} \cdot \dfrac{1}{\xi_{is}}}\right] \qquad i, j = 1, 2, \ldots, n,$$

where α_s is the value of exports of the sth commodity and ξ_{is} is the cross-elasticity of foreign demand (supply) for the jth export (import) with respect to the sth price. In a Paretian optimum, on the other hand,

$$p_j/p_i = -\mathrm{d}E_i/\mathrm{d}E_j, \qquad i, j = 1, 2, \ldots, n.$$

The conditions of an optimum will be satisfied, therefore, if an *ad valorem* tax of $100[\sum_s (\alpha_s/\alpha_i)/(1/\xi_{is})]\%$ is imposed on the ith commodity as it crosses the frontier, the tax to be reckoned on the *foreign* price.

Note that since no tax need be levied on the *numéraire* commodity, there need be only $(n-1)$ taxes in all. On the other hand, the choice of *numéraire* is arbitrary so that the $(n-1)$-dimensional vector of optimal taxes is not unique. Further, while the taxing authority *need* consider only $(n-1)$ commodities, it

[12] This paragraph is based on Graaff (1949–1950).

may impose taxes on all n commodities. In general, one tax (say, the ith) may be imposed at any arbitrary level; the remaining optimal taxes will then be functions of the ith tax.

Note also that, thanks to the presence of cross-elasticity terms, a Paretian optimum may require that some imports and exports be subsidized.

The special two-commodities case is of some interest. A single tax would suffice, and it could be levied indifferently on the exported or imported commodity. Reckoned on the foreign price, the optimal tax in this case is simply the reciprocal of the elasticity of the foreign supply of imports: $\tau = 1/\xi$. Much attention has been lavished upon this formula[13]. But it provides scant guidance to the discovery of the optimal τ, since it involves two, not one, unknowns. The value of ξ varies with the position on the foreign supply curve; the position on the foreign supply curve depends on the demand by the tariff-imposing country for imports; that, in turn, depends on the internal distribution of income; but, finally, the post-tariff distribution of income depends on the arbitrary pattern of lump sum taxes and subsidies. There is, then, not a single optimum τ but an infinity, A given τ, say 5%, may be optimal for one distribution of income, but in general will be either greater or smaller than the optimal τ for any other distribution. For the distribution represented by point u'' in fig. 5, for example, a 5% tariff is optimal, whereas the distribution represented by u''' calls for a 10% tariff. (Note that, in contrast to the case previously discussed, the utility possibility curves corresponding to the two tariff levels may intersect; if, as is assumed here, each rate is optimal for *some* distribution of income, they *must* intersect. About all that one can be sure of is that neither curve will loop inside the autarky curve – though they may touch it.) The utility possibility curve for tariff-restricted trade is then the envelope of the set of all utility possibility curves for specific τ's. These ideas are illustrated by fig. 5.

The tariff-imposing country is, of course, simply taking advantage of its monopoly position in world markets. What, then, happens to the optimum tariff if the production and sale of export commodities are in the hands of a monopolist? The monopolist will seek to equate the marginal cost of exports in terms of importables (that is, the marginal rate of transformation between exportables and importables) to the marginal revenue of exports in terms of imports (that is, the marginal terms of trade). Thus the monopolist in pursuit of maximum profit will impose a tax (rate of profit) on the foreigner equal to the

---

[13] Mill (1909, 1948) and Sidgwick (1887) early drew attention to the possibility, open to a single country, of gaining by imposing a tariff. It was left for Edgeworth (1925, p. 15) and Bickerdike (1906) to clinch the matter.

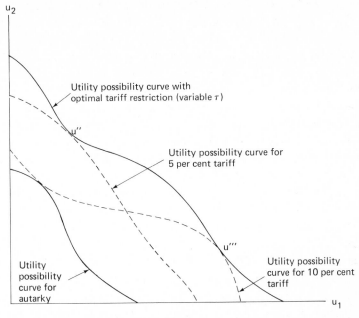

Fig. 5.

optimum tariff rate of competitive conditions. Under conditions of monopoly, then, the optimum tariff is zero (Polak, 1950–1951). Note, however, that the full Paretian optimum is not attained under monopoly, for consumers will equate their marginal rates of substitution not to the marginal rate of transformation but to the price ratio. There exists a case for paying a subsidy on sales to the domestic market, at a rate sufficient to equate price and marginal revenue (on home sales only), that is, at a percentage rate equal to (minus) the reciprocal of the elasticity of home demand for the export commodity.

Finally, the reader is reminded that the discussion of this section has been based on the assumption of given trading conditions. In particular, it has been assumed that the import duties levied by its trading partners do not change in response to changes in the home country's tariffs. None of the theorems of this section survive the recognition that the home country's trading partners may retaliate against the erection of a tariff barrier.

9. Final comments

It has been shown, under certain assumptions, that compensated trade, either free or restricted, is better than no trade. It is well, in conclusion, to emphasize that the proofs have been constructed under some fairly severe assumptions. The assumption of stable ordinal preference scales for individuals has ruled out of consideration what Mill considered to be the greatest of the benefits imparted by trade, the destruction of old preferences[14]. Similarly, no attention has been paid to the possible impact of trade on the state of technical knowledge and the rate of its accumulation. It has been assumed, as is customary, that returns to scale are constant, that the full employment of all resources is effected by flexible factor prices, and that there are no external economies or diseconomies, either of production or consumption[15]. Finally, it has been assumed throughout that lump sum taxes and subsidies are feasible. If the only kinds of taxes and subsidies available are those which carry with them a deadweight loss of allocative efficiency, then the theorems are true but irrelevant. The utility *feasibility* locus of the trade situation may well cut inside the no-trade feasibility locus (Samuelson, 1950).

References

Bickerdike, C. F. (1906), The theory of incipient taxes, *Economic Journal*, 16, Dec., 529–535.
Caves, R. E. (1960), *Trade and Economic Structure, Models and Methods*, Harvard University Press, Cambridge, Mass.
Edgeworth, F. Y. (1925), *Papers Relating to Political Economy*, II, Macmillan, London.
Enke, S. (1961), Trade gains in the short run: a reply to Mr. Kemp, *Canadian Journal of Economics and Political Science*, 27, Nov., 522–526.
Graaff, J. de V. (1949–1950), On optimum tariff structures, *Review of Economic Studies*, 17(1), 47–59.
Haberler, G. (1950), Some problems in the pure theory of foreign trade, *Economic Journal*, 60, June, 223–240.
Matthews, R. C. O. (1949–1950), Reciprocal demand and increasing returns, *Review of Economic Studies*, 17(2), 149–158.
Mill, J. S. (1909), *Principles of Political Economy* (Ashley ed.), Longmans, Green, London.
Mill, J. S. (1948), *Essays in Some Unsettled Questions of Political Economy*, London School of Economics and Political Science, London.
Olsen, E., (1958), Undenrigshandelens gevinst, *Nationaløkonomisk Tidsskrift*, 96 (1, 2), Aug., 76–79.
Polak, J. J. (1950–1951), The 'optimum tariff' and the cost of exports, *Review of Economic Studies*, 19 (1), 36–41.

[14] Mill (1909, Book III, ch. XVII, section 5).

[15] If external economies of scale are of sufficient strength to reverse the convexity of the production frontier and, withal, are not disturbing of the Paretian optimality conditions – a case which has been studied by Matthews (1949–1950) – the following obverse of the proposition of section (2), and (3) may be proved: through trade and lump sum taxes and subsidies, every individual in an imperfectly specialized country could be made *worse off* (or, in the limiting case, no better off) than in the absence of trade. The welfare implications of factor-price rigidities and external economies have been studied by Haberler (1950).

Samuelson, P. A. (1939), The gains from international trade, *Canadian Journal of Economics and Political Science*, 5, May, 195–205. Reprinted in: Ellis, H. S. and L. A. Metzler (eds.) (1949), *Readings in the Theory of International Trade*, The Blakiston Company, Philadelphia, 239–252.

Samuelson, P. A. (1950), Evaluation of real national income, *Oxford Economic Papers*, new series, 2, Jan., 1–29.

Samuelson, P. A. (1953), Prices of factors and goods in general equilibrium, *Review of Economic Studies*, 21, Oct., 1–20.

Sidgwick, H. (1887), *The Principles of Political Economy* (2nd ed.), Macmillan, London.

Chapter 9

VARIABLE RETURNS TO SCALE, COMMODITY TAXES, FACTOR MARKET DISTORTIONS AND THEIR IMPLICATIONS FOR TRADE GAINS*

1. Introduction

The contemplation of the static theory of the gains from international trade may induce a response of breathless admiration or a mood of deep despair, or both. It all depends on one's point of view: the subject is difficult and one cannot fail to admire the elegance and glitter of the theorems which have been established; on the other hand, the theorems rest on very special assumptions.

Specifically, it has been shown that, in the absence of external or internal economies and diseconomies of scale, in the absence of factor market distortions, and in the absence of consumption and production taxes:

(i) free trade is better (strictly, not worse) than no trade, in the sense that there always exists a system of ideal lump sum taxes and subsidies which would leave everybody not worse off after trade than before; and that

(ii) an improvement in a country's barter terms of trade is desirable, in the same sense.

We owe the first proposition to Paul Samuelson[1], the second to Anne Krueger and Hugo Sonnenschein. The assumptions listed above will be referred to as the *standard assumptions*.

When the standard assumptions are relaxed we are reduced to erroneous generalization[2] or the dissection of highly special cases[3]. The field is in a mess,

* *Swedish Journal of Economics*, 72 (Jan. 1970), 1–11, with T. Negishi.

[1] See Samuelson (1939, 1962) and Krueger and Sonnenschein (1967).

[2] Only in the case of variable returns to scale has there been a serious attempt to generalize the standard propositions. The essential references are to Graham (1923) and Tinbergen (1945, 1954). Most recent treatments contain simple variations on Tinbergen's theme, or parrot him quite uncritically.

In fact, Tinbergen's treatment is wrong in essentials. His much-reproduced diagram (Tinbergen, 1954, fig. 4, p. 181) is constructed on the assumption that the price ratio is equal to the ratio of marginal costs, which it clearly cannot be. Moreover, the locus of competitive outputs in that diagram has a shape which is inconsistent with the assumptions made about scale returns in the two industries. For more detail, see Herberg and Kemp (1969).

[3] See Kemp (1969, ch. 12).

littered with the debris of earlier debate yet empty of satisfactory generalizations.

Of course, we are in this field occupied with comparisons of second-best situations, and for some this observation will serve both as explanation and expiation. In the world of second best many strange things are possible. Nevertheless, one need not jump overboard in the belief that literally anything can happen and that generalization is impossible; at least, that is what we hope to show.

2. Variable returns to scale[4]

It is assumed that in industries $1, \ldots, k$ returns to scale are decreasing, that in industries $k + 1, \ldots, q$ returns to scale are constant, and that in industries $q + 1, \ldots, n$ returns are increasing. It is assumed, moreover, that entry to each industry is perfectly free so that, in equilibrium, profit is zero. If returns to scale are decreasing, they must be accompanied by diseconomies external to the firm; for internal diseconomies combined with freedom of entry imply constant returns to the industry (and firms of infinitesimal size). If, on the other hand, returns are increasing, the economies may be either internal to the firm or external to it. The form taken by the economies in this case, however, has no bearing on the analysis to follow: if the economies are of the internal variety, the industry will contain a single firm, but a firm constrained by the prospect of new entrants to equate price to average cost; and if the economies are external to the firm, price will in any case be forced to the level of average cost. Therefore, we need not specify the nature of the process generating the economies.

The assumptions just listed will be maintained throughout this section and will not be repeated in the statement of theorems.

The following notation will be employed:

$X = (X_1, \ldots, X_n)$ vector of outputs;
$D = (D_1, \ldots, D_n)$ consumption vector;
$A = (A_1, \ldots, A_n)$ vector of total inputs;
$A_{.j} = (A_{1j}, \ldots, A_{mj})$ vector of inputs in the jth industry;
$p = (p_1, \ldots, p_n)$ vector of commodity prices;
$w = (w_1, \ldots, w_m)$ vector of factor rentals.

---

[4] Some of the problems discussed in this section are treated also in Negishi (1969).

Values of the variables under autarky will be indicated by the superscript 0, free-trade values will be indicated by primes, and alternative free-trade values will be indicated by double primes.

Theorem 1. If the opening of trade results in the non-expansion of every industry $j = 1, \ldots, k$ and in the non-contraction of every industry $j = q + 1, \ldots, n$, so that

$$X'_j \leqslant X^0_j, \qquad j = 1, \ldots, k, \qquad X'_j \geqslant X^0_j, \qquad j = q + 1, \ldots, n, \tag{1}$$

then trade is necessarily non-harmful, in the sense that those who benefit from trade could afford to compensate those who suffer.

Proof. Suppose the contrary, that there exists an autarkic equilibrium which, in terms of individual utilities, cannot be reproduced or bettered under free trade. Then for all relevant free trade distributions of income, that is, distributions such that either everyone is not worse off or everyone is not better off than under autarky, the inequality

$$p'D' - w'A' < p'D^0 - w'A^0 \tag{2}$$

must be satisfied. Otherwise, free trade would be revealed as preferred to autarky. However, $X^0 = D^0$ and free trade is balanced so that

$$p'D' = p'X'. \tag{3}$$

Hence (2) may be rewritten as

$$p'X' - w'A' < p'X^0 - w'A^0 \tag{4}$$

that is, as

$$\sum_{j=1}^{k} (p'_j X'_j - w' A'_j) + \sum_{j=k+1}^{q} (p'_j X'_j - w' A'_j) + \sum_{j=q+1}^{n} (p'_j X'_j - w' A'_j)$$
$$< \sum_{j=1}^{k} (p'_j X^0_j - w' A^0_j) + \sum_{j=k+1}^{q} (p'_j X^0_j - w' A^0_j) + \sum_{j=q+1}^{n} (p'_j X^0_j - w' A^0_j). \tag{5}$$

However, freedom of entry ensures that in free trade equilibrium profit is zero in each industry:

$$p'_j X'_j - w' A'_j = 0, \qquad j = 1, \ldots, n.$$

If, faced with free trade prices and rentals, producers in the jth constant returns industry hold their outputs and factor inputs at levels appropriate to autarkic prices and rentals, their profit must be non-positive, that is

$$0 = p_j'X_j' - w'A_j' \geqslant p_j'X_j^0 - w'A_{\cdot j}^0, \qquad j = k+1, \ldots, q. \tag{6a}$$

A fortiori, given (1),

$$0 = p_j'X_j' - w'A_j' \geqslant p_j'X_j^0 - w'A_{\cdot j}^0, \qquad j = 1, \ldots, k; \qquad j = q+1, \ldots, n. \tag{6b}$$

Inequalities (6) contradict inequalities (5).   QED

We shall say that a country's barter terms of trade have improved if

$$p''X' > p''D'. \tag{7}$$

Theorem 2. If an autonomous improvement in a country's barter terms of trade results in the non-expansion of every industry $j = 1, \ldots, k$ and in the non-contraction of every industry $q+1, \ldots, n$ then the change is necessarily non-harmful, in the sense that those who benefit from the change could afford to compensate those who suffer.

Proof. Suppose the contrary, that there exists an initial free trade equilibrium which, in terms of individual utilities, cannot be reproduced or improved upon in the new free trade situation. Then for all relevant distributions of income the inequality

$$p''D'' - w''A'' < p''D' - w''A' \tag{8}$$

is satisfied. However, (7) holds and trade is balanced, so that

$$p''D'' = p''X''. \tag{9}$$

Hence (8) may be rewritten as

$$p''X'' - w''A'' < p''X' - w''A', \tag{10}$$

that is, as

$$\sum_{j=1}^{k} (p_j''X_j'' - w''A_j'') + \sum_{j=k+1}^{q} (p_j''X_j'' - w''A_j'') + \sum_{j=q+1}^{n} (p_j''X_j'' - w''A_j'')$$
$$< \sum_{j=1}^{k} (p_j''X_j' - w''A_j') + \sum_{j=k+1}^{q} (p_j''X_j' - w''A_{\cdot j}') + \sum_{j=q+1}^{n} (p_j''X_j' - w''A_{\cdot j}'). \tag{11}$$

By an argument similar to that which justified (6), however,

$$0 = p''_j X''_j - w'' A''_j \geq p''_j X'_j - w'' A'_j, \qquad j = 1, \ldots, n. \tag{12}$$

Inequalities (12) contradict inequalities (11). QED

Perhaps the most surprising features of theorem 1 are that it requires no assumptions about either the autarkic or free trade state of specialization, that it sidesteps any reference to the shape of either the locus of production possibilities or the locus of competitive outputs, and that no mention is made of the import–export status of any industry. It is perhaps worth drawing attention to the fact that in the statement of the theorem no restrictions are placed on the outputs of the $q - k$ constant returns industries.

Theorems 1 and 2 can be extended without difficulty to cover trade which is not free but restricted by tariffs, import quotas or exchange restrictions.

On the other hand, some plausible analogues to theorems 1 and 2 turn out to be false. Those theorems enable us to compare situations (pre- and post-trade, for example) which are characterized not only by variable returns to scale but also by the allocative distortions associated with average cost pricing. The theorems therefore tell us little about the implications for trade gains of variable returns *per se.* To get at that question one must imagine that, before and after the hypothetical disturbance (the opening of trade, for example), the distortions are precisely offset by a suitable system of taxes and subsidies. *But then theorems 1 and 2 are no longer true.* Even when (1) is satisfied the opening of trade (or an improvement in the terms of trade) may be harmful. Figure 1 provides an illustration from the world of two products and inelastic factor supplies.

Suppose that all industries enjoy increasing returns to scale and that they can be unambiguously divided into those with less strongly and those with more strongly increasing returns, each member of the second group enjoying more strongly increasing returns than every member of the first group. Suppose, moreover, that the opening of trade (or an improvement in the terms of trade) results in the non-expansion of the output of each industry in the first group, and in the non-contraction of the output of each industry in the second group. One is tempted to conjecture, in analogy to theorems 1 and 2, that under these conditions trade is necessarily gainful. Unfortunately the conjecture cannot be confirmed by the kind of argument used so far. Indeed there are reasons for believing the conjecture to be false. For when all industries enjoy increasing returns the contracting industries suffer a *loss* of efficiency, and whether this is outweighed in the welfare balance by the improvement in the efficiency of the expanding industries cannot be determined without a closer specification both of preferences and of technology.

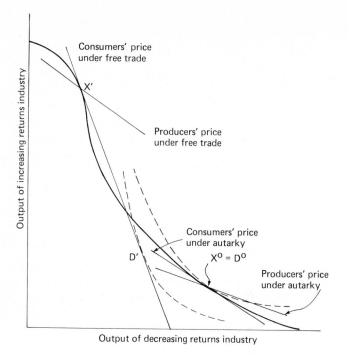

Fig. 1.

3. Commodity taxes

We now revert to the assumption of constant returns to scale but vary the standard assumptions by introducing commodity taxes.

Our notation must be extended to include consumption and production taxes, and to admit the distinction between prices as seen by consumers and prices as seen by producers:

$T_j \gtreqless 0$ *ad valorem* tax on the consumption of the jth commodity,

$$T = \begin{bmatrix} T_1 & 0 & \cdots & 0 \\ 0 & T_2 & \cdots & 0 \\ \vdots & \vdots & & \vdots \\ 0 & 0 & \cdots & T_n \end{bmatrix}$$ diagonal matrix, with T_j as the jth diagonal element,

$T_j^* \gtreqless 0$ *ad valorem* tax on the production of the jth commodity,

$$T^* = \begin{bmatrix} T_1^* & 0 & \cdots & 0 \\ 0 & T_2^* & \cdots & 0 \\ \vdots & \vdots & & \vdots \\ 0 & 0 & \cdots & T_n^* \end{bmatrix},$$

$p = (p_1, \ldots, p_n)$ vector of consumers' prices, $p^* = (p_1^*, \ldots, p_n^*)$ vector of producers' prices.

Suppose that the government has imposed a vector of consumption taxes but that all other standard assumptions hold. Then

Theorem 3. If the opening of trade results in the non-contraction of net tax revenue, calculated on the basis of post-trade prices, then trade is necessarily non-harmful, in the sense that those who benefit from trade could afford to compensate those who suffer. Net tax revenue cannot decline if consumption of the jth good fails to contract when T_j is positive and fails to expand when T_j is negative.

Proof. Suppose the contrary, that there exists an autarkic equilibrium which, in terms of individual utilities, cannot be reproduced or bettered under free trade. Then, for all relevant free trade distributions of income, the inequality

$$p'D' - w'A' < p'D^0 - w'A^0 \tag{2}$$

must hold. Now

$$p' = p^{*\prime}(I + T), \tag{13}$$

where I is the unit matrix. Hence

$$p^{*\prime}(I + T)D' - w'A' < p^{*\prime}(I + T)D^0 - w'A^0, \tag{14}$$

that is

$$p^{*\prime}D' + p^{*\prime}T(D' - D^0) - w'A' < p^{*\prime}D^0 - w'A^0. \tag{15}$$

Now $p^{*\prime}T(D' - D^0)$ is the increase in tax revenue calculated on the basis of post-trade prices. By assumption it is non-negative; hence

$$p^{*\prime}D' - w'A' < p^{*\prime}D^0 - w'A^0. \tag{16}$$

But free trade is balanced,

$$p^{*\prime}D' = p^{*\prime}X', \tag{17}$$

and autarkic production is equal to autarkic consumption,

$$D^0 = X^0. \tag{18}$$

Hence

$$p^{*\prime}X' - w'A' < p^{*\prime}X^0 - w'A^0. \tag{19}$$

Under constant returns and freedom of entry, however,

$$0 = p_j^{*\prime}X_j' - w'A_j' \geq p^{*\prime}X^0 - w'A_{\cdot j}^0, \qquad j = 1, \dots, n. \tag{20}$$

Inequalities (19) and (20) are in conflict; hence the main part of the theorem is proved. The second part of the theorem is obvious.   QED

Theorem 4. If an autonomous improvement in a country's barter terms of trade results in the non-contraction of net tax revenue calculated on the basis of the new prices then the change is necessarily non-harmful in the sense that those who benefit from the change could afford to compensate those who suffer. Net tax revenue cannot decline if consumption of the jth good fails to contract when T_j is positive and fails to expand when T_j is negative.

Proof. Suppose the contrary, that there exists an initial free trade equilibrium which, in terms of individual utilities, cannot be reproduced or bettered in the new free trade situation. Then for all relevant distributions of income the inequality

$$p''D'' - w''A'' < p''D' - w''A' \tag{8}$$

must hold. Now

$$p'' = p^{*\prime\prime}(I + T) \tag{21}$$

so that (8) may be rewritten as

$$p^{*\prime\prime}D'' + p^{*\prime\prime}T(D'' - D') - w''A'' < p^{*\prime\prime}D' - w''A'. \tag{22}$$

But by assumption the change in net tax revenue, $p^{*\prime\prime}T(D'' - D')$, is non-negative; hence

$$p^{*\prime\prime}D'' - w''A'' < p^{*\prime\prime}D' - w''A'. \tag{23}$$

Free trade is balanced,

$$p^{*\prime\prime}D'' = p^{*\prime\prime}X'', \tag{24}$$

and the terms of trade have improved,

$$p^{*\prime\prime}(X' - D') > 0. \tag{25}$$

Hence

$$p^{*''}X'' - w''A'' < p^{*''}X' - w''A'. \tag{26}$$

Under constant returns and freedom of entry, however,

$$0 = p_j^{*''}X_j'' - w''A_j'' \geq p_j^* X_j' - w''A_j'', \qquad j = 1, \ldots, n. \tag{27}$$

Inequalities (26) and (27) are in conflict and the non-trivial part of the theorem is proved. QED

Suppose, alternatively, that the government has imposed a vector of production taxes but that all other standard assumptions hold. Then the following theorems, companion to theorems 3 and 4, can be proved. The proofs contain no novelties and are withheld.

Theorem 5. If the opening of trade results in the non-contraction of net tax revenue, calculated on the basis of post-trade prices, then trade is necessarily non-harmful, in the sense that those who benefit from trade could afford to compensate those who suffer. Net tax revenue cannot decline if production of the jth good fails to contract when T_j^* is positive and fails to expand when T_j^* is negative.

Theorem 6. If an autonomous improvement in a country's barter terms of trade results in the non-contraction of net tax revenue, calculated on the basis of post-trade prices, then the change is necessarily non-harmful, in the sense that those who benefit from the change could afford to compensate those who suffer. Net tax revenue cannot decline if production of the jth good fails to contract when T_j^* is positive and fails to expand when T_j^* is negative.

4. Factor market distortions

Let us now assume that in each industry returns to scale are constant but that the reward of any particular factor, say the mth, may vary from industry to industry. The rental paid by the jth industry to the mth factor is denoted by $w_{mj}, j = 1, \ldots, n$. Without loss of generality we can renumber industries so that under free trade each industry pays to the mth factor not more than its predecessor:

$$w_{m,j+1} \leq w_{mj}, \qquad j = 1, \ldots, n-1, \tag{28}$$

with a strong inequality for some j.

Before proceeding to the substance of this section we clear out of the way two preliminary matters. First we note that the interindustrial differentials create a merely sham problem if they accurately reflect non-pecuniary advantages and disadvantages of employment in particular industries. To see this, we need only divide the mth factor into n subfactors according to the industry supplied, so that there are $n + m - 1$ factors in all. To avoid inessential complications, therefore, we assume that the owners of the mth factor are completely insensitive to the non-pecuniary aspects of employment.

We notice next that the persistence of the differentials is inconsistent with rational household choice; if in the circumstances described by (28) households behaved rationally the mth factor would be supplied only to the first industry. Accordingly, we now abandon an assumption we have carried through sections 2 and 3 – that the supply of each factor is a variable, depending on product prices and factor rewards – and assume instead that A_m, the supply of the mth factor, is a constant. The supplies of other factors remain variable.

Theorem 7. If for any $h, 1 < h < n$, the opening of trade results in the non-expansion of the employment of the mth factor in every industry $j = h, \ldots, n$ and in the non-contraction of the employment of the mth factor in every industry $j = 1, \ldots, h - 1$, so that

$$A'_{mj} \leq A^0_{mj}, \qquad j = h, \ldots, n, \qquad A'_{mj} \geq A^0_{mj}, \qquad j = 1, \ldots, h - 1,$$

then trade is necessarily non-harmful, in the sense that those who benefit from trade could afford to compensate those who suffer.

Proof. Suppose the contrary, that there exists an autarkic equilibrium which, in terms of individual utilities (which are, this time, functions of the individual's consumption of n goods and of his supply of $m - 1$ factors of production), cannot be reproduced or bettered under free trade. Then, since the household choice of D and $\bar{A}$ is assumed to be rational, for all relevant free trade distributions of income,

$$p'D' - \bar{w}'\bar{A}' < p'D^0 - \bar{w}'\bar{A}^0, \tag{29}$$

where $\bar{A} = (A_1, \ldots, A_{m-1})$ and $\bar{w} = (w_1, \ldots, w_{m-1})$. Otherwise, free trade would be revealed as preferred to autarky. On the other hand, from the assumptions of the theorem,

$$\sum_{j=1}^{h-1} w'_{mj}(A'_{mj} - A^0_{mj}) + \sum_{j=h}^{n} w'_{mj}(A'_{mj} - A^0_{mj}) > 0$$

which in turn yields

$$\sum_{j=1}^{n} w'_{mj} A'_{mj} > \sum_{j=1}^{n} w'_{mj} A^0_{mj}. \tag{30}$$

From (29) and (30),

$$p'D' - w'A' < p'D^0 - w'A^0 \tag{2}$$

and the argument proceeds as in the second half of the proof of theorem 1.

QED

Theorem 8. If for any $h, 1 < h < n$, an autonomous improvement in a country's barter terms of trade results in the non-expansion of the employment of the mth factor in every industry $j = h, \ldots, n$ and in the non-contraction of the employment of the mth factor in every industry $j = 1, \ldots, h - 1$, so that

$$A''_{mj} \leq A'_{mj} \qquad j = h, \ldots, n, \qquad A''_{mj} \geq A'_{mj} \qquad j = 1, \ldots, h - 1,$$

then the change is necessarily non-harmful, in the sense that those who benefit from trade could afford to compensate those who suffer.

Proof. Suppose the contrary, that there exists an initial free trade equilibrium which, in terms of individual utilities (which, again, are functions of the individual's consumption of n goods and of his supply of $m - 1$ factors), cannot be reproduced or improved on in the free trade situation. Then, for all relevant distributions of income, the inequality

$$p''D'' - \bar{w}''\bar{A}'' < p''D' - \bar{w}'\bar{A}' \tag{31}$$

is satisfied. From the assumptions of the theorem, we have

$$\sum_{j=1}^{n} w''_{mj} A''_{mj} > \sum_{j=1}^{n} w''_{mj} A'_{mj} \tag{32}$$

which, in conjunction with (31), yields again the inequality (8). The rest of the proof parallels that of theorem 2.   QED

Like theorems 1 and 2, these theorems bypass many questions which to earlier writers seemed central. For example, no mention is made of the import–export status of any industry, and no assumptions are made about the shape of the locus of competitive outputs. It may also be noted that nothing has been said about the hierarchy of rewards to the mth factor in the initial situation (autarky in theorem 7, the first of two free trade positions in theorem 8), and that nothing has been said about changes in the employment of factors other than the mth.

Theorems 7 and 8 have been stated in terms of interindustrial differences in the reward of a single factor. However, both theorems can be extended to cover interindustrial differences in the rewards of several (but not all) factors provided industries are ranked in the same way by each of the several factors.

5. Final remarks

In some of our proofs we have relied on the assumption that in each industry entry is completely free. This assumption is extreme, and may be thought crucial. We note, therefore, that all theorems carry over, with inessential changes, to the other polar world in which, in each industry, the number of firms is constant.

Appendix A: variable returns to scale, commodity taxes, factor market distortions and their implications for trade gains: a clarification*

In our recent paper (Kemp and Negishi, 1970) certain assumptions were introduced only implicitly. We now spell out those assumptions in detail. It suffices to reconsider theorem 1. Let $X = (X_1, \ldots, X_n)$ be the vector of outputs. These outputs are produced by a neo-classical, no-joint-products technology, with industries $1, \ldots, k$ displaying non-increasing returns to scale, industries $k + 1, \ldots, q$ constant returns, and industries $q + 1, \ldots, n$ non-decreasing returns. A superscript 0 indicates autarkic quantities and a prime indicates free-trade quantities. We then have (Kemp and Negishi, 1970, p. 3)

Theorem 1. If the opening of trade results in the non-expansion of every industry $j = 1, \ldots, k$ and in the non-contraction of every industry $j = q + 1, \ldots, n$, so that

$$X'_j \leqslant X^0_j, \quad j = 1, \ldots, k, \qquad X'_j \geqslant X^0_j, \quad j = q + 1, \ldots, n,$$

then trade is necessarily non-harmful, in the sense that those who benefit from trade could afford to compensate those who suffer.

The trouble with this statement of the theorem is that it does not specify X^0 and X' sufficiently closely. It does not make quite clear whether X^0 and X' are

---

* *Swedish Journal of Economics*, 73 (June 1971), 257–258, with T. Negishi.

specific production points or arbitrarily chosen members of sets of points; that is, it leaves unclear whether the autarky–free trade production comparisons are point–point, point–set, set–point or set–set. Nor is it stated whether X' is the free trade production point before compensation or after compensation. In fact, we had in mind point–point comparisons, with X' taken after compensation. However, it is possible to formulate related theorems in terms of each of the other types of comparison.

We now propose a more careful formulation of theorem 1. By a scheme of compensation we shall mean a vector of lump sum payments which ensures that either everyone is not worse off or everyone is not better off under free trade than under autarky.

Theorem 1 (revised). Suppose that there exists a particular scheme of compensation S such that the opening of trade results in the non-expansion of every industry $j = 1, \ldots, k$ and in the non-contraction of every industry $j = q + 1, \ldots, n$, so that

$$X'_j \leqslant X^0_j, \qquad j = 1, \ldots, k, \qquad X'_j \geqslant X^0_j, \qquad j = q + 1, \ldots, n.$$

Then trade is necessarily non-harmful, in the sense that there exists a scheme of compensation which leaves everyone not worse off than under autarky; S is such a scheme.

To construct a proof one need change only in trivial detail the proof already provided for theorem 1. Theorems 2–8 of Kemp and Negishi (1970) can be spelled out in similar fashion.

Appendix B: domestic distortions, tariffs, and the theory of optimum subsidy*

The purpose of this note is to question two related propositions of Bhagwati and Ramaswami (1963) and to rehabilitate a proposition of Hagen (1968). As a byproduct, some aspects of the theory of second-best or institutionally constrained optima may be clarified.

---

* *Journal of Political Economy*, 77 (Nov.–Dec. 1969), 1011–1013, with T. Negishi. Negishi's contribution was made while he was visiting the University of Minnesota.

Section B.1

Consider a small trading country subject to domestic imperfections arising from factor market distortions, externalities, and so forth. Bhagwati and Ramaswami have stated that, for such an economy, (1) a corrective tax-cum-subsidy is superior to a corrective tariff and (2) there may not exist a tariff which would yield an equilibrium superior to the free trade equilibrium. The second of these propositions seems to us to be incorrect. In the face of domestic distortions, and given the usual assumptions of trade theory, there always exists a positive or negative[5] second-best optimal tariff.

In support of proposition (2), and with production distortions in mind, Bhagwati and Ramaswami have argued that 'in the case of domestic distortions, $DRS = FRT \neq DRT$ under free trade. A suitable tariff can equalize FRT and DRT but would destroy the equality between DRS and FRT. Hence it is clear that no tariff may exist that would yield a solution superior to that under free trade' (Bhagwati and Ramaswami 1963, p. 45)[6]. On examination, however, this line of argument is seen to point not to (2) but to (1).

That proposition (2) is invalid may be established by a very simple line of reasoning. Consider an initial free trade equilibrium in which something is consumed of each commodity (the argument can be adjusted to cover boundary equilibriums). Suppose that this equilibrium is disturbed by the imposition of a tariff. At the initial equilibrium point, the relevant community indifference curve is tangential to the world price line; hence the rate of change of the consumption loss per unit increase in the tariff is zero. The rate of change of the production loss, however, is not zero, for in the initial equilibrium the locus of competitive outputs cuts the price line. Thus the net rate of change of welfare must be non-zero, and we may be sure that there exists a tariff which produces an equilibrium superior to that under free trade. It follows also that the constrained optimal tariff, if it exists, is non-zero.

Suppose that the net rate of change in welfare per unit increase in the tariff is positive under free trade, and let the rate of duty steadily increase. Eventually, the marginal production gain must vanish, while the marginal consumption loss

---

[5] One might be tempted to infer, from certain of their early passages, that Bhagwati and Ramaswami wish to restrict their statement to positive tariffs, leaving open the possibility that there may exist a negative tariff superior to free trade. See, for example, Bhagwati and Ramaswami (1963), pp. 45 and 46. Later, however, they make clear that they intend their statement to apply to both positive and negative tariffs. See Bhagwati and Ramaswami (1963), pp. 47 and 49.

[6] *DRS, FRT* and *DRT* stand, respectively, for the marginal domestic rate of substitution in consumption, the marginal rate of transformation through trade (slope of the foreign offer curve), and the marginal domestic rate of transformation in production.

is always non-negative. We may be sure, therefore, that a positive optimal tariff exists. We may be sure also that, provided something is consumed of each commodity, it is never optimal to completely offset the distortion. It is possible, indeed, that complete offsetting may be inferior to free trade.

Similar conclusions may be reached if under free trade the net rate of change of welfare is negative.

Section B.2

Hagen (1968) argued that if wage rates in import-competing manufacturing industry are higher than those in agriculture, it is in the public interest that manufacturing be protected by a prohibitive import duty. It was soon shown that, even in the face of distortions of the kind contemplated by Hagen, free trade may be preferable to no trade (see, for example, Fishlow and David, 1961, p. 541, n. 29; Bhagwati and Ramaswami, 1963, p. 49). Hagen's analysis and prescriptions, therefore, cannot be taken literally. It is clear from section B.1, however, that Hagen's argument can be successfully reformulated in terms of a positive, possibly non-prohibitive second-best tariff. In essence Hagen was right; he simply claimed too much.

Section B.3

Finally, consider a country with domestic distortions but with appreciable monopoly power in trade. Bhagwati and Ramaswami (1963, p. 45) have stated (without argument) that it may be impossible for such an economy to devise a tax-cum-subsidy that would yield an equilibrium superior to that of free trade. This statement also seems incorrect. There always exists a non-zero, second-best tax-cum-subsidy which yields an equilibrium superior to that of free trade. The proof is omitted.

References

Bhagwati, J. and V. K. Ramaswami (1963), Domestic distortions, tariffs and the theory of optimum subsidy, *Journal of Political Economy*, 71 (1), Feb., 44–50.
Fishlow, A. and P. A. David (1961), Optimal resource allocation in an imperfect market setting, *Journal of Political Economy*, 69 (6), Dec., 529–546.
Graham, F. D. (1923), Some aspects of protection further considered, *Quarterly Journal of Economics*, 37 (2), Feb., 199–227.
Hagen, E. E. (1968), An economic justification of protectionism, *Quarterly Journal of Economics*, 72 (4), Nov., 496–514.

Herberg, H. and M. C. Kemp (1969), Some implications of variable returns to scale, *Canadian Journal of Economics*, 2 (3), Aug., 403–415.

Kemp, M. C. (1969), *The Pure Theory of International Trade and Investment*, Prentice-Hall, Englewood Cliffs, NJ.

Kemp, M. C. and T. Negishi (1970), Variable returns to scale, commodity taxes, factor market distortions and their implications for trade gains. *Swedish Journal of Economics*, 72, Jan., 1–11.

Krueger, A. O. and Sonnenschein, Hugo (1967), The terms of trade, the gains from trade and price divergence, *International Economic Review*, 8 (1), Feb., 121–127.

Negishi, T. (1969), Marshallian external economies and gains from trade between similar countries, *Review of Economic Studies*, 36 (1), Jan., 131–135.

Samuelson, P. A. (1939), The gains from international trade, *Canadian Journal of Economics and Political Science*, 5 (2), May, 195–205.

Samuelson, P. A. (1962), The gains from international trade once again, *Economic Journal*, 72 (4), Dec., 820–829.

Tinbergen, J. (1945), *International Economic Cooperation*, Elsevier, Amsterdam.

Tinbergen, J. (1954), *International Economic Integration*, Elsevier, Amsterdam.

Chapter 10

SOME ISSUES IN THE ANALYSIS OF TRADE GAINS*

1. Introduction

It is well known that for a small country, with no power to influence world prices, free trade is optimal. From this it has seemed reasonable to infer (a) that any tariff-ridden situation is suboptimal and (b) that the higher is the tariff the smaller is the gain from trade. That, at any rate was the position I adopted in my *Pure Theory of International Trade*[1].

What can be said of the relative desirabilities of the free trading situation, the trading situation characterized by a uniform 5% import duty, that characterized by a 10% duty, etc.?

In the special case in which world prices are virtually independent of the volume of a country's imports and exports, a particularly simple answer can be given: the free trade situation is superior to the 5% situation, which in turn is superior to the 10% situation, and so on.

After reading Bhagwati's paper – and Vanek's recent book on customs unions[2] – I see no need to modify my 1962–1964 conclusions. I should not, however, seek to defend the logic by which I once tried to establish them. The best I can now say of the argument provided is that it is not so much wrong as lamentably incomplete.

What I now hope to show, in section 2, is that the maximum feasible utility of one individual, given arbitrary minimum feasible utilities of all other individuals, is greater in a low-tariff than in a high-tariff situation. As a byproduct; the derivation and possible shapes of the utility feasibility locus will be considered

* *Oxford Economic Papers*, 20 (July 1968), 149–161. I am grateful to Jagdish Bhagwati, Harry Johnson and Paul Samuelson for helpful correspondence.

[1] Kemp (1964, p. 169). A similar passage appears in Kemp (1962, p. 814).

[2] Vanek (1965). In ch. 4 and in the appendix Vanek has anticipated many of the points made in Bhagwati's section 3 and in section 2 of this paper. Of special relevance and interest are passages on pp. 80 and 202.

in some detail. I hope also to be able to set out conditions under which tariff-ridden equilibria are dynamically stable.

In the course of my 1962–1964 discussion of trade gains I proved that trade restricted by tariffs, quantitative controls, or exchange restrictions is better than no trade at all. On the other hand, Jagdish Bhagwati argues in his companion paper that for a small country the trade gain may be negative if trade is distorted by a tax on domestic production of either commodity or by a tax on domestic consumption of the imported commodity (or, equivalently, if trade is distorted by a subsidy to domestic production of either commodity or by a subsidy to domestic consumption of the exported commodity)[3].

In calculating the gain or loss from trade, however, Bhagwati compares an autarkic equilibrium unencumbered by taxes or subsidies of any kind with a tax- or subsidy-ridden free trade equilibrium. The gain or loss is then the joint result of the opening of trade and the imposition of taxes or subsidies. Without wishing to mount a methodological high horse or cast any doubt on the value of Bhagwati's calculations, it does seem to me that an equally interesting comparison is that of a tax or subsidy-ridden free trade situation with an equally tax- or subsidy-ridden autarkic situation. Only that comparison can reveal the gains *from trade alone.* The comparison is made in section 3.

Moreover, Bhagwati's practice of considering a tax or subsidy on the production or consumption of the *imported* or *exported* commodity may be found slightly confusing. For the superposition of an arbitrarily large tax or subsidy on an initial tax-free free trade situation may reverse the direction of trade: the pre-tax imported commodity may be the post-tax exported commodity. It seems preferable to consider the implications for trade gains of a tax or subsidy on a specific commodity, leaving the market to determine its export–import status. That at any rate will be our procedure in section 3. It will be shown that, even in the face of a consumption tax or (subject to a mild qualification) a production tax, free trade is potentially gainful.

In section 4 I consider a further question closely related to those considered in sections 2 and 3: does an improvement in a tariff-ridden country's terms of trade imply a potential gain?

2. Is a higher tariff worse than a lower tariff?

Suppose that a competitive economy produces two goods and trades one for the other at constant world prices. In fig. 1 the terms of trade are indicated by

---

[3] It is I think fair to say that in section 2 of his paper Bhagwati shows not that 'Kemp's theorem is . . . invalid' but that the theorem cannot be extended in the particular direction he considers.

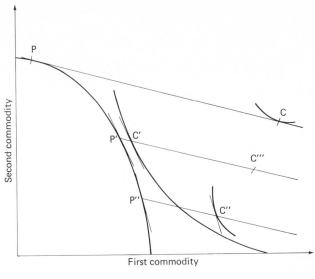

Fig. 1.

the slope of *PC*, and the free trade production and consumption equilibria lie, respectively, at *P* and *C*.[4]

If an import duty is imposed, the internal price ratio turns in favour of the imported commodity. Production now takes place at *P'* and consumption at *C'*, a point on the new trading line *P'C'''* at which the slope of the intersecting community indifference curve is equal to the slope of the internal or domestic price line.

If the import duty is raised the internal price ratio moves even further in favour of the imported commodity; production moves to *P''* and consumption to *C''*. As the figure makes clear, high-tariff welfare may be either greater or less than low-tariff welfare; moreover, for high-tariff welfare to exceed low-tariff welfare it is necessary that low-tariff consumption of the exported commodity exceed high-tariff consumption. But if consumption is greater at a higher price and lower real income the exported commodity must be inferior in consumption. However, while inferiority of the exported commodity is necessary to the paradoxical outcome it is not by itself sufficient.

In terms of utility feasibilities (fig. 2), we have shown that *U'*, a point attainable in the low-tariff situation, may lie inside or south-west of *U''*, a point attainable in the high-tariff situation.

---

[4] All indifference curves in fig. 1 are of the Scitovsky variety, but non-intersecting.

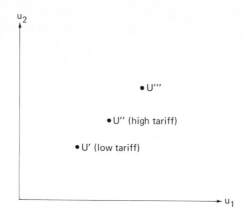

Fig. 2.

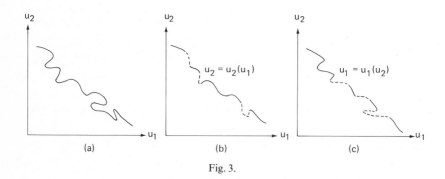

Fig. 3.

It is not difficult to see, however, that there also exists a feasible low-tariff point U'' north-east of U''. Thus, in terms of fig. 1, the income–consumption curve of the low-tariff situation passes south of C''. Therefore it must intersect $P'C'$ extended, possibly on the horizontal axis. The point of intersection, say C''', corresponds to U'''. A similar argument applies to each feasible high-tariff point. Thus every high-tariff equilibrium is dominated by at least one low-tariff equilibrium.

Let us define the utility feasibility locus as the locus of possible equilibrium utilities, given the rate of import duty. If inferiority is present this locus may incorporate several positively sloped stretches; it may even include one or more disconnected loops. Figs. 3(a) and 10 illustrate[5].

From this locus we may derive two further loci. The first of these tells us the

---

[5] The construction of the utility feasibility locus is described in the appendix.

maximum attainable values of u_2 for given minimum values of u_1 and is illustrated by fig. 3(b). The second locus is defined analogously. From it we may read off the maximum attainable values of u_1 for given minimum values of u_2 illustrated by fig. 3(c). We call these derived loci the *optimal loci*. In general the two optimal loci possess discontinuities and are not identical. If and only if the utility feasibility locus is monotonic are the optimal loci continuous and coincident.

In terms of these constructions we may paraphrase our main conclusion by saying that each low-tariff optimal locus lies uniformly outside both high-tariff optimal loci.

Thus we have confirmed that the paradoxical Vanek–Bhagwati outcome is possible, and have shown that it can emerge only if the exported commodity is inferior in consumption *and* if society is content with equilibria inside the optimal loci.

Does that conclusion carry over to a world of many traded commodities? The answer is: yes, provided the tariff is not prohibitive for any non-exported commodity. For when tariffs are raised uniformly, the domestic prices of imported goods all rise in the same proportion, with the prices of exported goods unchanged. Within each commodity group relative prices are constant, leaving only one relative price free to change – the price of imports in terms of exports. In effect we are back in a world of just two commodities to which the preceding analysis applies unchanged[6].

The stability or instability of an equilibrium can be investigated only in relation to a specific dynamic adjustment process. In this section we seek to show only that the Vanek–Bhagwati equilibrium may be stable. The process considered is therefore very simple: we assume that international payments are always in balance, so that the low-tariff consumption point of the country under consideration always lies on the trading line $P'C'''$ of fig. 1; we assume that there are no lags or frictions in the collection and distribution of tariff proceeds; and we assume that, whenever the slope of the community indifference curve exceeds that of the internal price line, the community tries to substitute the imported good for the exported good and vice versa. Suppose then that an initial equilibrium at C' is displaced slightly to the right along $P'C'''$, say to Z. If at C' the low-tariff Engel or income–consumption curve is steeper than $P'C'''$, the relevant indifference curve at Z must be steeper than the internal price line; hence the community will attempt to substitute the imported for the exported

---

[6] This paragraph contains a particular application of the well-known Leontief–Hicks theorem on composite commodities.

good, and consumption will move further away from C'. Evidently C' is in this case a point of locally unstable equilibrium.

If, on the other hand, the slope of the income–consumption curve at C' is less than that of $P'C'''$ we find by analogous reasoning that C' is a point of stable equilibrium. In this case, however, the income–consumption curve must cut $P'C'''$ again, to the right of C', before passing south of C''. This implies the existence of at least one additional low-tariff equilibrium which is Pareto-inferior to C''. Suppose we confine our attention to that low-tariff equilibrium point farthest to the right yet still inferior to C''. Clearly at that point the income–consumption curve must have steeper slope than $P'C'''$, so that the point is one of unstable equilibrium. Thus we may conclude that, if attention is confined to 'adjacent' low- and high-tariff equilibria, the Vanek–Bhagwati paradox requires that the low-tariff equilibrium be unstable.

In general, there may be any number of low-tariff equilibria which are Pareto-inferior to C''. Counting from the right, they must be alternately unstable, stable, unstable, ...

It is not difficult to show that the dividing line between stability and instability is defined by the relation $1 + tm = 0$, where t is the rate of import duty and m is the marginal propensity to consume the exported commodity. If $m < -1/t$ equilibrium is unstable; if the inequality points the other way, equilibrium is stable.

3. The gains from tax- or subsidy-ridden trade

Suppose that taxes (subsidies) are levied on (paid to) consumers of either or both of the two commodities. The country's budget constraint may be written

$$\sum_{i=1}^{2} p'_i(X'_i - D'_i) = 0, \tag{1}$$

where p'_i is the world price of the ith commodity, X'_i is the free trade production of the ith commodity and D'_i is the free trade consumption of the ith commodity. Free trade prices as seen by producers are the same as world prices. From the convexity of the production set, therefore,

$$\sum_{i=1}^{2} p'_i(X'_i - X^0_i) \geq 0, \tag{2}$$

where X^0_i is the autarkic production of the ith commodity. Moreover,

$$X^0_i - D^0_i = 0, \tag{3}$$

where D_i^0 is the autarkic consumption of the ith commodity. It follows from (1)–(3) that

$$\sum_{i=1}^{2} p'_i(D'_i - D_i^0) \geq 0.$$

That is, at world prices the community's autarkic consumption pattern would cost not more than the actual free trade consumption pattern. Since the p'_i are given, we may infer that the consumption possibility line of the free trade situation cuts (in an extreme case, touches) the autarkic indifference curve and that the community conceivably could consume more (not less) of both commodities than in the autarkic equilibrium. It only remains to show that there exists a competitive equilibrium on an indifference curve lying above (not below) the autarkic curve. Suppose that there does not exist such an equilibrium but that there exists an equilibrium on a lower indifference curve. Fig. 4 illustrates the possibility for the case in which a tax is imposed on the consumption of the first commodity. Since world prices are the same as producers' prices, trade takes place along the producers' price line $P'C'$. The free trade consumption equilibrium is represented by point C', on an indifference curve below the indifference curve II' which corresponds to the autarkic equilibrium at P^0. Note, however, that the Engel curve passing through C' must

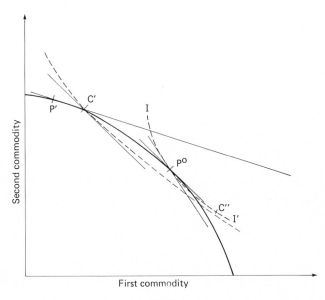

Fig. 4.

cut II' to the right of P^0, say in C'', so that over the relevant range the second commodity is inferior. The Engel curve, therefore, must eventually cut the line $P'C'$ a second time, above II', possibly on the horizontal axis. Thus there must exist at least one additional consumption equilibrium superior to the initial autarkic equilibrium. The geometric argument can be adjusted to cope with a tax on the consumption of the second commodity; the same conclusion (that trade is necessarily gainful) emerges. Moreover, the entire argument of this paragraph can be extended algebraically to cover an arbitrary number of commodities.

When we turn our attention to production taxes the picture which emerges is a little less tidy. We may suppose without loss that a tax is imposed on the production of the first commodity. (Equivalently, we may suppose that the production of the second commodity is subsidized.) An initial pre-trade equilibrium is indicated by point P^0 in fig. 5. The dotted Scitovsky indifference curve II' is based on the distribution of earned incomes in the initial equilibrium. The price ratio as seen by consumers is indicated by the slope of II' at P^0, the producers' price ratio by the slope of the production frontier. Suppose now that trade is opened and that, as a result, both price ratios move in favour of the first or taxed commodity. Then, as fig. 5 makes clear, trade is necessarily gainful.

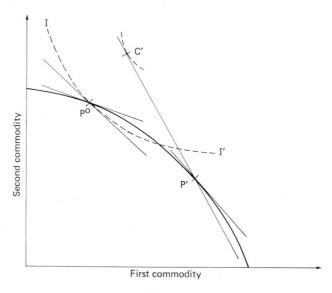

Fig. 5.

If, however, the opening of trade moves the two price ratios in favour of the second or untaxed commodity, the welfare outcome does not emerge so clearly. In this case trade shifts resources to the over-producing tax-protected industry. The implicit subsidy to that industry is passed on to foreign as well as to local consumers, suggesting that sometimes the subsidization of the foreigner may outweigh any gain from international *exchange*. The precise condition for this outcome is easy to find. If, as in fig. 6, the rate of tax is small enough to ensure that the world price line $P'C'$ intersects II', trade is gainful. If, as in fig. 7, the rate of tax is large enough to ensure that $P'C'$ does not intersect or touch II', trade is harmful. The critical rate of tax, for which trade is neither harmful nor gainful, depends on the difference between the world price ratio and the autarkic consumers' price ratio, and on the curvatures of the production frontier and II'.

We conclude that tax-distorted trade is necessarily gainful (a) if the opening of trade moves prices in favour of the relatively heavily taxed commodity or (b) if the rate of tax is sufficiently small. Since the critical tax rate depends on other things, however, only in case (a) can one infer from observable price changes along that a gain has accrued.

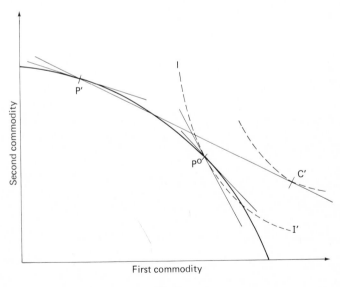

Fig. 6.

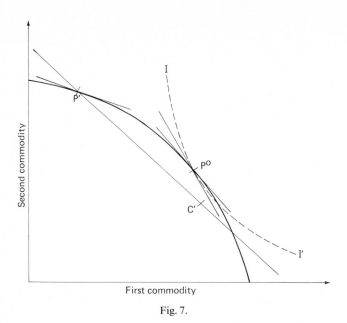

Fig. 7.

4. The effect on welfare of an improvement in the terms of trade

We owe to Anne Krueger and Hugo Sonnenschein the first rigorous demonstration that an improvement in a small country's terms of trade implies a potential
gain for that country (Krueger and Sonnenschein, 1967). A potential gain
accrues if the set of consumption bundles attainable after the change in the
terms of trade includes one which dominates the initial consumption bundle in
that it contains at least as much (algebraically) of every commodity and more of
at least one commodity. (It is understood that factor supplies are listed in each
bundle with negative sign.) It follows from the Krueger–Sonnenschein theorem
that the utility-feasibility surface of the situation with improved terms of trade
lies uniformly outside that corresponding to the initial terms of trade.

The proof provided by Krueger and Sonnenschein is based on the assumption of free and balanced trade. Suppose, however, that trade is not free but
impeded by tariffs. Is the theorem still valid? It can be shown that an
improvement in a tariff-ridden country's terms of trade may leave everyone
worse off, that for this outcome it is necessary that at least one good be inferior
in consumption, and that in any case it is always possible to find an equilibrium
after the improvement in the terms of trade which is Pareto-superior to an
initial equilibrium.

After the discussion of section 2, these conclusions will not be found surprising. The nature of the reasoning will be sufficiently indicated if we consider a very simple case: a small country with no appreciable influence on its terms of trade produces just one commodity, in constant amount; it exports part of its production in exchange for a second commodity; and it levies a duty on imports at a constant *ad valorem* rate. In terms of fig. 8, the country's output is *OP* and its trading and consumption opportunities are indicated by the straight line *PQ*. Under conditions of free trade, equilibrium would be reached at *C*, where a community indifference curve is tangent to the terms of trade line. But the effect of the tariff is to raise the internal relative price of imports above the world level. Therefore, the internal price ratio is represented by the slope of a line less steep than *PQ*, say *RS,* and the actual equilibrium is found on *PQ* at the point where the slope of the intersecting indifference curve is equal to that of *RS*. Suppose that *C'* is that point.

Now the terms of trade improve. The new trading possibilities are indicated by *PT* and the new internal price ratio by the slope of *UV*. The new equilibrium is found on *PT* at that point *C"* where the slope of the intersecting indifference curve is equal to that of *UV*. The new indifference curve may represent either an improvement or deterioration of welfare.

Figure 8 illustrates the possibility of deterioration. This anomalous result emerges, however, only when the export good is inferior (over the relevant

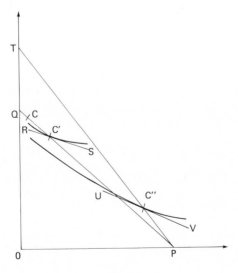

Fig. 8.

range). This is clear enough from fig. 8 if it is borne in mind that the slope of *RS* is *less* than that of *UV*. If neither good is inferior, an improvement in the terms of trade must increase welfare.

Moreover, even if a new equilibrium C'' involves a deterioration of welfare, there exists an alternative final equilibrium C''' such that everyone is better off than at C'. To see this, consider the income–consumption curve corresponding to the new domestic price ratio. Evidently it passes through C'' and to the left of C'. It therefore must eventually cut *PT* a second time, possibly at *T*. It follows that an alternative final equilibrium exists and that welfare is greater there than at C'.

5. Concluding remarks

The analysis of section 2 suggests a general proposition. Consider an initial competitive equilibrium which is a Paretian optimum. Now drive any number of wedges into the Paretian marginal equalities (and inequalities): a 5% sales tax on commodity 4, a 20% tax on commodity 7, etc. Evidently the new situation is Pareto-inferior to the initial situation. Finally, double the size of every wedge, so that the tax on the fourth commodity stands at 20%, etc. Then *the final situation is Pareto-inferior both to the initial situation and to the intermediate situation.* I have not proved this proposition – section 2 merely illustrates it for the case of a single wedge.

The paradoxes discussed in section 2 and 3 are members of a very large set. A single further example, from public finance, must suffice[7]. A simple closed economy, producing just two goods, is disturbed by the imposition of a 5% sales tax on one good. This depresses the price received by producers and reduces the output of the taxed good. It also reduces welfare: the initial situation is Pareto-preferred to the tax-ridden situation. If now the tax is raised to 10% it is possible that the producers' price of the taxed good will rise, that output will rise, and that everybody will be better off than before the tax increase. For this outcome, however, it is necessary that the untaxed good be inferior in consumption. Moreover among possible final equilibria there is one which is Pareto-preferred to that described.

---

[7] This example is being worked out in detail by Professors Hugo Sonnenschein and Edward Foster of the University of Minnesota.

Appendix: derivation of the utility feasibility locus

Consider an economy with just two individuals and with a fixed output of each of two commodities. Trade with the rest of the world takes place at fixed terms of trade $\pi = \pi_1/\pi_2$. Let τ_i be the rate of import duty on the ith commodity. Then the internal price ratio is

$p = \pi(1 + \tau_1)$ if the first commodity is imported,

$p = \pi/(1 + \tau_2)$ if the second commodity is imported,

$\pi(1 + \tau_1) \leq p \leq \pi/(1 + \tau_2)$ otherwise.

For such an economy we may construct a box diagram with dimensions given by the fixed outputs. Within this box we may draw four Engel curves, one for each individual for each of the two extreme price ratios, $\pi(1 + \tau_1)$ and $\pi/(1 + \tau_2)$. In fig. A1 are drawn the curves corresponding to $\pi(1 + \tau_1)$. $E_i^1 E_i^1$ is the Engel curve of the ith individual. The internal price ratio is represented by the slope of QQ; the international terms of trade are indicated by the common slope of the other straight lines.

Consider r_1^0 and r_2^0 in fig. A1. These represent a possible trading equilibrium with $r_1^0 r_2^0$, the net foreign trade vector, revealing that the first commodity is imported, the second exported. Corresponding to r_1^0 and r_2^0 in fig. A1 is r^0 on the utility feasibility curve in fig. A2. Now let r_1 move in a south-westerly direction along $E_1^1 E_1^1$, beginning at r_1^0, and let us trace out the corresponding equilibrium

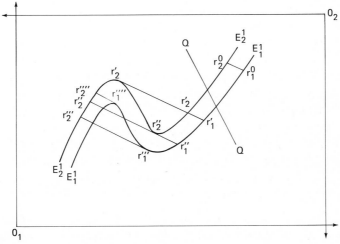

Fig. A1.

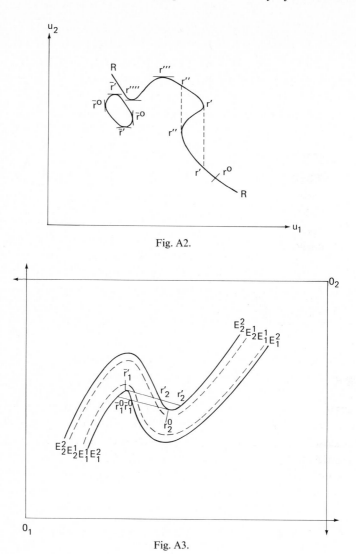

Fig. A2.

Fig. A3.

r_2 points on $E_2^1 E_2^1$. Until r_1 reaches r_1' this is a simple matter; the utility of the first individual steadily declines and that of the second individual steadily grows. To r_1', however, there correspond not one but two r_2 points; and to r_1 points between r_1' and r_1'' there correspond three equilibrium r_2 points, each with its associated trading vector and level of utility for the second individual. Continuing in this way we eventually trace out the *RR* curve of fig. A2.

The above construction was based on the assumption that the first commodity is imported. It is possible, however, that for some income distributions the second commodity will be imported. To explore this possibility we need the remaining pair of Engel curves, corresponding to an internal price ratio of $\pi/(1+\tau_2)$. These are drawn in fig. A3 and labelled $E_i^2 E_i^2$, with the old $E_i^1 E_i^1$-curves included for comparison. It is not difficult to see that only those r_1 points which lie between $\bar{r}_1^0$ and $\bar{r}_1^0$ and the corresponding r_2 points, represent possible trading equilibria, with net imports of the second commodity. As we allow r_1 to run through this restricted range, r_2 moves between the two $\bar{r}_2'$ points and traces out in fig. A2 a closed loop of utility possibilities. When added to the RR curve this loop gives us our complete set of feasible utility combinations. In the case illustrated the set is not connected.

That completes the derivation. It is to be emphasized that inferiority is necessary but not by itself sufficient to produce positively sloped stretches in the utility feasibility locus. And even when inferiority is sufficiently strong to produce positive slopes it may not be strong enough, or may not prevail over a sufficiently wide range of incomes, to produce a closed loop. Finally, even if the loop exists, it is disconnected only if $E_1^2 E_1^2$ and $E_2^2 E_2^2$ do not intersect. If $E_1^1 E_1^1$ and $E_2^1 E_2^1$ intersect, and if $E_1^2 E_1^2$ and $E_2^2 E_2^2$ intersect, the loop and RR can be connected by movements along the contract locus, with net foreign trade zero.

References

Kemp, M. C. (1964), *The Pure Theory of International Trade*, Prentice-Hall, Englewood Cliffs.

Kemp, M. C. (1962), The gain from international trade, *Economic Journal*, 72, (4), Dec., 803–819.

Krueger, A. O. and Sonnenschein, H. (1967), The terms of trade, the gains from trade and price divergence, *International Economic Review*, 8 (1), Feb., 121–127.

Vanek, J. (1965), *General Equilibrium of International Discrimination. The Case of Customs Unions*, Harvard University Press, Cambridge, Mass.

Chapter 11

THE GAINS FROM FREE TRADE*

1. Introduction

The literature concerning the gains from free trade divides naturally into two major parts, that pertaining to the opening of trade and that relating to autonomous variations in the prices facing a small country. In the first part, states of autarky are compared with states of free trade; in the second part, comparisons are made of alternative states of free trade. Almost nothing has been written concerning the welfare implications of variations in foreign demand when the country under consideration is of any size.

In this paper we develop a unified theory which encompasses all of the main known results concerning the gains from free trade, as well as several which appear to be new. In particular, we take a small step towards the welfare analysis of foreign demand variations for countries of any size. In dealing with small countries we find it convenient to introduce a family of price sets each of which is dual to a Scitovsky community indifference surface. The construct will, we think, find applications beyond those demonstrated in this paper.

The scope of the paper is conventional in that externalities and dynamic phenomena are excluded. We further omit any consideration of tariff-ridden trade. Section 2 contains a list of the more frequently used notations, as well as a statement of assumptions and a list of key definitions. Section 3 contains a proof of the well-known proposition that for countries of any size free trade is potentially better than no trade. To our knowledge, this is the first complete

* *International Economic Review*, 13 (Oct. 1972), 509–522, with H. Y. Wan, Jr. The paper was written at the University of California, Berkeley in the summer of 1970. During that period the authors were supported by National Science Foundation Grant GS-3018. Grateful acknowledgement is made to the University and Foundation. We acknowledge also helpful discussions with Daniel McFadden whose work on a related topic (which has since appeared in a joint article with Grandmont (1972)) inspired our proof of theorem 1.

proof of the proposition under assumptions of any generality. In section 4 we state and prove several propositions relating to the trading gains of small countries. Finally, in section 5 we return to the study of countries of any size and prove a theorem concerning the welfare implications of foreign demand variations of a particular type.

2. Notation and assumptions

The notation and assumptions have been kept as close as possible to those now more or less standard in the literature dealing with the existence and optimality of competitive equilibria[1]. However, it is now necessary to distinguish between tradeable and non-tradeable goods. Moreover much of the theory relating to trade gains involves comparisons of institutionally constrained or 'second-best' equilibria, or sets of equilibria. To facilitate such comparisons the standard assumptions and notation must be modified and extended.

We distinguish the home country and the rest of the world. Commodities are assumed to be either tradeable without cost or non-tradeable. We suppose that there are l commodities. The first l^0 of these are internationally tradeable, the next l^1 are non-tradeables associated with the home country, the last l^2 ($= l - l^0 - l^1$) are non-tradeables associated with the foreign country. (We do not wish to rule out the possibility that the same non-tradeable goods are available in both countries.) To avoid triviality, we assume that $l = l^0 + l^1 + l^2 \geq 2, l^0 \geq 2$.

It it assumed that in the home country there is a finite number m of consumers. The ith consumer is characterized by a closed, convex and lower-bounded set X_i of viable consumption vectors x_i, an l-dimensional endowment vector $\omega_i = \Delta_i + x_i$, where x_i is a member of X_i and Δ_i is a vector with the first ($l^0 + l^1$) elements positive and the remaining l^2 elements zero, and a complete, convex and continuous preference ordering $\gtrsim_i$ defined over X_i. *Ceteris paribus*, and under all circumstances, each individual prefers more of each of the l^0 tradeable commodities to less. Together with our assumption concerning ω_i, this rules out Arrow's counter-example (Arrow, 1951, p. 528). The possibility of consumption saturation is ruled out.

In addition it is assumed that there is a finite number n of producers. The jth producer is characterized by a set Y_j of feasible production vectors y_j; Y_j contains the null vector. The set of feasible aggregate production vectors

---

[1] See, for example, Debreu (1959).

$Y = \Sigma_j Y_j$ is assumed to be closed and convex and to satisfy the postulates of irreducibility of production and free disposal. We find it convenient to introduce also the set $Y_\omega = Y + \omega$, where $\omega = \Sigma_i \omega_i$, and the aggregate supply correspondence $\eta(p)$ (Debreu, 1959, p. 44). Evidently Y_ω is closed and convex.

All endowment, consumption and production vectors for the home country have zeros in the last l^2 positions.

The aggregate foreign excess demand correspondence is denoted by $\zeta_0(p)$, a set of l-dimensional vectors with zeros in positions $l^0 + 1, \ldots, l^0 + l^1$. It is assumed that ζ_0 (a) is closed, convex and lower-bounded for each p, (b) is homogeneous of degree zero in p, (c) satisfies the budgetary constraint that, for all $z \in \zeta_0(p)$, $p \cdot z \leq 0$ and (d) is upper semi-continuous in p.[2] The l-dimensional vector of prices is denoted by p and the subvector containing the first l^0 components of p is denoted by $\tilde{p}$. (The tilde notation will be used consistently all $z \in \zeta_0(p)$, $p \cdot z \leq 0$ and (d) is upper semi-continuous in p.[2] The l-dimensional vector of commodity prices or quantities.)

The state is recognized. However, its role is limited to the collection and disbursement of lump sums (side payments). For our purposes it suffices to consider one special system of side payments. The sums received and given by consumers $2, \ldots, m$ are such that, whatever the disturbance, each of those consumers can enjoy a specified constant level of well-being, usually associated with some initial autarkic or free trade equilibrium[3]. Let x_i^0 be the initial consumption vector of the ith consumer. Then we may define the not-worse-than-x_i^0 set $X_i(x_i^0) = \{x_i \in X_i : x_i \geq x_i^0\}$ and the post-transfer wealth of the ith consumer as $w_i = \min_{x_i \in X_i(x_i^0)} p \cdot x_i$, where $i = 2, \ldots, m$.[4] The first consumer, or *princeps*, then claims the residual income, i.e. $w_1 = \max_{x_1} p \cdot x_1$, where $x_1 \in [Y_\omega - \Sigma_2^m X_i(x_i^0)]$. We define the aggregate supply correspondence for the rest of the country *vis-à-vis princeps* as that set over which w_1 reaches its maximum, and denote it by $\zeta_-(p)$. The demand correspondence for the ith consumer is denoted by $\xi_i(p, w_i(p))$. In particular, the demand correspondence of *princeps* is denoted by $\xi_1(p, w_1(p))$.

---

[2] $\zeta_0(p)$ has these properties if foreign consumers and producers are subject to restrictions similar to those imposed on their home counterparts.

[3] In general, such a system of payments may not exist. However, for the disturbances we shall consider, existence is always assured.

[4] w_i may not exist for all p. Consider, however, the set of commodity bundles which are not worse than x_i^0 and which, given production techniques, foreign demand and the survival of other consumers, are feasible. This set is a compact subset of $X_i(x_i^0)$. In an equilibrium, as defined below, the chosen x_i must lie in that subset. One therefore may replace $X_i(x_i^0)$ with the compact subset just defined. Then w_i is defined for all p.

A trading equilibrium exists if there is a pair of price vectors (p', p'') such that

$$\Omega \equiv \xi_1(p, w_1(p')) \cap [\xi_-(p') - \zeta_0(p'')] \neq \emptyset, \tag{1}$$

where p' and p'' are domestic and foreign prices, respectively. A free trade equilibrium is a trading equilibrium with

$$p' = p''. \tag{2}$$

Free trade is potentially unharmful in relation to some initial equilibrium if Ω contains a vector x_1 such that $x_1 \gtrsim_i x^0_1$, where x^0_1 is the initial consumption vector of *princeps*.

We now seek to clarify the sense in which an economy will be called 'small'. Let $\tilde{p}$ and $\hat{p}$ be two given price subvectors, of dimensions l^0 and l^2 respectively. Let P^1 and P^m be the natural simplexes of dimensions l and m, respectively, and let $\theta \equiv (\theta_1, \ldots, \theta_m) \in P^m$. We define $P(\tilde{p}, \hat{p}) = \{p : p = (\rho\tilde{p}, \mu\hat{p}, \rho\hat{p}) \text{ for some } \hat{p}, \mu > 0, \rho > 0\}$, also

$$V = \{(p, \theta) \in P(\tilde{p}, \hat{p}) \times P^m : \xi_i(p, \theta_i \max_{y \in Y} p(y + \omega)) \neq \emptyset \text{ for all } i\}$$

and

$$Z_1 = \left\{z : z = (\tilde{z}, 0) \in \bigcup_{(p,\theta)\in V} \left[\sum_i \xi_i(p, \theta_i \cdot \max_{y \in Y} p(y + \omega) - \{\omega\} - \eta(p)\right]\right\}. \tag{3}$$

Definition 1. The domestic economy is small relative to the price *subvector pair* $(\tilde{p}, \hat{p})$ if $Z_1 \subseteq -\zeta_0(\tilde{p}, \cdot, \hat{p})$.

The foreign excess demand correspondence is written as $\zeta_0(\tilde{p}, \cdot, \hat{p})$ to indicate that it does not depend on the prices of home non-tradeables. In commonsense terms, a country is small if, whatever the home income distribution (consistent with the survival of each consumer), the resulting equilibria all share the same price subvectors for tradeables and foreign non-tradeables.

The symbol $a \equiv ((x_i), (y_i))$ denotes a particular *state* of the country. We shall write $a^1 \gtrsim a^2$ if and only if, for all i, $x^1_i \gtrsim_i x^2_i$ and x^1_i is in a^1, x^2_i is in a^2. Similarly, we shall write $a^1 \sim a^2$ if and only if, for all i, $x^1_i \sim_i x^2_i$ and x^1_i is in a^1, x^2_i is in a^2. Finally, we shall write $a^1 > a^2$ if and only if $a^1 \gtrsim a^2$ and, for some $i, x^1_i >_i x^2_i$, where x^1_i is in a^1 and x^2_i is in a^2. If $a^1 \gtrsim a^2$ we shall say that the substitution of a^1 for a^2 is Pareto-unharmful; if $a^1 > a^2$ we shall say that the substitution is Pareto-beneficial.

An autarkic equilibrium is a pair (a, p) such that

$$\sum_j y_j \in \eta(p), \qquad x_i \in \xi_i(p, w_i) \quad \text{for some } w_i, \qquad \sum_i x_i = \sum_j y_j + \omega. \tag{4}$$

An autonomous disturbance to the economy (e.g. the freeing of trade, a change in the world prices facing a small country) will be described as potentially unharmful if there exists a system of lump sum payments which would ensure that no person is harmed by the disturbance. A disturbance will be described as potentially beneficial if it is potentially unharmful and if, in addition, the system of payments would leave at least one person better off than before the disturbance.

Consider three price vectors p^1, p^2 and p^3, each normalized to lie in the natural simplex P^i. We shall say that p^2 is intermediate to p^1 and p^3 if it is possible to write p^2 as a strictly convex linear combination of p^1 and p^3:

$$p^2 = \lambda p^1 + (1-\lambda)p^3, \qquad 0 < \lambda < 1. \tag{5}$$

If (5) is satisfied we shall also say that p^3 deviates more from p^1 than does p^2, and that the replacement of p^1 with p^2 and of p^2 with p^3 involve price changes in the same direction.

Henceforth the superscript 0 will distinguish autarkic quantities and the superscript 1 the quantities of an initial free trade equilibrium.

3. Gains from the opening of trade – countries of any size

We shall prove

Theorem 1. Given the assumptions of section 2, for any autarkic equilibrium there can be found a free trade equilibrium in which no one is worse off, i.e. free trade is potentially unharmful in relation to no trade.

The proposition is well known (see Kemp, 1962, and Samuelson, 1962, conclusion 8), but it seems still to lack proof. Samuelson (1939) showed that for a small country with fixed amounts of the productive factors free trade is potentially unharmful in relation to no trade. Later, Kemp (1962, 1969) provided an 'almost proof' of the more general proposition by showing that no free trade equilibrium could be improved by returning to autarky, i.e. by showing that in utility space the autarkic utility possibility frontier could not pass above any free trade equilibrium point. However, a jump was then made to the conclusion of the theorem, that the free trade utility possibility frontier must pass above or through every possible autarkic equilibrium point. That the step needs justification is illustrated by fig. 1; evidently the autarkic equilibrium

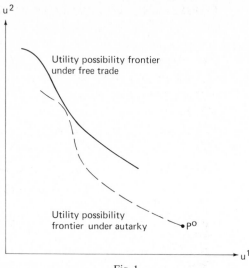

Fig. 1.

P^0 cannot be equalled or bettered under free trade. It is implicit in the proof we shall give that in drawing fig. 1 we have violated the assumptions of section 2[5].

Proof of theorem 1. It suffices to show that there exists a free trade equilibrium with prices p^* satisfying (1)–(2) and with $x_1 \in \Omega$, $x_1 \gtrsim_1 x_1^0$. The foreign excess demand correspondence is $\zeta_0(p)$ and the home excess demand correspondence may be defined as $\zeta_1(p) \equiv \xi_1(p, w_1(p)) - \zeta_-(p)$. Both are homogeneous of degree zero in p. Following Debreu (1959, ch. 5), there then exists an equilibrium price vector p^* such that $0 \in [\zeta_0(p^*) + \zeta_1(p^*)]$. That is, $x_1^* = z_-^* - z_0^*$, where $x_1^* \in \xi_1(p^*, w_1(p^*))$, $z_-^* \in \zeta_-(p^*)$ and $z_0^* \in \zeta_0(p^*)$. We then have

$$p^* \cdot x_1^* = p^* \cdot z_-^* \quad \text{(since } p^* \cdot z_0^* = 0\text{)}$$

$$\geq p^* \cdot \left(y^0 + \omega - \sum_{i=2}^{m} x_i^0 \right)$$

---

[5] It may be worth clarifying the relation of the above theorem to the principal propositions of the 1962 companion papers of Kemp (1962) and Samuelson (1962). As we have just noted, Kemp sought to prove what we have here called theorem 1. On the other hand, with the exception of his conclusion 8, Samuelson was concerned with the geometric properties and market-attainability of the outward boundary of the country's set of consumption possibilities. In particular, he showed that the autarkic consumption possibility set is a proper subset of the production-cum-trade consumption possibility set and that all Pareto-optimal points on the boundary of the latter set are attainable by means of lump sum transfers and optimal tariffs. Kemp was chiefly concerned with the welfare properties of second-best free trade equilibria, Samuelson with those of optimal tariff-restricted equilibria.

$$= p^* \cdot x_1^0 \quad \left(\text{since under autarky } y + \omega - \sum_{i=1}^{m} x_i = 0\right) \tag{5}$$

$$\geq \min_{x_1 \in X_1(x_1^0)} p^* \cdot x_1.$$

Thus x_1^*, the equilibrium consumption vector chosen by *princeps* under free trade, is not inferior to x_1^0, the consumption vector chosen under autarky.

QED[6]

We note that theorem 1 accommodates trade in both primary and produced factors of production[7].

---

[6] In a pioneering but neglected paper Vanek (1965, appendix to ch. iv) has stated a general theorem concerning utility possibility loci and remarked that our theorem 1 is an implication of it. Moreover, in important respects (including the use of the device of *princeps*) he has anticipated our line of argument. Now if one assumes that there always exists a competitive trading equilibrium Pareto-comparable to the autarkic state, his result does imply our theorem 1. However, the assumption of existence is not to be made lightly; indeed it is precisely at this point that Kemp's (1962) proof is defective. Moreover, the proof now offered can be generalized to accommodate *intra*-national externalities (see Wan, 1972); this is not true of Vanek's proof.

[7] In this paper we focus on the gains from free trade. However, we may note the following easy generalization of theorem 1.

Theorem 1′. Given the assumptions of section 2 and any vector of (non-negative) import duties, for any autarkic equilibrium there can be found a tariff-distorted trade equilibrium in which no one is worse off, i.e. fixed-tariff trade is potentially unharmful in relation to no trade.

Proof. Let $\tau_i (i = 1, \ldots, l^0)$ be the *ad valorem* rate of duty on imports of the ith commodity, calculated on the foreign price of tradeables $\bar{p}$. It has been shown by Sontheimer (1971, theorem 2) that, on the assumptions of the theorem, a trade equilibrium exists. In that equilibrium $p_i^{*\prime} = \lambda p^{*\prime\prime}(1 + \tau_i)$ if the ith commodity is imported and $p_i^{*\prime} = \lambda p_i^{*\prime\prime}$ if it is exported. Let I be the l^0-dimensional unit matrix and τ an l^0-dimensional diagonal matrix with τ_i or 0 in the ith diagonal place according as the ith commodity is or is not imported. Then

$$p^{*\prime} \cdot x_1^* = p^{*\prime} \cdot z_-^* - p^{*\prime} \cdot z_0^*$$

$$= p^{*\prime} \cdot z_-^* - \lambda p^{*\prime\prime} \cdot (I + \tau) \cdot z_0^* \quad \text{(applying Walras' law to the foreign economy, } p^{*\prime\prime} \cdot z_0 = 0\text{)}$$

$$\geq p^{*\prime} \cdot z_-^* \quad \text{(from the definition of } \tau\text{)}$$

$$\geq \min_{x_1 \in X_1(x_1^0)} p^{*\prime} \cdot x_1 \quad \text{(using (5))}.$$

QED

It is possible to prove similar theorems for non-negative export duties and for any scheme involving non-negative import and export duties.

4. Variations in foreign demand – small countries

We shall prove a series of propositions concerning the implications of an autonomous change in the world price vector, it being assumed that the home country is small in relation to both the initial and the new prices.

In an initial free trade equilibrium the aggregate home output vector is y^1 and the individual consumption vectors $x_i^1, i = 1, 2, \ldots, m$. The quantities of the new equilibrium are indicated by an asterisk. When prices change a side payment is made to each of individuals $2, \ldots, m$ just sufficient to leave his wellbeing undisturbed. The price change is then beneficial if and only if *princeps* is better off in the new equilibrium. We know that $p^* \cdot x_1^* = p^* \cdot z_1^*$. Hence *princeps* is better off in the new equilibrium if and only if $p^* \cdot z^* > \min_{x_1 \in X_1(x_1^1)} p^* \cdot x_1$, that is, if and only if

$$\max_{y \in Y, x_i \in X_i(x_i^1)} p^* \cdot \left(y + \omega - \sum_{i=1}^{m} x_i \right) > 0.$$

For this inequality to hold it suffices that

$$\max_{z = (\bar{z}, 0): z \in \left[Y_\omega - \sum_{1}^{m} X_i(x_i^1) \right]} p^* \cdot z > 0 \tag{6}$$

and this condition is also necessary. Let $a^1 = ((x_i^1), (y_i^1))$, and let $\tilde{\pi}^*$ be the normalized form of $\bar{p}^*$, so that $\sum_i^{l^0} \tilde{\pi}_i^* = 1$ and $\tilde{\pi}^*$ lies in the l^0-dimensional natural simplex P^{l^0}. Then (6) may be abbreviated to

$$\beta(\tilde{\pi}^*, a^1) > 0. \tag{7}$$

The index β dates back to Marshall (1923) and has been discussed by Viner (n.d.) and by Bhagwati and Johnson (1960). It is known to be a convex function of $\tilde{\pi}$. See Wan (1965), where β is called the maximum bonus.

We next define the set of not-better-than-a^1 world prices $N(a^1) = \{\tilde{\pi} : \beta(\tilde{\pi}, a^1) \leq 0\}$, the set of worse-than-$a^1$ world prices $\mathring{N}(a^1) = \{\tilde{\pi} : \beta(\tilde{\pi}, a^1) < 0\}$, and the set of equivalent-to-a^1 world prices $N(a^1) \backslash \mathring{N}(a^1) = \{\tilde{\pi} : \beta(\tilde{\pi}, a^1) = 0\}$. It will be shown that if $a^1 > a^0$ for some a^0 then $N(a^1) \backslash \mathring{N}(a^1)$ has no interior. The locus $\{\tilde{\pi} : \beta(\tilde{\pi}, a^1) = 0\}$ in P^{l^0} is dual to the Scitovsky contour, that is, the boundary of the set of not-worse-than-a^1 consumption vectors $\sum_{i=1}^{m} X_i(x_i^1)$.

We begin by proving three lemmata which collectively characterize the price sets $N(a^1)$ and $\mathring{N}(a^1)$ and which facilitate later proofs.

Lemma 1. Both $N(a^1)$ and $\mathring{N}(a^1)$ are convex.

Proof. Let $\tilde{\pi}'$, $\tilde{\pi}''$ and $\tilde{\pi}^\lambda$ be three world price vectors such that $\tilde{\pi}^\lambda = \lambda\tilde{\pi}' + (1-\lambda)\tilde{\pi}''$, $0 < \lambda < 1$. Then

$$\beta(\tilde{\pi}^\lambda, a^1) = \max_{z = (z,0): z \in \left[Y_\omega - \sum X_i(x_i^1)\right]} (\tilde{\pi}^\lambda, 0) \cdot z$$

$$= \tilde{\pi}^\lambda \cdot \tilde{z}^\lambda \quad \text{say}$$

$$= \lambda\tilde{\pi}' \cdot \tilde{z}^\lambda + (1-\lambda)\tilde{\pi}'' \cdot \tilde{z}^\lambda \tag{7}$$

$$\leq \lambda\beta(\tilde{\pi}', a^1) + (1-\lambda)\beta(\tilde{\pi}'', a^1).$$

If both $\beta(\tilde{\pi}', a^1)$ and $\beta(\tilde{\pi}'', a^1)$ are non-positive (negative) so must be $\beta(\tilde{\pi}^\lambda, a^1)$. QED

Lemma 2. Suppose that in a free trade equilibrium $\tilde{\pi} = \tilde{\pi}^1$, $a = a^1$ and $z = z^1 = (\tilde{z}^1, 0)$, where z is the excess supply vector of the home country. Then $\mathring{N}(a^1) \subseteq \{\tilde{\pi} \in P^{l^0} : \tilde{z}^1 \cdot \tilde{\pi} < 0\}$.

Proof. We have $(\tilde{z}^1, 0) \in [Y_\omega - \sum_{i=1}^m X_i(x_i^1)]$. Moreover, by definition $\beta(\tilde{\pi}, a^1) \geq \tilde{z}^1 \cdot \tilde{\pi}$. Thus if $\tilde{z}^1 \cdot \tilde{\pi} \geq 0$ then $\beta(\tilde{\pi}, a^1) \geq 0$ and $\tilde{\pi} \notin \mathring{N}(a^1)$. QED

Lemma 3. Either (a) $a^1 \sim a^0$, an autarkic state, and $\mathring{N}(a^1) = \mathring{N}(a^0) = \emptyset$ or (b) the equivalent-to-a^1 price set $[N(a^1) \backslash \mathring{N}(a^1)]$ has no interior.

Proof. (a) If $a^1 \sim a^0$, with $z^0 = 0$, then, from lemma 2, $\mathring{N}(a^1) = \mathring{N}(a^0) \subseteq \{\tilde{\pi} \in P^{l^0} : \tilde{\pi} \cdot 0 < 0\} = \emptyset$. Moreover, if $a^1 \sim a^0$, the equivalent-to-a^1 price set may have an interior. (b) From (a), $a^0 > a^1$ is not possible. Suppose, therefore, that $a^1 > a^0$ and that the assertion is false. Then there exists a price vector $\tilde{\pi}^2 \in 0(\tilde{\pi}^2) \subset [N(a^1) \backslash \mathring{N}(a^1)]$, where $0(\tilde{\pi}^2)$ is an open set. Associated with $\tilde{\pi}^2$ there is a state $a^2 \sim a^1$ and a trade vector $\tilde{z}^2 \neq 0$. Hence

$$\emptyset \neq \{\tilde{\pi} \in 0(\tilde{\pi}^2) : \tilde{z}^2 \cdot \tilde{\pi} > 0\} \not\subset N(a^2) = N(a^1),$$

a contradiction. QED

Theorem 2. Suppose that an initial free trade equilibrium is disturbed by an autonomous change in world prices.

(a) If the change in prices is potentially unharmful (potentially beneficial) then any greater change is also potentially unharmful (potentially beneficial) in relation to the initial equilibrium.

(b) If the new price vector is intermediate to some two reference price vectors,

where the substitution of the reference prices for the initial prices would not be potentially beneficial, then the change in prices is itself not potentially beneficial. If in addition one of the reference price vectors is such that its substitution for the initial price vector would not be potentially unharmful then the change in prices is itself not potentially unharmful.

(c) If the change in prices implies a non-deterioration of the terms of trade in the Laspeyres sense then the change is potentially unharmful (Krueger and Sonnenschein, 1967, theorem 2). If the change in prices implies an improvement of the terms of trade then the change is potentially beneficial.

Since the initial equilibrium may be one in which no trade takes place, we have

Corollary. Whatever the world prices, free trade is potentially unharmful in relation to autarky (Samuelson, 1939).

Proof of theorem 2. Let us denote by $\tilde{\pi}^2$ the new world price vector and write $\tilde{\pi}^\lambda \equiv \tilde{\pi}^2 + \lambda(\tilde{\pi}^2 - \tilde{\pi}^1), \lambda > 0$. Suppose that $\beta(\tilde{\pi}^2, a^1) > 0$. Then $\beta(\tilde{\pi}^\lambda, a^1) > 0$ also. For if $\beta(\tilde{\pi}^\lambda, a^1) \le 0$ then, from the convexity of $N(a^1)$ and the fact that $\beta(\tilde{\pi}^1, a^1) = 0$, $\beta(\tilde{\pi}^2, a^1) \le 0$, a contradiction. Thus if the change from $\tilde{\pi}^1$ to $\tilde{\pi}^2$ is potentially beneficial so is the change from $\tilde{\pi}^1$ to $\tilde{\pi}^\lambda$. Suppose alternatively that $\beta(\tilde{\pi}^2, a^1) \ge 0$. If $\beta(\tilde{\pi}^\lambda, a^1) < 0$, then, from (8) and the fact that $\beta(\tilde{\pi}^1, a^1) \equiv 0$,

$$\beta(\tilde{\pi}^2, a^1) \le [\lambda\beta(\tilde{\pi}^\lambda, a^1) + \beta(\tilde{\pi}^1, a^1)]/(1 + \lambda) < 0,$$

which is a contradiction.

(b) The first statement follows from the convexity of $N(a^1)$, the second from lemma 3(b) and the convexity of $\mathring{N}(a^1)$.

(c) By definition, the substitution of $\tilde{\pi}^2$ for $\tilde{\pi}^1$ involves the non-deterioration (improvement) of the home country's terms of trade if $\tilde{\pi}^2 \cdot \tilde{z}^1 \ge 0$ (respectively, $\tilde{\pi}^2 \cdot \tilde{z}^1 > 0$) where $\tilde{z}^1$ is the initial equilibrium excess supply vector of the home country. From lemma 2 $\tilde{\pi}^2 \cdot \tilde{z}^1 \ge 0$ implies that $\tilde{\pi}^2 \notin \mathring{N}(a^1)$. That proves the first proposition. Suppose that $\tilde{\pi}^2 \cdot \tilde{z}^1 > 0$ and that the sum $\tilde{\pi}^2 \cdot \tilde{z}_1$ is distributed to *princeps*. The preferences of *princeps* are convex and insatiable. Hence it is possible to make *princeps* better off with no one worse off.   QED

Theorem 2 contains a series of statements about comparisons which might be made between two alternative trading situations. In theorem 3, on the other hand, all statements relate to comparisons between three alternative situations. Before proceeding to the theorem, we find it convenient to state and sketch-prove

Lemma 4. If two states a^1 and a^2 are Pareto-comparable then:

(a) $a^2 \gtrsim a^1$ *implies* $\beta(\tilde{\pi}, a^1) \geq \beta(\tilde{\pi}, a^2)$ *for all* $\tilde{\pi}$,

(b) $a^2 > a^1$ *implies* $\beta(\tilde{\pi}, a^1) > \beta(\tilde{\pi}, a^2)$ *for all* $\tilde{\pi}$,

(c) $a^2 \sim a^1$ *implies* $\beta(\tilde{\pi}, a^1) = \beta(\tilde{\pi}, a^2)$ *for all* $\tilde{\pi}$,

(d) $\tilde{\pi}^1 \in \mathring{N}(a^2)$ *if and only if* $\tilde{\pi}^2 \notin N(a^1)$.

Proof. If $a^2 \gtrsim a^1$ then $\sum_{i=1}^{m} X_i(x_i^1) \supseteq \sum_{i=1}^{m} X_i(x_i^2)$. Similarly, if $a^2 > a^1$ then $\sum_{i=1}^{m} X_i(x_i^1) \supset \sum_{i=1}^{m} X_i(x_i^2)$; and if $a^2 \sim a^1$ then $\sum_{i=1}^{m} X_i(x_i^1) = \sum_{i=1}^{m} X_i(x_i^2)$. Statements (a), (b) and (c) follow straightforwardly from these three set relationships, respectively. Statement (d) follows from (a)–(c) and $\beta(\tilde{\pi}^1, a^1) = 0 = \beta(\tilde{\pi}^2, a^2)$.   QED

We can now state

Theorem 3. (a) Suppose that an initial free trade equilibrium is disturbed by an autonomous change in world prices. If the change in prices is Pareto-unharmful (Pareto-beneficial) with respect to the initial equilibrium then a further change in prices in the same direction is potentially unharmful (respectively, potentially beneficial) with respect to the second equilibrium.

(b) Consider a sequence of Pareto-unharmful price changes, the economy passing from $(a^1, \tilde{\pi}^1)$ through $(a^2, \tilde{\pi}^2)$, $(a^3, \tilde{\pi}^3), \ldots$ to $(a^T, \tilde{\pi}^T)$. Suppose that $a^t > a^1$ for some t, $1 < t \leq T$, so that $a^T > a^1$. Now consider any convex linear combination of the price vectors $\tilde{\pi}^1, \ldots, \tilde{\pi}^T$, say $\tilde{\pi}^\lambda$. Then the substitution of $\tilde{\pi}^\lambda$ for $\tilde{\pi}^T$ is not potentially beneficial with respect to the Tth equilibrium; and, if a positive weight is assigned to $\tilde{\pi}^t$ for any t such that $a^T > a^t$, the substitution is not potentially unharmful with respect to the Tth equilibrium.

Corollary 1. Suppose that autarky gives way to free trade, that the free trade prices differ from those prevailing under autarky and that the change is Pareto-beneficial with respect to autarky. If world prices move farther away from those of autarky then the second change is potentially beneficial with respect to the first free trade equilibrium.

Corollary 2. If an improvement of the terms of trade in the Laspeyres sense is Pareto-beneficial with respect to the initial equilibrium and if $l^0 = 2$ then a further improvement in the terms of trade (calculated with the same weights) is potentially beneficial with respect to the second equilibrium.

Part (a) of the theorem and corollary 2 have been proved by Krueger and

Sonnenschein (1967, theorems 1 and 3) under the assumption that primary factors are in fixed supply.

Proof of theorem 3. (a) From lemma 4(d), $\beta(\tilde{\pi}^1, a^2) \leq 0$ (respectively, $\beta(\tilde{\pi}^1, a^2) < 0$). The proposition then follows from theorem 2(a).

(b) Since $a^T > a^1$, a^T is not autarkic. Theorem 2(b) may then be applied iteratively to obtain the proof.   QED

For the special case in which there are just three traded commodities, the conclusions of this section may be illustrated in terms of the price simplex $P^1 = P^3$ depicted in fig. 2. Consider a sequence of five states $a^0, \ldots, a^4$ associated with the normalized world price subvectors $\tilde{\pi}^0, \ldots, \tilde{\pi}^4$ respectively. Suppose that $a^0, \ldots, a^4$ are Pareto-comparable and, in particular, that $a_0 < a^1 < \cdots < a^4$. Then $N(a^0) \subset N(a^1) \subset \cdots \subset N(a^4)$. Moreover, $\mathring{N}(a^0)$ is the only worse-than-a set which is empty and $[N(a^0) \backslash \mathring{N}(a^0)]$ is the only equivalent-to-a set which has interior points. The remaining constructions in fig. 2 correspond to the assumptions listed in the first column of table 1.

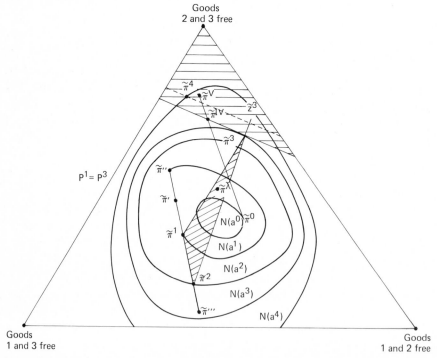

Fig. 2.

Table 1.
Illustration of results.

Facts	Theorem applied	Conclusion
$\bar{\pi}' = \lambda\bar{\pi}'' + (1-\lambda)\bar{\pi}^1, \lambda \in (0,1)$ $\bar{\pi}' \notin \mathring{N}(a^1)$	Theorem 2(a)	$\bar{\pi}'' \notin \mathring{N}(a^1)$
$\bar{\pi}^2 = \lambda\bar{\pi}''' - (1-\lambda)\bar{\pi}^1, \lambda \in (0,1)$ $\bar{\pi}^2 \notin N(a^1)$	Theorem 2(a)	$\bar{\pi}''' \notin N(a^1)$
$\bar{\pi}' = \lambda\bar{\pi}'' + (1-\lambda)\bar{\pi}^1, \lambda \in (0,1)$ $\bar{\pi}^1, \bar{\pi}'' \in N(a^1)$	Theorem 2(b)	$\bar{\pi}' \in N(a^1)$
$\bar{\pi}' = \lambda\bar{\pi}' + (1-\lambda)\bar{\pi}^2, \lambda \in (0,1)$ $\bar{\pi}^2 \in N(a^2), \bar{\pi}' \in \mathring{N}(a^2)$	Theorem 2(b)	$\bar{\pi}^1 \in \mathring{N}(a^2)$
$\bar{\pi}^{iv} \cdot \bar{z}^3 \geqq 0$	Theorem 2(c)	$\bar{\pi}^{iv} \notin \mathring{N}(a^3)$
$\bar{\pi}^4 \cdot \bar{z}^3 > 0$	Theorem 2(c)	$\bar{\pi}^4 \notin N(a^3)$
$\bar{\pi}^0$ is autarkic	Corollary to theorem 2	$\mathring{N}(a^0) = \emptyset$
$\bar{\pi}' = \lambda\bar{\pi}'' + (1-\lambda)\bar{\pi}^1, \lambda \in (0,1)$ $\bar{\pi}' \notin \mathring{N}(a^1)$	Theorem 3(a)	$\bar{\pi}'' \notin N(a^1)$ $(N(a')$ not shown)
$\bar{\pi}^2 = \lambda\bar{\pi}''' + (1-\lambda)\bar{\pi}^1, \lambda \in (0,1)$ $\bar{\pi}^2 \notin N(a^1)$	Theorem 3(a)	$\bar{\pi}''' \notin N(a^2)$
$\bar{\pi}^\wedge = \sum_1^3 \lambda_\psi\bar{\pi}^\psi, \lambda_\psi > 0, \sum_1^3 \lambda_\psi = 1$	Theorem 3(b)	$\bar{\pi}^\wedge \in \mathring{N}(a^3)$
$\bar{\pi}^2 \notin N(a^1), \bar{\pi}^3 \notin N(a^2)$ $\bar{\pi}^{iv} = \lambda\bar{\pi}^v + (1-\lambda)\bar{\pi}^0, \lambda \in (0,1)$ $\bar{\pi}^{iv} \in N(a^0)$	Corollary to theorem 3	$\bar{\pi}^v \notin N(a^{iv})$ $(N(a^{iv})$ not shown)

That theorem 3, corollary 2 cannot be extended to cover the case $l^0 > 2$ follows from the possibility that $\bar{\pi}^v \cdot \bar{z}^3 > \bar{\pi}^4 \cdot \bar{z}^3$ but $\bar{\pi} \in \mathring{N}(a^4)$. This is in fact the counter-example provided by Krueger and Sonnenschein (1967).

5. Demand variations – countries of any size

Let us suppose that the distributional policy of the home country is such that all equilibria are Pareto-comparable from the point of view of that country. And, varying our notation slightly, let us now denote the *post-compensation* excess demand correspondence of the home country by $\zeta_1(p)$, a set of l-dimensional vectors the last l^2 components of which are zero. Then $\zeta(p) = \zeta_0(p) + \zeta_1(p)$ is the world excess demand correspondence. Superscripts a and b indicate magnitudes *after* and *before* a variation of foreign demand. Thus p^a and p^b are equilibrium world price vectors after and before such a change.

It will be assumed that (a) foreign excess demand undergoes an unambiguous expansion, with home demand unchanged:

$$\zeta_0^a(p) \equiv \lambda(p)\zeta_0^b(p), \qquad \lambda(p) > 1 \quad \text{for all } p, \qquad \zeta_1^a(p) \equiv \zeta_1^b(p).$$

Such an expansion might be associated with the balanced growth of the foreign economy or, less plausibly, with an improvement in the means of international transportation. It will be supposed also that (b) post-variation world excess demand obeys a 'generalized law of demand', that is,

$$z^i \in \zeta^a(p^i), \qquad i = 1, 2, \quad \text{implies } (\bar{p}^2 - \bar{p}^1)(\bar{z}^2 - \bar{z}^1) < 0.$$

We may now state[8]

Theorem 4. On the above assumptions and if p^b is not autarkic the home country potentially benefits from an expansion of foreign demand. Trivially, if p^b is autarkic the home country is potentially unharmed by an expansion of foreign demand.

Proof. Suppose that p^b is not autarkic and let $(\bar{z}_0^b, \bar{z}_1^b)$ and $(\bar{z}_0^a, \bar{z}_1^a)$ be the foreign and home equilibrium excess demand vectors associated with p^b and p^a respectively. Then

$$\bar{z}^b \equiv \bar{z}_0^b + \bar{z}_1^b = 0, \qquad \bar{z}_0^b \neq 0 \neq \bar{z}_1^b, \qquad \bar{z}^a \equiv \bar{z}_0^a + \bar{z}_1^a = 0.$$

Let

$$z_0^{ab} \equiv \lambda(p^b)\bar{z}_0^b \in \zeta_0^a(p^b), \qquad z_1^{ab} = \bar{z}_1^b \in \zeta_1^a(p^b) \equiv \zeta_1^b(p^b),$$

so that

$$z^{ab} = (z_0^{ab} + z_1^{ab}) \in \zeta^a(p^b).$$

---

[8] In the famous ch. 18 of Book III of the *Principles*, J. S. Mill claimed (1909, p. 604)

... that the countries which carry on their trade on the most advantageous terms, are those whose commodities are most in demand by foreign countries, and which have themselves the least demand for foreign commodities. From which, among other consequences, it follows, that the richest countries, *caeteris paribus*, gain the least by a given amount of foreign commerce: since, having a greater demand for commodities generally, they are likely to have a greater demand for foreign commodities, and thus modify the terms of interchange to their own disadvantage. Their aggregate gains by foreign trade, doubtless, are generally greater than those of poorer countries, since they carry on a greater amount of such trade, and gain the benefit of cheapness on a larger consumption: but their gain is less on each individual article consumed.

Theorem 4 may be viewed as a restatement of the proposition contained in the first quoted sentence.

Then

$$0 \geq (p^a - p^b)(z^a - z^{ab})$$
$$= -(p^a - p^b)(z_0^{ab} + z_1^{ab})$$
$$= -(p^a - p^b)[(z_0^b + z_1^b) + (\lambda(p^b) - 1)z_0^b] \quad \text{(assumption (a))}$$
$$= [\lambda(p^b) - 1]p^a \cdot z_1^b \quad (p^b \cdot z_0^b = 0 \text{ and } z_1^b = -z_0^b).$$

That is, the terms of trade of the home country necessarily improve. Then

$$p^a x^a = p^a \omega + p^a y^a + p^a z_1^a$$
$$\geq p^a \omega + p^a y^b + p^a z_1^a \quad \text{(convexity of } Y\text{)}$$
$$> p^a \omega + p^a y^b + p^a z_1^b \quad \text{(improved terms of trade)}$$
$$= p^a x^b.$$

Hence, given the distributional policy of the home country, the new equilibrium is Pareto-preferred to the old. $\qquad$ QED[9]

It will be noticed that in the statement of theorem 4 the coefficient λ is allowed to depend on world prices. In a special case, for all p, $\lambda(p) = \lambda > 1$.

Addendum: The gain from trade in techniques of production

In formal analysis of the gains from trade it has been customary to suppose that in each trading country the set of production possibilities is independent of trading opportunities. It follows that conventional analysis does not cover the trade in productive techniques implicit in licensing agreements based on patents and copyrights.

---

[9] Theorem 4 has been stated in terms of a finite variation of foreign demand. Confining oneself to infinitesimal changes and differentiable excess demand functions, one may proceed as follows. In an initial equilibrium

$$z_1(p^*) + \lambda z_0(p^*) = 0, \qquad \lambda = 1, \qquad J \cdot p^* = 1,$$

where p^* is the equilibrium price vector and $J = (1, \dots, 1)$. Total differentiation with respect to λ yields

$$[\partial z/\partial p]\partial p/\partial \lambda = z_1, \qquad J \cdot (\partial p/\partial \lambda) = 0.$$

The Laspeyres terms-of-trade test becomes

$$(\partial p/\partial \lambda)'[\partial z/\partial p](\partial p/\partial \lambda) = z_1 \cdot (\partial p/\partial \lambda) < 0$$

for all $(\partial p/\partial \lambda)$ satisfying $J \cdot (\partial p/\partial \lambda) = 0$. This is equivalent to the requirement that the Jacobian $[\partial z/\partial p]$ be quasi-negative semi-definite under constraint. As is well known, the requirement is met if all commodities are gross substitutes for each other.

In seeking to extend existing theory to accommodate this kind of trade one encounters two difficulties. First, patents and copyrights typically confer monopoly–monopsony power on particular individuals or firms; hence techniques of analysis based on the assumption of perfect competition are inapplicable. Second, the privileges conferred by patents and copyrights are typically of finite duration; hence conventional timeless analysis, with its implicit assumption that conditions remain unchanged through time, is inappropriate if post-patent conditions are influenced by earlier licensing decisions. (One thinks here of learning by doing under licence.) These difficulties can be evaded by confining attention to small countries, which take as given both (conventional) commodity prices and the terms of licensing, and by assuming away the possibility that licensing decisions influence post-patent conditions of production or factor supply; and that is what I propose to do.

Let u be a quasi-concave Scitovsky social welfare function of the aggregate consumption vector c, let ω be an aggregate endowment vector, let Y be the net production set with elements y, and let p be a constant vector or world prices. In the absence of trade in techniques, but with free trade in conventional commodities, a small country may be viewed as solving

Problem 1

$$\max_{c,y} u(c) \quad \text{such that } y \in Y, \quad p(c - y - \omega) \leq 0, \quad c \geq 0.$$

Now suppose that an additional set of production possibilities Y^* is available to the country upon payment of a fee ω^*, a commodity vector which depends on y^*, $y^* \in Y^*$, and let us consider the revised problem,

Problem 2

$$\max_{c,y,y^*} u(c) \quad \text{such that } y \in Y, y^* \in Y^*, \quad p(c - y - y^* - \omega + \omega^*(y^*)) \leq 0.$$

The set $Y + Y^*$ can be replaced by a compact subset of itself (Debreu, 1959, sections 5.4 and 5.7); hence the maximum exists. It is easy to see that the solution to problem 2 yields a level of social welfare not less than does the solution to problem 1. In this weak sense, free trade in techniques is gainful[10].

---

[10] It can be shown also that free trade in techniques is gainful in relation to an initial situation of autarky.

References

Arrow, K. J. (1951), An extension of the basic theorems of classical welfare economics, in: Neyman, J. ed., *Proceedings of the Second Berkeley Symposium on Mathematical Statistics and Probability*, University of California Press, Berkeley, California, 507–532.

Bhagwati, J. and H. G. Johnson (1960), Notes on some controversies in the theory of international trade, *Economic Journal*, 70, March, 74–93.

Debreu, G. (1959) *Theory of Value*, Wiley, New York.

Kemp, M. C. (1962), The gain from international trade, *Economic Journal*, 72, Dec., 303–319.

Kemp, M. C. (1969), *The Pure Theory of International Trade and Investment*, Prentice-Hall, Englewood Cliffs, NJ.

Krueger, A. O. and H. Sonnenschein (1967), The terms of trade, the gains from trade and price divergence, *International Economic Review*, 8, Feb., 121–127.

Marshall, A. (1923), *Money, Credit and Commerce*, Macmillan, London.

Mill, J. S. (1909), *Principles of Political Economy*, Longmans, Green, London.

Samuelson, P. A. (1939), The gains from international trade, *Canadian Journal of Economics and Political Science*, V, May, 195–205.

Samuelson, P. A. (1962), The gains from international trade once again, *Economic Journal*, 72, Dec., 820–829.

Sontheimer, K. C. (1971), On the existence of international trade equilibrium with trade tax-subsidy distortions, *Econometrica*, 39, Nov., 1015–1036.

Vanek, J. (1965), *General Equilibrium of International Discrimination*, Harvard University Press, Cambridge, Mass.

Viner, J., *Studies in the Theory of International Trade*, Allen and Unwin, London.

Wan, H. Y., Jr. (1965), Maximum bonus – an alternative measure of trading gains, *Review of Economic Studies*, 32, Jan., 49–58.

Wan, H. Y. Jr. (1972), A note on trading gains and externalities, *Journal of International Economics*, 2 (May, 1972), 173–180.

Grandmont, J. M. and D. McFadden (1972), A technical note on classical gains from trade, *Journal of International Economics*, 2, May, 109–126.

Chapter 12

NOTES ON THE THEORY OF OPTIMAL TARIFFS*

1. Introduction

It is widely believed that, in the two commodities case, the optimal tariff must be non-negative – zero if world prices are beyond the control of the tariff-imposing country, positive otherwise. An exception is J. de V. Graaff who, in a little-noticed passage, has argued that the optimal tariff will be negative if Giffen effects are sufficiently strong. It will be shown that Graaff's argument is invalid but that circumstances can be imagined in which the optimal tariff must be negative.

It will be assumed that perfect competition prevails everywhere and, until section 5, that in the home or tariff-imposing country excise taxes are zero.

Section 2

We begin with the standard exposition. In fig. 1 the foreign country's offer curve is represented by $G'OG$. The optimal tariff restricts trade to the point where the marginal rate of transformation through trade (indicated by the slope of $G'OG$) is equal to the marginal rate of transformation through home production and to the marginal social rate of substitution in home consumption. Suppose that the optimal trading point is P, with the home country exporting the second commodity and importing the first. The home price of exports in terms of imports, say p, is indicated by the ratio AB/BP. The foreign price ratio, say p^*, is, on the other hand, indicated by OB/BP. But $p(1+\tau) = p^*$,

* *Economic Record*, 43 (Sept. 1967), 395–404. I acknowledge with gratitude helpful conversations with Professors John Chipman and Ken-ichi Inada.

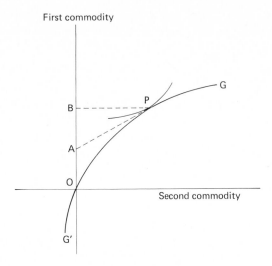

First commodity

Second commodity

Fig. 1.

where τ is the *ad valorem* rate of import or export duty. Hence the optimal rate of duty is $\tau = (p^*/p) - 1 = OA/AB$ which, necessarily, is positive[1].

Of course, the foreign offer curve need not possess the convenient shape displayed in fig. 1. Two alternative shapes are shown in figs. 2 and 3, both of them consistent with the requirement that only one offer should be forthcoming at each terms of trade[2]. In each case it is possible to find a trading point P' which *locally* maximizes the home country's welfare and to which there corresponds a negative tariff. However, in each case, the trading point P which provides a *global* maximum can be reached only with the aid of a positive tariff.

The foreign offer curves of figs. 1, 2 and 3 have two features in common: they pass through the origin, and their northern silhouettes are, except possibly at the origin, concave down. It is obvious on reflection that whenever the foreign

[1] The ideas sketched in this paragraph can be traced in their essence to Edgeworth (1925) and Bickerdike (1906, 1907). The exposition offered here is Graaff's (1957, pp. 133–135). In a puzzling final paragraph (p. 135) Graaff states that 'there is no reason why the relative curvature of the social indifference and foreign offer curves should not be such that the optimum, C, coincides with O, where no trade takes place. Then the familiar marginal equality is replaced by an inequality'. But if at O the slope of the relevant indifference curve exceeds the slope of the foreign offer curve, the optimum must lie in the third quadrant. If Graaff had drawn the whole of the foreign offer curve, not just that part which falls in the first quadrant, this would have been clear.

[2] That the foreign offer curve can take on these odd shapes is explained in Johnson (1959), in Kemp and Jones (1961), and in Komiya (1967).

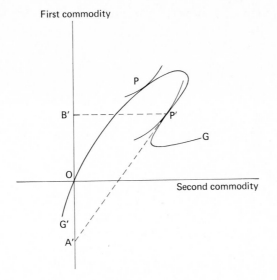

Fig. 2.

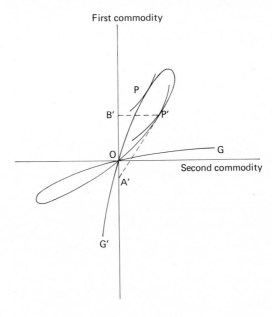

Fig. 3.

curve possesses these two features the optimal tariff must be non-negative. In our search for negative optimal tariffs, therefore, we must be prepared to sacrifice at least one of these features.

Section 3

In this section are described four alternative sets of circumstances in which the optimal tariff may be negative.

3.1. Case 1: foreign country imposes a tariff

If the foreign country itself imposes a tariff, its (tariff-distorted) offer curve need not be single valued. To see this, consider fig. 4. The terms of trade are indicated by the slope of QQ''', the internal price ratio in the foreign country by the steeper slope of the other straight lines. Q is the foreign production point, EE' is part of that foreign Engel curve which corresponds to the foreign internal price ratio, and Q', Q'' and Q''' are three possible consumption equilibria. Thus the possibility of multiple offers is established. (Note that inferiority of the first commodity in the foreign country is necessary, though not sufficient.) If,

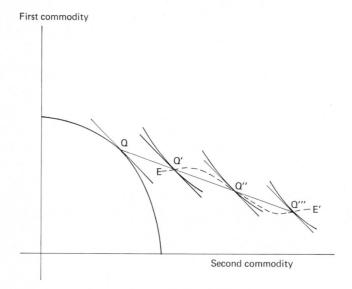

Fig. 4.

however, the foreign offer is multivalued, the offer curve may have the shape displayed in fig. 5, with negative optimal tariff.

It is something of a paradox, perhaps, that the imposition of a tariff by the foreign country might change from positive to negative the optimal tariff of the home country.

3.2. Case 2: strongly increasing returns abroad

It is well known that if returns are strongly increasing both the production possibility curve and the offer curve may depart from uniform convexity (see Matthews, 1950). In that case, as fig. 6 makes clear, the optimal tariff may be negative. Only if the optimum lies at the corner P', which corresponds to complete foreign specialization, may the optimal tariff be positive; then everything depends on the slope of the relevant home indifference curve.

3.3. Case 3: factor market imperfections abroad

A related case is that in which, as the result of convention or law, a foreign factor receives a higher reward in one industry than in another. The *con-*

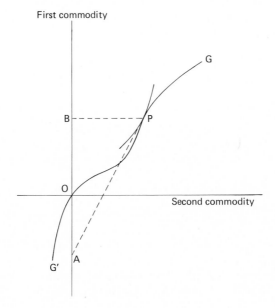

Fig. 5.

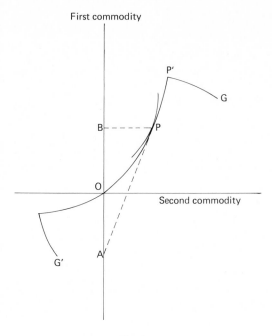

First commodity

P'

G

B - - - - - P

O

Second commodity

G'

A

Fig. 6.

strained curve of production possibilities may then be convex to the origin and give rise to an offer curve with the shape displayed in fig. 6. To see that a convex curve of production possibilities is indeed possible, one need only suppose that factor proportions are the same in each industry, so that given constant returns to scale, the unconstrained curve of production possibilities is a straight line, and then inject an interindustrial difference in rewards, however small (see Fishlow and David, 1961, p. 541, n. 29).

It is even possible that a negative optimal tariff may be associated with a lower wage in the foreign export industry. It is amusing to compare this possibility with the pauper labour argument for tariff protection.

3.4. Case 4: unilateral payments

The final example involves foreign offer curves which do not pass through the origin. Suppose that the foreign country is under obligation to pay to the home country each period an amount fixed in terms of the foreign country's export commodity. The foreign offer curve may then be as shown in fig. 7 – of conventional curvature but passing through *T*, where *OT* is the amount to be

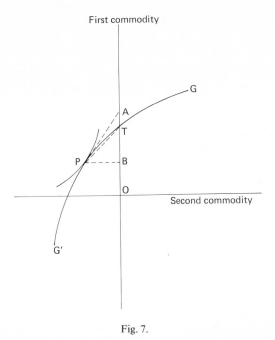

First commodity

G

A

T

P B

O

Second commodity

G'

Fig. 7.

transferred each period[3]. Suppose now that the optimum lies at P. The home country in effect trades from T to P at terms of trade indicated by the slope of PT, i.e. it has a net import of both commodities if we include the initial transfer OT as an import. The optimal rate of duty (on the first commodity, as usual) is

$$\tau = (p^*/p) - 1 = \left(\frac{BT}{PB} \middle/ \frac{AB}{PB}\right) - 1 = -(AT/AB)$$

which is negative.

Suppose, alternatively, that the home country must pay to the foreign country each period a sum fixed in terms of the home country's export commodity. The foreign offer curve will then be as shown in fig. 8, where OT is the amount to be transferred. If the optimum lies at P, with the home country a net exporter of both commodities, the optimal export duty (on the second commodity) will be (AT'/AB), which is negative.

While in this case the optimal tariff can be negative, it need not be so. For when both commodities are imported, or both exported, it is a matter of indifference whether a subsidy is paid to one industry or a tax levied upon the

---

[3] For further discussion of the generalized offer curve, see Kemp (1966b).

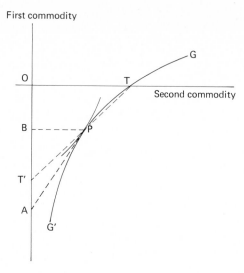

Fig. 8.

other. Note also that the possibility of a negative tariff does not arise if the transfer is denominated in the import commodity of the transferor. On the other hand, we note that when the amount transferred depends on commodity prices (as when it takes the form of dividend payments) the optimal tariff may be negative even though two-way trade persists (Jones, 1967).

Section 4

Graaff has argued that in a two-commodity world the optimal tariff can be negative 'only ... when imports are inferior goods in the domestic country – indeed, so markedly inferior that the Giffen paradox operates' (Graaff, 1957, p. 137n.; see also 1949–1950, pp. 54–55). Graaff's conclusion is based on Marshall's earlier conjecture (Marshall, 1926, pp. 382–383) that if the imported commodity is a Giffen good a tariff might increase import demand and thus turn the terms of trade against the tariff-imposing country. From this starting point Graaff seems to argue that, since an optimal tariff must restrict imports below the free trade level, the optimal tariff on Giffen goods must be negative. There are several things wrong with this line of reasoning; not least, Marshall's original conjecture is false (Kemp, 1966a, 1968). It suffices, however, to recall that any peculiarities of home demand are irrelevant to the determination of the sign of the optimal tariff. That the imported good is a Giffen good at home does not ensure that the optimal tariff is negative, or that it is positive. Inferiority in the foreign country of that country's imports may result in a negative optimal tariff in the home country, but that is another matter entirely.

Section 5

Most discussion of the optimal tariff has been conducted on the assumption that the tariff is the only tax levied in the home or policy-making country. The optimum in question was, therefore, a full Paretian optimum. That assumption was maintained in each of the four examples described in section 3. In this section, however, the assumption is dropped and an expression is obtained for the optimal tariff when a tax is imposed on the production of the exported commodity. The optimum is therefore of the second-best variety. The common sense expectation – that for sufficiently high rates of excise tax the optimal tariff is negative–is confirmed.

Figure 9 illustrates the argument. In the second quadrant are drawn a single consumption indifference curve and the familiar 'production block'. At point Q, the marginal rate of substitution in consumption R is minus the slope of the tangent to the indifference curve; and the marginal rate of transformation S is

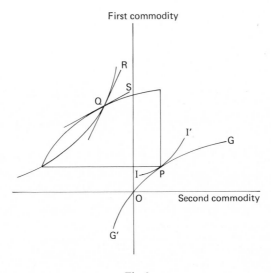

Fig. 9.

minus the slope of the tangent to the production possibility curve. Because of the excise tax $R > S$,

$$R = S(1 + t),$$ (1)

where t is the rate of tax on the second commodity. If now we slide the production block round the indifference curve, maintaining the relation (1) between R and S, we trace out the *constrained* trade indifference curve II'. To find the optimal tariff we need the slope of II'. Consider point P, which corresponds to point Q on the consumption indifference curve. If we change slightly the consumption C_1 of the first commodity, the consumption of the second commodity must change by $dC_2 = dC_1/R$. Moreover, from (1), the production X_1 of the first commodity must change by $dX_1 = R' dC_1/S'(1 + t)$ and the production of the second commodity by $dX_2 = dX_1/S = R' dC_1/SS'(1 + t)$, where primes indicate differentiation with respect to the consumption or production of the first commodity. The slope of II' is therefore

$$\frac{dC_1 - dX_1}{dC_2 - dX_2} = -\left[1 - \frac{R'}{S'(1 + t)}\right]\bigg/\left[\frac{1}{R} - \frac{R'}{SS'(1 + t)}\right].$$

Now in equilibrium $R = p$, which now represents the home price ratio as seen by consumers; and $S = p/(1 + t)$, the home price ratio as seen by producers. Hence the slope of II' reduces to

$$p\left[1 - \frac{R'}{S'(1 + t)}\right]\bigg/\left[1 - \frac{R'}{S'}\right].$$ (2)

In a trade optimum a trade indifference curve must be tangent to the foreign offer curve $G'OG$. Suppose that the optimum occurs at P, where II' and $G'OG$ touch. The slope of $G'OG$ is (Kemp, 1964, p. 302)

$$p^*[(1/\xi^*) + 1],$$ (3)

where ξ^* is the total price elasticity of foreign import demand. Equating (2) and (3), and recalling that $p^* = p(1 + \tau)$, we obtain

$$1 + \tau = \left\{\left[1 - \frac{R'}{S'(1 + t)}\right]\bigg/\left[1 - \frac{R'}{S'}\right]\right\}\bigg/\left(\frac{1}{\xi^*} + 1\right),$$ (4)

where τ is the optimal rate of duty. Now R' is negative, S' positive; hence $-R'/S'$ is positive. It follows that the numerator of (4) is a positive fraction which approaches $1/(1 - R'/S')$ as t goes to infinity. In an optimum $\xi^* < -1$; hence the denominator of (4) also is a positive fraction and approaches one as ξ^* goes to minus infinity. Clearly τ is negative for a sufficiently high rate of tax or for sufficiently elastic foreign import demand. If foreign demand is perfectly elastic, the optimal tariff must be negative if $t > 0$.

It will be obvious that if the home country were to subsidize the production of the imported commodity, the optimal tariff might again be negative.

Section 6

Suppose that the foreign country is a free trader, that constant returns prevail abroad, that there are no factor market imperfections abroad, and that no unilateral payments are made; but allow the number of commodities to exceed two. Then we must speak of the optimal tariff *vector*. Graaff has argued that the vector may contain negative elements (Graaff, 1949–1950, p. 53; and 1960, pp. 130–131). However, his argument is based on first-order conditions only; strictly speaking, therefore, his proposition must be considered unproved. To prove it, or to produce a counter-example, is a major outstanding intellectual challenge. If Graaff's proposition is proved correct, one would then like to know the answers to the following derived questions:

(a) Can all optimal tariff rates be zero – that is, can free trade be optimal – even when foreign demands and supplies are imperfectly elastic? Graaff has asserted that this is so (Graaff, 1949–1950, p. 53; and 1960, pp. 127, 130).

(b) Can net tariff revenue be negative in an optimum?

(c) Can all optimal tariff rates be negative?

References

Bickerdike, C. F. (1966), The theory of incipient taxes, *Economic Journal*, 16, Dec., 529–535.

Bickerdike (1907), review of A. C. Pigou, *Preferential and Protective Import Duties*, *Economic Journal*, 17, March, 98–102.

Edgeworth, F. Y. (1925), *Papers Relating to Political Economy*, II, Macmillan, London.

Fishlow, A. and P. A. David (1961), Optimal resource allocation in an imperfect market setting, *Journal of Political Economy*, 69, Dec., 529–546.

Graaff, J. de V. (1949–1950), On optimum tariff structures, *Review of Economic Studies*, 17 (1), 47–59.

Graaff, J. de V. (1957), *Theoretical Welfare Economics*, Cambridge University Press, London.

Johnson, H. G. (1959), International trade, income distribution, and the offer curve, *Manchester School*, 27, Sept., 241–260.

Jones, R. W. (1967), International capital movements and the theory of tariffs and trade, *Quarterly Journal of Economics*, 81, Feb., 1–38.

Kemp, M. C. and R. W. Jones (1962), Variable labor supply and the theory of international trade, *Journal of Political Economy*, 70, Feb., 30–36.

Kemp, Murray C. (1964), *The Pure Theory of International Trade*, Prentice-Hall, Engelwood Cliffs, NJ.

Kemp, M. C. (1966a), Note on a Marshallian conjecture, *Quarterly Journal of Economics*, 80, Aug.,
    481–484.
Kemp, M. C. (1966b), The gain from international trade and investment: a neo-Heckscher–Ohlin
    approach, *American Economic Review*, 56, Sept., 788–809.
Kemp, M. C. (1968), A partial theoretical solution of the problems of the incidence of import duties,
    in: J. N. Wolfe (ed.), *Value, Capital, and Growth. Papers in Honour of Sir John Hicks*, Edinburgh
    University Press, Edinburgh, 257–273.
Komiya, R. (1967), Non-traded goods and the pure theory of international trade, *International
    Economic Review*, 8, June, 132–152.
Marshall, A. (1926), *Memorandum on the Fiscal Policy of International Trade* (House of Commons
    No. 321, 1908). Reprinted in J. M. Keynes (ed.), *Official Papers by Alfred Marshall*, Macmillan,
    London. References are to the *Official Papers*.
Matthews, R. C. O. (1950), Reciprocal demand and increasing returns, *Review of Economic Studies*,
    17, Feb., 149–158.

Chapter 13

THE RANKING OF TARIFFS UNDER MONOPOLY POWER IN TRADE*

Kemp has argued that, for a country with no monopoly power in trade, a lower tariff is preferable to a higher tariff, in the sense that any distribution of individual utilities attainable with a higher tariff is attainable with a lower tariff, usually with something to spare (Kemp, 1962). Subsequently, Vanek (1965) and Bhagwati (1968) showed that if exportables are inferior (a) competitive equilibrium may not be unique, (b) one of the low-tariff equilibria may be inferior to one of the high-tariff equilibria and, therefore, (c) a reduction in the tariff might leave a country worse off. As a result (Bhagwati, 1968; Vanek, 1965; Kemp, 1968) Kemp's proposition has now been elaborated to read

the (best) utility possibility curve under a lower tariff will indeed lie outside that under a higher tariff, regardless of the inferiority of the exportable good in social consumption; but a competitive price system could well result in equilibria involving a higher welfare level under a higher tariff, unless inferiority of the exportable good in social consumption were ruled out.

Can anything be said about the ranking of tariffs when a country has monopoly power in trade? Or must one be content to know that an optimal tariff exists? This note shows that, under very modest restrictions on preferences and in spite of the necessity of ranking suboptimal policies, it is possible to establish the following propositions. Let the optimum tariff be t_w, the zero tariff t_0 and the (just) prohibitive tariff t_p.

Proposition 1. Successive increases in the tariff from the level t_0 will raise welfare until the level t_w is reached; successive increases in the tariff thereafter will reduce welfare until the level t_p is reached; higher tariffs merely involve continuing autarky and hence are partially ordered.

* *Quarterly Journal of Economics*, 83 (May 1969), 330–335, with J. Bhagwati.

Proposition 2. For a country with monopoly power in trade, therefore, the choice of a social welfare function will merely determine the magnitudes of t_w and t_p; hence one could regard tariffs as continuously laid in a chain from zero to infinity, with the social welfare function (for a specific country) serving, as it were, as a spike which lifts this chain up to the level of the optimal tariff and drops it to the floor at the level of the (appropriate) prohibitive tariff – as illustrated by fig. 1 for five hypothetical welfare functions.

These propositions are not *generally* valid. To establish the conditions under which they *are* valid, consider fig. 2, which shows the trade indifference curves U_w^I, U_0^I and U_p^I reached by country I successively under an optimum tariff, a zero tariff, and a prohibitive tariff. It is clear that proposition 1, and hence proposition 2, will hold *if and only if* an increase in country I's tariff will necessarily reduce the demand for imports. For, in such a case, an increase in

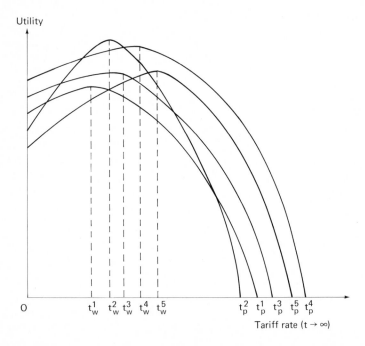

Fig. 1. Tariff ranking for a given country, with monopoly power in trade, under five alternative social welfare functions. Note that no cardinal significance is to be attached to the utility axis. The figure merely ranks, in terms of utility, tariffs ranging from zero to infinity for each social welfare function. It also shows the optimum tariffs for each of the five functions at t_w^5, t_w^4, t_w^3, t_w^2, t_w^1, and the corresponding prohibitive tariff levels at t_p^5, t_p^4, t_p^3, t_p^2 and t_p^1. The diagram could be readily extended to the second and third quadrants, to show the effects and ranking of export subsidies.

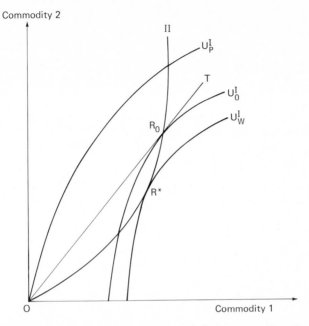

Fig. 2. This figure shows the optimum-tariff welfare level U_w^I, the zero-tariff welfare level U_0^I, and the self-sufficiency welfare level U_p^I for country I, the free trade terms of trade OT and country II's offer curve OII.

the tariff, starting from a zero tariff at R_0, will take the economy through higher and higher trade indifference curves until it reaches R^* and then through successively lower trade indifference curves to 0 and U_p^I.

Therefore, exceptions to proposition 1, and hence proposition 2, must constitute exceptions to the rule that an increase in the tariff will reduce the demand for imports. It can then be shown that this rule admits of exceptions only when the exportable commodity is inferior[1].

Hold the terms of trade constant at unity. Suppose that commodity 1 is imported and that commodity 2 is the *numéraire*. The internal price ratio is, therefore, $(1 + t)$, where t is the rate of duty. The demand for imports is $E_1(1 + t, I_2)$, where

$$I_2 = (1 + t)X_1 + X_2 + tE_1$$

---

[1] Note, therefore, that the argument sometimes made in balance-of-payments theory, that tariffs must be preferred to devaluation *until* the optimum tariff is reached, is valid only insofar as inferiority of the exportable good is ruled out.

is income in terms of the *numéraire* commodity, X_i is the output of good i and tE_1 is the tariff revenue. We have

$$\frac{dE_1}{dt} = \frac{\partial E_1}{\partial t} + \frac{\partial E_1}{\partial I_2}\frac{dI_2}{dt}, \qquad \frac{dI_2}{dt} = X_1 + E_1 + t\frac{dE_1}{dt}.$$

Hence

$$\frac{dE_1}{dt} = \frac{\partial E_1}{\partial t} + \frac{m_1}{1+t}\,X_1 + E_1 + t\frac{dE_1}{dt} = \left(\frac{\partial E_1}{\partial t} + \frac{m_1}{1+t}\,D_1\right)\Big/\left(1 - \frac{t}{1+t}\,m_1\right),$$

where m_1 is the marginal propensity to consume the first or imported commodity and D_1 is consumption of the first commodity. Introducing the Slutzky decomposition,

$$\frac{\partial E_1}{\partial t} = \frac{\partial E_1}{\partial t}\bigg| - \frac{m_1}{1+t}\,D_1, \quad \text{where } \frac{\partial E_1}{\partial t}\bigg|$$

is the pure substitution slope, we obtain, finally,

$$\frac{dE_1}{dt} = \frac{\partial E_1}{\partial t}\bigg|\Big/\left(1 - \frac{t}{1+t}\,m_1\right)$$

which is negative unless the export is very inferior.

Figure 3 illustrates the possibility, ruled out by our restrictions on consumption inferiority, that an increase in the rate of duty may give rise both to an

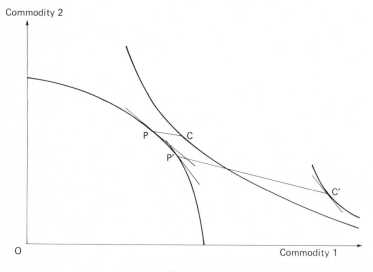

Fig. 3.

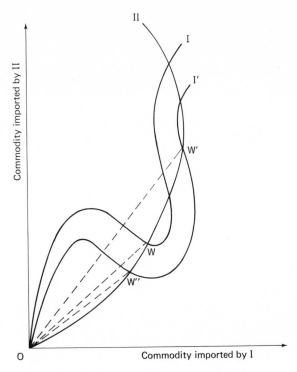

Fig. 4. *OI* is the low-tariff offer curve of country *I*, *OI'* is the high-tariff offer curve of country *I*, *OII* is the offer curve of country *II*.

increase in import demand and to a deterioration in the terms of trade of the tariff-imposing country. With the lower tariff, production takes place at *P*, consumption at *C*, and the terms of trade are indicated by the slope of *PC*. With the higher rate of duty, production takes place at *P'*, consumption at *C'*; and the (worsened) terms of trade are indicated by the slope of *P'C'*.

We have already stated that the possibility illustrated by fig. 3 can be ruled out if very modest restrictions are imposed on the community's preferences. We now offer two observations designed to emphasize just how modest those restrictions are[2]. First, we recall that '... the reciprocal demand curve traced out by a higher tariff rate will always lie inside the curve traced out by a lower tariff rate. ...' (Johnson, 1958, p. 34, fn. 7). It follows that the possibility illustrated by fig. 3 requires offer curves which yield multiple equilibria at given terms of trade, as in fig. 4 (points *W* and *W'* of fig. 4 correspond respectively

---

[2] The first observation emerged from a long correspondence with Harry G. Johnson.

to points C and C' of fig. 3). Second, it follows from our mathematical analysis that dE_1/dt is positive if and only if $1 - [tm_1/(1 + t)]$ is negative, that is, if and only if $1 + t(1 - m_1) < 0$. As Kemp has shown, however, this is precisely the condition for market instability when the terms of trade are given (Kemp, 1968).

Finally, we note that, even when an increase in the rate of duty is associated with a reduction in the demand for imports and a deterioration of the terms of trade, nevertheless there exists an alternative high-tariff equilibrium character-ized by reduced import demand and improved terms of trade (shown by point W'' in fig. 4). It follows that by choosing carefully from alternative equilibria one can ensure that, as the rate of duty is raised, welfare rises steadily, reaches a maximum, then declines until the duty is prohibitive.

References

Bhagwati, J. (1968), The gains from trade once again, *Oxford Economic Papers*, 20, July, 137–148.
Johnson, H. G. (1958), *International Trade and Economic Growth*, Allen and Unwin, London.
Kemp, M. C. (1962), The gains from international trade, *Economic Journal*, 72, Dec., 303–319.
Kemp, M. C. (1968), Some issues in the analysis of trade gains, *Oxford Economic Papers*, 20, July, 149–161.
Vanek, J. (1965), *General Equilibrium of International Discrimination. The Case of Customs Unions*, Harvard University Press, Cambridge, Mass.

Chapter 14

AN ELEMENTARY PROPOSITION CONCERNING THE FORMATION OF CUSTOMS UNIONS*

1. Introduction

In the welter of inconclusive debate concerning the implications of customs unions the following elementary yet basic proposition seems to have been almost lost to sight[1].

Proposition 1. Consider any competitive world trading equilibrium, with any number of countries and commodities and with no restrictions whatever on the tariffs and other commodity taxes of individual countries and with costs of transport fully recognized. Now let any subset of the countries form a customs union. Then there exists a common tariff vector and a system of lump-sum compensatory payments, involving only members of the union, such that each individual, whether a member of the union or not, is not worse off than before the formation of the union.

A detailed list of assumptions, and a relatively formal proof, may be found in section 2. Here we merely note that there exists a common tariff vector which leaves world prices, and therefore the trade and welfare of non-members, at their pre-union levels. If the net trade vector of the union is viewed as a (constant) endowment, it is then plausible that both the union as a whole and (after appropriate internal transfers) each member must be left not worse off by the removal of internal barriers to trade.

* *Journal of International Economics*, 5, to appear, with Henry Y. Wan, Jr. We acknowledge with gratitude the useful comments of Jagdish Bhagwati, John Chipman and two referees.
[1] The proposition, together with an indication of the lines along which a proof may be constructed, may be found in Kemp (1964, p. 176). A geometric proof for the canonical three-countries, two-commodities case has been furnished by Vanek (1965, pp. 160–165).

The proposition is interesting in that it contains no qualifications whatever concerning the size or number of the countries which are contemplating union, their pre- or post-union trading relationships, their relative states of development or levels of average income, and their propinquities in terms of geography or costs of transportation.

The proposition is also interesting because it implies that an incentive to form and enlarge customs unions persists until the world becomes one big customs union, that is, until world free trade prevails. More precisely, given any initial trading equilibrium, there exist finite sequences of steps, at each step new customs unions being created or old unions enlarged, such that at each step no individual is made worse off and such that after the last step the world is free trading. (In general, at each step some individual actually benefits.) Indeed, on the basis of these observations one might attempt to rehabilitate the vague pre-Vinerian view that to form a customs union is to move in the direction of free trade.

Evidently the incentive is insufficiently strong; tariffs and other artificial obstacles to trade persist. That the real world is not free trading must be explained in terms of:

(i) the game theoretic problems of choosing partners, dividing the spoils and enforcing agreements, and

(ii) the non-economic objectives of nations.
A role may be found also for:

(iii) inertia and ignorance concerning the implications of possible unions (in particular, concerning the long list of lump sum compensatory payments required); and, in the short run, for

(iv) the restraint exercised by international agreements to limit tariffs.
However (iv) can form no part of an explanation of the persistence of trading blocks in the long run.

Topics (i)–(iii) form a possible agenda for the further study of customs unions. For a preliminary analysis of (i) the reader may consult Caves (1971); and for suggestive work on (ii) he is referred to Cooper and Massell (1965), Johnson (1965) and Bhagwati (1968).

2. Proof of the proposition

Suppose that:

(ia) the consumption set of each individual is closed, convex and bounded below;

(ib) the preferences of each individual are convex and representable by a continuous ordinal utility function;

(ic) each individual can survive with a consumption bundle each component of which is somewhat less than his pre-union consumption bundle;

(ii) the production set of each economy is closed, convex, contains the origin and is such that positive output requires at least one positive input (impossibility of free production).

Consider a fictitious economy composed of the member economies but with a net endowment equal to the sum of the member endowments plus the equilibrium pre-union net excess supply of the rest of the world. In view of (i) and (ii), the economy possesses an optimum, and any optimum can be supported by at least one internal price vector (Debreu, 1959, pp. 92–93 and 95–96). Either the pre-union equilibrium of the member countries is a Pareto-optimal equilibrium of the fictitious economy (that is, corresponds to a maximal point of the utility possibility set), or it is not; in the latter case, a preferred Pareto-optimal equilibrium can be attained by means of lump sum transfers among individuals in the fictitious economy. That essentially completes the proof. It only remains to note that the required vector of common tariffs may be computed as the difference between the vector of pre-union world prices and the vector of internal union prices.

Commodities can be indexed by location. Hence the resource-using activity of moving commodities from one country to another is accommodated in the several production sets; no special treatment of cost of transportation is needed.

References

Bhagwati, J. (1968), Trade liberalization among LDCs, trade theory, and Gatt rules, in: J. N. Wolfe (ed.), *Value, Capital, and Growth. Papers in honour of Sir John Hicks*, Edinburgh University Press, Edinburgh, 21–43.

Caves, R. E. (1971), The economics of reciprocity: theory and evidence on bilateral trading arrangements, Harvard Institute of Economic Research, Discussion Paper No. 166.

Cooper, C. A. and B. F. Massell (1965), Towards a general theory of customs unions for developing countries, *Journal of Political Economy*, 73, 461–476.

Debreu, G. (1959), *Theory of Value*, Wiley, New York.

Johnson, H. G. (1965), An economic theory of protectionism, tariff bargaining, and the formation of customs unions, *Journal of Political Economy*, 73, 256–283.

Kemp, M. C. (1964), *The Pure Theory of International Trade*, Prentice-Hall, Englewood Cliffs, N.J.

Vanek, J. (1965), *General Equilibrium of International Discrimination. The Case of Customs Unions*, Harvard University Press, Cambridge, Mass.

Chapter 15

FOREIGN INVESTMENT AND THE NATIONAL ADVANTAGE*

In the March 1960 issue of the *Economic Record*, Sir Donald MacDougall provided an interesting analysis of the costs and benefits of foreign investment *from the point of view of the borrowing country* (MacDougall, 1960; see also the appendix). In this paper, which may perhaps serve as a companion piece to MacDougall's, I shall consider matters from the viewpoint of the lending country, and advance reasons for believing that capital-rich countries tend to invest too much of their wealth abroad, too little at home. Three quite independent lines of argument are deployed, all converging on the same conclusion.

It will be convenient (but not restrictive) to imagine that the lending country possesses a physically homogeneous capital stock consisting, say, of machines of a rather versatile kind. Part of this stock is invested abroad, the balance at home. It is desired to compare the free market and optimal foreign investments.

2. The argument from diminishing average return on foreign investment

Foreign investment exerts a depressing influence both on the price of the product to which the investment is directed and on the average physical productivity of the capital invested. The individual investor, however, is blind both to the influence of his investment on price and to its influence on productivity. He arrives at his decisions in the light of what, from the *nation's* point of view, is the *average* rate of return on foreign investment, namely the value of capital's marginal product abroad. In competitive equilibrium, the value of the marginal product of capital will be the same at home and abroad. But, from the national point of view, an optimum is attained only if the value of the marginal product at home is equated to the magnitude which is *marginal* to

* *Economic Record*, 38 (March 1962), 56–62.

the curve of total earnings abroad. It follows that, except in limiting cases, foreign investment is excessive and should be curbed.

That, briefly, is the first of the three grounds for restricting foreign investment. The argument might appear to overlook the possible favourable effect of the investment on the lending country's terms of trade. For example, it is widely believed that cheaper raw materials and consumer goods were among the greatest benefits which accrued to England from her nineteenth-century railway investments[1], yet such benefits must have been far from the calculations of most individual investors. Nevertheless, it will be argued that *whatever the direction of the investment* its amount is bound to be excessive; moreover, that the appropriate curb is the same in all cases.

It suffices to consider three cases:

(i) the borrowing country produces consumption goods of a kind which cannot be reproduced in the lending country;

(ii) the borrowing country produces raw materials vital to the lending country's industries and not of a kind produced in the lending country;

(iii) the borrowing country produces commodities which compete on world markets with the exports of the lending country.

Taken together these three 'pure' cases span the spectrum of situations in which we might be interested.

(i) Consider a world of two countries, the borrowing country and the lending country, each completely specialized in the production of a single consumption good. For later convenience, the lending country's product is called the first commodity, the borrowing country's the second. Production in each country is carried on with the aid of machines and certain other factors of production, the latter all in inelastic supply. It follows that the production function of the lending country may be written as $f_1(K_1 - K)$, where K_1 is the lending country's total stock of capital and K is the amount of capital sent abroad; and that the production function of the borrowing country may be written as $f_2(K_2 + K)$, where K_2 is the borrowing country's owned capital stock. The terms of trade, p, are defined as the price of the lending country's product in terms of the borrowing country's product, that is, as the price of the first commodity in terms of the second. The return on each machine invested abroad is the marginal product of machines,

$$f_2' = \frac{df_2}{d(K_2 + K)};$$

---

[1] Possibly more than one-half of England's foreign investments up to 1914 were in railways or in loans used for railway construction. See Nurkse (1954).

the total return on foreign investment is, therefore, Kf_2'. The total income of the borrowing country, in terms of its own product, is $(f_2 - Kf_2')$; and its demand for the imported product may be written as $D(f_2 - Kf_2'; p)$.

Now the lending country, by appropriate fiscal and commercial policy, can set the terms of trade p and the amount of foreign investment K at any levels it may choose (within the obvious limits defined by K_1 and K_2). The problem confronting the lending country, then, is that of maximizing some measure of communal welfare with respect to p and K, and of then finding the fiscal and commercial policies which will ensure that p and K are indeed at their welfare-maximizing values.

Suppose we postulate an index of welfare, u, which depends on the aggregate amount consumed of each commodity, and on nothing else. The consumption of its own product by the lending country is $(f_1 - D)$; and the amount of the borrowing country's product consumed by the lending country is $pD + Kf_2'$, that is, the value of the lending country's exports *plus* its foreign earnings. The welfare index, therefore, may be written as

$$u(f_1 - D; pD + Kf_2').$$

The first-order conditions of a maximum are

$$\frac{u_1}{u_2} = p\left(1 + \frac{1}{\eta}\right) = \frac{f_2'}{f_1'}\left[\frac{1 + (1 - m)\mu_2\epsilon_2}{1 - (f_2'/pf_1')m\mu_2\epsilon_2}\right], \tag{1}$$

where u_i is the partial derivative of u with respect to the aggregate consumption of the ith commodity (u_1/u_2 is therefore the marginal rate of substitution between the two commodities), $\eta \equiv (p/D) \cdot \partial D/\partial p$ is the price elasticity of the borrowing country's demand for imports, $m \equiv p[\partial D/\partial(f_2 - Kf_2')]$ is the borrowing country's marginal propensity to consume its imported commodity, $\epsilon_2 \equiv (K_2 + K)f_2''/f_2'$ is the elasticity of the marginal product of capital curve in the borrowing country (that is, the reciprocal of the elasticity of demand for capital in that country), $\mu_2 \equiv K/(K_2 + K)$ is the proportion of its capital stock that the borrowing country has borrowed and $f_1' = df_1/d(K_1 - K)$ is the marginal product of capital in the lending country.

The first of the two conditions is familiar from the theory of optimal tariffs; it requires that the marginal social rate of substitution in consumption should equal the marginal social rate of transformation through trade, and will be satisfied if a tax τ is imposed on imports (or exports) at an *ad valorem* rate of $100[-1/(1 + \eta)]\%$,

$$\tau = -1/(1 + \eta). \tag{2}$$

The second condition is only slightly more difficult to interpret. Note first that it can be rewritten as

$$f_1' = \frac{f_2'}{p}\left[\frac{\eta + (\eta + m)\mu_2\epsilon_2}{1+\eta}\right]. \tag{3}$$

Next, suppose that the foreign earnings are repatriated. Earnings per machine, expressed in terms of the second commodity, are f_2'; in terms of the first commodity, and after the import duty has been paid, they are f_2'/p. But suppose that foreign earnings are subjected to a special tax at a rate of $100t_1\%$. After both the import duty *and* the special tax have been paid, net earnings per machine would be $(f_2'/p)(1 - t_1)$. In competitive equilibrium net earnings will be the same in both countries, that is

$$f_1' = (f_2'/p)(1 - t_1). \tag{4}$$

It follows, from (3) and (4), that the optimal rate of tax is

$$t_1 = [1 - (\eta + m)\mu_2\epsilon_2]/(1 + \eta) \tag{5}$$

or, since $\eta + m = \bar{\eta}$, the compensated price elasticity of demand,

$$t_1 = (1 - \bar{\eta}\mu_2\epsilon_2)/(1 + \eta). \tag{6}$$

We know that $\bar{\eta} < 0$, $\epsilon_2 < 0$ and $\mu_2 \geq 0$; also that, in a trade optimum, $1 + \eta < 0$. Thus t_1 may be of either sign, depending on the specific values of η, m, etc. In particular, if $\mu_2 = 0$, that is, if the borrowing country relies only marginally on foreign sources of capital, t_1 *must* be negative. These are perhaps surprising conclusions. Bear in mind, however, that before foreign earnings are subject to the income tax, t_1, they have already suffered at the customs house. Negative or zero t_1 means merely that the optimal tariff is a sufficient deterrent to foreign investment. Any remaining element of paradox may be dispelled by noting that the combined rate of tax

$$\tau + t_1 = -\eta\mu_2\epsilon_2/(1 + \eta) \tag{7}$$

is necessarily positive, and that when no tariff is levied (because foreign demand is perfectly elastic, so that the optimal tariff is zero, or for any other reason) the appropriate rate of income tax

$$t_1 = -\mu_2\epsilon_2 \tag{8}$$

is always positive[2].

---

[2] Equation (8) may be obtained by studying the behaviour of (5) as $\eta \to -\infty$.

It is worth dwelling for a moment on the special case in which $\epsilon_2 = 0$, that is, in which the marginal product of capital abroad is insensitive to further investment. In that case, one feels, foreign investment should be unrestrained. This intuitive view is confirmed by appeal to (7) and (8): when an optimal tariff has been levied, the optimal income tax is negative and exactly undoes the work of the tariff, $\tau + t_1 = 0$; and when free trade prevails the optimum income tax is zero.

(ii) Suppose now that the borrowing country's export and sole product is a raw material essential to the lending country's product. The production function of the lending country now takes the more complicated form $f_1(K_1 - K, R)$, where $R = pD + Kf_2'$ is the volume of imported raw materials. But the welfare criterion is now very much simpler: the lending country must maximize $(f_1 - D)$ with respect to p and K.

Differentiating with respect to p yields

$$(\partial f_1/\partial R)D(1+\eta) - D\eta/p. \tag{9}$$

In the present case, however, $\eta \equiv -1$. Hence (9) reduces to D/p, which is always positive. It follows that there is no optimal p and therefore no optimal rate of import duty. Given any rate of duty, however large, there can be found a higher rate preferred to it. The lending country can secure to itself any proper fraction of world consumption by choosing a sufficiently high but finite export tax. In the limit, as the rate of tax goes to infinity, the fraction goes to one.

(iii) It remains to consider the possibility that the borrowing country produces a commodity which competes on the world market with the export of the lending country. Suppose, to adopt the simplest possible assumptions, that each country produces one commodity only, and that the same commodity is produced in each country. Since there is only one commodity, evidently there are no terms of trade to worry about. The lending country seeks to maximize $f_1 + Kf_2'$, as in the preceding case, but this time with respect to K only.

The first-order condition is

$$f_1' = f_2'(1 + \mu_2\epsilon_2). \tag{10}$$

If a tax at rate t_1 is imposed on repatriated earnings, the equality of marginal net earnings on investment in the two countries is expressed by the relation

$$f_1' = f_2'(1 - t_1). \tag{11}$$

It follows from (11) and (12) that the optimal rate of tax is

$$t_1 = -\mu_2\epsilon_2, \tag{12}$$

in complete parity with earlier results (cf. (8) and (12)).

So much for the argument from diminishing returns. Neither of the two remaining grounds for holding that capital-rich countries tend to over-lend need long detain us. The first is based on the risk of default, the second on the existence of foreign income taxes.

3. The argument from default and related risks

Default may take the straightforward form of failure on the part of foreign governments (or, with the connivance of their governments, foreign corporations) to meet their obligations to pay interest or repay capital; or it may take less obvious forms, such as the regulation of the rate structure of public utilities financed from abroad, or the imposition of taxation which discriminates against the incomes of non-residents.

Of course, in greater or lesser degree, the risk of default attends investment at home, too, and one might suppose that informed investors would direct their capital towards the highest returns, after making allowance for differences in risk. One might think, then, that the allocation effected by the international capital market, restrained by whatever taxes are suggested by diminishing returns, would be as close to ideal as may be.

The classic and, as far as I can see, irrefutable statement of the contrary view was provided by Keynes (1924) many years ago[3]:

Consider two investments, the one at home and the other abroad, with equal risks of repudiation or confiscation or legislation restricting profit. It is a matter of indifference to the individual investor which he selects. But the nation as a whole retains in the one case the object of the investment and the fruits of it; whilst in the other case both are lost. If a loan to improve a South American capital is repudiated, we have nothing. If a Poplar housing loan is repudiated, we, as a nation, still have the houses. If the Grand Trunk Railway of Canada fails its shareholders by reason of legal restriction of the rates chargeable or for any other cause, we have nothing. If the Underground System of London fails its shareholders, Londoners still have their Underground System.

[3] The problem of excessive foreign lending was, in Keynes' view, rendered particularly pressing by the Trustee Acts, which restricted trustee investments to Consols and the securities of colonial governments: 'It is not true that these great sums flow abroad as the result of a free and enlightened calculation of self-interest. They flow as the result of a particular social organization which – for the most part unintentionally – gives a bias in this direction.' (Keynes, 1924, p. 585).

4. The argument from foreign taxation[4]

Foreign taxation reduces the net yield of foreign investment from the viewpoint both of the community and of the individual investor. In itself, therefore, foreign taxation calls for no offsetting action by the government of the lending country. From the community's point of view, it is desirable that individual investors feel the full weight of foreign taxation.

Under international double taxation agreements, however, governments of lending countries typically allow full credit for taxes paid abroad. Thus the foreign tax serves as a disincentive to foreign investment only if the foreign rate of taxation exceeds the domestic rate. Even then, the disincentive is measured by the difference between the two rates of tax. As long as tax credits are allowed, there will be a gap between the marginal private and marginal social rates of return on foreign investment; and that gap is measured by the smaller of the domestic and foreign marginal rates of taxation. The implication is obvious: do not allow tax credits.

5. Qualifications

I conclude by making explicit two assumptions which have informed the foregoing analysis and the abandonment of which would call for perhaps considerable modifications of the conclusions drawn. The first of these is the assumption of perfect competition, both in the world capital market and in world commodity markets. To rush to the other extreme, suppose for a moment that both exports and foreign investment were at the discretion of a single individual. It is evident that he would take full account of diminishing returns and, in pursuit of private profit, would set the terms of trade and the level of foreign investment at the very levels which would maximize u. Neither a tariff nor a special tax would be necessary. Needless to say, most real world cases fall somewhere between the extremes of monopoly and competition.

I have assumed also that investors are equally well informed about foreign and domestic investment opportunities. It is, however, not inconceivable that ignorance of foreign opportunities is so profound that it dominates all other considerations, including those advanced in this note, and causes foreign investment to fall far short of its optimal level.

[4] Cf. MacDougall (1960, pp. 16–17).

Appendix: the benefits and costs of private investment from abroad: comment*

MacDougall (1960) has shown that capital imports may stop short of the point at which the borrowing country receives zero marginal net benefit. In particular, this possibility will be realized if capital imports are unimpeded, if perfect competition prevails, if returns to scale are constant, if external economies and taxation are absent, and if the terms of trade are independent of capital movements (MacDougall, 1960, section 2).

Suppose that MacDougall's conditions are satisfied. Should the borrowing country proceed to *encourage*, perhaps by subsidy, capital imports? That, at first encounter, would appear to be an obvious implication of his analysis. I shall argue, however, that a self-seeking borrowing country should tax all earnings of foreign-owned capital and, by implication, *curb* the capital inflow. Such a tax is the counterpart, on capital account, of the more familiar optimal tariff.

Suppose that each country produces a single commodity, and that that commodity is the same in each country[5]. Suppose further that the lending country possesses a physically homogeneous capital stock consisting, say, of machines of a versatile kind[6]. Part of this stock is invested abroad, the balance at home. It is desired to compare, from the viewpoint of the *borrowing* country, the free market and optimal foreign investments.

Production in each country is carried on with the aid of machines, and certain other factors of production, the latter all in inelastic supply. It follows that the production function of the lending country may be written as $f_1(K_1 - K)$, where K_1 is the lending country's total stock of capital and K is the amount of capital sent abroad; and that the production function of the borrowing country may be written as $f_2(K_2 + K)$, where K_2 is the borrowing country's owned stock of capital.

In competitive equilibrium, without artificial curb on (or encouragement of) capital movements, the world's stock of capital is so distributed between the two countries that the marginal return on investment is the same in both countries, that is, that $f_1' = pf_2'$, where p is the lending country's terms of trade and primes denote derivatives. Total foreign earnings are Kf_2'.

Suppose now that the government of the borrowing country seeks to

---

    * *Economic Record*, 38 (Mar. 1962), 108–110.
    [5] If all commodities are traded and if the terms of trade are constant, one may proceed as though there were a single commodity.
    [6] A justification of this assumption is offered in the main text of this chapter.

maximize that country's income by imposing a tax, at an *ad valorem* rate of $100t_2\%$, on the earnings of foreign capital. (Temporarily agnostic concerning the sign of t_2, we concede that the tax may turn out to be a subsidy.)

Foreign earnings net of tax are $K(1-t_2)f'_2$ and the net income of the borrowing country is $f_2 - K(1-t_2)f'_2$. The problem then is to maximize this expression with respect to t_2, subject to the revised marginal condition $f'_1 = p(1-t_2)f'_2$. The maximizing t_2 is readily found to be

$$t_2 = (-\mu_1\epsilon_1)/(1-\mu_1\epsilon_1),$$

where $\mu_1 = K/(K_1 - K)$ is the ratio of the lending country's foreign investments to its domestic investments, and $\epsilon_1 = (K_1 - K)f''_1/f'_1$ is the elasticity of the marginal product of capital curve in the lending country (that is, the reciprocal of the elasticity of demand for capital in that country).

Since $\mu_1 \geq 0$ and $\epsilon_1 < 0$, $t_1 \geq 0$; that is, in an investment optimum foreign earnings are *taxed*, not subsidized. In the limiting case in which the lending country contributes only marginally to the capital of the borrowing country, $\mu_1 = 0$ and the optimal tax is zero.

The same conclusion may be reached diagrammatically. In fig. A1 the world's capital stock is measured along the horizontal axis. The curve of the marginal product of capital in the lending country is M_1M_1: the corresponding curve in the borrowing country, referred to the origin O_2, is M_2M_2. In competitive

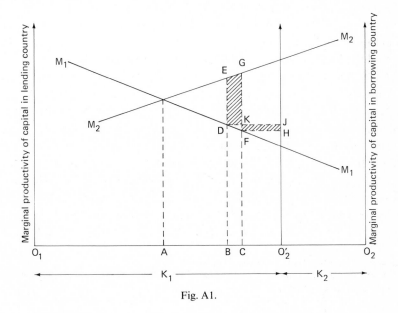

Fig. A1.

equilibrium, with no taxation of foreign earnings, the lending country invests AO_2' abroad. If, however, a tax t_2 is imposed, foreign investment shrinks to BO_2' and a gap $DE(= t_2 f_2')$ is opened between the two marginal products. Suppose now that t_2 is increased very slightly, to $(t_2 + dt_2)$, so that foreign investment is reduced further, to CO_2', and gap widens, to FG. Evidently net foreign earnings fall, from $BDJO_2'$ to $CFHO_2'$. The income of the borrowing country, on the other hand, is subject to two conflicting pressures: it increases by $FKJH$ ($= Kf_1'' \, dk$), but decreases by $DEGK$ ($= -t_2 f_2' \, dK$). In an optimum, these two pressures balance ($t_2 f_2' = -Kf_1''$, that is, by easy steps, $t_2 = (-\mu\epsilon_1)/(1 - \mu_1\epsilon_1)$).

References

Keynes, J. M. (1924), Foreign investment and the national advantage, *The Nation and Athenaeum*, 35, Aug. 9, 586.

MacDougall, G. D. A. (1960), The benefits and costs of private investment from abroad: A theoretical approach, *Economic Record*, 26, March, 13–35. Reprinted in *Bulletin of the Oxford University Institute of Statistics*, 22, Aug., 187–212.

Nurske, R. (1954), The problem of international investment today in the light of nineteenth-century experience, *Economic Journal*, 64, Dec., 744–758.

Chapter 16

THE GAIN FROM INTERNATIONAL TRADE AND INVESTMENT: A NEO-HECKSCHER–OHLIN APPROACH*

1. Introduction

That it may be to a single country's advantage to depress the volume of its foreign trade below the free trade level was known to Torrens, J. S. Mill, and Sidgwick (Torrens, 1821, pp. 281, 282; 1844, postscript to letter IX, especially pp. 329–338; Mill, 1848, pp. 21ff.; 1909, Book V, ch. 4, section 6; and Sidgwick, 1887, pp. 493ff.)[1]; and the more precise notion of an optimal degree of trade restriction (by means of an optimal tariff on imports or exports) goes back at least to Edgeworth (1925, pp. 13–16, 38, 39) and Bickerdike (1906, 1907). Rather later, it was recognized that a country may also gain by curbing its net international borrowing or lending[2], and that there may exist an optimal degree

* *American Economic Review*, 56 (Sept. 1966), 788–799. Section 3 revised. The author gratefully acknowledges the sustained assistance of Professor Henry Y. Wan, Jr., and of Professor Ronald Jones, especially with the more delicate arguments of section 3. The author acknowledges also the useful comments of Professors Takashi Negishi and John Chipman on the penultimate draft.

[1] The notion that a tariff may turn the terms of trade in favour of the tariff-imposing country has a confusing and little-known early history. The principle was clearly stated by Torrens in 1821 (Torrens, 1821) though the scope of the principle was unnecessarily restricted to circumstances in which the tariff-imposing country has 'a natural monopoly, either partial or complete'. The principle was reasserted by Torrens in an 1832 parliamentary speech (for details, see Robbins (1958, pp. 192–194)) and, for the special case in which all import demands are of unit elasticity, was elaborated with great precision in *The Budget* (Torrens, 1844) of 1844 (the important postscript to letter IX was written in 1843). In order of writing, though not of publication, Torrens' 1844 exposition was preceded by that of J. S. Mill. In the preface to *Essays on Some Unsettled Questions of Political Economy* (1844) Mill mentions that they were written in 1829–1830 and were being published in response to Torrens' *The Budget* (Torrens, 1844).

[2] See Keynes (1924, 1930); Iversen (1936, pp. 160–170); Cairncross (1935); Singer (1950); Nurske (1954); Schonfield (1959, 108–122). See also, however, Smith (1776, book II, ch. 5).

of restriction (by means of an optimal tax on foreign interest and profit receipts or payments) (MacDougall, 1960; Pearce and Rowan, 1966).

In this earlier literature, the gain from trade and the gain from international investment were implicitly assumed to be mutually independent and separately calculable. In conformity with this assumption, the calculation of the optimal degree of trade restriction and of the optimal curb on investment were treated as unrelated problems.

It is clear, however, that by changing the conditions of supply and the level of net income, both in the lending and in the borrowing country, international investment also may modify both the gain from trade and the optimal degree of trade restriction. On the other hand, the restriction of trade changes the terms of trade and the relative profitabilities of investment at home and abroad; it therefore may affect the optimal degree of restriction of international investment. 'Tariff factories' provide a simple and familiar example: the imposition of a tariff gives rise to an inflow of capital to finance the construction of branch plants behind the tariff wall; as a result, the terms-of-trade effect of the tariff is weakened, perhaps reversed. To treat trade and investment policies as separable and independent can be justified therefore only in a rough first approximation.

It is my purpose to formulate the problem of gain in a manner which will make clear the elements of interdependence, and to derive expressions for the optimal tariff and optimal tax.

In two earlier papers (Kemp, 1962a, 1962b; also 1964, chs. 13 and 14) this has been attempted for the simple case in which each country produces a single commodity. In this paper I shall instead work with a two-countries, two-commodities, two-factors model which is distinguished from the familiar Heckscher–Ohlin model, however, in that technology is allowed to differ between countries. The two factors recognized are labour and capital, the latter assumed to be homogeneous, perfectly durable, and smoothly substitutable for labour. Both factors are assumed to be in fixed supply: that is, the population of each country is stationary, and in each country net saving is zero. It is assumed that markets are perfectly competitive, all participants being well informed about world trading and investing opportunities. In particular, both factor markets are perfectly competitive, so that full employment is always assured, whatever commercial and fiscal policies are adopted. In keeping with the assumption of perfect competition, returns to scale are assumed to be constant. Finally, no account is taken of the possibility that one country may retaliate against the tariffs and taxes imposed by the other.

It will emerge that when account is taken of the elements of interdependence already referred to, either the optimal tariff or the optimal tax on foreign earnings, but not both, may be negative.

2. Geometric statement of the problem

Putting aside net new borrowing, grants, indemnities, and remittances, every country is subject to a budget constraint of the form

$$\text{(quantity of exports)} \; minus \; \text{(quantity of imports)} \times \text{(terms of trade)}$$
$$minus \; \text{(net international indebtedness)}$$
$$\times \quad \text{(average earnings on debt)}$$
$$= \quad 0.$$

The desired imports and exports of a country depend both on the terms of trade and on its net indebtedness. Suppose the latter is given. Then for each hypothetical value of the terms of trade we can plot desired imports and exports. By varying the terms of trade we can trace a locus of import–export combinations, each of which represents a potential international equilibrium (cf. fig. 1). This locus is a straightforward generalization of the familiar foreign trade offer curve. Note, however, that only when net indebtedness is zero does the curve pass through the origin and that, except in that special case, it is not possible to read off the terms of trade corresponding to a particular point on the locus by simply connecting that point by a straight line to the origin – the capital item in our equation complicates things. Note also that an equilibrium is possible in which the debtor country imports neither commodity; such an equilibrium would be located in the fourth quadrant of fig. 1.

Now take the foreign country's offer curve thus defined and slide it round the home country's production-possibilities curve in the manner made familiar by Baldwin (1952) and Samuelson (1962). In this way is generated an envelope – the home country's consumption-possibilities curve (*cc'* in fig. 2). Throughout this exercise, however, the net indebtedness of each of the two countries has been held constant. Suppose now that the home country invests a little more or less in the foreign country and that this is accomplished by shipping equipment from one country to the other. Evidently both the home country's production frontier and the foreign country's (generalized) offer curve will shift, and there will emerge a new envelope. Consider the envelope of all such envelopes (*CC'* in fig. 2). This truly describes the consumption possibilities facing the home country.

The problem is to find that combination of import duty (or subsidy) and

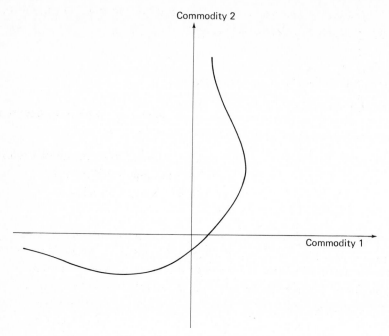

Fig. 1. Generalized offer curve.

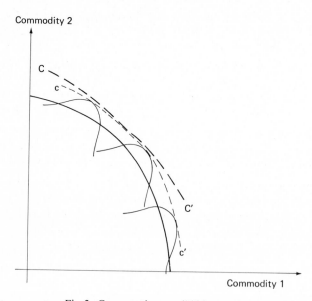

Fig. 2. Consumption possibilities curve.

income tax (or subsidy) which will move the home country to the favoured point on its generalized consumption-possibilities curve.

3. Solution of the problem: incomplete foreign specialization

Until further notice it will be assumed that, if it is a net creditor, the home or policy-making country either exports the second commodity or exports nothing; and that, if it is a net debtor, the home country exports the second commodity or exports both commodities. The second commodity is, in this sense, the 'natural' export of the home country.

For the time being it will also be assumed that each country produces something of both commodities.

Let X_i stand for the home output of the ith commodity and D_i for the home consumption of the ith commodity. $E_i (\equiv D_i - X_i)$ is then the home excess (or import) demand for the ith commodity. Let p stand for the price of the second commodity in terms of the first, r_1 for the return on one unit of capital (the marginal product of capital in terms of the first commodity), and K for the amount of capital invested abroad by the home country. (If K is negative, it stands for the amount of capital invested in the home country by the foreign country.) Asterisks relate the variables to the foreign country. Thus D_i^* stands for the foreign country's demand for the ith commodity and p^* for the world terms of trade. Finally, U is a concave Scitovsky (1941) (see also Samuelson (1956)) index of the home country's welfare, a function of the aggregate amounts consumed by the home country of each of the two commodities, and of nothing else:

$$U = U(D_1; D_2) = U(X_1 + E_1; X_2 + E_2).$$

The foreign country, however, is subject to the budget constraint

$$E_1^* + p^* E_2^* + r_1^* K = 0; \tag{1}$$

moreover, in market equilibrium

$$E_i + E_i^* = 0, \qquad i = 1, 2.$$

Hence the index may be written as

$$U(X_1 + p^* E_2^* + r_1^* K; X_2 - E_2^*).$$

Now foreign excess demand depends on the world terms of trade, on real income, and on the amount of capital invested abroad by the home country.

However, real income is itself related to the terms of trade and to the level of net international indebtedness; hence we may simply write $E_2^* = E_2^*(p^*, K)$. We note also that, since the foreign country is assumed to be incompletely specialized, r_1^* depends on p^*, but not on K.[3] We therefore may write $r_1^* = r_1^*(p^*, K)$, with $\partial r_1^*/\partial K = 0$ but $\partial r_1^*/\partial p^* \gtreqless 0$ if, respectively, the second commodity is relatively capital-intensive, the two commodities are equally capital-intensive, or the first commodity is relatively capital-intensive. Finally, we note that the home output of the second commodity depends on the output of the first commodity and on the amount of capital invested abroad; that is, $X_2 = \phi(X_1, K)$. ($\partial \phi/\partial X_1$ is the slope of the production possibilities curve; $-\partial \phi/\partial K$ is the marginal productivity of capital in terms of the second commodity, r_1/p.) It follows from all this that the welfare index can be written as a function of the three parameters X_1, p^* and K:

$$U[X_1 + p^*E_2^*(p^*, K) + r_1^*(p^*, K)K\,;\, \phi(X_1, K) - E_2^*(p^*, K)].$$

Each of the three parameters can be varied as an act of policy. The problem is to find those values of X_1, p^*, and K which maximize U.

It is worth noting, perhaps, that in this formulation of the problem the proceeds of the tariff and income tax are not explicitly recognized. This does not mean, of course, that matters of public finance are overlooked. The disposition of revenue is implicit in the selection of a social welfare function.

The first-order conditions of an interior maximum[4] may be written[5]

$$U_2/U_1 = -1/(\partial \phi/\partial X_1), \tag{2a}$$

$$U_2/U_1 = \frac{p^*}{\eta_2^*}\left(1 + \eta_2^* + \frac{K}{E_2^*}\frac{\partial X_2^*}{\partial K}\right), \tag{2b}$$

$$U_2/U_1 = p^*\left(\frac{\partial X_2^*}{\partial K} - \frac{r_1^*}{p^*}\right)\Big/\left(\frac{\partial X_2^*}{\partial K} - \frac{r_1}{p}\right), \tag{2c}$$

where $U_i \equiv \partial U/\partial D_i$, $\eta_2^* \equiv (p^*/E_2^*)(\partial E_2^*/\partial p^*)$ is the total price elasticity of

---

[3] With constant-returns technology, a given price ratio, and incomplete specialization, changes in the factor endowment give rise to changes in outputs but not to changes in factor proportions and (therefore) not to changes in marginal products.

[4] Those boundary cases in which the *home* country is completely specialized or in which K lies at one of the upper and lower limits determined by the initial endowments will be considered below.

[5] In writing eq. (2b) use has been made of the fact that $\partial X_2/\partial K = \partial r_1^*/\partial p^*$. This remarkable equality is proved in the appendix. In writing eq. (2c) use has been made of the fact that, given p^*, changes in K have no effect on net foreign real income and therefore no effect on foreign demand. Changes in K therefore affect $E_2^*(\equiv D_2^* - X_2^*)$ solely through X_2^*: $\partial E_2^*/\partial K = -\partial X_2^*/\partial K$. Use has been made also of the relation $-\partial \phi/\partial K = r_1/p$.

foreign import demand, and $\partial X_2^*/\partial K$ is the rate at which the foreign output of the second commodity responds to a unit change in the capital endowment, given the price ratio but assuming equilibrating adjustments in both industries.

The first of these three conditions states simply that the marginal social rate of substitution between the two commodities must equal the slope of the production frontier. This condition will be met under competitive conditions, when both are equal to the home price ratio.

The second condition may be interpreted as defining the optimal rate of duty. As we have just noted, $U_2/U_1 = p$; also, $p = p^*/(1 + \tau_1)$, where τ_1 is the *ad valorem* rate of import (or export[6]) duty. The second condition may be written, therefore, as

$$1/(1 + \tau_1) = (1 + \eta_2^* + \epsilon_2^*)/\eta_2^*,$$

where $\epsilon_2^* \equiv (K/E_2^*)(\partial X_2^*/\partial K)$ is the foreign elasticity of import production with respect to borrowed capital. It follows that the optimal rate of duty is

$$\tau_1 = -(1 + \epsilon_2^*)/(1 + \eta_2^* + \epsilon_2^*). \tag{3}$$

Now $\partial X_2^*/\partial K$, and therefore ϵ_2^*, may be of either sign: if the second commodity is relatively capital-intensive abroad, $\partial X_2^*/\partial K$ is positive; if the second commodity is relatively labour-intensive, $\partial X_2^*/\partial K$ is negative (Rybczynski, 1955). It follows that the optimal tariff may be of either sign, or zero.

Of special interest is the zero-indebtedness case, in which $K = 0$. For then $\epsilon_2^* = 0$ and the optimal rate of duty takes its familiar value

$$\tau_1 = -1/(1 + \eta_2^*). \tag{3'}$$

It is not surprising perhaps that free trade is optimal if the foreign import demand is perfectly elastic ($\eta_2^* = -\infty$) or, when the home country is a net creditor and imports *both* commodities, if the foreign supply of the second commodity is perfectly elastic ($\eta_2^* = +\infty$).

The interpretation of the third condition, contained in eq. (2c), is a little more intricate. Suppose that $K > 0$, that is, that the home country is a net creditor. Earnings per unit of capital, expressed in terms of the first commodity, are r_1^*. Suppose further that foreign earnings are subjected to a special income tax at a

---

[6] If, in the optimum, each country is an exporter, the tariff can be applied indifferently to the home country's imports of the first commodity or to its exports of the second commodity; the assignment of subscripts to τ is of no consequence. If, however, the home country is a net debtor and imports neither commodity, τ_1 must be interpreted as an *export* duty (levied on the *second* commodity). If, at the other extreme, the home country is a net creditor and exports neither commodity, the only possible interpretation of τ_1 is as an import duty (levied on the *first* commodity).

rate of $100t_1\%$. In competitive equilibrium the rate of return on capital will be the same in both countries; that is[7]

$$r_1 = r_1^*(1 - t_1).$$
                                                                    (4)

From eqs. (2b), (2c) and (3), on the other hand,

$$r_1 = r_1^*[1 + \epsilon_2^*(1 + \epsilon_2^*)/\mu_2\eta_2^*],$$
                                                                    (5)

where $\mu_2 \equiv r_1^*K/p^*E_2^*$ is the ratio of the earnings on capital invested abroad to the value of exports. It follows from eqs. (4) and (5) that the optimal rate of tax on foreign earnings is

$$t_1 = -\epsilon_2^*(1 + \epsilon_2^*)/\mu_2\eta_2^*.$$
                                                                    (6)

If $K < 0$, that is, the home country is a net debtor, it is the earnings on *foreign* capital which must be taxed. In competitive equilibrium

$$r_1(1 - t_1^*) = r_1^*,$$
                                                                    (7)

where t_1^* is the rate of tax. It follows from eqs. (5) and (7) that the optimal rate of tax is

$$t_1^* = \epsilon_2^*(1 + \epsilon_2^*)/[\mu_2\eta_2^* + \epsilon_2^*(1 + \epsilon_2^*)].$$
                                                                    (8)

The tax rates t_1 and t_1^* are the counterparts, on capital account, of the more familiar optimal tariff. Like τ_1, they may be of either sign. Note that when $|\eta_2^*| = \infty$, so that free trade is optimal, it also is optimal to refrain from tinkering with the international movement of capital. When $K = 0$, so that $\mu_2 = \epsilon_2^* = 0$, the optimal tax rates are, as one might have expected, indeterminate.

It should not be thought that when it is optimal for the home country to be a net debtor t_1 can be set arbitrarily, say at zero; nor that when it is optimal for that country to be a net creditor t_1^* can be set arbitrarily. There are strict limits within which the level of the 'spare' tax must be held. The essential point will be familiar from the study of free trade associations. Given the set of member countries' duties on trade with non-members, each country must impose 'equalizing' border taxes on trade between members in goods which, in part or in whole, are of non-member origin. Suppose that it is optimal for the home country to contrive to be a net debtor. Then, to remove any incentive for home capitalists to invest abroad it is necessary that

$$r_1 \geqq r_1^*(1 - t_1).$$
                                                                    (9)

---

[7] It is assumed here and later that no duty is levied on repatriated dividends. In the contrary case, considered in my earlier articles (Kemp, 1962a, 1962b), $r_1 = r_1^*(1 - t_1)/(1 + \tau_1)$.

On the other hand, to remove any incentive for foreign capitalists to revise their (optimal) investments in the home country it is necessary that $r_2(1 - t_1^*) = r_2^*$, where, for example, r_2 is the home rental of capital in terms of the second commodity; that is, since in equilibrium $r_1 = pr_2$, $r_1^* = p^* r_2^*$ and $p(1 + \tau_1) = p^*$, it is necessary that

$$r_1(1 - t_1^*) = r_1^*/(1 + \tau_1). \tag{10}$$

From eqs. (9) and (10) the required condition follows:

$$(1 + \tau_1)(1 - t_1)(1 - t_1^*) \leq 1. \tag{11}$$

If it is optimal for the home country to be a net creditor one arrives at the same condition. It will be obvious that eq. (11) places no effective restriction on t_1 when it is optimal to be a net creditor, and no effective restriction on the choice of t_1^* when it is optimal to be a net debtor. Indeed there will always be room for discretion in the choice of level of the 'spare' or 'back-up' tax after the other tax has been optimally chosen.

Inherent in eqs. (3), (6), and (8) is a quite confusing variety of possibilities. These are displayed in figs. 3(a) and (b). Figure 3(a) covers the case in which the home country is a net creditor and fig. 3(b) describes the possibilities when the home country is a net debtor. (Note, however, that fig. 3(a) does double duty: when E_2^* is negative all t_1 signs are reversed.) Depending on the values assumed by η_2^* and ϵ_2^*, it seems that any sign combination of rate of duty and tax rate is possible, that in particular both may be negative. But not all of these possibilities are plausible; indeed some regions may be ruled out altogether. This will now be shown.

First the elasticity of foreign import demand is decomposed into its pure substitution and income components. Thus

$$\eta_2^* = \frac{p^*}{E_2^*} \frac{\partial E_2^*}{\partial p^*} = \frac{p^*}{E_2^*} \left\{ \frac{\partial D_2^*}{\partial p^*} \bigg|_{y_1^* \text{const.}} + \frac{m_2^*}{p^*} \frac{\partial y_1^*}{\partial p^*} - \frac{\partial X_2^*}{\partial p^*} \right\} \tag{12}$$

$$= \bar{\eta}_2^* + \frac{m_2^*}{E_2^*} \frac{\partial y_1^*}{\partial p^*},$$

where

$$\bar{\eta}_2^* \equiv \frac{p^*}{E_2^*} \left\{ \frac{\partial D_2^*}{\partial p^*} \bigg|_{y_1^* \text{const.}} - \frac{\partial X_2^*}{\partial p^*} \right\}$$

is the pure elasticity of substitution, $m_2^* \equiv p^*(\partial D_2^*/\partial y_1^*)$ is the foreign marginal propensity to consume the second commodity, and y_1^* is the real income of the

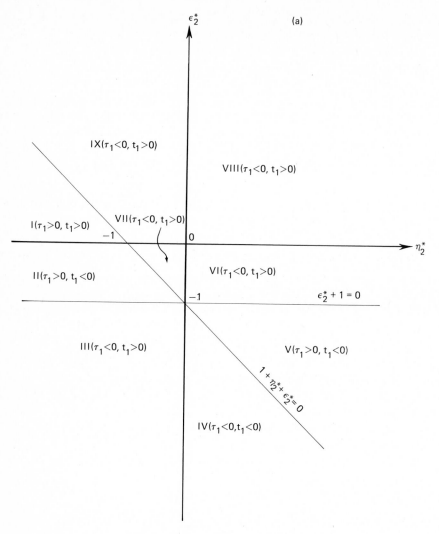

Fig. 3(a). Sign combination of τ_1 and t_1.

foreign country (that is, the cost, in terms of the first commodity, of the initial quantities consumed). Now

$$\partial y_1^*/\partial p^* = (\partial D_1^*/\partial p^*) + p^*(\partial D_2^*/\partial p^*) \quad \text{(by definition)} \tag{13}$$

$$= -E_2^*(1 + \epsilon_2^*)$$

from the budget restraint (1) and the duality relation of appendix A.

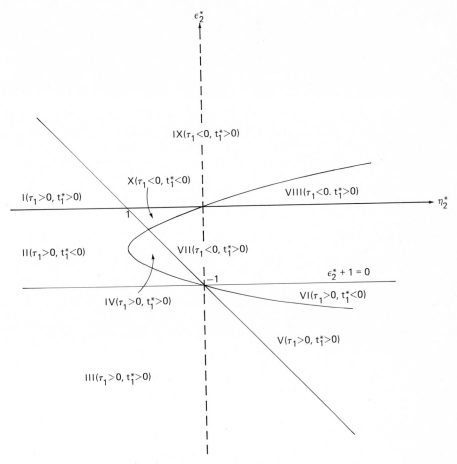

Fig. 3(b). Sign combinations of τ_1 and t_1^*.

Hence, substituting in eq. (12),

$$\eta_2^* = \bar{\eta}_2^* - m_2^*(1 + \epsilon_2^*). \tag{14}$$

Adding $(1 + \epsilon_2^*)$ to both sides we have also

$$1 + \eta_2^* + \epsilon_2^* = \bar{\eta}_2^* + m_1^*(1 + \epsilon_2^*). \tag{15}$$

Since $\bar{\eta}_2^*$ is the sum of the two pure substitution elasticities, of demand and production, it must be negative when E_2^* is positive and positive when E_2^* is negative. It then follows, from eq. (14), (a) that when E_2^* is positive, positive η_2^* requires negative $(1 + \epsilon_2^*)$ and therefore, from eq. (12), negative $(1 + \eta_2^* + \epsilon_2^*)$, and (b) that when E_2^* is negative, negative η_2^* requires positive $(1+\epsilon_2^*)$ and therefore, from eq. (15), positive $(1+\eta_2^*+\epsilon_2^*)$:

$$\text{if } E_2^*>0 \quad \text{then } \eta_2^*>0 \quad \textit{implies } 1+\eta_2^*+\epsilon_2^*<0, \tag{16a}$$

$$\text{if } E_2^*<0 \quad \text{then } \eta_2^*<0 \quad \textit{implies } 1+\eta_2^*+\epsilon_2^*>0. \tag{16b}$$

Further restrictions may be inferred from the requirements (i) that import and export subsidies must fall short of 100% (if they did not, competition would force the price of the subsidized commodity to zero or below) and (ii) that the rate of income tax must fall short of 100%. Thus, from eq. (3),[8]

$$-1<\tau_1=-(1+\epsilon_2^*)/(1+\eta_2^*+\epsilon_2^*) \tag{17}$$

and, from eqs. (6) and (8), respectively,

$$1>t_1=-\epsilon_2^*(1+\epsilon_2^*)/\mu_2\eta_2^* \tag{18a}$$

and

$$1>t_1^*=\epsilon_2^*(1+\epsilon_2^*)/[\mu_2\eta_2^*+\epsilon_2^*(1+\epsilon_2^*)]. \tag{18b}$$

It is possible that further restrictions on η_2^* and ϵ_2^* can be teased out of the higher order conditions for a maximum, but I have been unable to do so.

Finally, we note that

$$\epsilon_2^*=\frac{K}{E_2^*}\frac{\partial X_2^*}{\partial K}=\left(\frac{Kr_1^*}{p^*E_2^*}\right)\left(\frac{p^*}{r_1^*}\cdot\frac{\partial r_1^*}{\partial p^*}\right) \quad \text{(from appendix A).}$$

It follows that if $K>0$ and $\mu_2<-1$ (so that the home country is a creditor and imports both commodities) then the first bracketed expression is less than minus one and the second bracketed expression is greater than one in magnitude, implying that ϵ_2^* is greater than one in magnitude. The same is true when $K<0$ and $\mu_2<-1$.

When all restrictions are taken into account we are left with the possibilities displayed in figs. 4(a)–(d). Figure 4(a) illustrates the case in which, in the optimum, the home country is a net creditor, and continues to export the second commodity (so that $K>0$, $\mu_2>0$); fig. 4(b) illustrates the case in which the home country is a net creditor but imports both commodities (so that $K>0$, $\mu_2<-1$, and the optimum occurs in the fourth quadrant of fig. 1); fig. 4(c) illustrates the case in which, in the optimum, the home country is a net

---

[8] Alternatively, inequality (17) may be obtained by noting that the concavity of U rules out negatively sloped sections of the foreign country's offer curve (cf. fig. 1). The detailed proof is omitted.

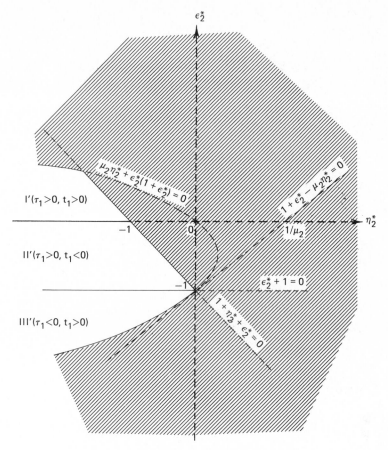

Fig. 4(a). $K > 0$, $\mu_2 > 0$.

debtor and exports the second commodity only (so that $K < 0, -1 < \mu_2 < 0$; and fig. 4(d) illustrates the remaining case in which the home country is a net debtor and exports both commodities (so that $K < 0$, $\mu_2 < -1$, and the optimum occurs in the second quadrant of fig. 1).

From figs. 4(a)–(d) we see that if two-way trade persists then the optimal tariff or the optimal tax (but not both) may be negative; that if one country imports both commodities then the optimal tariff but not the optimal tax may be negative; and that the optimal tariff and/or the optimal tax may be zero, that is, it is possible that free trade in goods and unrestricted mobility of capital are optimal.

It is noteworthy that in none of the four cases distinguished is the

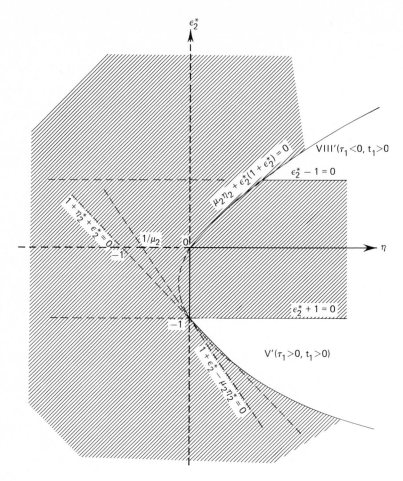

Fig. 4(b). $K > 0$, $\mu_2 < -1$.

elasticity of foreign import demand restricted to values algebraically less than minus one. This conclusion contrasts with a standard result of the theory of optimal tariffs and reflects the fact that a variation of the terms of trade affects not only foreign import demand but also the rate of return on foreign investment. Thus if sufficient additional investment income is generated thereby, it will pay the home country to push the terms of trade below the point of zero marginal export income.

That an optimal tariff or tax may be negative is paradoxical. To help dispel the paradox, consider the following line of thought, valid for the case of capital

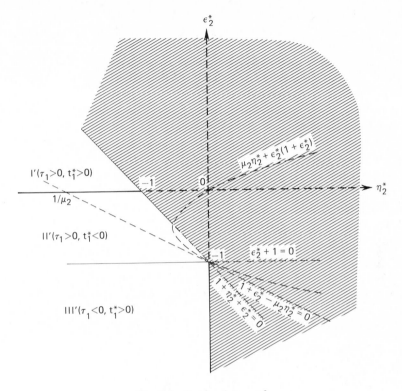

Fig. 4(c). $K < 0$, $-1 < \mu_2 < 0$.

export. When it parts with a unit of capital, the home country sacrifices production valued in terms of the first commodity at r_1. This loss must be weighed against the additional goods made available by the foreign country after its economy has adjusted to the increment of capital. The net addition to the flow of goods available to the home country is, in terms of the first commodity, $-[(\partial E_1^*/\partial K) + p(\partial E_2^*/\partial K) + r_1]$ or, since net foreign real income, and therefore foreign demand, is unaffected by the capital movement, $(\partial X_1^*/\partial K) + p(\partial X_2^*/\partial K) - r_1$. Now the rate of return abroad is $r_1^* = (\partial X_1^*/\partial K) + p^*(\partial X_2^*/\partial K)$. Hence the net social return on the marginal investment is $[r_1^* - r_1 + (p - p^*)(\partial X_2^*/\partial K)]$. In an optimum this expression must equal zero. It follows that the optimal tax, t_1, is positive if the home country places a lower valuation on the commodity the foreign production of which has increased than does the foreign country. This occurs if the home country's export good is capital-intensive abroad (so that $\partial X_2^*/\partial K > 0$) and a tariff is levied (so that $p < p^*$): region I' of fig. 4(a) and region V' of fig. 4(b); or if the

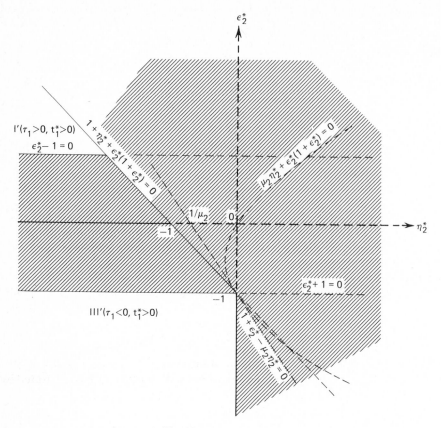

Fig. 4(d). $K < 0$, $\mu_2 < -1$.

export good is labour-intensive abroad (so that $\partial X_2^* / \partial K < 0$) and an export subsidy is paid (so that $p > p^*$): region III' of fig. 4(a) and region VIII' of fig. 4(b). Obversely, a subsidy on foreign earnings is optimal if the home country places a higher valuation on the commodity the foreign production of which has increased than does the foreign country. This occurs if the export good is labour-intensive abroad and an import duty is levied: region II' of fig. 4(a).

A similar line of thought may be developed for the case of capital import. It remains true than in an optimum $[r_1^* - r_1 + (p - p^*)(\partial X_2^* / \partial K)]$ must vanish. Hence the optimal tax t_1^* must be positive if the home country places a lower valuation on the commodity the foreign production of which has increased than does the foreign country. This occurs if the home country's export good is labour-intensive abroad and a tariff is levied (so that $p < p^*$): region I' of figs.

4(c) and 4(d); or if the home country's export good is capital-intensive abroad and an export subsidy is paid: region III' of figs. 4(c) and 4(d). Obversely, a subsidy on foreign earnings is optimal if the home country places a lower valuation on the commodity the foreign production of which has decreased than does the foreign country. This occurs if the home country's export good is capital-intensive abroad and a tariff is levied: region II' of fig 4(c).

The operation of an optimal system of tariffs and taxes may leave the Treasury out of pocket. Whether the home country is on balance a creditor or on balance a debtor, net revenue is

$$p^*E_2^*(1+\epsilon_2^*)(1+\epsilon_2^*+\mu_2)/\eta_2^*. \tag{19}$$

From figs. 4(a)–(d) it is clear that, in an optimum, $-p^*E_2^*/\eta_2^*$ is positive. Hence, if ϵ_2^* lies between -1 and $-(1+\mu_2)$, expression (19) is negative; otherwise, it is positive. When the home country is a net creditor and continues to export (fig. 4(a)), net revenue is necessarily positive if $\epsilon_2^* > 0$, that is, if the second commodity is relatively capital-intensive abroad; it is a necessary, but not sufficient, condition of negative net revenue that the second commodity be relatively labour-intensive abroad. When the home country is a net debtor and continues to import (fig. 4(c)), net revenue is necessarily positive if $\epsilon_2^* > 0$, that is, if the second commodity is relatively labour-intensive abroad; it is a necessary, but not sufficient, condition of negative net revenue that the second commodity be relatively *capital*-intensive abroad. In other cases (illustrated by figs. 4(b) and 4(d)) no statements of comparable simplicity seem possible.

So far we have confined our attention to interior optima. Specifically, we have put aside both the possibility that it is optimal for the home country to specialize completely and the possibility that the optimal K assumes one or other of the two extreme values determined by national capital endowments.

Fortunately our conclusions, with minor modifications, cover also the possibility of complete home specialization. For then $X_1 = 0$ and the welfare index becomes

$$U\{0 + p^*E_2^*(p^*, K) + r^*(p^*, K)K ; \phi(0, K) - E_2^*(p^*, K)\},$$

a function of two parameters only, p^* and K. The first-order conditions are identical with those contained in eqs. (2b) and (2c), hence the optimal tariff and tax are as set out in eqs. (3), (6) and (8). Eq. (2a) no longer holds, and must be replaced by a suitable inequality.

Similarly, if the optimal K lies at its upper limit, set by the home country's capital endowment, eq. (2c), and therefore eq. (6) must be replaced by an inequality. Eq. (6), for example, becomes

$$t_1 \geq \epsilon_2^*(1 + \epsilon_2^*)/\mu_2 \eta_2^*. \tag{6'}$$

If, on the other hand, K lies at its lower limit, set by the foreign country's capital endowment, eq. (8) becomes

$$t_1^* \geq \epsilon_2^*(1 + \epsilon_2^*)/[\mu_2 \eta_2^* + \epsilon_2^*(1 + \epsilon_2^*)]. \tag{8'}$$

It has been assumed also that the home country exports the second commodity. The analysis of the alternative possibility is, however, symmetrical with that already provided. All results may be obtained by simply permuting the subscripts in eqs. (3), (6) and (8).

4. Solution of the problem: complete foreign specialization

The discussion of section 3 was limited to the case of incomplete foreign specialization. The same general approach can be applied to the classical case in which the foreign country produces one commodity only. The cases differ, however, in two important respects. In the first place, the return on foreign investment, r_1^*, now depends on the level of net indebtedness, K, but not on the terms of trade, p^*; specifically $\partial r_1^*/\partial p^* = \partial X_1^*/\partial K = \epsilon_2^* = 0$, and $\partial r_1^*/\partial K < 0$. Second, it is no longer true that net foreign real income is, for given terms of trade, invariant under changes in K. Thus, if the foreign country is completely specialized in the production of the first commodity, we have

$$\frac{\partial E_2^*}{\partial K} = \frac{\partial D_2^*}{\partial K} = \frac{\partial D_2^*}{\partial I_1^*} \frac{\partial I_1^*}{\partial K} = \frac{m_2^*}{p^*}\left(-K\frac{\partial r_1^*}{\partial K}\right) = -\frac{m_2^*}{p^*} r_1^* \delta_1,$$

where $\delta_1 \equiv (K/r_1^*)(\partial r_1^*/\partial K)$ is the elasticity of the foreign rate of return with respect to foreign investment, and I_1^* is the income of the foreign country in terms of the first commodity.

In view of these differences, eq. (3) must be replaced by

$$\tau_1 = -1/(1 + \eta_2^*), \tag{3'}$$

eq. (2c) becomes

$$U_2/U_1 = r_1^*(1 + \delta_1 m_1^*)/[(r_1/p) - (m_2^* r_1^* \delta_1/p^*)], \tag{2c}$$

eq. (5) is replaced by

$$r_1 = r_1^*\{1 + \delta_1[m_1^* + m_2^*(1 + \eta_2^*)/\eta_2^*]\}, \tag{5'}$$

and eq. (6) becomes

$$t_1 = -\delta_1[m_1^* + m_2^*(1 + \eta_2^*)/\eta_2^*]. \tag{6''}$$

Finally, (8) is replaced by

$$t_1^* = \frac{\delta_1[m_1^* + m_2^*(1 + \eta_2^*)/\eta_2^*]}{1 + \delta_1[m_1^* + m_2^*(1 + \eta_2^*)/\eta_2^*]}. \tag{8''}$$

Eqs. (6'') and (8'') may be reached also by a line of reasoning similar to that pursued on pp. 205–209.

It is easily shown that in the present case, with complete specialization abroad, both the optimal tariff and the optimal tax must be positive. That is, it never pays to subsidize imports or exports, nor does it pay to subsidize borrowing or lending. To see that the optimal tariff must be positive, note first that if the foreign country is completely specialized, eq. (13) reduces to

$$\partial y_1^*/\partial p^* = -E_2^*,$$

and that (14) therefore reduces to

$$\eta_2^* = \bar{\eta}_2^* - m_2^* < 0; \tag{20}$$

eq. (16), on the other hand, reduces to

$$-1 < \tau_1 = -1/(1 + \eta_2^*). \tag{21}$$

From eqs. (20) and (21) it follows that $\eta_2^* < -1$.

To see that the optimal tax must be positive one need only note that $(1 + \eta_2^*)/\eta_2^* = 1/(1 + \tau_1) = p/p^* > 0$ and that $\delta_1 \gtrless 0$ as $K \lessgtr 0$.

That both the optimal tariff and the optimal tax must be positive is of considerable intrinsic interest for, at least since Ricardo, the case of complete specialization has possessed a special fascination for trade theorists. But the result is also interesting for the light it throws on some of our earlier conclusions; in particular, it helps us to see why a negative tax may be optimal when the foreign country produces something of both commodities. If the foreign country is completely specialized there is a direct link between K and r_1^*. An increase in the amount lent abroad inevitably depresses the rate of return, hence it can never pay to subsidize foreign lending. When foreign specialization is incomplete, however, the direct link is broken, and with that link goes the inevitability that the tax is positive. The several cases described in section 3 become possible.

5. Brief comments on the results

It has been shown how one may solve for the optimal K, p^* and X_1, and for the associated τ's and t's. It should be noted that the solutions depend on η_2^*, the elasticity of foreign import demand. Putting aside the special constant-elasticity case, however, the value of η_2^* depends on the price at which it is calculated. That in turn depends on the choice of U-function. Thus, the optimal rates of duty and tax vary with the specification of U. That the optimal tariff is in this sense not unique is well known; cf. Scitovsky (1941) and Graaff (1957, pp. 136, 137); we now see that the same is true of the optimal tax on foreign earnings.

Equations (3), (6) and (8) contain the term ϵ_2^*, based on $\partial X_2^*/\partial K$, both of which are unfamiliar. They are, however, easy to translate into parameters of production functions. This is done in appendix A.

The discussion has run in terms of comparative stationary states. Under stationary conditions the optimal tariff and tax are themselves stationary. It should be possible, however, to generalize the analysis to accommodate steadily growing or declining resource endowments and steadily improving technologies. If the assumptions of this paper are retained, the results are bound to be messy. If, however, the capital good is identified with one of the consumer goods – a characteristic simplification of modern growth theories – a fairly elegant analysis should be possible[9].

It has been assumed that in its choice of tariff and tax rate the policy-making country is constrained only by considerations of demand and technology. One can imagine, however, a second-best situation in which the policy-making country is further constrained by, for example, a commitment to free trade or to maximum rates of duty or by an international tax convention. The interesting questions then concern the extent to which a country can achieve its over-all commercial investment objectives with only the commercial (or investment) lever to manipulate or, more generally, with constraints on the extent to which the levers can be manipulated. The analysis can be extended to cope with such questions, though it might prove convenient to rewrite the U-function in terms of the alternative parameters X_1, τ_1, and t_1 (or t_1^*).

There are in our model not two but three traded goods, two consumption goods and the services of capital, and the optimal tax can be considered as an optimal tariff on trade in capital services. It is well known that if there are three traded consumption goods, it may pay to subsidize trade in one of them (Graaff,

---

[9] A first step in this direction has been taken by Negishi (1965).

1957). It now appears that the result can be extended by allowing one of the traded goods to be intermediate. On the other hand, it appears that the possibility of negative net revenue carries over to the case in which all traded goods are consumer goods.

If more than two countries are recognized the analysis becomes much more complicated, for then the pursuit of an optimum may require discrimination among the home country's trading partners. Thus, the optimal rate of duty on any particular good will depend on the amount invested in the supplying country; and the optimal tax on earnings derived from a particular foreign country will depend on the amount of trade carried on with that country and on the ϵ_i^* value of that country.

Finally, the reader is reminded of the long list of assumptions contained in section 1, in particular of the assumptions of full employment and perfect competition. He might try his hand at a Keynesian (or neo-Mercantilist) reworking of the paper, or he might ask himself how many of our conclusions would be helpful to an oil sheik in his negotiations with the larger oil companies.

Appendix A

In deriving eq. (2b) use was made of the dual relationship $\partial r_1^*/\partial p^* = \partial X_2^*/\partial K$. This appendix contains a proof of that equality. Actually, the relationship was stated and proved some years ago by Samuelson (1953, p. 10). But the proof was barely sketched and is, in any case, embedded in an especially difficult article. The following straightforward proof may therefore be of interest.

If the foreign country is completely specialized in the production of its export commodity, the proof is trivial. For then, $\partial X_2^*/\partial K = 0$ and, since $r_1^* = \partial X_1^*/\partial K$, $\partial r_1^*/\partial p^* = 0$. In what follows, it will be assumed that the foreign country produces something of both commodities.

Given constant returns to scale, the two foreign production relationships may be expressed as

$$X_i^* = k_i f_i(\rho_i), \qquad i = 1, 2, \tag{A1}$$

where X_i^* is the output of the ith commodity, k_i is the amount of capital employed in the ith industry, and ρ_i is the labour capital ratio in the ith industry. In a competitive equilibrium the following marginal equalities hold:

$$f_1' - p^* f_2' = 0, \qquad r_1^* = (f_1 - \rho_1 f_1') = p^*(f_2 - \rho_2 f_2'). \tag{A2}$$

$f'_i \equiv df_i/d\rho_i$ is the marginal productivity of labour in the ith industry; and $(f_i - \rho_i f'_i)$ is the marginal productivity of capital in the ith industry. Finally, we have two 'full employment' conditions:

$$k_1 + k_2 = K + \text{const.}, \qquad k_1\rho_1 + k_2\rho_2 = \text{const.} \tag{A3}$$

Treating K and p^* as parameters, and differentiating the entire system (A1–A3) with respect to K, we obtain

$$\partial X_2^*/\partial K = -\rho_1 f_2/(\rho_2 - \rho_1). \qquad\qquad \text{QED}$$

By similar reasoning,

$$\partial r_2^*/\partial(1/p^*) = \partial X_2^*/\partial K,$$

where r_2^* is the foreign marginal product of capital in terms of the second commodity.

Appendix B: international capital movements and the the theory of tariffs and trade: comment*

The post-Heckscher–Ohlin development of the theory of trade between two countries has relied heavily on the assumption that factors of production are not themselves internationally mobile. It is only in very recent years that efforts have been made to weaken this assumption. Professor Jones' recent article[10] contains the most complete break with the traditions of the subject and the most thorough exposition of the new theory.

Among the more striking of Jones' conclusions is the statement that in a tariff- or tax-ridden world it is either logically impossible or extremely unlikely that both countries will be incompletely specialized in production. It is always difficult to come to grips, in the context of pure theory, with statements about likelihood. And, in any case, it is not quite clear whether Jones intends to restrict his proposition to tariff- or tax-*optima*. In what follows, therefore, we shall simply state and prove a proposition which seems interesting in itself, without attempting to relate it to Jones' statement.

Suppose that technology differs from country to country. Then: if, *when trade is tariff-free and foreign earnings tax-free, international price equilibrium is unique and involves the incomplete specialization of both countries, the same*

* *Quarterly Journal of Economics*, 83 (Aug. 1969), 524–528, with K. Inada.
[10] Jones (1967). Also relevant are Mundell (1957), Kemp (1966), and Kemp (1968).

will be true after the imposition of a tariff or a tax provided the tariff and tax are sufficiently small.

In proving this proposition we shall assume that if the home country exports anything it exports the second commodity, and that if the foreign country exports anything it exports the first commodity. To ease the notational problem it will be assumed that the home country is a net creditor. The proof can be modified, however, to accommodate the alternative possibility. Let p represent the home price of the second commodity in terms of the first and r_i the home rate of return to capital in terms of the ith commodity. The home import duty is levied at the rate of $100\tau\%$ and the home tax on foreign earnings at the rate $100t\%$, with τ and t non-negative. Asterisks relate the variables to the foreign country, so that p^* is the world terms of trade, etc.

If trade is tariff-free and if foreign earnings are tax-free, $p = p^*$ and $r_1 = r_1^*$. If a tariff or a tax is imposed, however, we must write

$$(1+\tau)p = p^*$$

and[11]

$$(1+\tau)r_1 = (1-t)r_1^*$$

or

$$\log(1+\tau) + \log p = \log p^* \tag{B1}$$

and

$$\log(1+\tau) + \log r_1 = \log(1-t) + \log r_1^*. \tag{B2}$$

Suppose first that the relative factor intensities of the two industries differ from one country to the other and that in an initial tax- and tariff-free equilibrium both countries are incompletely specialized. Let the price ratios prevailing in this initial equilibrium be $p^0 = p = p^* = (p^*)^0$. If this equilibrium is disturbed by the imposition of a sufficiently small tax and tariff it is possible to find a terms of trade $p^* = (p^*)'$ and a home price ratio $p = p' = (p^*)'/(1+\tau)$ such that eqs. (B1) and (B2) are satisfied (see fig. B1).

---

[11] Foreign earnings per unit of capital are, in money terms, $p_1^*(1-t)r_1^*$; in terms of the first commodity, they are $p_1^*(1-t)r_1^*/p_1 = (1-t)r_1^*/(1+\tau)$. In equilibrium, this expression must be equal to r_1. In Jones' formulation there is no counterpart to eq. (2); his condition is $r_1 = (1-t)r_1^*$. Jones' condition is the correct one if it is supposed that foreign earnings are repatriated in kind and free of duty; or if it is supposed that, in spite of its creditor status, the home country exports something of the second commodity and taxes its exports. The difference in formulation is, in the present context, inessential.

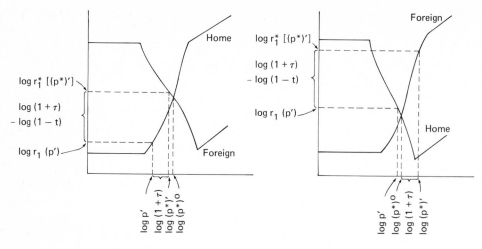

Fig. B1(a).   Fig. B1(b).

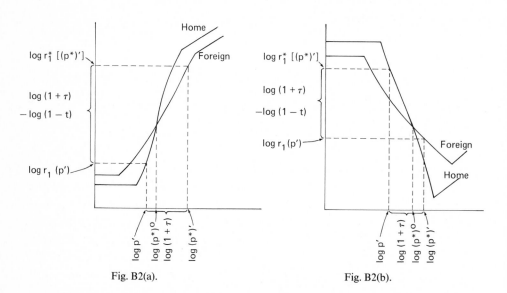

Fig. B2(a).   Fig. B2(b).

Figure B2 illustrates the alternative possibility, that the relative factor intensities of the two industries are the same everywhere.

It may be objected that world demand and supply may not be equated at $(p*)'$. To overcome this objection it is necessary to examine in more detail the special properties of the model. It should be noted in particular that when both countries are incompletely specialized the international allocation of capital is, at any given terms of trade, indeterminate: any sufficiently small change in the allocation will leave marginal products (and therefore rates of return) unchanged in both countries, hence any one of an infinity of allocations would suit the owners of capital equally well. On the other hand, changes in the allocation of capital result in changes in the world excess demand for each commodity. Hence, provided the tax and tariffs are sufficiently small, there will exist an allocation which will bring the commodity markets into equilibrium at the terms of trade $(p*)'$. In this argument we have twice required that τ and t be sufficiently small. It must be understood therefore that τ and t lie in the intersection of the two (τ, t)-sets defined by these requirements.

The proof has relied on an interesting recursive property of the model. Thus, eqs. (B1) and (B2), which reflect technological conditions only, determine the terms of trade $p*$. Given the terms of trade, we may then obtain the international allocation of capital K from the conditions of equilibrium in the commodity markets. This property disappears if one or both countries are completely specialized in production, for in that case marginal factor productivities are not independent of K.

References

Baldwin, R. E. (1952), The new welfare economics and gains in international trade, *Quarterly Journal of Economics*, 66, Feb., 91–101.

Balogh, T. and P. P. Streeten (1960), Domestic versus foreign investment, *Bulletin Oxford University Institute of Statistics*, 22, Aug., 213–224. Revised version in Streeten, P. (1961), *Economic Integration*, Leyden, ch. 4.

Bickerdike, C. F. (1906), The theory of incipient taxes, *Economic Journal*, 16, Dec., 529–535.

Bickerdike, C. F. (1907), review of A. C. Pigou, *Preferential and Protective Import Duties*, 27, March, 98–102.

Cairncross, A. K. (1953), *Home and Foreign Investment 1807–1913*, Cambridge, ch. 9. Reprinted from *Review of Economic Studies*, 3 (Oct. 1935), 67–78.

Edgeworth, F. Y. (1925), *Papers Relating to Political Economy*, Vol. 2, London.

Graaff, J. de V. (1957), *Theoretical Welfare Economics*, Cambridge.

Iversen, C. (1936), *Aspects of the Theory of International Capital Movements*, London.

Jasay, A. E. (1960), The social choice between home and overseas investment, *Economic Journal*, 70, March, 105–113.

Kemp, M. C. (1962a), Foreign Investment and the national advantage, *Economic Record*, 38, March, 56–62.

Kemp, M. C. (1962b), The benefits and cost of private investment from abroad: comment, *Economic Record*, 38, March, 108–110.

Kemp, M. C. (1964), *The Pure Theory of International Trade*, Englewood Cliffs.

Kemp, M. C. (1965), A guide to Negishi, *Economic Record*, 41, Dec., 632–633.

Kemp, M. C. (1966), The gain from international trade and investment: a neo-Heckscher–Ohlin approach, *American Economic Review*, 56, Sept., 788–809.

Kemp, M. C. (1968), A partial theoretical solution of the problems of the incidence of import duties, in: Wolfe, J. N. (ed.), *Value, Capital and Growth. Essays in Honour of Sir John Hicks*, Edinburgh University Press, Edinburgh, 257–273.

Jones R. W. (1967), International capital movements and the theory of tariffs and trade, *Quarterly Journal of Economics*, 81, Feb., 1–38.

Keynes, J. M. (1924), Foreign investment and the national advantage, *The Nation and Athenaeum* 35, 9 Aug., 584–587.

Keynes, J. M. (1925), Some tests for loans to foreign and colonial governments, *The Nation and Athenaeum*, 35, 17 Jan., 564–565.

Keynes, J. M. (1930), *Treatise on Money*, Vol. 1, London, 343–346.

Lerner, A. P. (1936), The symmetry between import and export taxes, *Economica*, n.s., 3, Aug., 306–313.

MacDougall, G. D. A. (1960), The benefits and costs of private investment from abroad: a theoretical approach, *Economic Record*, 36, March, 13–35. Reprinted in *Bulletin Oxford University Institute of Statistics*, 22, Aug., 187–212.

Mill, J. S. (1848), *Essays on Some Unsettled Questions of Political Economy*, London.

Mill, J. S. (1909), *Principles of Political Economy* (ed. Sir W. J. Ashley), London.

Mundell, R. A. (1957), International trade and factor mobility, *American Economic Review*, 67, June, 321–337.

Negishi, T. (1965), Foreign investment and the long-run national advantage, *Economic Record*, 41, Dec., 628–632.

Nurske, R. (1954), The problem of international investment today in the light of nineteenth-century experience, *Economic Journal*, 64, Dec., 744–758.

Pearce, I. F. and D. C. Rowan (1966), A framework for research into the real effects of international capital movements, in: Tullio Bagiotti, ed., *Essays in Honour of Marco Fanno*, pp. 505–535, Padua.

Robbins, R. (1958) *Robert Torrens and the Evolution of Classical Economics*, London.

Rybczyski, T. N. (1955), Factor endowments and relative commodity prices, Economica, n.s. 22, Nov., 336–341.

Samuelson, P. A. (1953), Prices of factors and goods in general equilibrium, *Review of Economic Studies*, 21, Oct., 1–20.

Samuelson, P. A. (1956), Social indifference curves, *Quarterly Journal of Economics*, 70, Feb., 1–22.

Samuelson, P. A. (1962), The gains from international trade once again, *Economic Journal*, 72, Dec., 820–829.

Schonfield, A. (1959), *British Economic Policy Since the War*, rev. ed., London.

Scitovsky, T. (1941), A reconsideration of the theory of tariffs, *Review of Economic Studies*, 9, Summer, 89–110. Reprinted in Ellis, H. S. and L. A. Metzler (eds.), *Readings in the Theory of International Trade* (1949), Philadelphia, 359–389.

Sidgwick, H. (1887), *The Principles of Political Economy*, 2nd ed., London.

Simpson, P. B. (1962), Foreign investment and the national economic advantage: a theoretical analysis, in: Mikesell, R. F. (ed.), *US Private Investment Abroad*, Eugene, Oregon, ch. 18.

Singer, H. W. (1950), The distribution of gains between investing and borrowing countries, *American Economic Review, Proceedings*, 40, May, 473–485.

Smith, A. (1776), *An Inquiry into the Nature and Causes of the Wealth of Nations*, London.

Torrens, R. (1821), *An Essay on the Production of Wealth*, London.

Torrens, R. (1844), *The Budget. On Commercial and Colonial Policy*, London.

Chapter 17

LEARNING BY DOING: FORMAL TESTS FOR INTERVENTION IN AN OPEN ECONOMY*

1. Introduction

Some ten years ago I offered a brief examination of the Mill–Bastable infant-industry dogma (Kemp, 1964)[1]. Drawing a sharp distinction between the benefits of learning which are confined to the firm which is doing, and the benefits of learning which accrue to other firms, that is, between dynamic internal and dynamic external economies of production, I argued that, under competitive conditions with complete knowledge by producers, dynamic internal economies could not serve to justify the protection of infant firms. I admitted that infants might lack the foresight and means to wait out the period of learning and, on social grounds, may deserve protection. However, I noted that the case for protection is then based not on dynamic internal economies but on the presence of uncertainty and the imperfection of capital markets.

During the intervening years this proposition has had its ups and downs. In particular, it has been denied by Negishi (1968, 1972) and Ohyama (1972), and upheld by Long (1975).

In this note I propose to look again at the policy implications of dynamic internal economies without, however, burdening myself with the more special assumptions which pervade the infant-industry literature. In the context of a two-period model, I develop two general tests which may be applied to any proposal for intervention. The first test if failed disqualifies the proposal; the

* *Keio Economic Studies*, 11 (1) (Oct. 1974), 1–7. This note has its origin in talks given at the Delhi School of Economics in August 1967 and at the University of Essex in the spring of 1968. In its preparation I have been greatly influenced by the papers of Negishi (1968) and Long (1975). For most useful comments I am indebted to Jagdish Bhagwati (in Delhi) and to Henry Y. Wan, Jr., Geoffrey Fishburn, Ngo Van Long and Michihiro Ohyama.
[1] The treatment in Kemp (1964) is a refined version of that in Kemp (1960).

second test if passed justifies intervention. It is shown that the first test cannot be met if the policy-making country applies a system of optimal tariffs and if its producers have complete knowledge and are not myopic. The relevance of the analysis to economies with privately owned wasting resources is noted.

2. The model

Consider a country (the 'home' country) which potentially produces, consumes and trades (freely, with the rest of the world) n commodities. Time is divided into two periods, the present and the future. Symbols with the subscript 1 relate to the present, those with the subscript 2 to the future. Thus

c_1 = present consumption vector of the home country;

e_1 = present endowment vector of the home country;

y_1 = present net production vector of the home country, with the ith element positive, negative or zero as the ith commodity is on balance an output, an input or neither;

m_1 = present vector of net home imports with the ith element positive or zero as the ith commodity is on balance imported, exported or neither;

p_1 = vector of present consumers' prices in the home country, equal to producers' gross prices (that is, gross of tax and subsidy), equal to world prices in the case of freely traded goods;

Y_1 = set of feasible present production vectors in the home country.

The symbols c_2, e_2, y_2, m_2, p_2, Y_2 are defined analogously. It is possible that some elements of y_i are inherently non-positive and that some elements of m_i are inherently zero ($i = 1, 2$). For example, given the home country's technology it may not be feasible to produce certain commodities in positive amounts, and some commodities may be non-tradeable.

In each period non-increasing returns prevail, so that the net production possibility sets Y_i are convex; in addition they are assumed to be closed. Since there are no externalities of production it is unnecessary to distinguish individual firms. To give expression to the possibility of learning, the set of future production possibilities is supposed to be conditional upon the present net output vector and is therefore written $Y_2(y_1)$. It follows that the set of feasible production vectors $\{(y_1, y_2): y_1 \in Y_1, y_2 \in Y_2(y_1)\}$ need not be convex.

Individual preferences are strictly convex[2]. Moreover, the distribution of income is so controlled that if interference with the allocation of resources leaves one individual better off (respectively, worse off) then it leaves no

---

[2] For the necessary conditions derived in section 3 even convexity can be dispensed with.

individual worse off (better off). It follows that the community behaves like a single individual with strictly convex preferences. The set $C(c_1, c_2)$ contains those two-period consumption vectors which are preferred to the given vector (c_1, c_2). The set $\bar{C}(c_1, c_2)$ contains those two-period consumption vectors which are preferred to or indifferent to (c_1, c_2).

Suppose that in an initial free trade tax-free competitive equilibrium

$$c_i = c^0_i, \quad e_i = e^0_i, \quad y_i = y^0_i, \quad m_i = m^0_i, \quad p_i = p^0_i,$$
$$i = 1, 2. \tag{1}$$

Consider now any alternative feasible pattern of production which, we suppose, can be imposed on the economy by some mixture of taxes and subsidies on production. We wish to rank the associated competitive equilibrium against the initial equilibrium. Quantities associated with the new equilibrium will be indicated by primes. For example, the new pattern of production is denoted by (y'_1, y'_2), with $y'_1 \in Y_1$ and $y'_2 \in Y_2(y'_1)$.

3. The tests

3.1. A necessary condition

We begin by developing a condition which must be satisfied if the substitution of (y'_1, y'_2) for (y^0_1, y^0_2) is to be judged desirable. Now if the change is desirable, $(c'_1, c'_2) \in C(c^0_1, c^0_2)$ and $\sum p^0_i c'_i > \sum p^0_i c^0_i$. Noting that $c_i = y_i + e_i + m_i$ and that $e'_i = e^0_i$, this inequality may be written

$$\sum p^0_i(y'_i - y^0_i) + \sum p^0_i(m'_i - m^0_i) > 0. \tag{2a}$$

That is, interpreting m^0_i and m'_i as input–output vectors of a special kind, if the change in allocation is desirable then it is profitable at the initial prices. Since $\sum p^0_i y^0_i \geq 0$ (non-negative profits in a competitive equilibrium) and since $\sum p^0_i m^0_i = 0$ (the balance of payments is zero), (2a) reduces to

$$\sum p^0_i y'_i + \sum p^0_i m'_i > \sum p^0_i y^0_i \geq 0. \tag{2b}$$

That is, if the change in allocation is desirable then the new allocation is profitable at the old prices. Of course, profitability at the old prices does not imply profitability at the new.

In the limiting small-country case the prices of tradeable goods (but not necessarily of non-tradeable goods) are independent of the allocation of resources in the home country. In another limiting case, $m'_i = 0$ ($i = 1, 2$), that

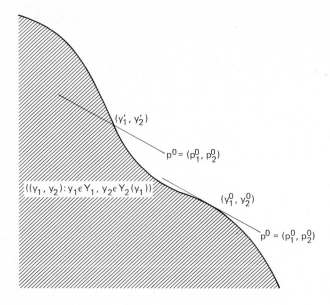

(y'_1, y'_2)

$p^0 = (p^0_1, p^0_2)$

$((y_1, y_2): y_1 \epsilon Y_1, y_2 \epsilon Y_2(y_1))$

(y^0_1, y^0_2)

$p^0 = (p^0_1, p^0_2)$

Fig. 1.

is, the home economy is closed after intervention (but not necessarily before intervention). In each case $\sum p^0_i m'_i = 0$ and (2b) reduces to

$$\sum p^0_i y'_i > \sum p^0_i y'_i \geqq 0. \tag{2c}$$

That is, if the new consumption vector is preferred to the old then the new production vector is profitable at the old prices.

Suppose that producers have complete knowledge and are not myopic. Then at the old prices (y^0_1, y^0_2) is profit-maximizing and

$$\sum p^0_i y^0_i \geqq \sum p^0_i y'_i. \tag{3}$$

It follows that, for a small country or for one which after intervention would be autarkic, inequality (2c) can never be satisfied and intervention never justified[3].

---

[3] Ohyama (1972, pp. 63–64) has argued that even in small countries (with non-myopic businessmen) intervention may be justified. However, there appears to be a slip in his reasoning. The inequality at the bottom of p. 63 should be

$$p''(z'' - z') + p''(a'' - a') \geqq -p''(w'' - w').$$

The first term on the left may be positive since p'' is the vector of domestic consumers' prices which by assumption differs from the vector of prices received by producers in the infant industry. I am grateful to Professor Ohyama for his assistance in tracking down the slip.

For a large open economy it is still possible that (2a) may be satisfied in spite of (3). However, this could be the case only if the home country had failed to take advantage (by tariffs on trade) of its monopoly–monopsony power in trade. The imposition of production taxes and subsidies might then be justified on second-best grounds.

The assumption that producers have complete knowledge and are not myopic is conventional in general economic theory, and also in the more rigorous treatments of the infant-industry dogma. However, in a context of learning by doing, where the hand teaches the brain and producers are of limited imagination, the assumption is not altogether plausible. Suppose then that producers are only local maximizers or are unaware that Y_2 depends on y_1. In the future producers must adjust to unforeseen changes in their production set Y_2. Present expectations of future spot prices will be falsified and any futures contracts concluded in the present will prove to be suboptimal. It follows that one can no longer infer from $(c_1', c_2') \in C(c_1^0, c_2^0)$ that $\sum p_i^0 c_i' > \sum p_i^0 c_i^0$, so that (2a) ceases to be a necessary condition of intervention and intervention cannot be ruled out even in a small or autarkic country.

3.2. A sufficient condition

Let us suppose that the necessary condition (2a) is either satisfied or irrelevant. That is, our attention is for the time being restricted to an economy which either is large, free-trading and non-autarkic, or is guided by producers who are myopic or unaware of the learning process, or both.

For $(c_1^0, c_2^0) \notin \bar{C}(c_1', c_2')$ it suffices that $\sum p_i' c_i' > \sum p_i' c_i^0$ so that, following the reasoning behind (2a),

$$\sum p_i'(y_i' - y_i^0) + \sum p_i'(m_i' - m_i^0) > 0. \tag{4a}$$

That is, if the change in allocation is profitable at the new prices it is desirable. Alternatively, we may note that under free trade $\sum p_i'(m_i' - m_i^0)$ is positive or negative as the home country's terms of trade improve or deteriorate as a result of the change, and say that the change is desirable if the additional loss on pure production, calculated at the new prices, is more than offset by the gains from improved terms of trade. Since $\sum p_i' m_i' = 0$ (the balance of payments is zero), (4a) reduces to

$$\sum p_i'(y_i' - y_i^0) - \sum p_i' m_i^0 > 0. \tag{4b}$$

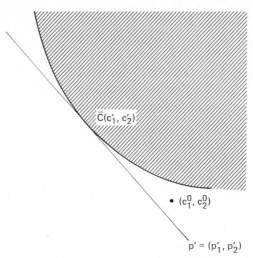

Fig. 2.

Of course, (4a) and (4b) are sufficient but (in general) not necessary. Fig. 2 suggests the possibility that the change is desirable but (4a) and (4b) not satisfied.

In the limiting small-country case, $p'_i = p^0_i$ for tradeable goods and (4b) reduces further to

$$\sum p'_i(y'_i - y^0_i) > 0. \tag{4c}$$

In that case intervention is desirable if the new production vector is less unprofitable than the old when evaluated at the new prices. The same inequality is obtained if in the *absence* of intervention the home country is self-sufficient, so that $m^0_i = 0$ $(i = 1, 2)$.

The conclusions reached so far are summarized in

Proposition 1. For intervention to be justified it is necessary that the inequality

$$\sum p^0_i y'_i + \sum p^0_i m'_i > \sum p^0_i y^0_i \geqq 0 \tag{2b}$$

be satisfied. This inequality cannot be satisfied if the home country applies a system of optimal tariffs and if its producers have complete knowledge and are not myopic. Intervention is justified if the inequality

$$\sum p'_i(y'_i - y^0_i) - \sum p'_i m^0_i > 0 \tag{4b}$$

is satisfied. If the home country is small or if after intervention it is self-

sufficient, (2b) *reduces to*

$$\sum p_i^0 y_i' > \sum p_i^0 y_i^0 \geqq 0 \qquad (2c)$$

and (4b) *reduces to*

$$\sum p_i'(y_i' - y_i^0) > 0. \qquad (4c)$$

Suppose that the home country is small but its producers myopic or ill-informed. They must be dislodged from (y_1^0, y_2^0) and driven to a preferred point (y_1', y_2'). Suppose that (y_1', y_2') is a global optimum for the community. Since the learning process is supposed to be internal to the firm, that point is also a global optimum for each firm. Suppose further that firms adjust without delay to price stimuli. Then the optimal tax-subsidy intervention is very short-lived, a series of mere flash signals following closely one upon the other, each designed to move producers one step closer to (y_1', y_2'). Strictly, under the extreme conditions assumed, intervention spanning any finite interval of time results in suboptimal transitional production. In fact, of course, adjustment is not instantaneous; the optimal policy takes time to do its work and itself varies with time, in a manner determined by the speed with which firms react to price stimuli and by the properties of the production set.

In the more recent literature on infant industries it has been customary to 'decompose' the production set into two sets one of which (that of the infant industry) incorporates learning, the other not[4]. Producers employing activities included in the latter set are neither taxed nor subsidized; the pattern of their production is the same whether or not the infant industry is supported, provided only that prices do not change. Evidently this technology is a special case of that described in section 2. Let α and β relate production sets to the non-learning and learning (infant) sectors, respectively. Then we may write

$$Y_1 = Y^\alpha + Y_1^\beta, \qquad Y_2 = Y^\alpha + Y_2^\beta(y_1^\beta).$$

The reader may develop the specialized forms of tests (2a) and (4a) without difficulty.

The argument of this section has been developed in terms of a model with just two periods, the present and the future. However, there is no difficulty in extending the argument to cover any number of periods. In general, the production set of the jth period is denoted by $Y_j(y_1, \ldots, y_{j-1})$ for $j > 1$; then the

---

[4] See, for example, Long (1975), Negishi (1968, 1972) and Ohyama (1972).

key formulae (2a) and (4a) carry over unchanged, with the summations running over the number of periods.

Finally, it may be noted that the description of the home country's technology offered in section 2 is sufficiently general to accommodate privately owned wasting resources not included in the endowment vectors e_i. The case for intervention in a context of wasting resources is identical (except for trivial matters of sign) with the case for intervention in a context of learning by doing.

4. Perspective

Attention has been focused on dynamic *internal* economies of production. It is well known that, when the economies are *external* to the firm, intervention generally is justified. It remains to note, however, that if the externalities can be 'internalized' by bargaining then the conclusions of section 3 apply. In particular, in a small country with knowledgeable and non-myopic producers intervention is never justified.

References

Kemp, M. C. (1960), The Mill–Bastable infant-industry dogma, *Journal of Political Economy*, 68, (1), Feb., 65–67.

Kemp, M. C. (1964), *The Pure Theory of International Trade*, Prentice-Hall, Englewood Cliffs, NJ, ch. 12.

Long, N. Van (1975), Infant industry protection, dynamic internal economies and the non-appropriability of consumers' and producers' surpluses, *Economic Record*, 51 (134), June, 256–262.

Negishi, T. (1968), Protection of the infant industry and dynamic internal economies, *Economic Record*, 44, (105), March, 56–67.

Negishi, T. (1972), *General Equilibrium Theory and International Trade*, North-Holland Publishing Company, Amsterdam, ch. 6.

Ohyama, M. (1972), Trade and welfare in general equilibrium, *Keio Economic Studies*, 9 (2), 37–73.

Chapter 18

INTERNATIONAL TRADE WITH A WASTING BUT POSSIBLY REPLENISHABLE RESOURCE*

1. Introduction

At the core of conventional trade theory is a simple two-by-two model of production. Each of two commodities is produced (non-jointly) with the aid of two primary or non-produced factors of production, say labour and a resource (land). The availability of the primary factors changes neither with the passage of time nor with use. There arises no problem of husbanding or conserving factors of production or, more generally, of optimally allocating them over time. Under conventional regularity assumptions it is optimal to fully exploit the factors at each instant; and this is achieved as a byproduct of competitive profit maximization.

In this paper we disturb the traditional model in one important respect. The resource is now treated as a wasting (but possibly replenishable) asset. For each country and possibly (depending on the nature of property rights in the resource) for each firm there arises the problem of husbanding the resource. Moreover, it is no longer certain that unhindered profit maximization results in rates of utilization and replenishment (and, therefore, net saving) which are socially optimal. As a corollary, it is not clear that unhindered profit maximization gives rise to the optimal patterns of specialization and trade or, indeed, to the optimal direction of trade.

Our objectives are easily stated. We first seek to characterize the socially optimal time profiles of resource utilization and replenishment and of production and trade. We then compare these profiles with their *laissez-faire* counterparts and infer the policies of optimal intervention under alternative assumptions about property rights and entrepreneurial foresight.

* *International Economic Review*, 16 (3) (Oct. 1975), 712–732, with Hideo Suzuki. We are indebted to Yasuo Uekawa for many useful comments.

We follow convention in recognizing two produced commodities. The second commodity is a raw material produced by labour and the resource. The first commodity is a consumption good; it is produced by labour and the raw material. In addition, labour may be devoted to the (artificial) replenishment of the resource. We also follow convention in recognizing two primary factors, labour and the resource. Labour is a true primary factor. The resource, on the other hand, may be artificially replenished as well as self-replenishing; it is therefore a hybrid, neither pure primary factor nor pure produced input.

We abstract throughout from conservation motives; resources are valued only as a means of obtaining consumption, directly by production or indirectly by trading the raw material. It seems to us that conservation motives, broadly defined in terms of social utility functions with the resource as an argument, should not be associated just with wasting assets. However, full allowance is made for the possibility of natural replenishment and for the possibility that production of the raw material becomes increasingly difficult as the resource approaches exhaustion. In many treatments of wasting assets these possibilities are ignored or glossed over.

Throughout the paper we confine our attention to small countries with no appreciable influence on world prices. For the time being, world prices are taken to be constant over time. (This assumption is relaxed in section 4.)

2. The optimal trajectory: non-replenishable resources[1]

For the time being we suppose that both natural and artificial replenishment of the resource are impossible; that is, we confine our attention to resources of which petroleum and other mineral deposits, rather than forests and fisheries, are the prototypes. This assumption permits a considerable simplification of the analysis and allows us to isolate those complications associated with replenishment. The possibility of replenishment will be considered in section 3.

The production function for the first or consumption good is $f(l, v)$, where l is the amount of labour employed in the first industry and v is the amount of raw material used. The function f is supposed to be homogeneous of degree one in l and v, quasi-concave and to satisfy the Inada conditions. Choosing labour units so that the constant total supply of labour is one, the output of the

---

[1] The problem treated in this section has been studied by Vousden (1974), but under the restrictions that replenishment is impossible and that productivity in production of the raw material is independent of the remaining stock of the resource. See also Kemp and Suzuki (ch. 24) and Long (1974).

second commodity (the raw material) is given by $(1-l)g(r)$, where g is an increasing, concave function of the stock of resource r, with $g(0) = 0$, $g'(0) = \infty$, $g(\infty) = \infty$ and $g'(\infty) = 0$. After choosing raw-material units appropriately, the time rate of resource depletion may be expressed as

$$-\dot{r} = (1-l)g(r), \qquad \dot{r} \equiv dr/dt.$$

The social problem is to find the optimal time paths of l and v subject to the above differential equation, to an initial value of the resource stock, say r_0, and to obvious non-negativity constraints on l and v. Optimality is to be judged, quite conventionally, in terms of the integral of discounted social utility u.[2] Thus we seek

$$\max_{l,v} \int_0^\infty e^{-\rho t} u(c)dt, \qquad \rho > 0, \tag{1}$$

subject to

$$\dot{r} = -(1-l)g(r), \tag{2}$$

$$0 \leq l \leq 1, \tag{3}$$

$$v \geq 0, \tag{4}$$

$$r(0) = r_0, \tag{5}$$

where ρ is the rate of discount and

$$c = f(l, v) + p[(1-l)g(r) - v] \tag{6}$$

is the level of total or per capita consumption (equal to production of the consumption good plus export of the raw material), and where p is the constant world price of the raw material in terms of the consumption good. The social utility function $u(c)$ is assumed to be bounded above, to possess a positive first derivative and to be strictly concave, and to satisfy

$$\lim_{c \to 0} u'(c) = \infty. \tag{7}$$

Among the conditions which an optimal path must satisfy we have[3]

[2] To justify such a criterion one is not driven to posit the immortality of individuals. It suffices to suppose that a constant population contains a balanced age distribution of individuals with the same finite lifetime, that the same instantaneous utility function is valid for each day of the life of a particular individual and for all individuals, and that the objective of policy is to maximize the integral of discounted social utilities where the social utility at any point of time is simply the finite sum of individual utilities at that point of time.

[3] See, for example, Hadley and Kemp (1971, theorem 4.3.1).

$$\dot{r} = -(1-l)g(r), \tag{8}$$

$$\dot{\mu} = \rho\mu - [pu'(c) - \mu](1-l)g'(r), \tag{9}$$

$$u'(c)(\partial/\partial l)f(l, v) - [pu'(c) - \mu]g(r) \begin{cases} \geq 0 & \text{if } l = 1, \\ = 0 & \text{if } 0 < l < 1, \\ \leq 0 & \text{if } l = 0, \end{cases} \tag{10}$$

$$u'(c)[(\partial/\partial v)f(l, v) - p] \begin{cases} = 0 & \text{if } v > 0, \\ \leq 0 & \text{if } v = 0, \end{cases} \tag{11}$$

$$\lim_{t \to \infty} e^{-\rho t} \mu r = 0. \tag{12}$$

The multiplier $\mu(t)$ may be interpreted as the current social valuation of the resource in terms of utility and will play an important role in our later discussion of optimal intervention (section 4).

From the information contained in (7)–(12) we seek to construct a (μ, r)-phase diagram. We begin by dividing the (μ, r) plane into regions of complete and incomplete specialization. From the homogeneity of $f(l, v)$,

$$l(\partial f/\partial l) = f - v(\partial f/\partial v). \tag{13}$$

If only the first good is produced, after application of (11) and the fact that the total labour force is one (13) reduces to

$$\partial f/\partial l = f - pv. \tag{14}$$

That is, when only the first good is produced, $\partial f/\partial l$ is equal to total output. Let us write $w \equiv \partial f/\partial l$. Then we may define

$$\mu_1(r) = \inf\left\{\mu : \frac{\partial f}{\partial l} \geq \left(p - \frac{\mu}{u'(w)}\right)g(r)\right\} \tag{15a}$$

and graph the lower boundary of the set of points (μ, r) consistent with complete specialization in the production of the first commodity. Similarly, we may define

$$\mu_2(r) = \sup\left\{\mu : \frac{\partial f}{\partial l} \leq \left[p - \frac{\mu}{u'(pg(r))}\right]g(r)\right\} \tag{15b}$$

and graph the upper boundary of the set of points consistent with complete specialization in the production of the second commodity. Here $pg(r)$ is the value of output, in terms of the consumption good, when only the raw material is produced. From (15a) and (15b) we obtain, respectively,

$$w = \left[p - \frac{\mu_1(r)}{u'(w)}\right]g(r) \tag{16a}$$

and

$$w = \left[p - \frac{\mu_2(r)}{u'(pg(r))}\right]g(r). \tag{16b}$$

Now fig. 1 depicts the relationship between r and national income when specialization is complete in one commodity or the other. Bearing in mind the relationships of fig. 1 and the strict concavity of $u(c)$, we may infer from (16) that

$$0 > \mu_1(r) > \mu_2(r) \quad \text{if } r < \tilde{r}, \qquad 0 = \mu_1(r) = \mu_2(r) \quad \text{if } r = \tilde{r},$$
$$0 < \mu_2(r) < \mu_1(r) \quad \text{if } r > \tilde{r}, \tag{17}$$

where $\tilde{r}$ is the unique solution to the equation $w = pg(r)$. It is easy to check, moreover, that $\mu_1(r)$ is monotonic increasing and asymptotic both to the μ-axis

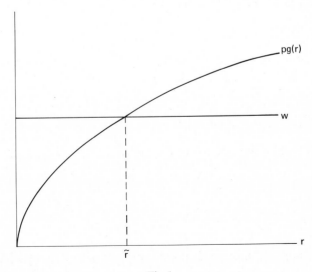

Fig. 1.

and to $pu'(w)$, and that $\mu_2(r)$ is increasing for $0 \leq r \leq \tilde{r}$ and asymptotic both to the μ-axis and to the r-axis. Putting together our information about $\mu_1(r)$ and $\mu_2(r)$, we obtain the regions of specialization displayed in fig. 2. Everywhere above and on the locus $\mu_1(r)$, except at the point $(\mu, r) = (0, \tilde{r})$, only the consumption good is produced; everywhere below and on the locus $\mu_2(r)$, except at $(\mu, r) = (0, \tilde{r})$, only the raw material is produced; and in the regions between the two loci, and at $(\mu, r) = (0, \tilde{r})$, both commodities are produced.

Consider now the locus of points (μ, r) such that $\dot{\mu} = 0$. From (9), $\dot{\mu} = 0$ when $\mu = 0 = 1 - l$, that is, to the left of $\tilde{r}$ the locus $\dot{\mu} = 0$ coincides with the r-axis. At the point $(\mu, r) = (0, \tilde{r})$, $\dot{\mu} = 0$ if only the consumption good is produced; otherwise, $\dot{\mu} < 0$. For any value of r greater than but sufficiently close to $\tilde{r}$, there exists μ, $\mu_1(r) > \mu > \mu_2(r)$, and an associated l, $0 < l < 1$, such

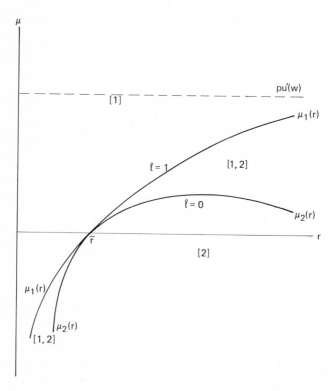

Fig. 2. Region [1]: only the consumption good is produced. Region [2]: only the raw material is produced. Region [1, 2]: both the consumption good and the raw material are produced.

that $\dot{\mu} = 0$. However, there is a critical value of r, say r^*, such that the associated μ is equal to $\mu_2(r^*)$ and the associated l is equal to one. Thereafter, the locus $\dot{\mu} = 0$ declines monotonically and approaches the r-axis asymptotically. From (8), on the other hand, $\dot{r} = 0$ if and only if just the consumption good is produced; otherwise, $\dot{r} < 0$.

Consider now fig. 3. For $r(0) > \tilde{r}$, the optimal trajectory is indicated by the heavy dashed curve. The trajectory ends at the stationary point $(\mu, r) = (0, \tilde{r})$, and that point is reached in finite time. Until the stationary point is reached, only the raw material is produced; and, of course, the entire output of that commodity is exported in exchange for the consumption good. When the stationary point is reached, an abrupt transition is made to a second phase characterized by the contrary specialization, with some part of the output of the consumption good exported in exchange for the raw material. At no point

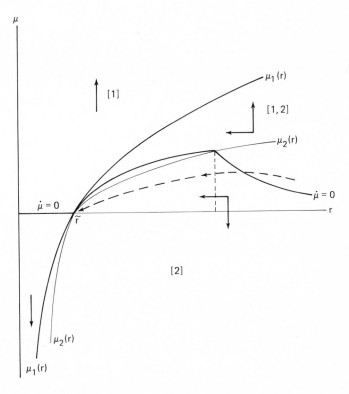

Fig. 3.

of time is it optimal to produce both commodities[4]. For $r(0) \leq \bar{r}$, only the second phase is relevant. The economy is initially at a stationary point $(\mu, r) = (0, r_0)$ and stays there, producing only the consumption good and importing the raw material.

We have not proved that the 'optimal' trajectory of fig. 3 is indeed optimal. However, the present problem is a special version of the problem to be discussed in section 3, and it will be shown that if a trajectory satisfies the necessary conditions of the more general problem it is globally optimal. We may conclude that, along the optimal trajectory:

(a) production is always completely specialized;
(b) there can take place at most one switch of specialization;
(c) after some finite time only the consumption good is produced;
(d) the resource is never exhausted.

3. The optimal trajectory: replenishable resources

We now complicate our analysis considerably by recognizing the possibility of both natural and artificial replenishment of the resource. The time rate of natural replenishment is written $\phi(r)$, where ϕ is a strictly concave function of r, initially increasing then decreasing and ultimately negative with $\phi(0) = 0$ and

---

[4] It is common in optimal control problems for elements of linearity (or convexity) in the Hamiltonian to produce jumps in the control variables. In the present case the jumps can be traced to the homogeneity of $f(l, v)$. If instead f were taken to be a general concave function, the jumps would disappear. Then, for sufficiently large $r(0)$, the optimal path would pass through regions of complete specialization in raw material production and of incomplete specialization and would approach (but never reach) a stationary point of complete specialization in the production of the consumption good.

To show this, we write

$$\mu_1(r) = \frac{u'(f(1, v) - pv)}{g(r)} (pg(r) - f_l(1, v)),$$

$$\mu_2(r) = \frac{u'(pg(r))}{g(r)} (pg(r) - f_l(0, v))$$

and redefine $\bar{r}$ as the solution of $\mu_1(r) = 0$. $(\bar{r}, 0)$ is again a stationary point of the system and the endpoint for the problem. However, from the concavity of f, $df_l/dl < 0$; and, making use of the fact that $dc/dl = f_l - pg(r)$, it can be shown that $\mu_1(r) > \mu_2(r)$ for all $r > 0$. Hence, for $r > \bar{r}$, the optimal path must pass through the region of incomplete specialization; and, once in that region, the system never leaves it.

Of course, as time goes by more labour is allocated to production of the consumption good and less to production of the raw material. If initially the raw material is exported there must exist a critical moment at which the country becomes self-sufficient, thereafter exporting the consumption good.

$0 < \phi'(0) < \infty$. That is, near $r = 0$ the resource regenerates naturally in an approximately exponential fashion but, from the beginning, the pressure of a limited environment makes itself felt and, eventually, the pressure is such that net procreation is ruled out altogether. A typical ϕ-function is graphed in fig. 4.

To accommodate the possibility of artificial replenishment we introduce a third constant-returns industry, with the resource as output and labour as input. Modifying our earlier notation slightly, we now let l_1 be the labour employed by the first or consumption-good industry, l_2 the labour employed by the second or raw-material-producing industry and, therefore, $1 - l_1 - l_2$ the labour employed by the resource-replenishing third industry. Then the rate of artificial replenishment is simply $\theta(1 - l_1 - l_2)$, where θ is a positive constant, and the time rate of resource depletion is $-\dot{r} = l_2 g(r) - \phi(r) - \theta(1 - l_1 - l_2)$.

The new social problem is to find

$$\max_{l_1, l_2, v} \int_0^\infty e^{-\rho t} u(c) dt, \qquad \rho > 0, \tag{18}$$

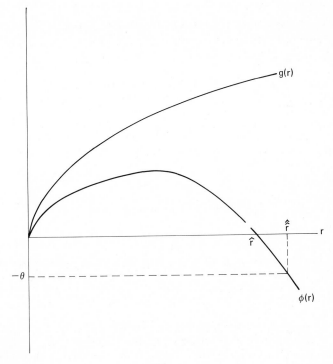

Fig. 4.

subject to

$$\dot{r} = -l_2 g(r) + \phi(r) + \theta(1 - l_1 - l_2), \tag{19}$$

$$l_i \geqq 0, \qquad i = 1, 2, \tag{20}$$

$$1 - l_1 - l_2 \geqq 0, \tag{21}$$

$$v \geqq 0, \tag{22}$$

$$r(0) = r_0, \tag{23}$$

where

$$c = f(l_1, v) + p[l_2 g(r) - v]. \tag{24}$$

The Hamiltonian and Lagrangian are, respectively,

$$H = u(c) + \mu[-l_2 g(r) + \phi(r) + \theta(1 - l_1 - l_2)]$$

and

$$L = H + \delta(1 - l_1 - l_2).$$

Among the conditions which an optimal path must satisfy we have

$$\dot{r} = -l_2 g(r) + \phi(r) + \theta(1 - l_1 - l_2), \tag{25}$$

$$\dot{\mu} = [\rho - \phi'(r)]\mu - [pu'(c) - \mu]l_2 g'(r), \tag{26}$$

$$u'(c)(\partial/\partial l_1)f(l_1, v) - \mu\theta - \delta \leqq 0 \quad \text{with equality if } l_1 > 0, \tag{27}$$

$$u'(c)pg(r) - \mu[g(r) + \theta] - \delta \leqq 0 \quad \text{with equality if } l_2 > 0, \tag{28}$$

$$u'(c)[(\partial/\partial v)f(l_1, v) - p] \leqq 0 \quad \text{with equality if } v > 0, \tag{29}$$

$$\delta \geqq 0 \quad \text{with equality if } 1 - l_1 - l_2 > 0, \tag{30}$$

$$\lim_{t \to \infty} e^{-\rho t} \mu r = 0. \tag{31}$$

As in section 2 we begin by dividing the (μ, r)-plane into regions of complete and incomplete specialization. Two cases must be distinguished according as $\theta > w/p$ ('high productivity in artificial replenishment') or $\theta \leqq w/p$ ('low productivity in artificial replenishment'). Figs. 5(a) and (b) are the products of some remarkably tedious calculations, a sketch of which may be found in the appendix. The loci $\mu_1(r)$ and $\mu_2(r)$ appear again, supplemented, however, by three additional boundary curves. On most of the boundaries just one commodity is produced, that is, either $l_1 = 1$ or $l_2 = 1$. The exception is the vertical segment labelled [1, 2, 3] in fig. 5(a). At its lower extremity, just the raw material is produced; but at every other point on the segment the allocation of labour between the three activities is, within limits, indeterminate. This indeterminacy is of no consequence. Note also that, when productivity in replenishment is low ($\theta \leq w/p$), it is never optimal to artificially replenish the resource and at the same time produce the raw material; that is, it is never optimal to play at the same time the roles of predator and husbandman.

We turn now to the construction of the loci $\dot{r} = 0$ and $\dot{\mu} = 0$. Let us consider first the locus $\dot{r} = 0$ and, for the time being, confine our attention to the case (illustrated by fig. 4) in which $g(r) > \phi(r)$ for all $r > 0$, so that replenishment is always inadequate if only the raw material is produced. Let $\hat{\hat{r}}$ be the maximum maintainable value of the resource, so that

$$\phi(\hat{\hat{r}}) + \theta = 0 \tag{32}$$

and let $\hat{r}$ be the maximum maintainable value of the resource in the absence of

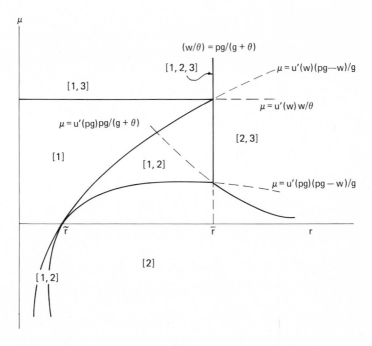

Fig. 5(a). $\theta > w/p$. Region [1]: only the consumption good is produced. Region [2]: only the raw material is produced. Region [1, 2]: only the consumption good and the raw material are produced. Region [1, 3]: only the consumption good and the resource are produced. Region [2, 3]: only the raw material and the resource are produced. Region [1, 2, 3]: all three commodities are produced.

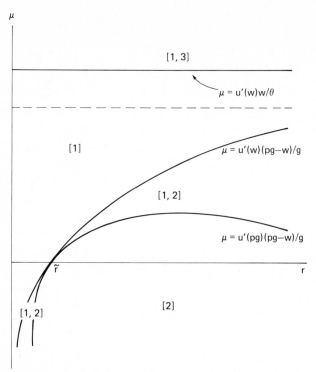

Fig. 5(b). $\theta \leq w/p$. Region [1]: only the consumption good is produced. Region [2]: only the raw material is produced. Region [1, 2]: only the consumption good and the raw material are produced. Region [1, 3]: only the consumption good and the resource are produced.

artificial replenishment, so that

$$\phi(\hat{r}) = 0. \tag{33}$$

Suppose that $\hat{r} < \bar{r}$, where $\bar{r}$ is defined in the appendix and displayed in fig. 5(a), and suppose that only the consumption good and raw material are produced (so that $l_1 + l_2 = 1$). From (25) we see that, for each r, $0 < r < \hat{r}$, there exists a value of l_1 greater than zero and less than one such that $\dot{r} = 0$. For all such r, therefore, the locus $\dot{r} = 0$ lies inside the region [1, 2]. At $r = \hat{r}$, the locus intersects the boundary between regions [1] and [1, 2] and becomes a vertical line until region [1, 3] is reached. Thereafter it increases monotonically and approaches the vertical line $r = \hat{\hat{r}}$ monotonically. If, alternatively, $\hat{r} \geqq \bar{r}$ the locus is a smooth curve without the vertical jump at $r = \hat{r}$. Fig. 6 displays the several possibilities. Fig. 6(a) is drawn on the assumption that $\theta > w/p$, fig. 6(b) on the assumption that $\theta \leqq w/p$.

We have assumed that $g(r) > \phi(r)$ for all $r > 0$. In general, however, the equation $g(r) = \phi(r)$ may have any number of positive solutions. To appreciate the implications of multiple solutions it suffices to suppose that there are two distinct solutions, r_1 and r_2, as in fig. 7. Then, if only the raw material is produced, $\dot{r} = 0$ when $r = r_1$ and when $r = r_2$, $\dot{r} < 0$ when $r < r_1$ and when $r > r_2$, and $\dot{r} > 0$ when $r_1 < r < r_2$. The locus $\dot{r} = 0$, then, has one of the discontinuous forms displayed in figs. 8(a) and (b).

Let us turn now to eq. (26) and the locus $\dot{\mu} = 0$. The locus has two branches; for this reason it is convenient to consider separately the two cases $r^{**} > \tilde{r}$ and $r^{**} \leq \tilde{r}$, where r^{**} is defined by the equation $\rho = \phi'(r^{**})$.

Suppose that $r^{**} > \tilde{r}$. Then the two branches of the locus $\dot{\mu} = 0$ have no points in common, one branch lying entirely in the region $0 \leq r \leq \tilde{r}$ and the other entirely in the region $r \geq r^{**}$. For $0 \leq r \leq \tilde{r}$, $\dot{\mu} = 0$ when $\mu = 0$ and only the consumption good is produced; moreover, to every r, $0 < r < \tilde{r}$, there corresponds a negative μ and an l_2, $0 < l_2 < 1$, such that $\dot{\mu} = 0$, with $\mathrm{d}\mu/\mathrm{d}r > 0$ along the locus $\dot{\mu} = 0$. So much for the first branch; let us consider now the second branch. From (26) it is easy to see that in regions [1] and [1, 3], where nothing is produced of the raw material, $\dot{\mu} = 0$ when $r = r^{**}$. In regions [2] and

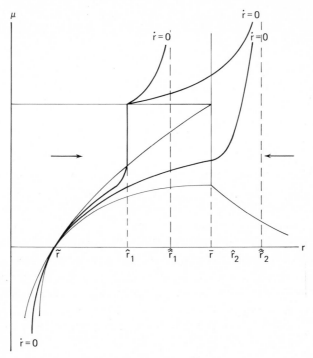

Fig. 6(a). $\theta > w/p$.

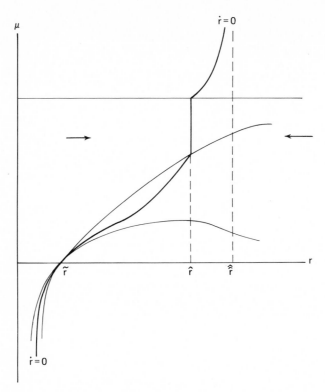

Fig. 6(b). $\theta \leq w/p$.

[1, 2], where no artificial replenishment takes place, the locus is negatively sloped and asymptotic to the r-axis. Finally, in region [2, 3], where nothing is produced of the consumption good, the locus $\dot{\mu} = 0$ is defined by

$$(\rho - \phi')\mu - [pu'(l_2pg) - \mu]l_2g' = 0.$$

However, in this region $u'(l_2pg)pg - \mu g = \theta\mu$. Hence, $\dot{\mu} = 0$ if and only if $\rho - \phi' = \theta l_2(g'/g)$. The sign of $d\mu/dr$ along the locus in this region cannot be determined; however, it is easily seen that, if $r^{**} \geq \tilde{r}$, the locus is asymptotic to $r = r^{**}$. Moreover, the locus cannot remain in region [2, 3] but for some sufficiently large r enters region [2] and, as we have noted, is there asymptotic to the r-axis. Three alternative loci (one for each of three alternative values of r^{**}) are displayed in fig. 9(a). (If $\theta \leq w/p$, only the first of the three loci is possible.)

Consider now the alternative possibility, that $r^{**} \leq \tilde{r}$. Then the two branches of the locus $\dot{\mu} = 0$ intersect at the point $(\mu, r) = (0, r^{**})$. One branch is exactly

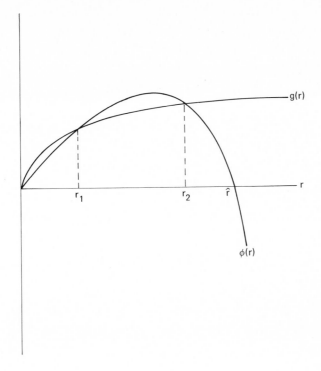

Fig. 7.

as in the non-replenishment case (see fig. 3). The other branch runs vertically up from (μ^{**}, r^{**}), where $\mu^{**} \equiv \mu_2(r^{**})$; and, for $0 < r < r^{**}$, it lies entirely in the region $[1, 2]$ with negative slope. Fig. 9(b) displays the locus $\dot{\mu} = 0$ for this case.

It is now a simple matter to construct the complete phase diagram. Consider first the simplest case, in which $g(r) > \phi(r)$ for all $r > 0$. Putting together the loci of figs. 6 and 9, and bearing in mind that $r^{**} < \hat{r} < \hat{\hat{r}}$, we find that there always exists a unique stationary point and a unique optimal path converging on that point. Moreover, we see that the stationary point must lie either in region $[1, 2]$ or in region $[2, 3]$; that is, at the stationary point specialization is always incomplete, with the raw material produced in combination with either the consumption good or the resource (but not both). In contrast to our findings in section 2, the stationary point cannot be one of complete specialization in the production of the consumption good. If the stationary point lies in region $[1, 2]$, as it must when labour is of low productivity in artificial replenishment, then trade may be in either direction or, in a singular case, absent altogether. Figs.

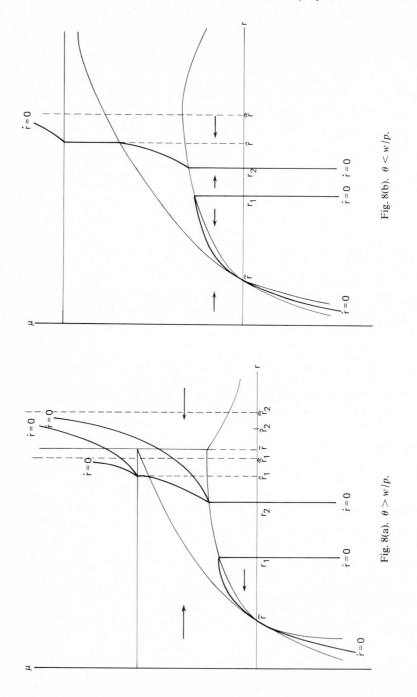

Fig. 8(a). $\theta > w/p$.

Fig. 8(b). $\theta < w/p$.

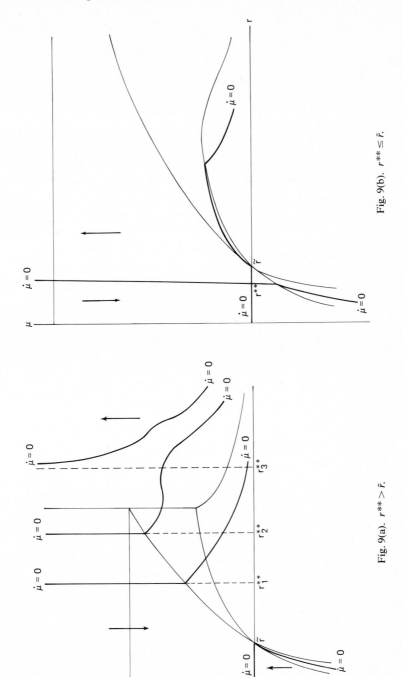

Fig. 9(a). $r^{**} > \tilde{r}$.

Fig. 9(b). $r^{**} \leq \tilde{r}$.

10(a)–(c) display the possibilities when $\theta > w/p$, figs. 11(a) and (b) when $\theta \leq w/p$.

Let us now abandon the assumption that $g(r) > \phi(r)$ for all $r > 0$ and admit the possibility that, even when the entire labour force is devoted to the production of the raw material, yet for some r the resource continues to grow as a result of natural replenishment. Superimposing the loci of figs. 8 and 9, we find that two new possibilities emerge. Not unexpectedly, a stationary point may now be found in region [2]; that is, in the long run it may be optimal to specialize completely in the production (and export) of the raw material. In addition, we find that the stationary point need not be unique and that the destination of an optimal trajectory may depend on its starting point, that is, on the initial stock of the resource. Fig. 12 illustrates both possibilities. In spite of these novelties, however, our main conclusion stands: the stationary point cannot be one of complete specialization in the production of the consumption good[5].

To complete our analysis it remains to demonstrate that the 'optimal' paths of figs. 10 and 11 are indeed optimal. It suffices to show that the Hamiltonian of the problem

$$H = u[l_1 w + l_2 pg(r)] + \mu[\phi(r) + \theta(1 - l_1 - l_2) - l_2 g(r)]$$
$$= u(\cdot) - \mu l_2 g(r) + \mu[\theta(1 - l_1 - l_2) + \phi(r)] \tag{34}$$

is concave in r for each t when $l_1(t)$, $l_2(t)$ and $\mu(t)$ are assigned their values along the 'optimal' paths[6]. Now $\mu(t) \geq 0$ along the 'optimal' paths; hence the first, third and fourth terms of (34) are concave. The second term, on the other hand, is convex if $l_2 > 0$. It will be shown that, nevertheless, $u(\cdot) - \mu l_2 g(r)$ is concave. We proceed under the assumption that $l_2 > 0$. We have

$$(\partial/\partial r)[u(\cdot) - \mu l_2 g(r)] = (u'p - \mu)l_2 g'$$

which, since $(u'p - \mu)g \geq u'w > 0$ when $l_2 > 0$, is positive. Moreover,

$$(\partial^2/\partial r^2)[u(\cdot) - \mu l_2 g(r)] = l_2[(u''p - \mu)g'' + u''p^2 g']$$

which, since $u'' < 0$ and $g'' < 0$ by assumption and since $u'p - \mu > 0$, is negative. It follows that $u(\cdot) - \mu l_2 g(r)$, and therefore H, is concave in r.

---

[5] None of the qualitative conclusions of this section is sensitive to the substitution of a general concave $f(l, v)$ for the homogeneous function of the text (cf. footnote 4). Only some of the quantitative detail changes. In particular, if f is concave then $\mu_1(r) > \mu_2(r)$ for all $r > 0$ and the line [1, 2, 3] of fig. 5(a) is no longer straight and vertical throughout its length but slopes negatively for sufficiently small μ.

[6] See, for example, Arrow and Kurz (1970, proposition II. 6).

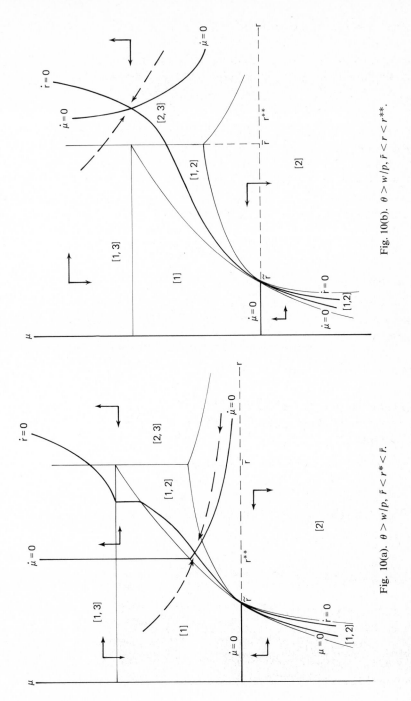

Fig. 10(a). $\theta > w/p$, $\tilde{r} < r^* < \bar{r}$.

Fig. 10(b). $\theta > w/p$, $\bar{r} < r < r^{**}$.

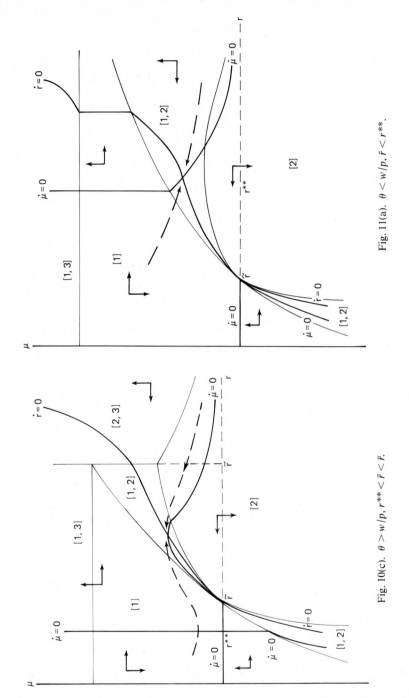

Fig. 11(a). $\theta < w/p, \tilde{r} < r^{**}$.

Fig. 10(c). $\theta > w/p, r^{**} < \tilde{r} < \bar{r}$.

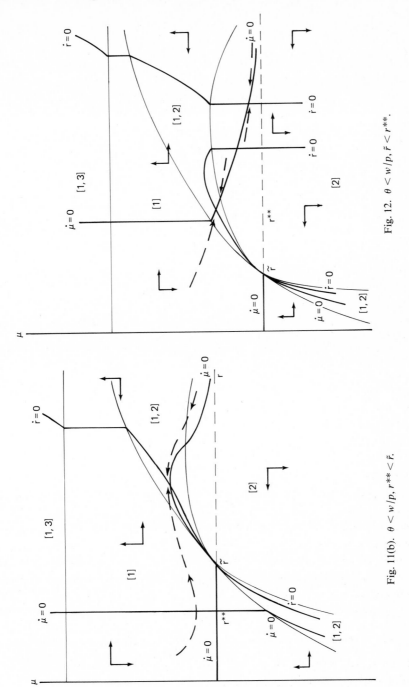

Fig. 11(b). $\theta < w/p, r^{**} < \tilde{r}$.

Fig. 12. $\theta < w/p, \tilde{r} < r^{**}$.

4. Competitive allocations and optimal intervention

We have characterized the time path of the socially optimal allocation of labour between the three activities. Does this allocation differ from the competitive allocation and, if so, what form should intervention take? It is instructive to consider an extreme case. Suppose (i) that the resource is, like some mineral deposits, parcelled out as private property and (ii) that producers are homogeneous, far-sighted (plan to an infinite horizon) and seek to maximize the same utility functionals as the government. Then the competitive allocation of resources is socially optimal. In particular, trade is gainful.

Evidently the conditions of competitive optimality are severe. If one or more of the conditions is not met, intervention is called for, and the appropriate form of intervention depends on which of the above conditions is not met. Suppose, for example, that condition (ii) is met but that the resource is like some ocean fishing grounds, freely available to all producers and not subject to private property rights. Then the appropriate intervention is by means of a tax on the use of the resource and a subsidy to the artificial replenishment of the resource, each at the rate μ per unit. In the absence of appropriate intervention, trade is possibly harmful. Suppose, as a further example, that producers apply a higher rate of discount than the government. Then, clearly, a subsidy to borrowing is required.

5. The implications of world-wide resource depletion

We have assumed that world prices are both beyond the control of the (small) country under consideration and constant through time. However, might it not be more appropriate to suppose that the relative price of the raw material is steadily rising? The answer to this question depends on the nature of the resource. If the resource is replenishable, one may suppose that the rest of the world is in long-run stationary equilibrium with constant prices. If the resource is not replenishable such an equilibrium does not exist and the assumption of constant prices is less easy to defend. Accordingly, we have reworked the analysis of section 2 on the more general assumption that the world price of the raw material is changing exponentially through time:

$$p(t) = p(0)\,e^{\zeta t}, \qquad \zeta \geqq 0. \tag{35}$$

Without reproducing the detailed analysis, we can indicate briefly some of the implications of introducing (35).

If $\zeta > 0$, the (r, μ)-phase diagram changes from one moment to the next, with $\tilde{r}$ moving asymptotically to the origin and the horizontal asymptote for $\mu_1(r)$ drifting up. For $r(0) > \tilde{r}(0)$, to the optimal trajectory of fig. 3 there must now be added a final segment which coincides with the r-axis. Clearly it is no longer optimal, after some point of time, to specialize in producing the consumption good; whatever the value of $r(0)$, there exists some point of time (possibly $t = 0$) after which it is always optimal to produce both the consumption good and the raw material. As a result, the stock of the resource sinks asymptotically to zero.

6. Final remarks

In conclusion, we sketch a possible reinterpretation of our conclusions and then indicate some directions which further exploration may take.

In sections 2 and 3 no place was found for capital goods other then the resource itself and this neglect may appear to be a serious weakness of the analysis. However, under the small-country assumption maintained throughout this chapter, it makes no essential difference to the analysis whether capital goods appear as inputs or not. It suffices perhaps that this fact be demonstrated for the simpler case in which replenishment is not possible.

Introducing a homogeneous capital-good input, let us rewrite the production functions of the first and second industries as $f(k_1, l, v)$ and $h(k_2, 1-l) \cdot g(r)$, respectively, where k_i is the amount of capital employed in the ith industry and the functions f and h are homogeneous of degree one. We now seek

$$\max_{l,v,k_1,k_2} \int_0^\infty e^{-\rho t} u(c)\,\mathrm{d}t, \qquad \rho > 0, \tag{1'}$$

subject to

$$\dot{r} = -h(k_2, 1-l) \cdot g(r) \tag{2'}$$

and to (3)–(5), where c is now given by

$$c = f(k_1, l, v) + p[h(k_2, 1-l) \cdot g(r) - v] - iq(k_1 + k_2)$$

and i is the given world rate of interest and q the given world price of the capital good (in terms of the consumption good). Among the necessary conditions for an optimum we find

$$u'(c)[(\partial f/\partial k_1) - iq]\begin{cases} = 0 & \text{if } k_1 > 0, \\ \leq 0 & \text{if } k_1 = 0, \end{cases} \tag{36}$$

$$u'(c)[(\partial f/\partial v) - p]\begin{cases} = 0 & \text{if } v > 0, \\ \leq 0 & \text{if } v = 0, \end{cases} \tag{37}$$

$$u'(c)[(\partial h/\partial k_2)g - iq]\begin{cases} = 0 & \text{if } k_2 > 0, \\ \leq 0 & \text{if } k_2 = 0. \end{cases} \tag{38}$$

Now $\partial f/\partial k_1$ and $\partial f/\partial v$ are functions of k_1/l and v/l, and $\partial h/\partial k_2$ is a function of $k_2/(1-l)$. Given p, q, i and r, the factor ratios are determined by (36)–(38). Given the two prices and the rate of interest, therefore, the two production functions $f(k_1, l, v)$ and $h(k_2, 1-l) \cdot g(r)$ can be rewritten as $\kappa_1 l$ and $\kappa_2(1-l)g(r)$, where κ_1 and κ_2 are constants, without in any way changing the problem. But that is precisely the form of the production functions in section 2 (where $\kappa_1 \equiv f(1, v/l)$) and $p = \partial f(1, v/l)/\partial(v/l))$.

In conclusion we briefly indicate some directions which further exploration might take. First, one might allow for the optimal choice of 'resource farming' methods. We have assumed that there exists a relationship of constant proportionality between the output of the raw material and the rate of depletion of the resource. In many realistic situations, however, the relationship is variable; there is a trade-off between the amount of the resource wasted and the input of labour[7]. There remains also the difficult problem of introducing more general non-separable utility functionals[8]. And, finally, there is the need to allow for uncertainty concerning the current and future extent of the resource stock and concerning future prices and technology[9].

Appendix

In this appendix we sketch the reasoning applied to the construction of the regions of specialization displayed in fig. 5. Basic to all calculations are the inequalities (27)–(30). We begin by noting that, as an implication of (7), it is never optimal to produce only the resource.

[7] To be specific, one might adopt a production function of the form $l_2 g(r, \dot{r})$.

[8] The substitution of a linear for a strictly concave utility function does not affect the general character of our conclusions. It merely forces together the twin loci $\mu_1(r)$ and $\mu_2(r)$ and thus restricts the region [1, 2] in which it is optimal to produce both the consumption good and the raw material.

[9] The analysis of section 2 and 3 has been reworked by Suzuki (1974) under the assumption that the resource is of unknown size.

If only the consumption good is produced,

$$\mu \leqq u'(w)(w/\theta), \tag{A1}$$

$$\mu \geqq u'(w)[(pg - w)/g], \tag{A2}$$

yielding regions [1] of figs. 5(a) and (b).

If only the raw material is produced,

$$\mu \leqq u'(pg)[pg/(g + \theta)], \tag{A3}$$

$$\mu \leqq u'(pg)[(pg - w)/g], \tag{A4}$$

yielding regions [2] of figs. 5(a) and (b).

If only the consumption good and raw material are produced,

$$u'(l_1 w + (1 - l_1)pg)w = u'(l_1 w + (1 - l)pg)pg - \mu g \geqq \theta\mu. \tag{A5}$$

From (A5), the concavity of $u(c)$ and the facts displayed in fig. 1,

$$u'(pg)[(pg - w)/g] \leqq \mu \leqq u'(w)[(pg - w)/g], \tag{A6}$$

$$\mu \begin{cases} \leqq u'(w)(w/\theta) & \text{if } r > \tilde{r}, \\ \leqq u'(pg)(w/\theta) & \text{if } 0 < r < \tilde{r}, \end{cases} \tag{A7}$$

$$\mu \begin{cases} \leqq u'(w)[pg/(g + \theta)] & \text{if } r > \tilde{r}, \\ \leqq u'(pg)[pg/(g + \theta)] & \text{if } 0 < r < \tilde{r}. \end{cases} \tag{A8}$$

Now suppose that $p > w/\theta$. Then there exists one and only one value of r, say $\bar{r}$, such that

$$pg(r)/[g(r) + \theta] = w/\theta. \tag{A9}$$

Note also that (A9) holds if and only if

$$[pg(r) - w]/g(r) = w/\theta \tag{A10}$$

so that

$$pg(\bar{r})/[g(\bar{r}) + \theta] = w/\theta = [pg(\bar{r}) - w]/g(\bar{r}). \tag{A11}$$

Moreover,

$$w/\theta > pg(r)/[g(r) + \theta] > [pg(r) - w]/g(r) \quad \text{if } r < \bar{r} \tag{A12a}$$

and

$$w/\theta < pg(r)/[g(r) + \theta] < [pg(r) - w]/g(r) \quad \text{if } r > \bar{r}. \tag{A12b}$$

With the aid of (A12) we can now show that, for $r > \bar{r}$, (A6)–(A8) are incompatible. Suppose the contrary. Then, for $r > \bar{r}$,

$$\mu = u'(l_1 w + (1 - l_1)pg[(pg - w)/g],$$

$$\leq u'(l_1 w + (1 - l_1)pg)[pg/(g + \theta)] \tag{A13a}$$

and

$$\mu \leq u'(l_1 w + (1 - l_1)pg)(w/\theta), \tag{A13b}$$

whence, for $r > \bar{r}$,

$$(pg - r)/g \leq [pg/(g + \theta)](w/\theta), \tag{A14}$$

contradicting (A12b). Thus we may conclude that, for $r > \bar{r}$, production of both the consumption good and the raw material (but not the resource) is impossible. From this remark, and from (A6)–(A8), we may construct the regions [1, 2] of figs. 5(a) and (b).

If only the consumption good and the resource are produced,

$$u'(l_1 w)w = \theta\mu \geq u'(l_1 w)pg - \mu g. \tag{A15}$$

From (A15), the concavity of $u(c)$ and the facts of fig. 1, we obtain

$$\mu = u'(l_1 w)(w/\theta) \geq u'(w)(w/\theta), \tag{A16}$$

$$\mu \geq u'(l_1 w)[(pg - w)/g] \geq u'(w)[(pg - w)/g], \tag{A17}$$

$$\mu \geq u'(l_1 w)[pg/(g + \theta)] \geq u'(w)[pg/(g + \theta)]. \tag{A18}$$

We now apply (A12) to show that that if $\theta > w/p$, (A16)–(A18) are incompatible to the right of $\bar{r}$, implying that, for $r > \bar{r}$, production of both the consumption good and the resource (but not the raw material) is impossible. Suppose the contrary. Then, for $r > \bar{r}$,

$$\mu = u'(l_1 w)(w/\theta) \geq u'(l_1 w)[(pg - w)/g], u'(l_1 w)[pg/(g + \theta)] \tag{A19}$$

implying that

$$w/\theta \geq (pg - w)/g, pg/(g + \theta) \tag{A20}$$

which contradicts (A12b). Thus we arrive at the regions [1, 3] of figs. 5(a) and (b).

If only the raw material and the resource are produced,

$$u'(l_2 pg)pg - \mu g = \theta\mu > u'(l_2 pg)w. \tag{A21}$$

From (A21), the concavity of $u(c)$ and the facts displayed in fig. 1,

$$\mu = u'(l_2 pg)[pg/(g + \theta)] \geq u'(pg)[pg/(g + \theta)], \tag{A22}$$

$$\mu \geqq u'(l_2 pg)(w/\theta) \geqq u'(pg)(w/\theta), \tag{A23}$$

$$\mu \leqq u'(l_2 pg)[(pg - w)/g], \tag{A24a}$$

$$u'(l_2 pg)[(pg - w)/g] \geqq u'(pg)[(pg - w)/g]. \tag{A24b}$$

We now apply (A12) to show that (A22)–(A24) are incompatible to the *left* of $\bar{r}$, implying that, for $r < \bar{r}$, production of both the raw material and the resource (but not the consumption good) is impossible. Suppose the contrary, that (A22)–(A24) are compatible for $r < \bar{r}$. Then, for $r < \bar{r}$,

$$\mu = u'(l_2 pg)[pg/(g + \theta)] \leqq u'(l_2 pg)[(pg - w)/g], \tag{A25}$$

contradicting (A12a). Thus we arrive at regions [2, 3] of figs. 5(a) and (b). Notice that, when $\theta < w/p$, there is no region [2, 3] because, in that case, $\bar{r}$ does not exist.

Finally, if all three commodities are produced,

$$u'(l_1 w + l_2 pg)w = u'(l_1 w + l_2 pg)pg - \mu g = \theta \mu. \tag{A26}$$

Eliminating μ from (A26), we obtain

$$u'(l_1 w + l_2 pg)[(pg\theta - wg - w\theta)/\theta] = 0 \tag{A27}$$

which holds if and only if (A10) holds. As we have noted, when $\theta > w/p$, (A10) is satisfied by one and only one value of r, namely $\bar{r}$; and, when $\theta \leqq w/p$, (A10) has no solution. Thus, when $\theta > w/p$, the region [1, 2, 3] degenerates to the vertical line segment indicated in fig. 5(a); and, when $\theta \leqq w/p$, the region vanishes.

References

Arrow, K. J., and M. Kurz (1970), *Public Investment, the Rate of Return and Optimal Fiscal Policy*, Johns Hopkins Press, Baltimore.

Hadley, G., and M. C. Kemp (1971), *Variational Methods in Economics*, North-Holland Publishing Company, Amsterdam.

Kemp, M. C., and H. Suzuki (ch. 24), Optimal international borrowing with a wasting resource.

Long, N. V. (1974), International borrowing for resource extraction, *International Economic Review*, 15, Feb., 168–183.

Suzuki, H. (1974), International trade with a wasting but possibly replenishable resource: the case of uncertainty about the extent of the resource, University of New South Wales.

Vousden, N. (1974), International trade and exhaustible resources: a theoretical model, *International Economic Review*, 15, Feb., 149–167.

Chapter 19

TRADE GAINS IN A PURE CONSUMPTION-LOAN MODEL*

I. Introduction

The question of trading gains has been discussed almost always in the context of a static model of international trade. Here I consider the question in relation to a consumption-loans model of the Samuelson type (see Samuelson (1958) and Gale (1973)) and show that, in spite of the propensity of that model to generate paradoxes (see, for example, Gale (1971)), the familiar welfare propositions of static trade theory carry over to it.

The essence of the argument can be put very simply. Any closed-economy competitive equilibrium involves a market redistribution of the community's aggregate endowment for each period among the individuals surviving into that period. In any open economy it is possible to achieve the closed-economy competitive allocation by means of taxes and subsidies. Any open-economy 'trading' away from that allocation must then be to the advantage of each individual.

2. A closed economy

There is only one commodity, a perishable consumption good which cannot be produced and cannot be stored from one period to another. In each period of his finite life span, each individual receives a fixed amount of that commodity. Each individual is born with perfect foresight and with stable preferences defined over his lifetime consumption profile. In particular, he knows with certainty his own life span, his own income profile and all prices or interest rates which will prevail during his lifetime. Individuals may differ in prefer-

 * *Australian Economic Papers*, 12 (June 1973), 124–126. The helpful comments of Henry Y. Wan, Jr. and a referee are gratefully acknowledged.

ences, life span, date of birth and income profile. The birth rate may be constant or variable.

There exists a clearing house or market secretariat which buys and sells (against some unit of account) at prices (rates of interest) which clear the market, that is, equate to zero the net purchases of the secretariat during each period.

Let n be the maximum life expectancy of any individual; let $y_{it}^i \geqslant 0$ and $c_{it}^i \geqslant 0$ be respectively the income and consumption during the jth period of his life of the ith individual born in period t; and let r_t be the one-period rate of interest during period t. Then we have, for period t, the market-clearance condition

$$\sum_i c_{it}^1(r_t, r_{t+1}, \ldots, r_{t+n-2}) + \sum_i c_{i,t-1}^2(r_{t-1}, \ldots, r_{t+n-3})$$

$$+ \cdots + \sum_i c_{i,t-n+1}^n(r_{t-n+1}, r_{t-n+2}, \ldots, r_{t-1})$$

$$= \sum_i y_{it}^1 + \sum_i y_{i,t-1}^2 + \cdots + \sum_i y_{i,t-n+1}^n. \tag{1}$$

This is a difference equation of order $2(n-1)-1$ in the rate of interest. To solve, we need $2(n-1)-1$ boundary restrictions on the c's or r's. Only the details of our argument, not our qualitative conclusions, depend on the manner in which these restrictions are generated and on their content[1]. We may suppose that some $2(n-1)-1$ consecutive r's are arbitrarily chosen by the secretariat, so that the eqs. (1) can be used to determine recursively all earlier and later r's.

---

[1] One might suppose that at some specific point in time the first births miraculously took place, trading with the market secretariat being possible from this biological time origin, $t = 1$. Then the system of market-clearance equations becomes

$$\sum_i c_{i1}^1(r_1, r_2, \ldots, r_{n-1}) = \sum y_{i1}^1,$$

$$\sum_i c_{i1}^2(r_1, r_2, \ldots, r_{n-1}) + \sum_i c_{i2}^1(r_2, r_3, \ldots, r_n) = \sum y_{i1}^2 + \sum y_{i2}^1,$$

$$\cdots$$

$$\sum_i c_{i1}^n(r_1, r_2, \ldots, r_{n-1}) \cdots + \sum c_{in}^1(r_n, r_{n+1}, \ldots, r_{2(n-1)}) = \sum y_{i1}^n + \cdots + \sum y_{in}^1, \tag{2}$$

$$\sum_i c_{i2}^n(r_2, r_3, \ldots, r_n) + \cdots + \sum c_{i,n+1}^1(r_{n+1}, r_{n+2}, \ldots, r_{2(n-1)+1}) = \sum y_{i2}^n + \cdots + \sum y_{i,n+1}^1,$$

etc.

One might then suppose that the secretariat simply supplies arbitrary values for $r_1, r_2, \ldots, r_{n-2}$, leaving $r_{n-1}, r_n, \ldots$ to be determined recursively by the first, second, ... equation. Or one might

3. An open economy

Suppose now that from period $t = t_0$ the country under study is opened to 'trade' (free or restricted) with other countries and (in keeping with the assumption of perfect foresight) that the opening of trade in period t_0 is perfectly foreseen throughout their lives by all individuals who are born under the old regime but will live for at least two periods under the new regime (so that r_{t_0} will influence their decisions), that is, all individuals born not earlier than period $t_0 - n + 2$ and not later than period $t_0 - 1$. Suppose further that the post-trade profile of interest rates is forced through the same grid of boundary values as the autarkic profile. It is then clear that the opening of trade potentially affects all rates of interest prevailing during and after period $t_0 - n + 2$.

Is it possible on welfare grounds to compare the free-trade and autarkic equilibria? The answer seems to be 'Yes'. For during and after period $t_0 - n + 2$ it is possible to so redistribute the country's aggregate endowment for that period that each individual has exactly what he would have consumed under autarky. If after redistribution an individual engages in borrowing and lending, consuming either more or less than under autarky, he does so by choice and is therefore not worse off than under autarky. Of course, the trade-with-redistribution profile of interest rates will differ from the trade-without-redistribution profile (from period $t_0 - n + 2$ on) and from the autarky-without-redistribution profile.

Technically, the above argument is incomplete without a demonstration that autarkic and (post-redistribution) trading equilibria exist. However, that demonstration poses no problems which have not been handled in the literature (see, for example, Kemp and Wan (1972)).

---

suppose that time has a foreseen biological end, as well as a beginning.

Let doomsday be the period $t = T$. Births might continue right up to Doomsday or, more consistently with the assumption of perfect foresight, the last births might occur during period $T - n + 1$. In the latter case, the system (2) terminates with the equation

$$\sum c_{i,T-n}^n(r_{T-n}, \ldots, r_{T-2}) + \sum c_{i,T-n+1}^{n-1}(r_{T-n+1}, \ldots, r_{T-1}) = \sum y_{i,T-n}^n + \sum y_{i,T-n+1}^{n-1}.$$

Instead of starting the system at the biological time origin, one might imagine that the possibility of trading is introduced only during some period $t = t_1$ after the biological zero and that until then individuals simply consume their incomes. If the trading origin is at least n periods after the biological origin, the system of market-clearance equations is of the form (1) with $t = t_1, t_1 + 1, \ldots$ Then sufficient boundary conditions could be provided by the secretariat. For example, the secretariat might simply announce arbitrary values for $r_{t_1}, r_{t_1+1}, \ldots, r_{t_1+n-3}$.

4. Concluding remarks

The assumption that there is only one consumption good is inessential to our conclusions. In fact, all c_{it}^j and y_{it}^j can be as well interpreted as vectors as scalars. Thus our conclusion that free trade is gainful comprehends both the conventional atemporal exchange of commodities as well as the intertemporal exchange emphasized above.

On the other hand, the market secretariat has been endowed with perfect foresight concerning future excess demands. Even for a Samuelson–Gale world, with identical individuals born in each period and a constant relative age distribution of the population, this assumption might be thought a little extravagant.

References

Gale, D. (1971), General equilibrium with imbalance of trade, *Journal of International Economics*, 1, May, 141–158.

Gale, D. (1973), Pure exchange equilibrium of dynamic economic models, *Journal of Economic Theory*, 6, Feb., 12–36.

Kemp, M. C. and H. Y. Wan, Jr. (1972), The gains from free trade, *International Economic Review*, 13, Oct., 509–522.

Samuelson, P. A. (1958), An exact consumption-loan model of interest with or without the social contrivance of money, *Journal of Political Economy*, 66, Dec., 467–482.

PART III

INTERNATIONAL TRADE
UNDER CONDITIONS OF UNCERTAINTY

Introduction to Part III

To anyone who has not himself attempted to reformulate the central theorems of trade theory to accommodate elements of uncertainty it must seem quite extraordinary that such a reformulation has not long ago been provided by others; but no one who has made the attempt will be in the least surprised. The recognition of uncertainty seems to have a devastating effect on many of our most cherished propositions. Moreover, unless one is prepared to confine oneself to very primitive economies (of the Torrens–Ricardo kind, for example) or to adopt very special assumptions about the source and extent of uncertainty, about preferences and about market institutions, it does not seem possible to find much by way of replacement.

The first two essays collected in this part are based on generalized Torrens–Ricardo models of production and carry a simple cautionary message: that under conditions of uncertainty, long-run comparative advantage is a very unreliable predictor of the competitive or optimal patterns of production and trade. These essays may be read in conjunction with papers by Ruffin (1974a, 1974b), Turnovsky (1974) and Kemp (1974). Ch. 22, on the other hand, reverts to the standard Heckscher–Ohlin model of production and draws out some of the implications for production and trade of a dose of technological uncertainty. It may be read in conjunction with a paper by Batra (1974). The next two chapters, which with equal advantage might have been placed in part II, deal with the optimal husbanding of wasting resources of unknown extent. The final essay develops models of the behaviour of a single market (perhaps the foreign exchange market) under conditions of uncertainty. The analysis of that essay has been extended by Farrell (1966), Glahe (1966), Obst (1967), Schimmler (1973) and Williamson (1973).

References

Batra, R. N. (1974), Resource allocation in a general equilibrium model of production under uncertainty, *Journal of Economic Theory*, 8, May, 50–63.

Farrell, M. J. (1966), Profitable speculation, *Economica*, 33, May, 183–193.

Glahe, F. R. (1966), Professional and nonprofessional speculation, profitability and stability, *Southern Economic Journal*, 33, July, 43–48.

Kemp, M. C. (1974), Price uncertainty in an extended Torrens–Ricardo model of production and international trade, University of New South Wales.

Obst, N. (1967), A connection between speculation and stability in the foreign exchange market, *Southern Economic Journal*, 34, July, 146–149.

Ruffin, R. J. (1974a), International trade under uncertainty, *Journal of International Economics*, 4, Aug., 243–259.

Ruffin, R. J. (1974b), Comparative advantage under uncertainty, *Journal of International Economics*, 4, Aug., 261–273.

Schimmler, J. (1973), Speculation, profitability, and price stability – a formal approach, *Review of Economics and Statistics*, 55, Feb., 110–114.

Turnovsky, S. J. (1974), Technological and price uncertainty in a Ricardian model of international trade, *Review of Economic Studies*, 41, April, 201–217.

Williamson, J. (1973), Another case of profitable destabilizing speculation, *Journal of International Economics*, 3, Feb., 77–84.

Chapter 20

PRODUCTION AND TRADE PATTERNS UNDER UNCERTAINTY*

1. Introduction

What happens to the propositions of trade theory when the traditional assumption of certainty is relaxed? In this paper we direct this question to the classical or Torrens–Ricardo version of the theory. The classical theory is a most suitable guinea pig since the strong assumptions on which it is based yield implications for trade and production patterns which, compared to those of the more general Heckscher–Ohlin theory, are unambiguous.

Of course, we cannot take over the classical theory just as it is. It must be suitably modified so that uncertainty may be grafted in a non-trivial way. The modifications we have chosen relate to the timing and short-run reversibility of decisions concerning the allocation of labour to competing activities.

Suppose then that:

(i) There are just two trading countries, each composed of identical consuming–producing units which may, however, differ from country to country.

(ii) Each country is capable of producing two tradeable commodities. With each commodity there is associated a no-joint-products activity vector in which a single primary factor, labour, and possibly the other commodity appear as inputs. The commitment of labour to each activity must be made one period before production takes place; in the period during which production takes place, labour may be withdrawn from an activity, but it cannot be transferred to the competing activity. In short, *ex ante* labour is mobile between activities, *ex post* it is immobile. However, actual input and output are contemporaneous.

(iii) Each country produces in addition a purely domestic or non-tradeable commodity. The output of this commodity is, like Cournot's spring water,

* *Economic Record*, 49 (June 1973), 215–227, with N. Liviatan.

exogenously determined, beyond the control of the individual consuming–producing units, and does not absorb labour or either tradeable good. The supply of this commodity to consumers is random and affects their choices concerning the two producible commodities. This is how uncertainty enters the model.

(iv) Labour is internationally immobile and in fixed aggregate supply.

(v) Either all product markets are spot, that is, all contracts to buy and sell are contemporaneous with the exchange itself, *or* all product markets are forward, that is, all contracts are made one period before the exchange takes place.

The assumptions are not quite those of Torrens and Ricardo. In particular, we have departed from the strict letter of classical trade theory in recognizing both purely domestic and intermediate goods and in introducing a lag between the commitment of labour and the associated output of each of the two tradeable commodities. Nevertheless, in the absence of uncertainty (when the supply of the non-tradeable commodity is constant) our assumptions yield all the familiar classical conclusions.

In particular, the relevant (long-run) production possibility frontiers are straight lines based on free mobility of labour between activities. Moreover, comparative advantage in production in the long run means the same thing and plays the same role as in classical theory.

We shall show, however, that under conditions of uncertainty and imperfect mobility the implications of the classical theory are no longer valid. In particular, long-run comparative advantage in production has little predictive value concerning the pattern of trade or specialization. To dramatize our analysis we shall show that the pattern of trade and specialization under uncertainty may be just the reverse of the pattern of trade and specialization under certainty. This will be shown to be so whether markets are organized on a spot or a futures basis.

From these results we infer that one should not generally expect to be able to explain empirical patterns of trade in terms of some crude notion of comparative advantage, as was the case for example in the controversy concerning the Leontief paradox. We also infer that planned patterns of trade and specialization cannot properly be based on static considerations alone[1].

---

[1] In a valuable pioneering paper Brainard and Cooper (1968) have studied the implications of price uncertainty for the patterns of trade and production of a small country of the Heckscher–Ohlin type. Their paper differs from ours not only in its assumptions about production but also in taking price uncertainty as given, without relating it to the underlying randomness of preferences, technology or factor endowments, and in its reliance on quadratic utility functions and the mean-variance analysis of choice under uncertainty.

2. Equilibrium of a single country in isolation: spot markets

We begin by drawing a distinction between short-run and long-run production possibilities. Consider fig. 1. If the entire labour force were allocated to the production of the first tradeable commodity, the net output of that commodity would be $\bar{X}_1$, and the (negative) net output of the second tradeable commodity would be $\underline{X}_2$, where $-\underline{X}_2$ is the amount of the second commodity needed to produce $\bar{X}_1$ of the first commodity. The vector OA_1 then represents the first activity normalized on the total labour force. Similarly, if the entire labour force were devoted to the second activity, the net outputs of the two commodities would be represented by the point $(\underline{X}_1, \bar{X}_2)$ and the second activity by the vector OA_2. For an open economy, the long-run locus of net production possibilities is the straight-line segment A_1A_2; for a closed economy, the long-run locus is that part of A_1A_2 cut off by the axes, that is, B_1B_2. During any particular time period, however, the allocation of labour between industries is fixed by decisions of the preceding period. Labour cannot be immediately transferred from one activity to another; at most it can be withdrawn from an activity and allowed to stand idle, thus ensuring some

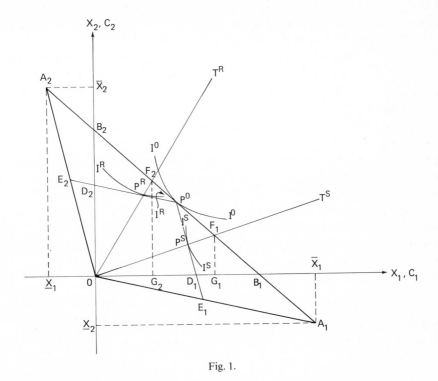

Fig. 1.

saving of the intermediate or produced input. Suppose that one-half of the labour force has been committed to each activity, so that the long-run production point is P^0. Then, for an open economy, the locus of short-run production possibilities is $E_1 P^0 E_2$, where $E_1 P^0$ is parallel to OA_2 and $E_2 P^0$ is parallel to OA_1; for a closed economy, the locus is $D_1 P^0 D_2$. Of course, there is a different locus of short-run production possibilities for each allocation of labour, that is, for each choice of P^0 on $A_1 A_2$.

We consider now the equilibrium of a single country in isolation, say country A. Since all consuming-producing units in A are alike, we may introduce a single utility function $U(C_1, C_2; C_3)$ and interpret C_i either as aggregate consumption of the ith commodity or as a constant multiple of consumption by the typical unit. The function U is assumed to be not separable with respect to C_3. Under conditions of technological certainty we may set $C_3 = X_3^0$, where X_3^0 is the exogenously given constant output of the purely domestic good, and thus obtain a 'partial' utility function of the amounts consumed of the two tradeable commodities, that is, $U(C_1, C_2; X_3^0)$. Then, superimposing a family of indifference curves on fig. 1, we find that the community reaches a production–consumption equilibrium at P^0, where the locus of long-run production possibilities $B_1 B_2$ forms a tangent to the indifference curve $I^0 I^0$. The loci of short-run production possibilities play no role in the determination of an uncertainty-free equilibrium.

In order to maintain comparability of the certainty and uncertainty models we introduce uncertainty in such a way as to leave the production technology of the two tradeable commodities unaffected. For this purpose we suppose that the exogenously given supply of the third commodity is random, taking the values X_3^R and X_3^S (R and S for 'rain' and 'shine') with probabilities W^R and W^S ($= 1 - W^R$), where $0 < W^R < 1$. Utility may then be written as $U(C_1, C_2; C_3^j)$ where $C_3^j = X_3^j$, and $j = $ R, S. If $X_3 = X_3^R$ we have a partial indifference map consisting of curves such as $I^R I^R$ in fig. 1, while if $X_3 = X_3^S$ the entire indifference map changes and we have curves such as $I^S I^S$.

Given the choice of P^0 by the economic units, the locus of short-run production possibilities in the following period is $D_1 P^0 D_2$ (fig. 1). If, in the following period, $X_3 = X_3^R$, the equilibrium production–consumption point is P^R on $D_2 P^0$ and p^R, the equilibrium price of the first commodity in terms of the second, is proportional to the slope of $D_2 P^0$. If, alternatively, $X_3 = X_3^S$, the equilibrium production–consumption point is P^S on $D_1 P^0$ and the equilibrium price p^S is indicated by the slope of $D_1 P^0$. Let OT^R be the Engel curve or expansion path defined by p^R and $C_3 = X_3^R$; and let OT^S be the Engel curve defined by p^S and $C_3 = X_3^S$. The locus of long-run production possibilities $A_1 A_2$

intersects OT^R and OT^S at F_2 and F_1, respectively. Then it is clear that, for any P^0 between F_1 and F_2, the equilibrium price ratio is $p^R(p^S)$ with probability $W^R(W^S = 1 - W^R)$.

How should the economic units choose P^0? We first note that, in general equilibrium, the units will consider only those P^0 between F_1 and F_2. For suppose that they choose a point P^0 to the left of F_2 on A_1A_2. If $X_3 = X_3^R$, the market equilibrium price must be greater than p^R; and, if $X_3 = X_3^S$, the equilibrium price is p^S. In either case, a point P^0 not so far to the left is preferred. Thus the supposition that the economic units choose a point to the left of F_2 leads to a contradiction when the market is in equilibrium. Similarly for a P^0 to the right of F_1. Hence the price in any equilibrium is p^R with probability W^R and p^S with probability $W^S = 1 - W^R$.

We suppose that each economic unit seeks to maximize its expected utility. Let $U^*(p^j, P^0)$ be the maximum utility for given P^0 and p^j, $j = R, S$. Then the problem facing the typical economic unit is to find

$$\max_{P^0} \{W^R U^*(p^R, P^0) + W^S U^*(p^S, P^0)\}. \tag{1}$$

By a suitable choice of U we can ensure that a solution value of P^0 lies in the interior of F_1F_2. We then have a stationary equilibrium characterized by the clearance of all markets; a stable and known probability distribution of prices, with the probability of p^R being W^R and the probability of p^S being W^S; the maximization by each economic unit of its utility subject to the prevailing price ratio and to the locus of short-run production possibilities defined by the solution to (1). We note that, for a single economy containing identical economic units, the 'spot' equilibrium just described is the same as the Arrow–Debreu 'futures' equilibrium, and that both equilibria are Pareto-optimal.

3. Trading equilibrium: spot markets

Let us now introduce a second country, say B, and the possibility of free trade in the first and second commodities. To keep the argument as simple as possible, we suppose that country B is small in relation to A, in the sense that B could sell any part of its maximum output of either commodity at the A-price ratio p^R or p^S. The technology of country B is displayed in fig. 2. Denoting by $s(P_iP_j)$ the absolute value of the slope of any straight-line segment, referred to

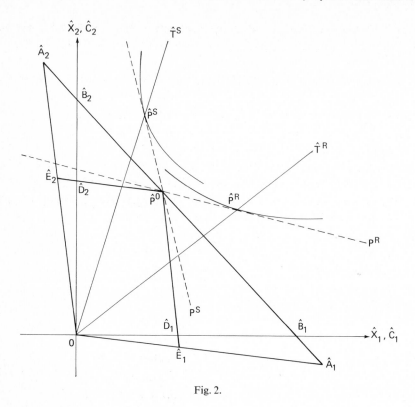

Fig. 2.

the horizontal axis, we assume that

$$s(\hat{E}_2\hat{P}^0) < p^R = s(E_2P^0) < s(A_1A_2) < s(\hat{A}_1\hat{A}_2) < s(E_1P^0) = p^S < s(\hat{E}_1\hat{P}^0).$$

$$(2)$$

(A circumflex distinguishes the quantities relating to country B.) It follows that the price ratio facing country B fluctuates above and below the level indicated by $s(\hat{A}_1\hat{A}_2)$.

As a further simplification, we suppose that in country B there is no technological uncertainty at all. (Of course B, a price-taker, must still cope with uncertainty concerning prices.) The partial utility function of B is then $\hat{U}(\hat{C}_1, \hat{C}_2; \hat{X}_3^0) = \hat{U}(\hat{C}; \hat{X}_3^0)$, with $\hat{X}_3^0$ a constant. If $\hat{E}_1\hat{P}^0\hat{E}_2$ is the locus of short-run production possibilities in country B then at prices p^R and p^S the equilibrium consumption vectors are indicated by points $\hat{P}^R$ and $\hat{P}^S$ respectively. The equilibrium points change if the commitment of labour changes. In the long-run equilibrium the small country chooses its P^0 to maximize expected utility at the p^J price ratios determined in the large country. (It may be noted that for the small country this stationary equilibrium with trade is different from the one that would prevail in an Arrow–Debreu model of contingent markets.)

In the case of certainty we know that the relevant production slopes are $s(A_1A_2)$ and $s(\hat{A}_1\hat{A}_2)$ and that if the latter is larger then country B will specialize in producing the second commodity. The same will be true under uncertainty if both p^R and p^S are smaller than $s(\hat{A}_1\hat{A}_2)$. However, if p^j fluctuates above and below $s(\hat{A}_1\hat{A}_2)$ then country B will ordinarily diversify its production between the two industries. Moreover its production need not be dominated by its 'comparative advantage' in the second commodity. To take an extreme case, it is even possible that country B will completely specialize in the first commodity (in which it has a comparative disadvantage under certainty)[2].

4. An example

In this section we develop a numerical example of complete trade reversal. Let the utility function of country A be

$$U(C_1, C_2; C_3) = \log C_1 + \delta(C_3) \log C_2, \tag{3}$$

where

$$\delta(C_3) > 0, \quad (d/dC_3)\delta(C_3) > 0, \quad (d^2/dC_3^2)\delta(C_3) < 0 \tag{4}$$

so that U is strictly concave, displaying relative risk aversion in all of its arguments. The equation of the locus of long-run production possibilities is, say,

$$X_2^* = \alpha - \beta X_1^* \tag{5}$$

and the budget constraint is

$$\begin{aligned} C_2^R + p^R C_1^R = X_2^* + p^R X_1^* \quad \text{when } X_3 = X_3^R \\ C_2^S + p^S C_1^S = X_2^* + p^S X_1^* \quad \text{when } X_3 = X_3^S. \end{aligned} \tag{6}$$

---

[2] Conclusions of this type could have been obtained simply by confronting the small country with randomly fluctuating prices, without inquiring into the source of the randomness. However, while this partial-equilibrium approach would have spared us some tedious calculation, it would have left the job half done. Moreover, to display a world trading equilibrium under conditions of uncertainty seemed in itself to be a useful exercise. Finally, we wished to preserve symmetry in our treatments of spot and futures markets.

The demand functions derived from (3), (5) and (6) are

$$C_1^R = \frac{\alpha + (p^R - \beta)X_1^*}{p^R[1 + \delta(X_3^R)]}, \qquad C_2^R = \delta(X_3^R)p^R C_1^R \tag{7a}$$

and

$$C_1^S = \frac{\alpha + (p^S - \beta)X_1^*}{p^S[1 + \delta(X_3^S)]}, \qquad C_2^S = \delta(X_3^S)p^S C_1^S, \tag{7b}$$

Substituting from (7) into (3) and taking account of (5), we obtain

$$E\{U\} = \sum_{j=R,S} W^j \left[\log \frac{\alpha + (p^j - \beta)X_2^*}{p^j(1 + \delta^j)} + \delta^j \frac{\alpha + (p^j - \beta)X_1^*}{1 + \delta^j} \right]$$

$$\equiv V(X_1^*). \tag{8}$$

Hence

$$(d/dX_1^*)V(X_1^*) = \sum_j \left[\frac{W^j(1 + \delta^j)(p^j - \beta)}{\alpha + (p^j - \beta)X_1^*} \right] \tag{9}$$

and it can be verified that $d^2V/dX_1^{*2} < 0$. At an interior maximum, expression (9) is equal to zero; hence

$$\text{opt } X_1^* = - \frac{\alpha \sum_j W^j(1 + \delta^j)(p^j - \beta)}{(p^R - \beta)(p^S - \beta) \sum_j W^j(1 + \delta^j)}. \tag{10}$$

We assume, as in fig. 1, that $p^R < \beta < p^S$; hence the denominator of (10) is positive. We also assume, as in fig. 1, that p^R and p^S correspond to the slopes of the locus of short-run production possibilities and that the slopes of OT^R and OT^S are given, by (7), as $\delta^R p^R$ and $\delta^S p^S$, respectively. To ensure the existence of a feasible solution for the economy as a whole, we require that

$$\delta^S p^S < X_2^*/X_1^* < \delta^R p^R. \tag{11}$$

Applying (5) and (10) to (11), we obtain

$$\delta^S p^S < \frac{W^R(1 + \delta^R)(p^R - \beta)(-p^S) + W^S(1 + \delta^S)(p^S - \beta)(-p^R)}{W^R(1 + \delta^R)(p^R - \beta) + W^S(1 + \delta^S)(p^S - \beta)} < \delta^R p^R. \tag{12}$$

Suppose now that

$$W^S = 1 - W^R = 0.83, \qquad \delta^R = 6, \qquad \delta^S = 1, \qquad \delta^S = 3, \qquad \beta = 2. \tag{13}$$

It may be verified that these values are consistent with (12). They therefore yield an internal equilibrium of country A between the two expansion paths.

Let us turn to the small country B. The utility function of B is assumed to be

$$U(C_1, C_2; C_3) = \log C_1 + \delta \log C_2. \tag{14}$$

For B, $\delta^R = \delta^S = \delta$; hence the counterpart to (10) is

$$\text{opt } X_1^* = -\frac{\alpha \sum_j W^j(p^j - \hat{\beta})}{(p^R - \hat{\beta})(p^S - \hat{\beta})} = -\frac{\alpha(\bar{p} - \hat{\beta})}{(p^R - \hat{\beta})(p^S - \hat{\beta})}, \tag{15}$$

where $\bar{p} \equiv \sum_j W^j p^j$. As in figs. 1 and 2, we require that

$$p^R < \beta < \hat{\beta} < p^S. \tag{16}$$

Suppose further that neither productive process involves intermediate inputs, so that the locus of long-run production possibilities in country B is confined to the non-negative quadrant and the maximal value of $\hat{X}_1^*$ is

$$\hat{X}_{1m}^* = \hat{\alpha}/\hat{\beta}. \tag{17}$$

For a corner solution at $\hat{X}_{1m}^*$ it is necessary and sufficient that opt $\hat{X}_1^* \geqq \hat{X}_{1m}^*$ or, in view of (15) and (17), that

$$-\hat{\beta}(\bar{p} - \hat{\beta})/(p^R - \hat{\beta})(p^S - \hat{\beta}) \geqq 1. \tag{18}$$

From (13) we calculate that $\bar{p} = 2 \cdot 66$. Suppose now that $\hat{\beta} = 2 \cdot 1$. The left-hand side of (18) is then $1 \cdot 18$ and the inequality is satisfied. Since $p^R = 1$ and $\beta = 2$, $\hat{\beta} = 2 \cdot 1$ also satisfies (16). Hence country B specializes completely in the production of the first commodity, in spite of the fact that $\hat{\beta} > \beta$.

5. Alternative model incorporating futures markets

The foregoing analysis rested on the assumption that, while the allocation of labour is determined under conditions of uncertainty, trade itself is conducted *ex post* or spot, under conditions of complete certainty. In this section we swing to the other extreme and assume that all contracts to exchange the two traded commodities are entered into *ex ante* and involve the Arrow–Debreu type of contingent claims on future goods (see Arrow, 1953 and Debreu, 1959). In our earlier model we allowed trade within given states of nature but not across states of nature. We now introduce the latter possibility by defining commodities 1 and 2 in terms of their physical characteristics, location and state of nature and by assuming that all contracts to buy and sell are entered into before the actual production of the commodity. The third commodity is now supposed to be not subject to exchange.

The assumptions of Arrow and Debreu are, of course, unrealistic. Nevertheless they are attractive because they are simple and because, from a welfare point of view, they represent an idealization of the real world. Indeed, since the risk model of Arrow and Debreu preserves so many features of the model of risk-free competitive equilibrium one might suppose that it is incompatible with trade reversal of the type discussed earlier.

We begin by studying A (the large country) in isolation. For simplicity we now consider the extreme case in which neither commodity 1 nor commodity 2 is needed as an intermediate input in the production of the other commodity. (This assumption can be relaxed.) Then the locus of short-run production possibilities is rectangular, as in fig. 3. We denote by p_i^R and p_i^S the prices contracted now to be paid next period for the delivery next period of a unit of the ith commodity in the two alternative states of nature. Then $p_i^R + p_i^S$ is the price to be paid for the certain delivery of a unit of the ith commodity. Every economic unit is endowed with the same utility function $V(C^R, C^S, C_3^R, C_3^S)$ which, we suppose, takes the special von Neumann form

$$V = W^R U(C^R; C_3^R) + W^S U(C^S; C_3^S). \tag{19}$$

(C^j denotes the vector $[C_1^j, C_2^j]$.) If today the economic unit sells X_1^* on the

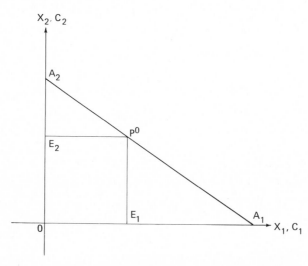

Fig. 3.

futures market, it receives tomorrow an income of

$$I = \sum_{i=1}^{2} (p_i^R + p_i^S)X^*, \tag{20}$$

where $X_2^* = \alpha - \beta X_1^*$ along the locus of long-run production possibilities (A_1A_2 in fig. 3). We consider now the problem of maximizing V with respect to C^R and C^S for given X_1^* and, to this end, introduce the Lagrangian

$$L = W^R U(C^R; X_3^R) + W^S U(C^S; X_3^S) - \lambda \left[\sum_{i=1}^{2} (p_i^R C_i^R + p_i^S C_i^S) - I \right]. \tag{21}$$

The first-order conditions for an interior maximum are

$$\frac{U_1^R}{U_2^R} = \frac{p_1^R}{p_2^R}\frac{U_1^S}{U_2^S} = \frac{p_1^S}{p_2^S}\frac{U_1^R}{U_1^S} = \frac{p_1^R}{p_1^S}\frac{W^S}{W^R}, \tag{22}$$

where $U_1^R \equiv \partial U(C_1^R, C_2^R; X_3^R)/\partial C_1^R$, etc. Differentiating the optimal value of L with respect to X_1^* and applying the appropriate envelope theorem, we obtain

$$(\partial/\partial X_1^*)(\text{opt } L) = \lambda(\partial I/\partial X_1^*) = \lambda[(p_1^R + p_1^S) + \beta(p_2^R + p_2^S)]. \tag{23}$$

Thus for an interior solution it is necessary that the prices satisfy $\partial I/\partial X_1^* = 0$ or

$$\beta = (p_1^R + p_1^S)/(p_2^R + p_2^S), \tag{24}$$

a condition with an obvious counterpart under certainty. Finally, the equilibrium of the economy is determined by (22), (24) and the market clearing conditions

$$C_i^R = C_i^S = C_i^*, \qquad i = 1, 2. \tag{25}$$

Including (5), we have altogether nine equations and nine variables: C_i^R and C_i^S (four variables), X_1^* (two variables) and three price ratios. (In sections 2 and 3, because of the separation of the states of nature, it was possible to choose two separate *numéraires*; here we may choose only one.)

Let us now reintroduce country B. Since B is small in relation to A, all prices are determined in the manner just described. For B we retain our earlier assumption that each commodity is needed in the production of the other. Thus $\hat{a}_{ij}$ is the amount of good i required per unit of good j. The loci of short-run production possibilities are typified therefore by $\hat{E}_1\hat{P}^0\hat{E}_2$ in fig. 4, where $s(\hat{E}_2\hat{P}^0) = \hat{\alpha}_{21}$ and $s(\hat{E}_1\hat{P}^0) = 1/\hat{\alpha}_{12}$. The figure is drawn on the further assumption that

$$0 < p_1^R/p_2^R < \hat{\alpha}_{21} < 1/\hat{\alpha}_{12} < p_1^S/p_2^S < \infty. \tag{26}$$

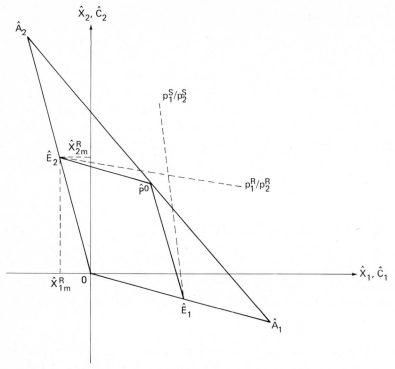

Fig. 4.

Let the equation of the locus of long-run production possibilities be

$$\hat{X}_2^* = \hat{\alpha} - \hat{\beta}X_1^* \tag{27}$$

and denote by $\hat{X}_{2m}^R$ the value of $\hat{X}_2$ at $\hat{E}_2$ and by $\hat{X}_{1m}^S$ the value of $\hat{X}_1$ at $\hat{E}_1$. It can be calculated that

$$\hat{X}_{1m}^R = \frac{a_{12}}{1 - \hat{a}_{12}\hat{a}_{21}} [-\hat{\alpha} + (\hat{\beta} - \hat{a}_{21})\hat{X}_1^*],$$

$$\hat{X}_{2m}^R = \frac{1}{1 - \hat{a}_{12}\hat{a}_{21}} [\hat{\alpha} - (\hat{\beta} - \hat{a}_{21})\hat{X}_1^*],$$

$$\hat{X}_{1m}^S = \frac{\hat{a}_{12}}{1 - \hat{a}_{12}\hat{a}_{21}} \left[\hat{\alpha} - \left(\hat{\beta} - \frac{1}{\hat{a}_{12}}\right)\hat{X}_1^*\right], \tag{28}$$

$$\hat{X}_{2m}^S = \frac{\hat{a}_{12}\hat{a}_{21}}{1 - \hat{a}_{12}\hat{a}_{21}} \left[-\hat{\alpha} + \left(\hat{\beta} - \frac{1}{\hat{a}_{12}}\right)\hat{X}_1^*\right].$$

The income of country B is

$$\hat{I} = \sum_{i=1}^{2} (p_i^R \hat{X}_i^R + p_i^S \hat{X}_i^S). \tag{29}$$

(The short-run transformation function containing $\hat{X}_i^R$ and $\hat{X}_i^S$ depends, of course, on $\hat{X}_1^*$.)

Suppose now that the utility function of B is of the same general form as that of A, that is, $\hat{V}(\hat{C}^R, \hat{C}^S, \hat{C}_3^R, \hat{C}_3^S)$, and let us maximize $\hat{V}$ subject to given $\hat{X}_1^*$. This can be done in stages: first, $\hat{I}$ is maximized; then $\hat{V}$ is maximized, given $\hat{I}$. From the first stage we obtain $\hat{I}(\hat{X}_1^*)$, and from the second $\hat{V}(\hat{I})$. Thus

$$\frac{\partial \hat{V}}{\partial \hat{X}_1^*} = \frac{\mathrm{d}\hat{V}(\hat{I})}{\mathrm{d}\hat{I}} \frac{\mathrm{d}\hat{I}(\hat{X}_1^*)}{\mathrm{d}\hat{X}_1^*}. \tag{30}$$

Now $\mathrm{d}\hat{V}(\hat{I})/\mathrm{d}\hat{I}$ is obviously positive; hence the economic unit will continue to increase (decrease) $\hat{X}_1^*$ as long as $\mathrm{d}\hat{I}(\hat{X}_1^*)/\mathrm{d}\hat{X}_1^*$ is positive (negative). We may therefore concentrate on the second stage of maximization.

We note that the maximization of $\hat{I}$ with respect to $\hat{X}_i^R$ and $\hat{X}_i^S$, given $\hat{X}_1^*$, involves two separable constraints, which may be written in general form as

$$\Phi(\hat{X}^R; \hat{X}_1^*) = 0, \qquad \Phi(\hat{X}^S; \hat{X}_1^*) = 0. \tag{31}$$

It follows that if $\hat{I}$ is maximized with respect to $\hat{X}_i^R$ and $\hat{X}_i^S$, then $\Sigma p_i^R \hat{X}_i^R$ must be maximized subject to $\Phi(\hat{X}^R; \hat{X}_1^*) = 0$ and $\sum p_i^S \hat{X}_i^S$ must be maximized subject to $\Phi(\hat{X}^S; \hat{X}_1^*) = 0$. Thus, given $\hat{X}_1^*$, we may independently maximize the income components associated with each of the two states of the world. From fig. 4 it is clear that, in the first state, the optimal production point is $\hat{E}_2$ and that, in the second state, the optimal point is $\hat{E}_1$. The net amounts produced are given by (28) above. Substituting from (28) into the expression for income, we obtain

$$\max_{\hat{X}_i^R, \hat{X}_i^S} \hat{I} = \text{const.} + \frac{1}{1 - \hat{a}_{12}\hat{a}_{21}} \left[(\hat{\beta} - \hat{a}_{21})(p_1^R \hat{a}_{12} - p_2^R) \right.$$
$$\left. + \left(\hat{\beta} - \frac{1}{\hat{a}_{12}} \right)(p_2^S \hat{a}_{21} - p_1^S)\hat{a}_{12} \right] \hat{X}_1^* = \text{const.} + k\hat{X}_1^*, \tag{32}$$

say, where, from the construction of fig. 4,

$$\hat{\beta} - \hat{a}_{21} > 0, \qquad p_1^R \hat{a}_{12} - p_2^R < 0, \qquad \hat{\beta} - (1/\hat{a}_{12}) < 0,$$
$$p_2^S \hat{a}_{21} - p_1^S < 0 \quad \text{and} \quad 1 - \hat{a}_{12}\hat{a}_{21} > 0.$$

We note that, since k is constant, the small country must always specialize completely, as in the classical model (but in contrast to the conclusions of section 3). We note also that the sign of k depends not only on $\hat{\beta}$ and the prices but also on the parameters $\hat{a}_{ij}$ of the locus of *short-run* production possibilities. Thus the direction of specialization in B depends partly on the ease of short-run adjustment in that country and is not simply dependent on the relative magnitudes of β and $\hat{\beta}$. It follows that an example of trade reversal can be constructed.

We now provide such an example. Suppose that $\hat{\beta} > \beta$, so that, under certainty, country B specializes in the production of the second commodity. Suppose further that there exists in country A an interior equilibrium, so that $\beta = (p_1^R + p_1^S)/(p_2^R + p_2^S)$. Then

$$\hat{\beta} > (p_1^R + p_1^S)/(p_2^R + p_2^S). \tag{33}$$

In addition, from fig. 4,

$$p_1^R/p_2^R < \hat{a}_{21} < \hat{\beta} < 1/\hat{a}_{12} < p_1^S/p_2^S. \tag{34}$$

Now if country B is to specialize in the production of the *first* commodity then k must be positive, that is,

$$(\hat{\beta} - \hat{a}_{21})(p_1^R\hat{a}_{12} - p_2^R) + (\hat{\beta} - 1/\hat{a}_{12})(p_2^S\hat{a}_{21} - p_1^S)\hat{a}_{12} > 0. \tag{35}$$

Thus the problem of constructing an example of trade reversal reduces to that of finding positive values of $\hat{\beta}$, $\hat{a}_{ij}$, p_i^R and p_i^S which satisfy (33), (34) and (35). The following values meet that requirement:

$$p_1^R = 1.9, \qquad p_2^R = 1, \qquad \hat{a}_{21} = 3.5, \qquad \hat{\beta} = 4, \qquad 1/\hat{a}_{12} = 5,$$

$$p_1^S = 6, \qquad p_2^S = 1. \tag{36}$$

6. Concluding remarks

In conclusion we note that, simply by considering X_3 as a random preference parameter, it is possible to interpret our models in terms of uncertainty about tastes. On this interpretation, however, the plausibility of (1) as a criterion of country A's welfare is much reduced, and we do not wish to emphasize the possibility.

References

Arrow, K. J. (1953), Le rôle des valeurs boursières pour la répartition la meilleure des risques, *Econométrie*, 41–48, Centre nationale de la Recherche Scientifique, Paris. Reprinted in English as 'The role of securities in the optimal allocation of risk-bearing', *Review of Economic Studies*, 31 (April, 1964), 91–96.

Brainard, W. C., and R. N. Cooper (1968), Uncertainty and diversification in international trade, *Studies in Agricultural Economics, Trade and Development*, Food Research Institute, Stanford University, 8, No. (3), 257–285.

Debreu, G. (1959), *Theory of Value*, Wiley, New York, ch. 7.

Chapter 21

PATTERNS OF PRODUCTION AND TRADE UNDER CONDITIONS OF RESOURCE UNCERTAINTY*

1. Introduction

In an earlier paper, Kemp and Liviatan (1973) studied some of the implications for patterns of production and trade of randomness in individual preferences and in production sets. Here it is proposed to consider another fundamental source of uncertainty – randomness in factor endowments. The phenomenon is of great importance to all countries – of even greater importance, perhaps, than randomness of preferences, of production sets, or of world prices[1] – but it is of special importance to poor, predominantly agricultural countries. The discussion is in terms of a generalized Torrens–Ricardo model of production, with just one way of producing each commodity. The general conclusions reached are much the same as in Kemp and Liviatan (1973). Thus it is shown that, under conditions of resource uncertainty, long-run comparative advantage has little predictive value concerning patterns of trade and specialization and that, in particular, such patterns may be just the reverse of those indicated by long-run comparative advantage.

2. One primary factor of production

It is convenient to begin with the trivial case in which there is a single primary factor of production. For the time being, then, we consider a small trading country composed of identical consuming–producing units, facing known and

* The helpful suggestions of Yew-Kwang Ng and Yasuo Uekawa are gratefully acknowledged.

[1] On a general-equilibrium view of the world economy, price uncertainty is not fundamental but is derived from the randomness of preferences, technique and resource endowments. However this does not mean that one cannot properly examine the responses of a small country to the randomness of world prices.

constant world prices and capable of producing either and both of two traded commodities with the aid of a single primary factor, say land. In terms of area, the total land endowment, as well as the endowment of each consuming–producing unit, is fixed. However, the amount of arable land varies with the weather and perhaps with other random environmental factors. Under any given weather conditions the locus of production possibilities is a determinate straight line, but in response to variations in the weather the locus undergoes random parallel displacements. Associated with the mean amount of arable land there is the long-run locus of production possibilities; this is identified with the locus of production possibilities under conditions of resource certainty. Finally, it is supposed that each consuming–producing unit must divide its land between the two commodities before the weather is known, that is, under conditions of uncertainty. (When the state of the weather is known, the proportion of arable land allocated to the ith industry will prove to be the same as the proportion of land area allocated.) Given the allocation, the units simply wait for the weather to declare itself and then trade from a known production point at the constant terms of trade.

It is evident that in this case each consuming–producing unit will find it to its advantage to completely specialize in the production of whichever commodity is favoured by a relative price greater than its constant marginal opportunity cost (and that, if neither commodity is distinguished in this way, the pattern of production is indeterminate). Since the identity of the favoured commodity (or the fact that neither commodity is favoured) is independent of the amount of uncertainty, the need to pre-commit resources is not a handicap. Thus we have

Proposition 1. Suppose that there is a single primary factor of production. Then it is always optimal to completely specialize in production, however great the uncertainty; and, if production is necessarily specialized, both the pattern of production and the pattern of trade are independent of the amount of uncertainty.

3. Two primary factors of production

This comforting conclusion must be heavily qualified if land is only one of several primary factors. Let us now introduce a second primary factor, say labour; and let us suppose that labour is available in constant amount and, for the time being, that the allocation of labour can be delayed until the weather has declared itself. Fig. 1 displays the labour constraint OLL' together with the long-run or average or 'under certainty' land constraint OTT'.

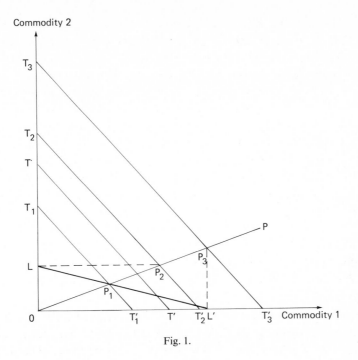

Fig. 1.

As in section 2, land must be committed before the state of the weather is known. Given the technology, the relative allocation of land can be represented by a positively sloped straight line through the origin; suppose, for purposes of illustration, that the allocation of land is described by the ray OP. Consider now the three lines T_1T_1', T_2T_2' and T_3T_3'. If it were not for the fact that land must be pre-committed, these would form the outer boundaries of realized land constraints, each associated with some particular state of the weather. Because of pre-commitment, however, the true realized or *post factum* land constraints are the rectangles with north-east corners at P_1, P_2 and P_3, respectively.

Associated with a particular state of the weather and given a particular pattern of land commitment there is a set of short-run production possibilities. This set is obtained as the intersection of the (triangular) labour constraint and the relevant (rectangular) land constraint. Evidently the set may be triangular, rectangular or triangular with one or both acute corners shaved off. Thus for all land constraints contained in the rectangle OP_1 the set coincides with the land constraint (that is, the labour constraint is ineffective); for all land constraints larger than the rectangular area OP_1 but smaller than the rectangular area OP_2

the set is triangular with both corners lopped (fig. 2); for all land constraints larger than or equal to the rectangular area OP_2 but smaller than the rectangular area OP_3 the set is triangular with one corner lopped (fig. 3); and, finally, for all land constraints larger than or equal to the rectangular area OP_3 the set coincides with the triangular labour constraint (that is, the land constraint is ineffective).

Given these facts about sets of short-run production possibilities, and given the world commodity price ratio, how much land should be allocated to each of the two commodities, that is, what should be the slope of the ray OP?

It is clear that if the price line has a slope not less than the outer boundaries of the land constraints then it is optimal to allocate all of the available land to the first commodity, and that if the price line has a slope not greater than the outer boundary of the labour constraint then it is optimal to allocate all of the available land to the second commodity. For such extreme price ratios the optimal policy is the same as under certainty (when the land constraint is OTT').

Suppose then that the slope of the price line falls somewhere between those of LL' and TT'. Under that supposition, if it is always the case (whatever the state of the weather) that only the labour constraint is effective, or if it is always the case that only the land constraint is effective, then clearly it is optimal to specialize completely, pre-committing all of the available land to one

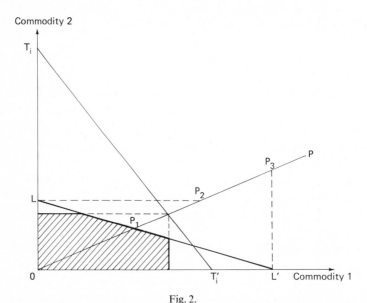

Fig. 2.

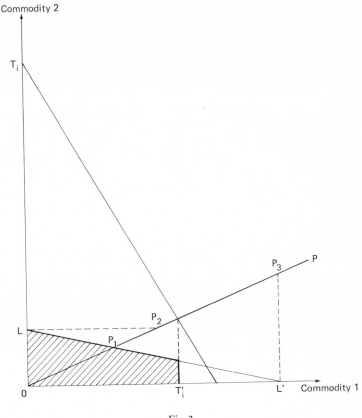

Fig. 3.

industry, the industry favoured depending on the constraint which is operative.

Again under the supposition that the slope of the price line lies between the slopes of LL' and TT', but at the other extreme, if it is always the case that both constraints are operative then it is optimal to incompletely specialize, pre-committing some of the available land to each industry and post-commiting some of the available labour to each industry, with the amount of labour committed to any particular industry depending of course on the state of the weather. One can be more precise. Let $OT_lT'_l$ and $OT_uT'_u$ in fig. 4 be the smallest and largest possible *ante factum* land constraints, the actual *ante factum* land constraint fluctuating between these extremes. Then it is easy to check that, whatever the commodity price ratio, it is suboptimal to pre-commit land in a manner which can be represented by a ray lying outside the cone P_lOP_u. The optimal ray must lie in that cone, its precise location depending on

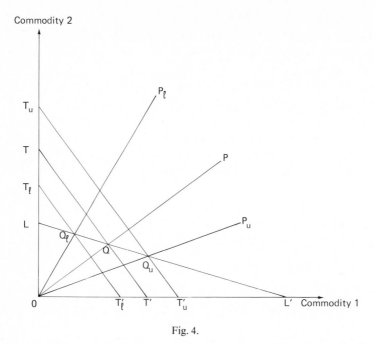

Fig. 4.

the price ratio. In particular, it is possible to drive the optimal ray as close as is desired to OP_l (or OP_u) by choosing a price ratio sufficiently close to that represented by the slope of LL' (respectively, $T_l T'_l$ or $T_u T'_u$). Under certainty, on the other hand, the optimal ray is always OP. Clearly, then, only in singular cases will the optimal allocation of land under uncertainty coincide with the optimal allocation of land under certainty.

Under the same supposition, there remains one residual possibility, that sometimes only one *ante factum* constraint is effective but that neither the labour nor the land constraint is always the only effective constraint. In that case, the optimal specialization may be complete or incomplete, depending on the commodity price ratio. Moreover it is easy to construct examples in which it is optimal to specialize completely under conditions of resource certainty but not under conditions of uncertainty, and vice versa. Thus we have

Proposition 2. Suppose that there are two primary factors of production, labour and land, that land (but not labour) must be pre-committed, and that land (but not labour) is in random supply. If the commodity price ratio lies outside the bounds set by the ante factum labour and land constraints then it is optimal to specialize in one commodity or the other, and the optimal specializa-

tion is the same however great the uncertainty. The same is true if the commodity price ratio lies between the bounds set by the two constraints but one particular constraint is always ineffective. In other cases, resource uncertainty may radically change the optimal pattern of specialization; in particular, it may be optimal to completely specialize under conditions of uncertainty but not under conditions of certainty, and vice versa.

Proposition 2 has been argued on the supposition that land but not labour (that is, the factor in random supply but not the factor in non-random supply) must be pre-committed. However, the conclusions of the proposition remain valid if the supposition is turned upside down. Indeed, as this suggests, they remain valid if each factor must be pre-committed, so that both an optimal ray for labour and an optimal ray for land must be found. (In fact it is optimal to choose the same ray for labour as for land.)

4. Generalizations – uncertainty about the quality of factors

The resource uncertainty studied in sections 2 and 3 is of a very pure kind: the quantity of arable land varies randomly, but its quality is invariant. In practice, of course, variations in the weather bring in their train variations not only in the quantity of arable land but also in the relative suitability of the land for alternative crops. Associated with each state of the weather there is, in effect, a particular kind of land with its own characteristic relative and absolute efficiencies in the two industries. In this section an attempt is made to accommodate this feature of reality. With the extra freedom offered by a more general formulation it is possible to establish even more dramatic contrasts between the optimal allocation of resources under certainty and the optimal allocation under conditions of uncertainty.

In view of the above remarks, there is no loss in ignoring labour. Thus two traded commodities are produced with the aid of land, the quality of which varies with the weather. In any given weather conditions the locus of production possibilities is a straight line; but the locus shifts randomly, not necessarily in parallel fashion, in response to variations in the weather. For simplicity, it is assumed that just two types of weather (and therefore just two qualities of land) are possible. It either rains or it shines, with probabilities of occurrence w^R and w^S, respectively. If it rains, the locus of production possibilities is $P^R P^R$ in fig. 5; if it shines, the locus is $P^S P^S$, not necessarily

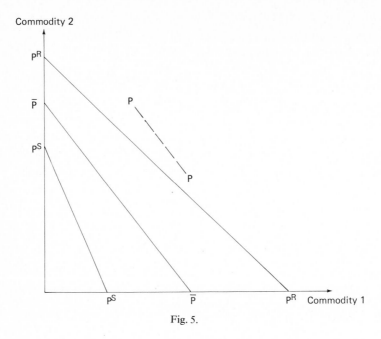

Fig. 5.

parallel to $P^R P^R$ but possibly intersecting it. The average or long-run locus is $\bar{P}\bar{P}$. The constant terms of trade are indicated by the slope of PP.

As in sections 2 and 3, the typical consuming–producing unit is confronted by a two-stage problem. The allocation of land area must be completed before the weather is known and, therefore, before the quality of the land is known; the allocation is irrevocable. Given the allocation, the task of the consuming–producing unit is simply to wait for the weather to declare itself and then trade from a known production point at the given terms of trade.

Let us consider the particular example displayed in fig. 6. The figure is drawn on the assumptions that, in the second industry, the productivity of land area is independent of the weather and that $w^R = \frac{1}{2} = w^S$. If it were not for the fact of pre-commitment, the locus of production possibilities would be PP^R when it rains, PP^S when it shines, and $P\bar{P}$ on the average. The world price ratio is assumed to differ in magnitude only very slightly from the slope of $P\bar{P}$, with the difference favouring the first commodity. In the absence of uncertainty, with P^R and P^S coinciding with $\bar{P}$, the country would produce only the first commodity and trade from $\bar{P}$ to the consumption point $\bar{C} = (\bar{C}_1, \bar{C}_2)$, where an indifference curve is tangential to the world price line $P\bar{P}$. Let us now reintroduce uncertainty and suppose that the community is composed of

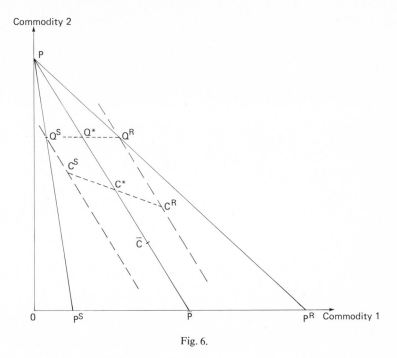

Fig. 6.

risk-averting individuals, with a strictly concave utility function u. Then each unit will find it to its advantage to specialize completely in producing the second commodity, trading from P back to the uncertainty-free consumption point $\bar{C}$. To understand this, suppose the contrary, that it is optimal to allocate some land area to the production of the first commodity so that, when it rains, the point of actual production is Q^R and the point of consumption C^R (say) and, when it shines, the point of production is Q^S (horizontally to the left of Q^R) and the point of consumption C^S (say). Let Q^* be the point of intersection of $P\bar{P}$ with $Q^S Q^R$ and let C^* be the point of intersection of $P\bar{P}$ with $C^S C^R$. Then, since the lines $Q^S C^S$, $Q^* C^*$ and $Q^R C^R$ are parallel, and since $Q^S Q^R$ is parallel to the horizontal axis,

$$w^R/w^S = Q^S Q^*/Q^* Q^R = C^S C^*/C^* C^R.$$

Thus $C^* = w^S C^S + w^R C^R$ and, from the concavity of u,

$$u(C^S)w^S + u(C^R)w^R < u(C^*) \leqq u(\bar{C}).$$

This is a contradiction; hence it is not optimal to allocate land to the production of the first commodity. Thus we have

Proposition 3. Suppose that there is a single primary factor of production, land area, that land must be pre-committed and that the quality of land is random. Then it may be optimal to specialize in the production (and export) of one commodity under conditions of certainty and in the production (and export) of the other commodity under uncertainty.

The general conclusion of sections 2 and 3, that long-run comparative advantage is an unreliable predictor both of trade patterns and of patterns of specialization, is reinforced.

Reference

Kemp, M. C. and N. Liviatan (1973), Production and trade patterns under uncertainty, *Economic Record*, 49, June, 215–227.

Chapter 22

SOME GENERAL-EQUILIBRIUM IMPLICATIONS OF TECHNOLOGICAL UNCERTAINTY*

1. Introduction

That the standard (Heckscher–Ohlin–Samuelson) model of production has not been extended to accommodate uncertainty is surprising – until one attempts such an extension. Then one's initial enthusiasm tends to be stifled by the inherent difficulty of the task and the fact that soon becomes evident that few strong theorems of standard theory survive an immersion in uncertainty. I derive a few mouse-like and perhaps self-evident propositions here, concerning the implications of technological uncertainty for outputs and the distribution of factor incomes in an open economy[1].

2. Analysis: small country

The initial context is a familiar one. A small economy produces two com-modities, the first a consumption good and the second an investment good, with

* The helpful comments of Wilfred Ethier, Geoffrey Fishburn, Ngo Van Long, James Melvin and Hiroshi Ohta are gratefully acknowledged.

[1] Batra (1974) covers some of the ground of this paper. However, his theorems 1, 2 and 4 seem to lack adequate proof. In particular, the right-hand side of his equations (19) is zero if initially there is no uncertainty so that, in Batra's notation, $\alpha_1 \equiv \mu_1$. Batra's error seems to stem from his adoption of the particular parameterization of uncertainty introduced by Sandmo (1971). As Sandmo himself has observed (1971, p. 59), the parameterization breaks down in the limiting case of certainty.

Moreover, Batra's theorem 3 seems to depend on the assumption that there exists a special class of risk-averse entrepreneurs who absorb all risks and who own neither of the two factors of production but hire them at fixed predetermined rentals. This implies the absence of market institutions which make possible the spreading of risks over all individuals. In a community of risk-averse individuals there is evidently an incentive to create such institutions and thus make possible the payment of rentals which depend on the revealed state of the world. However with risks widely spread it does not appear possible to prove anything like Batra's theorem 3. In particular it does not seem possible to prove it under the conditions of proposition 2 below.

the aid of two primary factors of production and under constant returns to scale. The production function of the first industry is subject to a random multiplicative (and therefore factor-neutral) disturbance.

For any particular value of the random variable it is possible to construct a locus of production possibilities; in particular, this is so when the random variable takes its mean value. Let $\bar{x}_i$ be the mean output of the ith industry, and

$$\bar{x}_2 = x_2(\bar{x}_1) \tag{1}$$

the locus of production possibilities, when the random variable takes its mean value. (The function $x_2(\bar{x}_1)$ is supposed to be decreasing and strictly concave[2]. The actual outputs of the first and second industries are then $(1 + \rho z)\bar{x}_1$ and $x_2(\bar{x}_1)$, respectively, where z is a random variable with mean zero and ρ, $\rho \geq 0$, is a parameter increases in which imply mean-preserving spreads of the random variable $1 + \rho z$. Commodity units are chosen of equal value. The total output of the economy, in terms of either commodity, is therefore

$$x \equiv (1 + \rho z)\bar{x}_1 + x_2(\bar{x}_1). \tag{2}$$

Factors of production must be allocated to the two industries before the realization of the random variable. Since the disturbance is factor-neutral it always is optimal to so allocate factors that mean production lies on the frontier[3]. The task of the community, therefore, reduces to that of maximizing its expected utility with respect to $\bar{x}_1$ and subject to (1). Social utility w is supposed to be a strictly concave function of income in terms of the first or consumption good, that is, of x. From (2), income depends on $\bar{x}_1$ and z; hence utility may be expressed indirectly as a function of the same variables. Thus the task of the community is to find

$$\max_{\bar{x}_1 \ z} \mathrm{E}\{w[x(\bar{x}_1, z)]\} \tag{3}$$

with the function x defined by (2).

The first- and second-order conditions for an interior maximum are, respectively,

$$\mathrm{E}\{w'(x) \cdot [1 + \rho z + x_2'(\bar{x}_1)]\} = 0 \tag{4}$$

---

[2] For some parts of the several propositions to be proved it is required only that $x_2(\bar{x}_1)$ be weakly concave. In the interests of a clean and orderly development, however, the stronger assumption is retained throughout.

[3] If the disturbance were factor-biased, it would be optimal to so allocate factors that, when the random variable takes its mean value, the output point lies inside the frontier.

and

$$\Delta \equiv E\{w''(x) \cdot [1 + \rho z + x_2'(\bar{x}_1)]^2\} + E\{w'(x) \cdot x_2''(\bar{x}_1)\} < 0, \tag{5}$$

where $w'(x) \equiv dw/dx$, $x_2'(\bar{x}_1) \equiv dx_2/d\bar{x}_1$, etc. Since by assumption $x_2''(\bar{x}_1) < 0$ and $w''(x) < 0$, the second-order condition is necessarily satisfied. Let $\bar{x}_1^*$ and $\bar{x}_2^* = x_2(\bar{x}_1^*)$ be the maximizing values of the two average outputs. In the special case of certainty, $\rho = 0$ and, since $x_2'(\bar{x}_1)$ is not random, (4) reduces to the familiar tangency requirement

$$1 + x_2'(\bar{x}_1) = 0. \tag{4'}$$

In fig. 1, $\bar{x}_1^{**}$ *and* $\bar{x}_2^{**}$ are the maximizing outputs defined by (4') and (1).

It can be shown that if under conditions of complete certainty optimal production is incompletely specialized then it must be so under conditions of uncertainty, however great the uncertainty. The reason is that even risk-averse decision-makers are prepared to accept sufficiently small favourable gambles. Formally, let us suppose that $\bar{x}_i^{**} > 0$ ($i = 1, 2$) and that $\bar{x}_1^* = 0$, $\bar{x}_2^* = x_2(0) > 0$ for some positive ρ. Then

$$\begin{aligned}
E\{w'(x) \cdot [1 + \rho z + x_2'(\bar{x}_2)]\} &= E\{w'[x_2(0)] \cdot [1 + \rho z + x_2'(0)]\} \\
&= w'[x_2(0)] \cdot [1 + x_2'(0) + \rho E\{z\} \\
&= w'[x_2(0)] \cdot [1 + x_2'(0)] \quad (\text{since } E\{z\} = 0) \\
&> 0 \quad (\text{since } x_2(\bar{x}_1) \text{ is strictly concave}). \tag{6}
\end{aligned}$$

implying that $[\bar{x}_1 = 0, \bar{x}_2 = x_2(0)]$ is not optimal. The proof is completed by showing that if under conditions of complete certainty optimal production is incompletely specialized then $\bar{x}_1^* < \bar{x}_1^{**}$ when $\rho > 0$, implying that $\bar{x}_2 = 0$ is suboptimal. Suppose that, when $\rho > 0, \bar{x}_1^* = \bar{x}_1^{**}$ (so that $\bar{x}_2^* = \bar{x}_2^{**}$), where $\bar{x}_i^* > 0$ ($i = 1, 2$). We then have

$$E\{w'(x^*) \cdot [1 + \rho z + x_2'(\bar{x}_1^*)]\} = \rho E\{w'(x^*)z\} \quad (\text{from (4')})$$

$$< 0 \quad (\text{from the strict concavity of } w, \text{ the fact that } E\{z\} = 0 \text{ and the fact that } x^* \text{ is increasing in } z) \tag{7}$$

in violation of (4); and equality can be restored only by setting

$$\bar{x}_1^* < \bar{x}_1^{**}. \tag{8}$$

While inequality (8) is valid for all $\rho > 0$, in general $\bar{x}_1^*$ is not a monotone function of ρ.

On average, a risk-averse community is less well off under uncertainty than

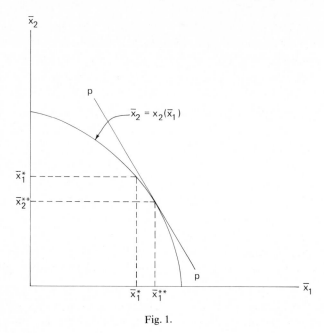

Fig. 1.

under conditions of certainty. Moreover, the relationship between expected social utility and uncertainty is monotone, whatever the degree of uncertainty and whatever the response of relative (or average) risk aversion to changes in consumption. By way of proof, we have

$$(\mathrm{d}/\mathrm{d}\rho)E\{w(x^*)\} = E\{w'(x^*) \cdot [(1 + \rho z + x_2'(\bar{x}_1^*))(\mathrm{d}\bar{x}_1^*/\mathrm{d}\rho) + z\bar{x}_1^*]\}$$

$$= \bar{x}_1^* \, E\{w'(x^*) \cdot z\} \quad \text{(from (4))}$$

$$< 0 \quad \text{(from (7))}. \tag{9}$$

Thus we arrive at[4]

Proposition 1. Suppose that in the absence of uncertainty optimal production is incompletely specialized. Then factor-neutral technological uncertainty con-

---

[4] In this proposition uncertainty-ridden optima are contrasted with the particular uncertainty-free equilibrium defined by $\rho = 0$. It may be asked whether that particular uncertainty-free equilibrium has any special claims to our attention. In this connection, note that, given $\bar{x}_1$, output x is positively and linearly related to z, so that a mean-preserving spread of z implies a mean-preserving spread of x. On the other hand, as Rothschild and Stiglitz (1970) have shown, only mean-preserving spreads of x invariably leave a risk-averse community worse off. Since the uncertainty-free situation with $\rho = 0$ is the limit of a sequence of mean-preserving contractions of x it seems natural to choose it as the standard for comparisons with uncertainty-ridden situations.

fined to one industry depresses the optimal average output of that industry below the level appropriate to conditions of certainty; but optimal production remains incompletely specialized, however great the uncertainty. Moreover, expected social utility is a decreasing function of the uncertainty.

The proposition is quite independent of the concrete assumption that the first or disturbed industry produces the consumption good. Indeed, the proposition is valid whatever the nature of the commodities produced by the two industries. If each industry produces a consumption good then, as a corollary to proposition 1, factor-neutral technological uncertainty may reverse the pattern of a small country's (average) trade, the disturbed industry giving way to the other industry as (on the average) provider of exports.

Will the optimal allocation of resources, defined by (4) and (1), emerge in a market economy? Obviously not, if no control is exercised over the distribution of income. Suppose, then, that social utility is of the Scitovsky kind, with all individual utilities increasing and decreasing together; and suppose further that after each realization of the random variable the market economy is subjected to lump sum redistributive transfers computed in the light of the given social utility function. Then the decision-makers in each industry, whoever they may be, will have a sufficient incentive to seek the maximum of expected utility. Moreover, factors will be paid their optimal marginal products in terms of the product of the uncertainty-free industry and the (random) ratio of the marginal products of the two factors will be the same in each industry. Thus we have, as a further corollary of proposition 1,

Proposition 2. Suppose that a market economy behaves as though it is maximizing the expected value of Scitovsky social utility and that in the absence of uncertainty something would be produced of each commodity. Then factor-neutral technological uncertainty confined to one industry reduces the average output of that industry below the level which would prevail in the absence of uncertainty; but production remains incompletely specialized, however great the uncertainty. It follows that factor-neutral technological uncertainty confined to one industry lowers (raises) the real reward, in terms of whatever commodity, of the factor employed relatively intensively (unintensively) by the risky industry. Finally, expected social utility is a decreasing function of the uncertainty.

Of course, this proposition is also quite independent of the assumption that the first industry produces a consumption good.

3. Extensions

To extend the two propositions to accommodate technological uncertainty in both industries is an obvious next step. However, the required calculations are extremely tedious and yield definite conclusions only under severely restrictive assumptions about the functions $w(x)$ and $x_2(\bar{x}_1)$. Here it is simply noted without proof that if in the absence of uncertainty optimal production is incompletely specialized and if there is non-positive correlation between the random variables, say z_1 and z_2, associated with the first and second industries then optimal production remains incompletely specialized, however great the uncertainty and however great the disparity between uncertainty in the first and in the second industries.

The analysis extends much more readily to general $m \times n$ economies (where m is the number of primary factors and n the number of products). Suppose again that the set of production possibilities is strictly convex[5]. Then the first proposition carries over without qualification to economies producing any number $n (n > 1)$ of commodities. (Since commodity prices are held constant, and since the disturbance is confined to one industry, there are still essentially only two industries.) It should be noted, however, that while a change in the output of the first industry implies an opposite change in the *aggregate* output of the remaining $n - 1$ industries (and therefore in the output of at least one of them) it does not imply an opposite change in the output of *each* of the remaining industries. Similarly, the second, third and last sentences of the second proposition extend to economies with more than two produced commodities. The fourth sentence remains valid if there are just two primary factors.

Most surprisingly, perhaps, the propositions carry over to economies possessed of monopoly–monopsony power in trade. Let π be the world price of the second commodity (the investment good) in terms of the first (the consumption good); in general, π depends on the amount produced (and exported) of the second commodity. Income in terms of the first commodity is $(1 + \rho z)\bar{x}_1 + \pi \bar{x}_2$ and the task of the community is to find

$$\max_{\bar{x}_1} \operatorname*{E}_{z}\{w[(1 + \rho z)\bar{x}_1 + \pi(x_2(\bar{x}_1)) \cdot x_2(\bar{x}_1)]\}. \tag{10}$$

The first- and second-order conditions for an interior maximum are, respectively,

$$\operatorname{E}\{w'(\ ) \cdot y\} = 0 \tag{11}$$

---

[5] This is a strong assumption when $m < n$. However, the remark in footnote 2 is still relevant.

and

$$\Delta' \equiv E\{w''(\ ) \cdot y^2\} + E\{w'(\ ) \cdot [(\pi' \cdot \bar{x}_2 + \pi)x_2'' + (2\pi' + \pi''\bar{x}_2)(x_2')^2]\} < 0,$$
(12)

where

$$y \equiv 1 + \rho z + [\pi'(\bar{x}_2) \cdot \bar{x}_2 + \pi(\bar{x}_2)]x_2'.$$
(13)

Now $\pi' \cdot \bar{x}_2 + \pi$ is the marginal revenue (in terms of the first commodity) derived from exports and in an optimum must be positive. Moreover, $2\pi' + \pi''\bar{x}_2$ reflects the curvature of the foreign offer curve and usually is taken to be negative. Thus under conventional assumptions about the foreign offer curve, and from the assumed concavity of $x_2(\bar{x}_1)$ and $w(\ )$, the second-order condition is necessarily satisfied. In the special case of complete certainty, $\rho = 0$ and (11) reduces to the 'optimal tariff' condition

$$1 + (\pi'\bar{x}_2 + \pi)x_2' = 0.$$
(11')

Reasoning similar to that of section 2 can now be applied to establish proposition 1 under the present more general assumptions. As a corollary, in any optimum under uncertainty the terms of trade must be less favourable to the policy-making country than in the optimum associated with certainty; and if relative risk aversion is a non-decreasing function of income then the terms of trade decline in monotone fashion as uncertainty increases. Similarly, proposition 2 can be established, it being understood that the government maintains a constant optimal tariff on imports of the first commodity[6].

In the above analysis of the large-country case only full optima have been considered. This leaves open the question whether analogues to propositions 1 and 2 are available when no advantage is taken of the country's monopoly–monopsony position. Here I simply report, without tiresome proof, that indeed there are 'second-best' counterparts to the 'first-best' propositions just discussed[7].

[6] In general, under conditions of uncertainty, the optimal *ad valorem* import duty, the optimal specific duty, the optimal import quota and the optimal export quota yield different optima, even after abstraction from differences in the distributional implications of the four controls. (This implies that at least some of the controls yield only 'second-best' optima and that for the achievement of a full optimum it may be necessary to apply more than one control.) In the particular model of section 2, however, the several optima coincide; there is therefore no need to be more specific about the nature of the optimal tariff imposed.

[7] In section 2 the state of technique was treated as a random variable and price as a parameter. However it is possible to reverse the roles of price and technique and obtain propositions

References

Arrow, K. J. (1965), *Aspects of the Theory of Risk-Bearing*, Yrjö Jahnssonin Säätio, Helsinki.

Batra, R. N. (1974), Resource allocation in a general equilibrium model of production under uncertainty, *Journal of Economic Theory*, 8, 50–63.

Pratt, J. W. (1964), Risk aversion in the small and in the large, *Econometrica*, 32, 122–136.

Rothschild, M. and J. E. Stiglitz (1970), Increasing risk: I a definition, *Journal of Economic Theory*, 2, 225–243.

Sandmo, A. (1971), On the theory of the competitive firm under price uncertainty, *American Economic Review*, 61, 65–73.

concerning the implications of price uncertainty. For example, if the consumption good is chosen as *numéraire* and if under certainty the price ratio is equal to the mean of the uncertain price ratio then it is possible to prove the following counterpart of proposition 1:

If in the absence of uncertainty optimal production is incompletely specialized then price uncertainty raises the optimal output of the consumption good above the level appropriate to complete certainty, but with optimal output remaining incompletely specialized; moreover, both the optimal output of the consumption good and expected social utility are increasing functions of the uncertainty.

Note, however, that for this proposition, as for the large country proposition of section 3, it is essential that there be only one consumption good. If both commodities can be consumed, w is no longer a function of a single variable linear in the random price ratio, and the results of Rothschild and Stiglitz are inapplicable; moreover there is then no single natural choice of certain price ratio.

Chapter 23

HOW TO EAT A CAKE OF UNKNOWN SIZE*

1. The problem

An individual possesses a cake. He does not know how big the cake is. However, to each conceivable cake size s he is able to attach a subjective probability[1]. The owner of the cake wishes to formulate an optimal consumption plan knowing that, when he finishes the cake, his rate of consumption will drop to zero. Such a plan specifies the rate at which he will consume at each point of time if he has not already finished the cake.

It is shown in section 2 that there exist conditions under which the owner of the cake should plan for a positive but declining rate of consumption. Under these conditions, then, a result valid under certainty extends to situations in which the cake is of unknown size. However, the conditions are not completely trivial. In general, it may be optimal to plan for a rate of consumption which is sometimes increasing.

The problem is generalized in section 3 to accommodate the possibility that more than one individual has access to the cake. A solution, based on assumptions of the Cournot type, is proposed. Possible applications of the analysis are indicated in section 4.

2. Analysis of the problem

Let us suppose that the owner of the cake seeks to maximize an integral of discounted expected 'instantaneous' utilities, where the instantaneous utility at time t, say u_t, depends only on the rate of consumption at time t, say c_t, so that

* For helpful comments I am indebted to Dimitri Bertsekas, David Gale, Warren Hughes, Ngo Van Long, Richard Manning, Yew-Kwang Ng, Michihiro Ohyama, Robert Solow, Hideo Suzuki, Takashi Takayama and Henry Wan.
[1] For convenience only, s is taken to be a scalar (volume or weight, for example).

$u_t = u(c_t)$. The function u is supposed to be increasing and strictly concave. Let us suppose also that the individual is immortal, so that his task is to maximize[2]

$$\int_0^\infty e^{-\rho t}\, E\{u(c_t)\}\, dt, \qquad \rho \geqq 0, \tag{1}$$

where ρ is the constant rate of discount and E is the expectation operator.

Let $C_t = \int_0^t c_v\, dv$ be the cumulative consumption at time t; and let $\pi(s;C)$ be the subjective probability that initially, at time $t = 0$, the cake was greater than s in size, given that an amount $C, C \leqq s$, has been consumed already and that the cake is not yet seen to be finished. In particular, $\pi(s;0)$ is the subjective probability that initially the cake was of size greater than s given that none of the cake has been eaten. It will be assumed that $\pi(s;0)$ possesses continuous partial derivatives $\partial\pi(s;0)/\partial s$ and, of course, that

$$\pi(0;0) = 1, \tag{2a}$$

$$\lim_{s\to\infty} \pi(s;0) = 0, \tag{2b}$$

$$(\partial/\partial s)\pi(s;0) \leqq 0. \tag{2c}$$

Then a plan formulated at time $t = 0$ to consume at the rate $c_t > 0$ at time t will be carried out with subjective probability $\pi(C_t;0)$. If the plan is carried out, the utility yield is $u_t = u(c_t)$; otherwise, the yield is $u(0)$, which is supposed to be finite and, given that assumption, can be set equal to zero without further loss. The utility expected from the entire plan is, therefore,

$$\int_0^\infty e^{-\rho t}\, u(c_t)\pi(C_t;0)\, dt, \qquad \rho \geqq 0. \tag{3}$$

Suppose that the owner of the cake seeks that consumption trajectory c_t^* which maximizes (3) subject to the side conditions

$$\dot{C}_t = c_t, \tag{4}$$

$$c_t \geqq 0. \tag{5}$$

Among the conditions which must be satisfied by such a trajectory we have, in

---

[2] Given the restrictions imposed on π, the cake owner's problem under uncertainty may have a solution even when $\rho = 0$. This contrasts with the situation under certainty (see Gale, 1967).

addition to (4) and (5),

$$\dot{\mu} = \rho\mu - u(c)\frac{\partial}{\partial s}\pi(s;0)\bigg|_{s=C} \tag{6}$$

$$u'(c)\pi(C;0) + \mu\begin{cases} = 0 & \text{if } c > 0, \\ \leq 0 & \text{if } c = 0, \end{cases} \tag{7}$$

$$C_0 = 0, \tag{8}$$

$$\lim_{t\to\infty} e^{-\rho t}\mu C = 0. \tag{9}$$

Suppose that there exists an optimal path satisfying (4)–(9). Perhaps there exists an s, say $\hat{s}$, not greater than $\bar{s}$ and such that $\pi(C,0) = 0$ for all $C > \hat{s}$. Then the actual path of consumption c_t^{**} will coincide with the optimal path c_t^*. Otherwise, there will arrive a moment of sorrow T when $C_t^* = \bar{s}$ and $c_t^* > 0$. Then the rate of consumption will drop to zero and stay there; that is, $c_t^{**} = c_t^*$ for $t \leq T$ and $c_t^{**} = 0$ for $t > T$.[3]

Under conditions of certainty, with $\rho > 0$, c_t^* is monotonely decreasing. Does this property of optimal paths extend to conditions of uncertainty? From (6) and (7), if $\pi(C^*;0) > 0$,

$$\dot{c}^* = -\left[\rho\mu - (u(c^*) - c^*u'(c^*))\frac{\partial}{\partial s}\pi(s;0)\bigg|_{s=C^*}\right]\bigg/u''(c^*)\pi(C^*;0). \tag{10}$$

---

[3] Notice that no allowance is made for plan revision. The reason is that no revision is needed. Suppose that at time $\tau > 0$ the cake is still not seen to be exhausted. The owner of the cake is then faced with the problem of finding

$$\max_{c_t} \int_\tau^\infty e^{-\rho t} u(c_t)\pi(C_t; C_\tau)\, dt,$$

subject to the side conditions $\dot{C}_t = c_t$, $c_t \geq 0$, $C_\tau = C_\tau^*$. However,

$$\pi(C_t;0) = \pi(C_t; C_\tau)\pi(C_\tau;0).$$

The maximand therefore reduces to

$$\frac{1}{\pi(C_\tau;0)}\int_\tau^\infty e^{-\rho t} u(c_t)\pi(C_t;0)\, dt.$$

Since by assumption $c_t^*(t \geq 0)$ is a solution to the original problem, the truncated path $c_t^*(t \geq \tau)$ must be a solution to the new problem. Replanning is unnecessary.

In putting together the above proof I have adapted and transplanted the argument of Long (1974, section 3). This argument is formulated in discrete time and in the context of a different but related problem. The relationship between the problem of Long (1974) and that of this paper is discussed in section 5.

Evidently $\mu < 0$ and $c^* > 0$; and, from the concavity of $u(c)$, $u - cu'$ is positive. Moreover, in general $\partial\pi(s\,;0)/\partial s|_{s=c}$ is not bounded below. Hence one cannot rule out the possibility that, for some t, $\dot{c}_1^*$ is positive. That is, *the monotone behaviour of c_1^* under certainty* (when $\partial\pi(s\,;0)/\partial s|_{s=c} = 0$ and $c_1^{**} = c_1^*$) *is not necessarily duplicated under certainty.* From (10) we see also that for $\dot{c}_1^* > 0$ it is necessary that $\dot{\mu} > 0$. *In the limiting case in which $\rho = 0$ and to which there is no counterpart under certainty, $\dot{c}_1^*$ and therefore $\dot{\mu}$ are necessarily positive.*

A simple example will convey the essential point – that optimal consumption may be sometimes increasing. Suppose that the owner of the cake believes that there is an even chance that the cake is very small (say of size 1) or very big (say of size 10^6). Then he must proceed cautiously at first; but once he has confirmed that there is more than one unit of cake, he can afford to be less frugal and step up his rate of consumption[4].

The more precise proposition, that in the absence of time preference the optimal consumption trajectory (if it exists[5]) is monotonely increasing, may be understood with the aid of a simple thought experiment. Let us suppose that the rate of consumption is constant over two disjoint equal intervals of time $[t_1, t_1 + \Delta t]$ and $[t_2, t_2 + \Delta t]$, where $t_1 < t_2$, and let us contemplate the transfer of a small quantum of consumption from one interval to another, with the rate of consumption at all other points of time left unchanged. If the transfer is from the earlier (later) to the later (earlier) period, the expected utility will increase (decrease) for all t, $t_1 + \Delta t < t < t_2$; moreover, a transfer from the earlier (later) to the later (earlier) period will increase (decrease) the expected utility at any point of the interval $[t_2, t_2 + \Delta t]$ by more than it will decrease (increase) the expected utility at the corresponding point of $[t_1, t_1 + \Delta t]$. It is therefore advantageous to transfer consumption from the earlier to the later period[6].

The assumption that the owner of the cake is immortal is immaterial. A similar analysis is possible, and similar conclusions may be obtained, if it is supposed that the individual has a finite lifetime, whether certain or not. The assumption that $u(0)$ is finite is not completely innocuous. However, it can be made acceptable by imagining the cake added to an otherwise steady diet with finite utility[7].

---

[4] I owe the above example to David Gale. From the point of view of conventional control theory, the example contains undesirable discontinuities. That these could be removed (at some cost in terms of simplicity and intuitive appeal) will be obvious.

[5] For solubility when $\rho = 0$ it is necessary that $\pi(s\,;0) > 0$ for all s.

[6] This paragraph is based on the suggestions of Michihiro Ohyama.

[7] If $u(0) = -\infty$, as when $u(c) = \log c$, the problem either has no solution or involves uncertainty

Our analysis can be extended to accommodate certain kinds of natural growth or decay. Let C_t now stand for cumulative net consumption less cumulative natural growth (possibly negative). If the time rate of natural growth can be expressed as a function ϕ of cumulative net consumption and of time t, we have, instead of (4),

$$\dot{C}_t = c_t - \phi(C_t, t). \tag{4'}$$

As a consequence, in (6) ρ is replaced by $\rho + \partial\phi/\partial C$. The possibility of non-monotone c_t^* persists[8].

Sensitivity experiments of several kinds are possible. We pause here only to note that an increase in the rate of discount has the effect of tilting the optimal consumption path in favour of earlier periods[9].

Custom condones the choice of the sum of discounted expected utilities as maximand. However, custom is based on considerations of tractability rather than plausibility and one wonders how robust is our conclusion (that optimal planned consumption is not necessarily monotone) when substitution is made of alternative maximands. Consideration is now given to two alternative maximands each of which (in its certainty form) has found some favour in the recent literature on economic control.

It is a serious weakness of the Ramseyan utility functional that it rules out the possibility of complementarity between consumption during different periods (or at different points) of time. Modifications of Ramsey's functional have been proposed recently by Wan (1970), Samuelson (1971), Glycopantis (1972) and Ryder and Heal (1973). One particularly simple modification consists in adding as an argument of the instantaneous utility function the weighted sum

---

in a merely trivial way. Suppose that there is no positive number such that the cake is known with certainty to be of at least that size. Then, for all conceivable planned-consumption paths, (3) fails to converge. Suppose, alternatively, that such a positive number exists. For any plan such that at some point in time cumulative planned consumption exceeds that number (3) again fails to converge. In this case, therefore, the problem is simply to spread over time the consumption of the supremum of certain cake sizes; that is, the problem is one of optimally consuming a cake of *known* size.

[8] Two special cases may be noted. If the natural growth of the cake depends only on cumulative net consumption of the cake and the relationship is exponential, so that $\phi = \gamma C$, $\gamma \gtreqless 0$, then $\partial\phi/\partial C = \gamma$, and, in (6), ρ is replaced by $\rho + \gamma$. (Solubility of the problem then implies that $\rho + \gamma \geq 0$. See footnote 2.) And if natural growth and decay are autonomous (that is, purely time dependent) then $\partial\phi/\partial C = 0$.

[9] I note here, as a corollary of the possibility of non-monotonic c_t^*, that the convention of allowing for an increase in uncertainty by substituting a 'suitably' higher (but still constant) rate of discount has no general theoretical justification. Under certainty, consumption is necessarily monotonic, however high the rate of discount.

of past consumption. Limiting oneself to a system of uniform weights[10], (3) becomes

$$\int_0^\infty e^{-\rho t} u(c_t, C_t) \pi(C_t; 0) \, dt, \qquad \rho \geqq 0. \tag{3}$$

The necessary conditions (6) and (7) become

$$\dot{\mu} = \rho\mu - \left[\pi(C; 0) \frac{\partial}{\partial C} u(c; C) + u(c; C) \frac{\partial}{\partial s} \pi(s; 0) \Big|_{s=C} \right] \tag{6'}$$

and

$$\pi(C; 0) \frac{\partial}{\partial c} u(c; C) + \mu \begin{cases} = 0 & \text{if } c > 0, \\ \leqq 0 & \text{if } c = 0, \end{cases} \tag{7'}$$

respectively. Suppose that a solution exists. Then (10) becomes

$$\dot{c}^* = \left[\pi(C; 0) \left(\frac{\partial}{\partial C} u(c; C) - \frac{\partial^2}{\partial c \, \partial C} u(c; C) \right) + u(c; C) \right.$$

$$\left. - \left(cu \frac{\partial}{\partial c} u(c; C) \right) \frac{\partial}{\partial s} \pi(s; 0) \Big|_{s=C} - \rho\mu \right]$$

$$\div \pi(C; 0) \frac{\partial^2}{\partial c^2} u(c; C). \tag{10'}$$

Evidently $\dot{c}^*$ may still be of either sign. Moreover, if $\partial u(c; C)/\partial C < 0$ then it is still true that optimal consumption monotonely increases if $\rho = 0$.

The Ramseyan functional has been subjected to a quite different line of attack by Rawls (1971). Extending the Rawlsian max–min criterion to accommodate uncertainty we might consider[11]

$$\max_c \min_t \mathop{E}_{\bar{s}} \{u(c_t)\} = \max_c \min_t u(c_t) \pi(C_t; 0).$$

Then, along an optimal path,

$$u(c_t) \pi(C_t; 0) \equiv u(\dot{C}_t) \pi(C_t; 0) = \text{constant},$$

---

[10] For the conclusions reached in this paragraph any system of weighting is permissible.

[11] Professor Solow has pointed out to me that, alternatively, one might take, as the appropriate general:zation of the max–min criterion,

$$\max_c \mathop{E}_{\bar{s}} \{\min_t u(c_t)\}$$

and that the two generalized criteria are not equivalent. (The min and E operations do not commute because min is non-linear.)

implying that consumption is either zero or growing. If there exists a value of C such that $\pi(C; 0) = 0$ then optimal consumption is zero. Only when there is a positive probability of the cake being of any size, however large, is it optimal to consume *any* of it – and in that case consumption must grow.

3. One cake and n consumers

Let there be n consumers with access to the communal cake. None knows the initial size of the cake, but at any particular point of time each individual knows how much has been consumed. How will the consumers behave, individually and collectively? Is their collective behaviour socially optimal? I propose to answer these questions on Cournotesque assumptions familiar from the theory of differential games.

Suppose that at the point of time t the ith individual seeks to formulate a consumption plan without allowing for the fact that, as the result of others' consumption, he may become progressively better informed about the initial size of the cake. We obtain, in place of (4)–(8),

$$\dot{C}_{iv} = c_{iv}, \tag{4''}$$

$$C_{iv} \geq 0, \tag{5''}$$

$$\dot{\mu}_i = \rho_i \mu_i - u_i(c_{iv}) \frac{\partial}{\partial s} \pi_i(s; C_t)\Big|_{s = C_{iv} + \sum_{j \neq i} C_{jt}} \tag{6''}$$

$$u'_i(c_{iv}) \pi_i\left(C_{iv} + \sum_{j \neq i} C_{jt}; C_t\right) + \mu_i \begin{cases} = 0 & \text{if } c_{iv} > 0, \\ \leq 0 & \text{if } c_{iv} = 0, \end{cases} \tag{7''}$$

$$C_{jt} \text{ known}, \quad j = 1, \ldots, n, \tag{8''}$$

where $v \geq t$, $i = 1, \ldots, n$ and, for example, C_{it} is the cumulative consumption of the ith individual at time t. However, as time goes by, C_t grows and the plan must be revised. Allowing for the continual revision of plans, so that only the first moment of each plan is retained, (4'')–(7'') reduce to

$$\dot{C}_{it} = c_{it}, \tag{4'''}$$

$$c_{it} \geq 0, \tag{5'''}$$

$$\dot{\mu}_i = \rho_i \mu_i - u_i(c_{it}) \frac{\partial}{\partial s} \pi_i(s; C_t)\Big|_{s = C_t}, \tag{6'''}$$

$$u'(c_{it}) \pi_i(C_t; C_t) + \mu_i \begin{cases} = 0 & \text{if } c_{it} > 0, \\ \geq 0 & \text{if } c_{it} = 0. \end{cases} \tag{7'''}$$

To close the system we simply add the accounting relationship

$$C_t = \sum_{i=1}^{n} C_{it}. \tag{11}$$

In the symmetrical case in which the n individuals are identical, subscripts may be dropped so that the system $((4''')-(7'''), (11))$ reduces further to

$$\dot{C} = nc, \tag{12}$$

$$c \geqq 0, \tag{13}$$

$$\dot{\mu} = \rho\mu - u(c)\frac{\partial}{\partial s}\pi(s;C)\Big|_{s=C}, \tag{14}$$

$$u'(c)\pi(C;C) + \mu\begin{cases} = 0 & \text{if } c > 0, \\ \leqq 0 & \text{if } c = 0. \end{cases} \tag{15}$$

Except for the constant multiplier n in (12), and the appearance of $\pi(s;C)$ in place of $\pi(s;0)$, we are back to the one-person problem of section 2. Let us now add to the restrictions (2)

$$\pi(C;C) \leqq 1, \tag{2a'}$$

$$\lim_{C\to\infty} \pi(C;C) = 0, \tag{2b'}$$

$$\frac{\partial}{\partial s}\pi(s;C)\Big|_{s=C} \leqq 0, \qquad \frac{\partial}{\partial C}\pi(s;C)\Big|_{s=C} \geqq 0,$$

$$\left(\frac{\partial}{\partial s}\pi(s;C) + \frac{\partial}{\partial C}\pi(s;C)\right)\Big|_{s=C} \leqq 0. \tag{2c'}$$

(Since $\pi(s, C)$ is defined only for $s \geqq C$, $\partial\pi(s;C)/\partial s|_{s=C}$ and $\partial\pi(s;C)/\partial C|_{s=C}$ are to be taken as right- and left-hand derivatives, respectively.) It is then easily shown that c_i^{***}, *the solution to* (12)–(15), *is not necessarily monotone.*

For a social optimum, when the population is homogeneous, it is necessary and sufficient that (12)–(15) hold with one change: in (15), μ must be replaced by $n\mu$. Thus only when $n = 1$ do (12)–(15) define a social optimum. When $n > 1$ the cake is consumed too fast. To achieve an optimal rate of cake consumption, it suffices to create private property rights in the cake. The same objective can be achieved by taxing consumption of the cake if there exist other goods in terms of which the tax might be expressed. The appropriate rate of tax increases with n.

4. Possible applications

(a) Consider an economy with one true primary factor labour, available in known and constant amount, and one wasting resource. Labour and the resource combine to produce a single consumption good. What can be said about the optimal rate of depletion of the resource and about the optimal time path of output?

The answer to this question is already at hand. Let c_t be the rate of depletion. Then we may introduce a production function

$$x_t = f(c_t), \tag{16}$$

where f is supposed to be increasing and strictly concave, and we may express our utility function as

$$u_t = u(f(c_t)) \equiv v(c_t). \tag{17}$$

Since $v(c_t)$ is strictly concave (see, for example, Hadley and Kemp (1971, theorem 2.17.3)) our new problem reduces to the one-person cake-eating problem of section 2. In particular, the optimal rate of depletion, and therefore the optimal rate of output, is not necessarily monotone in time.

(b) That the optimal rate of depletion is not necessarily monotone remains true of multisectoral economies. However, in such more general economies the optimal path of any particular output is rigidly tied to the rate of depletion only in special cases. Let us consider one such case. Suppose that labour and a wasting resource combine to produce two goods which can be sold on world markets at prices beyond the control of the individual country. Then, for any choice of *numéraire*, the relationship f between output x_t and the rate of depletion c_t is as depicted in fig. 1. If the optimal rate of depletion is declining through time then so is total output. Moreover, from the Samuelson–Rybczynski theorem, the rate of depletion is positively correlated with the output of the relatively resource-intensive good. It follows that, if the rate of depletion is non-monotone with respect to time, a particular commodity might switch from the export to the import trade then later switch again.

(c) Discussion of the gains from international trade has been confined to a setting in which the individual actors are blessed with complete information concerning the opportunities open to them. The key theorem then asserts that under conditions of *laissez faire* and in the absence of externalities, international trade is potentially beneficial to each trading country.

For the purposes of this theorem information may be complete even though each actor makes his decisions under conditions of irreducible uncertainty

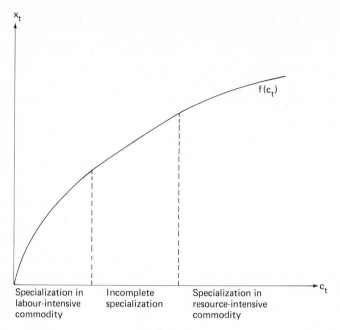

Fig. 1.

stemming from random mechanisms in nature. It suffices that each actor knows the relevant probability distributions. In fact, any proof of the gainfulness of trade under conditions of certainty can be extended along well-known Arrow–Debreu lines to accommodate uncertainty (see, for example, Arrow (1953) and Debreu (1959, ch. 7)).

Matters may be very different if the actors are ill-informed, whether about random or about non-random variables. Consider the situation described under (b) above. The consumption path c_t^* is optimal in relation to the incomplete information available to the cake owner and summarized by $\pi(s; 0)$. In relation to the true size of the cake, however, the path is suboptimal. In particular, a commodity may be imported when it should be exported. It is then easily seen that the opportunity to trade may exacerbate misallocations based on the incompleteness of knowledge and that trade may be potentially harmful.

(d) The calculations of section 3 have an obvious bearing on the descriptive and prescriptive analysis of wasting common-property resources (like fisheries) and of wasting restricted-common-property resources (like oil and gas fields).

(e) There is a class of search situations in which information concerning the amount of a resource can be obtained not as a byproduct of consumption of the resource but by the expenditure of other resources. In these situations the central problem is to choose the optimal time profile of expenditure and, in particular, the optimal point at which to abandon the search altogether. At what point should an oil prospector stop drilling, leave a dry hole and try elsewhere? Evidently such questions are closely related to that which troubled the cake eater of section 2 and can be approached along a similar route. Similarly with industrial re(search) problems. At what stage should the search for a cheaper method of producing a commodity be abandoned and past expenditures written off?

5. Final remarks

Consider again the cake-eating problem of section 2. The probability that the plan will have to be abandoned during any future interval of time depends on cumulative planned consumption at the beginning and end of that interval, but it does not depend on the duration or futurity of the interval.

There is a class of problems, some members of which have been studied recently, in which matters are exactly reversed: the probability that the plan will have to be abandoned during any future interval of time depends on the duration and futurity of the interval but not on the plan itself. Thus Long (1975) has studied the optimal production plan of a firm which owns a resource subject to the threat of nationalization, where the risk of nationalization is independent of the plan; and Dasgupta and Heal (1974) have studied the optimal production plan for a country which owns a resource which at some uncertain future time will be rendered obsolete by some possibly unknown competing resource.

Evidently these two classes of problems contain extreme cases, members of a general class of problems in which the stated probability depends both on the plan and on the duration and futurity of the interval of interest. This general class of problems can be handled by the methods of section 2 if only $\pi(C;0)$ is replaced by $\tilde{\pi}(C;0;t)$, with

$$\lim_{s \to \infty} \tilde{\pi}(s;0;t) = 0 = \lim_{t \to \infty} \tilde{\pi}(s;0;t) \tag{2b*}$$

and

$$(\partial/\partial s)\tilde{\pi}(s;0;t) \leq 0, \qquad (\partial/\partial t)\tilde{\pi}(s;0;t) \leq 0 \tag{2c*}$$

instead of (2b) and (2c), respectively. In the general case, we have, in place of (10),

$$\dot{c}^* = -\left[\rho\mu - (u(c^*) - c^*u'(c^*))\frac{\partial}{\partial s}\,\pi(s;0;t)\Big|_{s=C^*}\right.$$

$$\left. + u'(c^*)\frac{\partial}{\partial t}\,\tilde{\pi}(C^*;0;t)\right]\Big/u''(c^*)\tilde{\pi}(C^*;0;t) \tag{10*}$$

and the italicized conclusion of section 2 follows *a fortiori*.

Tacking in another direction, suppose that it is believed that at some unknown future time the community's coal reserves will be supplemented by the discovery of oil, that is, that a second cake, again of unknown size, will become available. Without going into details I can report that it is possible to extend the techniques of section 2 to accommodate this and even more general problems. The details may be found in Kemp (1974).

References

Arrow, K. J. (1953), Le rôle des valeurs boursières pour la répartition la meilleure des risques, *Econométrie*, 41–48, Centre Nationale de la Recherche Scientifique, Paris.

Dasgupta, P. and G. Heal (1974), The optimal depletion of exhaustible resources, *Review of Economic Studies*, Symposium on the economics of exhaustible resources, 3–28.

Debreu, G. (1959), *Theory of Value*. Wiley, New York.

Gale, D. (1967), On optimal development in a multi-sector model, *Review of Economic Studies*, 34, Jan., 1–18.

Glycopantis, T. (1972), Optimal conditions in certain models with intertemporarily dependent tastes, *Western Economic Journal*, 10, June, 139–155.

Hadley, G. and M. C. Kemp (1971), *Variational Methods in Economics*, North-Holland, Amsterdam.

Kemp, M. C. (1974), A further generalization of the cake eating problem under uncertainty, University of New South Wales.

Long, N. V. (1975), The pattern of resource extraction under uncertainty about possible nationalization, *Journal of Economic Theory*, 10, Feb., 42–53.

Rawls, J. (1971), *A Theory of Justice*, Harvard University Press, Cambridge, Mass.

Ryder, H. E. and G. M. Heal (1973), Optimal growth with intertemporarily dependent preferences, *Review of Economic Studies*, 40, Jan., 1–31.

Samuelson, P. A. (1971), Turnpike theorems even though tastes are intertemporarily dependent, *Western Economic Journal*, 9, March, 21–25.

Wan, H. Y. (1970), Optimal saving programs under intertemporarily dependent preferences, *International Economic Review*, 11, Oct., 521–547.

Chapter 24

OPTIMAL INTERNATIONAL BORROWING WITH A WASTING RESOURCE*

1. Introduction

Consider a small country with an exhaustible resource. Ore in the ground earns no interest; there is, therefore, an incentive to extract it as quickly as possible. On the other hand, extraction may be subject almost from the beginning to static diminishing returns, implying that the undiscounted total cost of extracting the resource can be minimized by spreading extraction thinly over time. This suggests that there is some optimal rate of extraction, perhaps time dependent, which nicely balances these two conflicting pressures. The purpose of this note is to give some precision to this notion and, in particular, to characterize the optimal time paths of extraction, foreign indebtedness and consumption.

In section 2 it is supposed that the resource is of known extent. This absurd assumption is relaxed in section 3. To avoid inessential complications it is supposed that, quite apart from any prospective contribution of the exhaustible resource itself, the country enjoys a steady stream of non-tradeable consumption goods at a rate which is adequate for subsistence and which can be neither artificially diminished nor artificially augmented.

A question of special interest concerns the relative desirability of selling the mine at the outset and of working the mine with the aid of borrowed capital. It is shown that, whereas under conditions of certainty the two courses of action are equivalent, to sell the mine at the outset (and thereafter live on bond interest) is always the preferred course of action under conditions of uncertainty and risk aversion. The argument is, at bottom, a very simple and familiar one: a risk-averse individual or collection of individuals should diversify its sources of uncertain income. However, the simplicity of the argument is shrouded in the detail of the exposition.

2. Analysis: certainty

The country has a constant labour force l and a known amount r_0 of some exhaustible resource. Labour and capital goods are applied to the resource to produce a raw material; however, the difficulty of extraction depends on the amount of the raw material already removed. Suppressing l, the production function for the raw material at time t may be written therefore as

$$f(k_t, r_t),\tag{1a}$$

where k_t is the amount of capital employed at time t and r_t is the balance of the resource at time t. Suppose that

$$f(k, 0) = 0,\tag{1b}$$

$$\left.\begin{array}{ll} \partial f/\partial k > 0, & \lim_{k \to 0}(\partial f/\partial k) = \infty, \\[1mm] \partial^2 f/\partial k^2 < 0, & \partial f/\partial r \geqq 0, \\[1mm] \partial^2 f/\partial k\, \partial r \geqq 0, & \end{array}\right\} \quad \text{if } k, r > 0.\tag{1c}$$

(These restrictions are consistent with increasing, decreasing or constant returns to scale in the three factors of production.) Once installed, machines cannot be uprooted and sold. Machines do not depreciate.

The raw material can be sold on the world market at a price beyond the control of the policy-making country. Similarly, capital and consumption goods can be purchased at given prices. Commodity units are chosen of equal value. Finally, the country can borrow and lend at a given rate of interest i provided that the country's net indebtedness does not exceed the current value of the resource[1]. Let b_t be the net credit position of the country at time t, in terms of some consumption good, and let c_t be the rate of consumption (over and above the pre-existing steady rate) at time t.

The country must determine the optimal time paths of k, b and c. Optimality is to be gauged in terms of the conventional integral of discounted instantane-

---

[1] This is almost an implication of the small-country assumption. Strictly speaking, we need the additional assumption that the borrowing country is not expected to repudiate all or a part of the loan or, if there is risk of repudiation, the extent of the risk is independent of the amount borrowed.

ous utilities or felicities

$$\int_0^\infty e^{-\rho t} u(c)\,dt, \qquad \rho \geqq 0, \tag{2}$$

where ρ is the rate of discount or time preference. Suppose that $u'(c) > 0$ and that $u''(c) < 0$ and, to ensure that solutions are internal, that

$$\lim_{c \to 0} u'(c) = \infty. \tag{3}$$

In view of the small-country assumption the problem can be tackled in two stages. In the first stage, given the production function (1) and the rate of interest i, a time path is chosen for k such that v, the present value of the mine, is maximized. In the second stage, given $v^* \equiv \max_k v$, the optimal paths of b and c are calculated. In particular, one can imagine that the mine (together with labour services in perpetuity) is sold at time zero for v^* and then treat in the second stage a generalized cake-eating problem (generalized because, left to itself, the cake grows at rate i). For, from the point of view of the policy-making country, it is a matter of indifference whether the mine is sold at the outset or worked with the aid of borrowed capital – the paths of optimal consumption and optimal extraction are the same.

Consider stage 1. In view of (1c) it is optimal to install all equipment at the outset, at time zero (implying that the optimal rate of extraction is non-increasing over time). The optimal installation yields

$$v^* = \max_k v = \max_k \left\{ \int_0^T f(k, r)\, e^{-it}\, dt - k \right\}, \tag{4}$$

where

$$\dot{r} = -f(k, r) \tag{5}$$

and

$$r_0 \text{ is given,} \tag{6}$$

and where T is the life span of the mine and, since the equipment has no scrap value, can be taken to be infinity. Now let us add to v^* the initial net credit balance of the country, thus obtaining the initial value of b, say b_0, the cake to be eaten.

If b_0 is positive, we move to stage 2. The problem is to find

$$\max_c \int_0^\infty e^{-\rho t} u(c)\, dt, \qquad \rho \geqq 0, \tag{7}$$

subject to

$$\dot{b} = ib - c \tag{8}$$

and

$$b_0 \text{ is given.} \tag{9}$$

The Euler equation can be written

$$\dot{c} = (\rho - i)u'(c)/u''(c), \tag{10}$$

whence the optimal consumption path, if it exists[2], is increasing, decreasing or constant as ρ is less than, greater than or equal to i. Moreover, as is easily seen, b is increasing, decreasing or constant as c is increasing, decreasing or constant.

3. Analysis: uncertainty

Suppose now that the initial extent of the resource is unknown. If f, a known function, depends on both k and r then the value of r_0 can be computed exactly by momentarily investing a small positive amount and observing the associated value of f; any initial uncertainty about the extent of the resource can be of only the most fleeting kind. To introduce resource uncertainty in a non-trivial way it is necessary to couple it with technological uncertainty and/or delete r as an argument of f. To enable us to focus on resource uncertainty, f will be assumed to take the special form

$$f(k, r) = \begin{cases} \phi(k) & \text{if } r > 0, \\ 0 & \text{if } r = 0, \end{cases} \tag{1'}$$

where $\phi(k)$ is increasing, concave and such that $\lim_{k \to 0} \phi'(k) = \infty$. (Relationship (1'), like (1), is consistent with increasing, decreasing or constant returns to scale in the three factors of production.) However, the conclusions of this

---

[2] An optimal path exists if $u'(c)/cu''(c)$ is constant for all c (as when $u(c) = c^\alpha$, $\alpha < 1$) and if $(\rho - i)u'(c)/cu''(c) < i$.

section remain valid if the production function at time t takes the more general form $f(k_t, r_t, z_t)$, where z_t is a random variable the realized value of which indicates the technical information available at time t.

To avoid inessential complications it will be assumed that everyone, whether at home or abroad, holds to the same subjective probability distribution concerning r_0. Even so, it is no longer a matter of indifference to the policy-making country whether the mine is sold at the outset or worked with the aid of borrowed capital. For a risk-averse country, it is optimal to shed all risk by selling the mine at the outset. We proceed to a detailed demonstration.

There is a world rate of interest for riskless loans, say i. This rate can be used to calculate r^{**}, the maximum expected value of the mine (together with labour services in perpetuity). Instead of (4) we have[3]

$$v^{**} \equiv \max_k \operatorname*{E}_{r_0} \left\{ \int_0^\infty f(k, r)\, e^{-it}\, dt - k \right\}, \tag{4'}$$

where E is the instruction to take the mathematical expectation. Let the maximizing value of k be denoted by k^{**}. Since even risk-averse individuals are prepared to engage in 'infinitesimal' fair bets, and since the mine-owning country is small the mine can be sold for v^{**} at the outset. Thereafter the country is faced with a generalized cake-eating problem under certainty.

Consider now the alternative policy of working the mine with borrowed capital. The rate of interest at which borrowing can take place depends on the risk of default as perceived by the lender. Under the assumptions of this note the risk of involuntary default is positive and unavoidable moreover, it depends on the consumption path planned by the mine-owning country. For the time being, however, let us waive this complication and suppose that the mine-owning country can borrow k^{**} at the rate of interest appropriate to riskless loans. Having borrowed that sum and invested it in opening the mine, the mine-owning country receives, in addition to its certain subsistence income, an *uncertain* stream of income $f(k^{**}, r) - i \cdot k^{**}$ with expected value v^{**}. Evidently the risk-averse mine-owning country is better off with an optimally consumed cake of size v^{**} than with a prospect of uncertain consumption and expected present value not greater that v^{**}. That is, the optimal policy is to sell

[3] Even with (1c) necessarily satisfied, it may be suboptimal to install all equipment at the outset; that is, it is no longer true that the optimal rate of planned extraction is necessarily constant (cf. ch. 23). The possibility that the optimal rate of extraction is sometimes increasing is here ignored. To allow for it would merely complicate the argument.

the mine at the outset. If the risk of default, and rates of interest greater than i, are now introduced, the conclusion follows *a fortiori*[4].

We have focused on uncertainty about the extent of the resource. Evidently this is only one of many types of uncertainty relating to the extraction and sale of the raw material. We note therefore that, whatever the type of uncertainty, the conclusion is the same: a small country should sell the mine at the outset. Moreover, the country need not be small in all respects. In particular, the conclusion is independent of the assumption that the raw material can be sold at a given world price–it remains valid even if the policy-making country is a monopolist.

For reasons of nationalism, etc. the country may yet, of course, prefer to work the mine on borrowed money, that is, it may consciously choose the economically second-best course of action; but that is another matter[5].

Moreover, the conclusion does rest on the assumption that residents of the mine-owning country are everywhere risk-averse. Alternatively, suppose that locally, in a neighbourhood of the initial steady rate of consumption, they are risk-lovers but that elsewhere they are risk-averters. Then it may be optimal to sell, not all of the resource, but only enough to eliminate the risk of wild swings of consumption far into the regions of risk aversion.

4. Additional miscellaneous remarks

In accommodating international borrowing and lending sections 2 and 3 go beyond the earlier analyses of Kemp and Suzuki (1975) and Suzuki (1974) respectively. On the other hand, the present discussion is confined to non-replenishable resources.

---

[4] The possibility of default destroys the convenient separability of consumption and production decisions upon which we have hitherto relied. When the possibility of default is recognized, the task of the mine-owning country is to choose k and a planned consumption path such that

$$\mathop{\mathrm{E}}_{r_0} \int_0^\infty u(c)\,\mathrm{e}^{-\rho t}\,\mathrm{d}t$$

is maximized subject to the borrowing constraint

$$k = \mathop{\mathrm{E}}_{r_0} \int_0^\infty (f(k,r) - c)\,\mathrm{e}^{-it}\,\mathrm{d}t.$$

[5] It may be noted, however, that along the second-best path both the amount of capital applied to the resource and the rate of extraction of the resource are smaller than when the mine is sold at the outset.

After the present note was drafted there appeared a paper by Long (1974) covering similar ground. However, Long's analysis of the small-country case differs from ours in several important details. Firstly, he focuses on the production decision to the exclusion of the consumption decision; moreover, he confines himself to the case of complete certainty. Secondly, he supposes in effect[6] that capital goods can be resold at any time at original cost. Thirdly, he assumes that the productivity of capital in the extraction of the raw material is independent of r, the remaining stock of the resource. Finally, he introduces a rising supply curve of capital justifying it (for a small country) in terms of the increasing risk of default. In our opinion, however, the risk of default is zero when all future technology, as well as the future stock of the resource, are known with certainty[7].

References

Kemp, M. C. and H. Suzuki (1975), International trade with a wasting but possibly replenishable resource, *International Economic Review*, 16 (3), Oct., 712–732.

Long, N. V. (1974), International borrowing for resource extraction, *International Economic Review*, 15, (1), Feb., 168–183.

Suzuki, H. (1974), International trade with a wasting but possibly replenishable resource: the case of uncertainty about the extent of the resource, University of New South Wales.

[6] In effect, because Long supposes that equipment is rented rather than bought from the proceeds of loans. Given his assumption that equipment can be freely moved, the difference is inessential.

[7] One can imagine that, in Long's world, the foreign owners of equipment recognize the possibility that the government of the resource-owning country may fail to return the rented equipment. The risk of expropriation may generate a rising supply curve of capital. For this observation we are indebted to Ngo Van Long.

Chapter 25

SPECULATION, PROFITABILITY AND PRICE STABILITY*

1. Introduction

Speculative activity may contribute to the stability of price, or it may promote and feed on instability. But how may one determine, for a specific market over a specific period of time, whether on balance the activities of speculators have been stabilizing or destabilizing?

It has been maintained by Friedman (1953, p. 175 and also 1960, p. 135) that destabilizing speculation must be unprofitable since it involves selling at low prices and buying at high prices[1]. If this proposition were valid, and if it were also true that stabilizing speculation is always profitable (because it involves buying at low prices and selling at high), the question would take a more tractable form. For then the empirical investigators need only identify the sign of speculative profits: if they were positive, the speculators must have contributed to price stability; if profits were negative, speculators must have added to instability.

Unfortunately, neither proposition is generally true; counter-examples will be produced in sections 3 and 4. They may be untrue, however, only under conditions which in practice are most unlikely to be satisfied. If this were so, speculators' profits might yet serve as a useful, if not infallible, guide to the

* *Review of Economics and Statistics*, 45 (May 1963), 185–189. I am grateful to Professor William Baumol for helpful comments on an earlier draft.

[1] Friedman adds a footnote warning that '... this is a simplified generalization on a complex problem. A full analysis encounters difficulties in separating "speculative" from other transactions, defining precisely and satisfactorily "destabilizing speculation" and taking account of the effects of the mere existence of a system of flexible rates as contrasted with the effects of actual speculative transactions under such a system.' While this footnote reveals an awareness of several of the fundamental difficulties which beset both analytical and empirical work in this field, it does not amount to a qualification of Friedman's assertion. That assertion is, as we shall see, false.

stabilizing or destabilizing effects of speculators' activities. This possibility is examined in section 4.

In section 5 there is outlined an alternative, more direct approach to the problem of determining the effects of speculation on stability. It possesses the incidental but substantial advantage of not requiring the direct measurement of speculative profits and losses.

2. Definitions

A moment's thought will convince one of the vagueness of our intuitive notions of what constitutes speculative activity, and of the difficulty of constructing a definition which is both widely acceptable and a convenient basis for analysis. Attempts to provide formal definitions of the notions of stability and speculators' profits encounter almost as many and as acute difficulties.

Intuitively we think of speculators as buying (or refraining from selling[2]) in the expectation of later selling (or refraining from buying) at a higher price; or perhaps as selling, in anticipation of a decline in demand, earlier than would otherwise be economical[3]. Individual speculators (or collusive groups of speculators) may or may not consider that the future price is under their control. A non-speculator, on the other hand, is viewed as buying only for purposes of immediate consumption or production, and as selling with no thought of later repurchasing the same or similar goods.

Striking out from this intuitive basis, Friedman and Telser (see Telser (1959, p. 300); also Baumol (1957, p. 269 and 1959, p. 302)) have noted that a *non-speculator* will not be influenced by the prices he expects to prevail at some future date, nor, therefore, by recent price trends; and propose that the excess demand of non-speculators be written as a function (say, N) simply of current price and, to embrace seasonal, trend, and purely random factors, of time itself. Aggregate excess demand at time t might then be written as

$$N[p(t), t] + S(t),$$

where $p(t)$ is the price at time t and the residual $S(t)$ is speculative excess demand at t. These definitions are perhaps not ideal[4] but are retained throughout this note.

---

[2] A farmer, for example, might withhold his crop from the market in the expectation of a price increase.

[3] If, for example, a constructor believes that the bottom is about to fall out of the market for new houses, he might accelerate the rate at which half-completed houses are being completed, possibly by hiring expensive overtime labour, in an effort to sell while the market is still buoyant.

[4] See, in this connection, the remarks of Baumol (1959, pp. 301–302).

Speculators' profits may be defined either in terms of money or in terms of the traded commodity. I choose money for this purpose. But, whatever the choice of *numéraire*, the definition must imply a rule for valuing changes over the period studied in speculators' holdings of the second (non-*numéraire*) commodity. To avoid the arbitrariness attaching to such a rule, I shall define speculators' profits as the net money value of sales, where the calculation is to be performed only for periods with the same beginning and ending holdings, that is, for periods over which net speculative purchases are zero[5].

There remains for consideration the definition of *stability* itself. With an eye on the welfare effects of speculation, one might define speculation as stabilizing if the actual time path of price lay 'closer' to the 'ideal' path than in the absence of speculation. But such a definition would involve a radical departure from usage, as well as laying more traps than I can hope to evade. I am led, therefore, to define price stability, in purely statistical terms, as the inverse of the average squared deviation from the mean. Perhaps it will not cause confusion if, although price may contain no random element, I call this average the 'variance'. I merely note that the definition has one important defect: for repetitive periodic price movements, the variance is independent of the frequency of the fluctuation – provided, of course, that the calculation is carried out over some integral multiple of the period of the cycle[6].

3. Profitable speculation is not necessarily stabilizing

Some readers will have followed the recent exchange of views between William Baumol and Lester Telser on the subject of this section (Baumol, 1957, pp. 269, 270; Telser, 1959, pp. 300, 301; Baumol, 1959, pp. 301, 302). It will be recalled that in his initial paper Baumol provided a certain counter-

---

[5] Slightly more generally, one might have defined profit as a pair of numbers, the first of which is the change over the period studied in the speculators' cash holdings, and the second of which is the change in their holdings of the second commodity. Profit would be called positive if one number were positive and the other non-negative; and one profit (x, y) would be adjudged greater than another (x', y') if $x > x'$, $y \geq y'$ or $x \geq x'$, $y > y'$.

[6] Suppose, for example, that price follows a regular sine path $p(t) = \sin bt$. The period of the cycle is $2\pi/b$ time units. (Alternatively, the frequency of the fluctuation is $b/2\pi$ per unit of time). We have

$$\operatorname{var} p = \frac{b}{2\pi} \int_0^{2\pi/b} \sin^2 bt \, \mathrm{d}t = \frac{1}{2},$$

whence $(\mathrm{d}/\mathrm{d}b)(\operatorname{var} p) = 0$.

example to Friedman's assertion that destabilizing speculation must be un-profitable. The example rested on the assumptions: (a) that the supply of the commodity traded is independent of price and in fact varies sinusoidally with time; (b) that non-speculative demand depends linearly on price alone; and (c) that speculative demand reaches a peak just after price has reached its minimum, and reaches a minimum just after price has reached its peak. Baumol was able to show that, for a limited time and given appropriate initial prices, speculators might make profits and yet add to the instability of price. This appeals to me as a perfectly good counter-example. Telser, however, has objected to the example on the ground that *eventually* the sinusoidal com-ponent of the solution would be dominated by the exponential term and, hence, that Baumol's speculators would be led to accumulate inventories in-definitely.

Telser's objection seems to me quite irrelevant. A counter-example need not display any kind of generality; in particular, it need not be valid for all initial values of price[7].

Be that as it may, I shall produce in this section a counter-example which is quite immune to the kind of objection raised by Telser. Suppose that the excess demand of non-speculators is independent of time and has the Giffenesque graphical form of $N(p)$ in fig. 1[8]. In the absence of speculation there are three possible equilibrium prices, p_1, p_2, and p_3. p_1 and p_3 represent stable equilibria, p_2 represents an unstable equilibrium. Suppose that at the moment when we take up the narrative price stands at p_1 and that excess speculative demand is negligible. The equilibrium is disturbed by a surge of speculative demand S; suppose, in particular, that the aggregate excess demand curve, $N(p) + S$, now lies sufficiently far to the right that it intersects the price axis only once, at p_4.

---

[7] It is possible perhaps to interpret Baumol's 'Reply' (1959, pp. 301, 302) as conceding Telser's arguments. Professor Baumol has informed me in correspondence, however, that he sticks by his two main counter-examples and, hence, to his basic position.

A second attempt to dispose of Friedman by counter example is that of Stein (1961). Stein asks us to suppose that an initial equilibrium is disturbed by private speculative sales of foreign exchange. The exchange offered by the speculators is purchased by an exchange authority. After the private bear manoeuvre has been completed, the authority takes fright at its depleted reserves and devalues the foreign currency. After the devaluation, the speculators buy back the foreign currency at a profit. Evidently the speculators have made a profit at the expense of exchange stability. Nevertheless, Stein's is not a valid counter-example. For the exchange authority, *also*, has acted as a speculator and, moreover, its operations have been unprofitable. Taken together, private profits and public losses cancel out.

[8] In a different context, Houthakker has recently made use of a similar construction; see Houthakker (1961, p. 170).

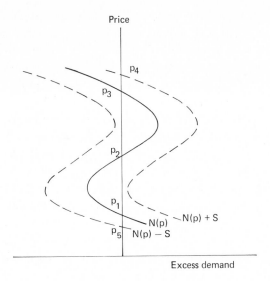

Fig. 1.

Excess demand appears and the price begins to rise; if there were no change in speculators' bullishness, it would settle eventually at p_4. In fact, we suppose, speculators withdraw from the market as soon as p_2 is passed. The excess demand curve reverts to its initial position, but price continues to rise until p_3 is reached. However, at this stage the speculators are holding inventories purchased at various prices, all of them less than or equal to p_2. The speculators now reverse the whole operation. They enter the market as sellers, and the aggregate excess demand curve moves to the left, to the position occupied by $N(p) - S$ in fig. 1. The scale of their operations, we suppose, is sufficient to reduce the number of intersections to one, labelled p_5. Excess supply appears and the price begins to fall; if there were no further change in speculators' bearishness, the price would settle eventually at p_5. In fact the speculators again withdraw from the market after p_2 has been passed; the excess demand curve again reverts to its initial position, but the price continues to fall until p_1 is regained. Thus the price cycle has been completed. The speculators have bought at prices less than or equal to p_2, and sold at prices in excess of or equal to p_2. Evidently their operations have been profitable. They also have been destabilizing.

In this example some demanders or some suppliers are frustrated in their desire to buy or sell. It is perhaps worth pointing out, therefore, that our counter-example does not require that non-speculators be frustrated; it would be as valid if *only* the late-coming speculators were frustrated[9].

Note, finally, that in the example provided, non-speculative excess demand is assumed to be non-linear in the price. The role of this assumption will be discussed further in section 4.

4. Unprofitable speculation is not necessarily destabilizing

In the land of counter-examples one is free to vary assumptions at will. Let us then break with the assumptions of section 3 and assume instead that non-speculative demand is linear in price, but depends on time too:

$$N[p(t), t] = -a \cdot p(t) + f(t), \qquad a > 0.$$

No restrictions are placed on $f(t)$. Under these assumptions it is possible to show that unprofitable speculation may yet be stabilizing.

In the absence of speculation price would follow the path

$$p(t) = f(t)/a.$$

Now we introduce a speculative excess demand function, $S(t)$, which is subject to no restrictions other than that already described: over the period studied, say from t_0 to t_1,

$$\int_{t_0}^{t_1} S(t) \, dt = 0. \tag{1}$$

When speculative activity is superimposed on the previously non-speculative market, the time path of price, say $p_s(t)$, is given by

$$p_s(t) = [f(t) + S(t)]/a$$

that is, by

$$p_s(t) - S(t)/a = p(t). \tag{2}$$

---

[9] Counter-examples which involve the occasional frustration of non-speculative demand may be very easily constructed. Thus, suppose that the process of market adjustment is described by the relation $p(t) - p(t-1) = E(t-1)$, where E stands for aggregate excess demand. Non-speculative excess demand, we suppose, is linear in price and independent of time. Initially the market is in a speculation-free equilibrium. A single speculator now enters the market and succeeds in buying one unit of the commodity, at a price $p(t)$. In the following period the price is higher $[p(t+1) > p(t)]$; the speculator enters the market again and sells. Later the price returns to its initial level. The profitable, speculative manoeuvre has added to the instability of price.

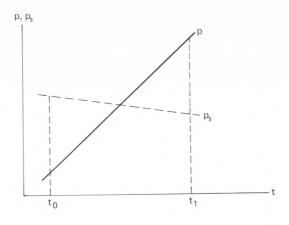

Fig. 2(a).

By virtue of (1), the average price over the period t_0 to t_1 is the same as in the absence of speculation:

$$\bar{p} - \bar{p}_s. \tag{3}$$

Speculators' profits are

$$\Pi = -\int_{t_0}^{t_1} p_s(t) S(t) \, \mathrm{d}t = -(t_1 - t_0) \operatorname{cov}(p_s, S). \tag{4}$$

Squaring both sides of (2), integrating from t_0 to t_1, and taking note of (3) and (4), we obtain

$$\frac{1}{a^2} \operatorname{var} S + \operatorname{var} p_s + \frac{2\Pi}{a(t_1 - t_0)} \operatorname{var} p. \tag{5}$$

Now the first two terms on the left-hand side of (5) are positive. It follows that, even if speculators make losses ($\Pi < 0$), var p_s may be less than var p; that is, unprofitable speculation may yet be stabilizing. The possibility is illustrated by fig. 2. Fig. 2(a) depicts the case in which $f(t)$ is a simple linear trend[10], fig. 2(b) the case in which $f(t)$ is a sine wave, and fig. 2(c) the case in which $f(t)$ contains a discontinuity. In each case, speculation 'goes too far', reversing the direction of the trend, displacing the sine wave by π time units, and converting a 'step up' into a 'step down'.

[10]If the trend were expected by speculators to continue indefinitely, speculators would never unload and (1) would never be satisfied. The theorem would be valid but irrelevant.

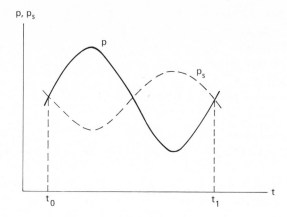

Fig. 2(b).

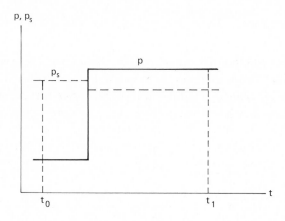

Fig. 2(c).

The conclusion of the preceding paragraph was derived from the assumption that non-speculative demand is linear in price. It is evident, however, that the production of a valid counter-example does not depend on that assumption; to assure oneself that this is so, imagine the introduction of a 'very slight' non-linearity. Nor was it really necessary to wade through a lengthy algebraic derivation; that unprofitable speculation may yet be stabilizing is perhaps sufficiently obvious from fig. 2(b).

The algebra has, however, thrown up a possibly useful result as a by-product[11]: *if non-speculative demand is linear in price (with a > 0) and contains a component dependent on t only, profitable speculation cannot fail to be stabilizing; if* $\Pi > 0$, *var* $p_s <$ *var* p.[12]

The importance of the theorem lies in the possibility that linearity may sometimes be a reasonable assumption, at least over the range of prices observed during the particular period studied. Whenever the assumption is reasonable, it would seem, the empirical investigator need only assure himself of the profitability of speculation in order to infer that speculation has been stabilizing.

A final warning. It has been established in this section that, under certain assumptions, speculative profits imply greater stability of price. It has *not* been shown that maximum profit results in maximum stability. The latter is achieved only when p_s is constant. But if p_s is constant, speculative profits must be zero. Maximum profits imply some residual variation in price[13].

5. A short cut

We wish to know whether, for a specific market and over a specific period of time, the activities of speculators have exerted a stabilizing or destabilizing influence on price. So far we have found only that the profits earned by speculators are a somewhat equivocal guide. When we reflect further that there may be very substantial obstacles in the way of estimating speculators' profits, we may well wonder whether we may not be better served by a more direct approach to the problem. It is proposed in this final section to sketch very briefly just such an approach.

As a first step, one might estimate from the available time series a (possibly non-linear) aggregate excess demand function for the commodity, say E. The arguments of the function would include, no doubt, the prices of the recent past: $p(t-1)$, $p(t-2)$, etc. Having estimated the parameters of E, one could

---

[11] A similar result has been obtained by Telser (1959). Telser's proof is based on the very special assumption that either there is a single profit-maximizing speculator, or speculators act collusively as though there were a single speculator. It is perhaps fair comment on Telser's paper that he nowhere emphasizes the crucial importance of the $f(t)$ term in the non-speculators' demand function. Without it, neither Telser's nor my theorem can be proved.

[12] It will be recalled that the counter-example of section 3 involved a non-linear excess demand function.

[13] Telser (1959) has shown that, in the linear case, maximum profits are earned if and only if $S(t) = -a[p_s(t) - \bar{p}_s]$.

estimate non-speculative demand, N, by substituting $p(t)$ for $p(t-i)$ in E. Speculative excess demand, $S(t)$, would then emerge as a residual: $S \equiv E - N$. Following this procedure, one would emerge with estimates of the time paths of both speculative and non-speculative excess demand and, also, with an estimate for each period of the price that would have emerged in the absence of speculation. The variance of the latter could then be computed and compared with the variance of the recorded price.

Having proceeded that far it would be a simple matter to estimate speculators' profits for each time period. Such estimates are, however, quite unnecessary to the above comparison.

References

Baumol, W. J. (1957), Speculation, profitability and stability, *Review of Economics and Statistics*, 39, Aug., 263–271.
Baumol, W. J. (1959), Reply, *Review of Economics and Statistics*, 39, Aug., 301–302.
Friedman, M. (1953), *Essays in Positive Economics*, University of Chicago Press, Chicago, 157–203.
Friedman, M. (1960), In defense of stabilizing speculation, in: Pfouts, R. W. (ed.), *Essays in Economics and Econometrics*, University of North Carolina Press, Chapel Hill.
Houthakker, H. S. (1961), Systematic and random elements in short-term price movements, *American Economic Review*, 51, May, 164–172.
Stein, J. L. (1961), Destabilizing speculative activity can be profitable, *Review of Economics and Statistics*, 43, Aug., 301–302.
Telser, L. G. (1959), A theory of speculation relating profitability and stability, *Review of Economics and Statistics*, 41, Aug., 295–301.

SUBJECT INDEX